BUSINESS AND ITS PUBLIC

HARVARD BUSINESS REVIEW EXECUTIVE BOOK SERIES

BUSINESS AND ITS PUBLIC

DOUGLAS N. DICKSON
Editor

JOHN WILEY & SONS
New York • Chichester • Brisbane • Toronto • Singapore

Library of Congress Cataloging in Publication Data:

Main entry under title:

Business and its public.

   (Harvard business review executive book series)
   Includes indexes.
   1. Public relations—Addresses, essays, lectures.
2. Industry—Social aspects—Addresses, essays, lectures.
3. Corporate image—Addresses, essays, lectures.
I. Dickson, Douglas N.   II. Series.

HD59.B865   1984   659.2'85   83-23487
ISBN 0-471-88749-8

Printed in the United States of America

10 9 8 7 6 5 4 3 2 1

Foreword

For sixty years, the *Harvard Business Review* has been the farthest reaching executive program of the Harvard Business School. It is devoted to the continuing education of executives and aspiring managers primarily in business organizations, but also in not-for-profit institutions, in government, and in the professions. Through its publishing partners, reprints, and translation programs, it finds an audience in many languages in most countries in the world, occasionally penetrating even the barrier between East and West.

The *Harvard Business Review* draws on the talents of the most creative people in modern business and in management education. About half its content comes from practicing managers, the rest from professional people and university researchers. Everything *HBR* publishes has something to do with the skills, attitudes, and knowledge essential to the competent and ethical practice of management.

This book consists of 34 articles that offer advice on how to shape the complex relationships linking the modern corporation to its various publics. Managers have often been engrossed in public relations and public affairs programs without critically examining either substance or purpose. This collection offers insight from some of the most distinguished HBR authors into the philosophical and practical importance of public relations. Nurturing or protecting the identity of a company is an executive function growing in importance as all those concerned about business become increasingly observant of company performance.

Neither abstruse nor superficial, the articles chosen for this volume are intended to be usefully analytical, challenging, and carefully prescriptive. Every well-informed business person can follow the exposition in its path away from the obvious and into the territory of independent thought. I hope that readers can adapt these ideas to their own unique situations and thus make their professional careers more productive.

KENNETH R. ANDREWS, Editor
Harvard Business Review

Contents

Part Six   Relations with Stockholders

BUSINESS
AND ITS
PUBLIC

Introduction

DOUGLAS N. DICKSON

Perhaps nothing has characterized the post World War II period of American business more than a preoccupation with public relations. After companies lost the positive public image earned through their war effort—a positive image that had helped, in part, erase black marks suffered during the worst part of the Depression (from disclosures of the actions of stock speculators) and after (from vocal corporate opposition to FDR)—top executives began to accept the position that better relations, and a sound public position, could be had if they were willing to work for it.

The road to true acceptance did not come easily, however. A love-hate relationship between business and the public is natural in the United States. Many times throughout our history, companies have come under attack because they are the backbone of the economic system. Especially with the predominance of big business enterprises in the late nineteenth century, with the subsequent muckraking disclosures of price fixing and poor business practices of monopolies, and the reverses of the Depression, the public has blamed business for whatever economic ills trouble America.

Executives constantly complain that the public is after them, as if that were a new phenomenon. But, as Alfred Chandler has written, "(Even) in 1912—one of the rare national elections where there were four, rather than two, major candidates—all four promised in somewhat different ways to regulate business."

Up until the postwar period, most companies simply threw up their hands, formed their wagons in a circle, and tried to keep out the public. But after World War II, some executives changed their attitudes toward their public relations just as they did in many other areas of business (for example, encounters with the federal government). Relations could be managed, like anything else, and somehow defused of their negative impact.

The emphasis placed on public relations increased and took on more importance when public distrust magnified into anger during the 1960s. Initial revelations about pollution and corporate involvement with chemical warfare

1

during the Vietnam War, along with the rise of consumerism in the late 1960s and a corresponding increase in federal regulation helped lend credence to the idea that companies had to do something to make their public image more positive. Because some companies (even those within the same industry) managed to escape vilification, the executives of companies that were not so lucky could not really dispute the importance of good public relations. Few could comfortably say that they no longer cared what the public thought.

But recognizing that they should care and actually caring are not the same thing. These executives were simply interested in getting out of corporate hot water.

Most companies instituted formal programs to monitor various publics (whether consumers, employees, or the federal government) in order to react more effectively to a crisis. Many set up offices in Washington to monitor and influence the legislative process. Budgets were increased, more executive time spent on public relations.

Not all of this activity was reactive, of course. Many executives began to support cultural and leisure activities more openly than they had in the past, and looked for opportunities to promote a better image with the communities in which they operated. The field of public relations was widened to include relations with current and potential stockholders; most big companies now spend a great deal of time monitoring the way analysts perceive their organization. In response, they allotted middle management time for the presentation of the most positive corporate image to the investing public, often pushing traditional vehicles like annual reports or institutional advertising up to the realm of "corporate art nouveau."

Whatever the form, however, management's preoccupation of the 1950s and 1960s with public relations gradually became an obsession, and reached a zenith when, at the beginning of the 1970s many chief executive officers maintained that they spent more than 50% of their time in handling some kind of public relations activity.

But has it worked? Is the American public more satisfied with companies than before? There seems to be a new public interest in the subject of business, and a parallel rise in distrust of government. Government is not seen as being capable of doing much, while some companies are said to hold the key to long-term stability. Like the period of the 1920s, investors are pouring money into the stock market.

Many people no longer shun the pursuit of a business career, and need to understand how business works in order to succeed. They become interested in the possibilities of their own businesses, thinking that it can often provide the freedom they need to do what they want. Business magazines have flourished in the last decade, and business stories are given greater prominence in the media. Common sense seems to indicate that if a company is doing something well, the environment is right for it to tell its story more easily than ever before.

Very little of this rosy picture is the result of public relations, however. In the same way that companies turned to PR out of blatant self-interest, so the interest shown by the public in business comes from the same self-center. In the light of the harsh economic realities of the 1970s, many of us have simply realized that we need a job to survive. A better understanding of how that job works will allow us to compete more realistically in the market.

Most big, as opposed to small, business is still looked on with distrust. When surveyed, much of the American public maintains the traditional adversary stance (with the momentary exception of high-technology companies). At bottom, Americans cannot easily change their historic love-hate feeling about companies. Added recently to the injury of the criticism that business has unleashed environmental and consumer chaos on unsuspecting communities, has been the insult of the charge that outmoded American management practices have led to corporate failure before the onslaught of foreign competition and, along the way, the economic ruin of our country. Recent revelations that executives are being paid fortunes when they leave a company in the wake of a takeover, help buttress all the negative opinions of Americans about big business and its excess.

Given this operating environment, it's no wonder that most managers remain dissatisfied with the way their public relations work. Executives complain bitterly about the negative reactions toward them from various publics. In a recent survey of top management opinion, executives overwhelmingly stated that their public relations programs did not achieve desired goals. Most seem to agree with Irving Shapiro, who commented in *HBR* that "Business . . . is [still] seen as an uncontrolled power that bends the political process to its will and is not sincerely concerned with the quality of its products or the safety of the people whose lives it affects—which is to say, just about everybody.''

Why All This Wheel Spinning?

But why have many of the good intentions of companies borne such little measurable fruit with the public? Especially given a good climate of opinion? Is the public simply ungrateful? Will it always bite the hand that feeds it?

Admittedly, business seems to have to fight a losing battle in the United States. Accomplishments are too often missed, while failures are touted for all to hear. Most institutions come under attack when things go bad (as the economy has) and business will come under attack as long as things go wrong. Besides, the American public will always idealize the image of anything small fighting anything big (whether it's Elliot and E.T., the frontier hero carving his way out of the wilderness, or the struggling entrepreneur) while distrusting anything big and institutionalized (whether it's Washington bureaucrats, landowners, or business.)

Despite that, companies still expect that PR can work miracles and that it can produce a positive response even when the company has done something that is obviously stupid or wrong. Those that complain need to look at certain companies that capably maintain a positive image with the American public and American investors. It's not just the industry in which the company operates, either. Philip Morris sells products that cause death; yet its image remains basically sound. Mobil and Shell are both oil companies that have benefited from high oil prices, yet Mobil is seen as a neanderthal institution while Shell is "enlightened."

Why the difference? For one thing, executive obsession with the public's image of the company has often blinded the manager to the reality of the organization's performance, which, after all, is what the public is most interested in. Trying to get the best publicity for a company is not the same thing as trying to improve the company's processes, or its relations with its employees, or the best strategy for the future, success with which will help insure the best kind of public relations.

For another, companies have not learned the lessons of the past very well. Many still react to the public in a negative way, that is, not by telling the truth or doing good works, but rather by being suspicious of the public's motives, trying to manipulate opinion rather than understanding and profiting from it, and simply using public relations to cover up mistakes. In that way, executives make the same kind of public relations blunders they have for years. They institute formal programs without backing them up with the right kind of support. Real problems are handled essentially in an ad hoc fashion. PR obscures reality, rather than illuminating it. Executives don't look far enough down the road; they don't use their own assets on an ongoing basis. For example, most don't take the time to listen to criticisms of corporate policies that come from dissenters *within* the corporation, criticisms that often precede, and are harbingers of, problems outside the company. They become frustrated with public relations managers because they can't deliver, and then turn to public relations firms, which don't have industry expertise, to bail them out.

Not every company makes these kinds of mistakes. But the overall record of business is still unsatisfying. And business itself remains unsatisfied with the result.

So, what's the answer? For companies to ignore the public and simply concentrate on making quality products? To worry about improving relations with their employees, and properly motivating personnel? Obviously, no good company can ignore either. But, while companies must pursue all of these avenues, they cannot realistically ignore the public. Now that the Pandora's box has been opened, companies cannot close it.

Instead, managers have to learn to practice the art well, by putting it in its proper place as an adjunct to a good strategic program. Companies must not let public relations become an obsession, but recognize it for what it is, and when and how it is important. Managers should practice it in a way that will benefit the public and the corporation.

Here is a good dramatization of the problem:

> When business is bad, or at least does not live up to expectations, management tries to do everything it can to find the cause of the trouble and provide the remedy. On such occasions, however, many executives seem to have a weakness for patent medicines. They tend to look for ready-made solutions as described in the latest . . . "how-to" publications. These cures often work, partly because the formulas contain some ingredients which are of real value. But sometimes they can do great harm. If the ailment is serious, something drastic may be required to save the business; and wasting time on faddist measures may prove fatal.
>
> Image making is one of the more dangerous types of management panaceas. It gives the false impression that a fundamental change is being made, for creating a new image of oneself seems deceptively like creating a new self. . . . Management needs to do more than change its image to change itself. Recognizing its blind spots and learning useful new skills are essentials.

A couple of paragraphs from the latest critique of managers in the pages of *HBR*? Maybe a page torn from *In Search for Excellence*? No, that is David Finn, a long time public relations practitioner, writing in 1961 to the readers of *HBR*, trying to show them where public relations is needed, and where it goes astray.

In fact, some of the best advice on practicing the art of public relations has appeared in the pages of the *Harvard Business Review*. Most (if you ignore some of the archaic references to current events) continues to be valid. The reason is fairly simple. Good public relations is founded on a philosophic recognition by top management that telling the simple truth about the corporation, both about its potential and its difficulties, will win the right kind of public recognition.

Unlike some other business practices, public relations is not, by definition or practice, a science. Sound advice does not become obsolete. Certainly, research can give the executive current answers about the best way to position a company in relation to particular markets. But, to work, public relations needs to be implemented effectively by sophisticated professionals, knowledgeable about the company and its strategy as well as about the media.

We've culled the issues of *HBR* since the first recognition by companies of the importance of public relations. I've found that the advice given in the late 1940s and 1950s is among the best written on the subject. It is thoughtful and philosophical, and perhaps brings public relations down to earth. Only by recognizing the practical possibilities of public relations can a company implement an effective program.

It is in the implementation of a good public relations program that the articles in this collection can help—not by providing the latest figures on U.S. demographics, or the rundown on which congressional representative is the most effective on which committee. But rather by providing sound advice, not only on the rationale behind practicing the best kind of public relations, but also how to implement and manage the program effectively.

Is There a Problem?

The starting point for effective public relations is a recognition by management that there is a real problem to be solved. Public distrust does not often come willy-nilly, but rather when the company has made a mistake. The mistake itself may not be large, but it may be an indication that something within the company is wrong and should be corrected. Companies should not get wound up in grandiose cosmetic plans to deal with the symptoms, but rather concentrate on acknowledging difficulty, and then on taking steps to cure the disease.

Many executives still spend a great deal of time wondering whether they should be concerned about public reaction. But they are wheel spinning. It's been a long time since companies could ignore their constituencies. And there is little doubt that they must at least consider the interaction of their management decisions with the public. From a philosophic point of view, it is impossible to ignore the fact that companies have other responsibilities beyond those of providing quality products, a good return for shareholders, or jobs for employees.

Despite lip service paid to the wonders of the free-market system, executives distrust its vagaries. But they should learn to understand them. Especially given today's economic realities, when the good, often lifelong, reputations of many companies and executives are beginning to fall apart, it is obvious that many organizations will have to spend a great deal of time searching for ways to engender renewed public confidence. A bad reputation does not simply affect the company's share price. It affects the ability to operate; to attract, keep, and motivate good quality personnel; to maintain good relations with customers; to beat out competitors and win over the government. In fact, a good reputation is a necessary prerequisite for continued smooth operations.

Just admitting that fact is not enough. Because, without a deeper understanding of the rationale behind it, companies can lapse into public relations programs that are nothing more than image making. A good reputation can be had only if it is pursued properly and for the right reasons. A company does not begin to improve its public relations by hiring a flashy PR manager, or an even flashier CEO. Top management must first understand the company's own internal identity and culture and then its place in society and the marketplace. Without this understanding or recognition that a strong internal identity is important, a company can never interact effectively with the outside world. The discussion of culture and identity is outside the scope of a book on public relations, but understanding that one exists is fundamental to understanding what good public relations can be.

This internal understanding may begin with an understanding of the place, or distinct role, that companies play in American society. They create value for a whole host of publics in the United States. Whether it's their own employees or customers, or the people living in a community near each manufacturing installation, the company shares some responsibility for doing its job well, insofar as it affects each. The only way to tell whether a good job is being done is for the company to listen to the opinions of those within the company who interact with these various levels. Good external relations begins with sound internal management.

Almost 30 years ago, the eminent business historian Thomas Cochran wrote a landmark article in *HBR*, "Business and the Democratic Tradition," in which he castigated companies for ignoring the strengths of that tradition. He found that, despite their place in a democratic society, companies had done little to make themselves democratic. And that this failure was directly related to their failure to gain solid reputations with the American public. Most companies have rarely enjoyed a good reputation, because they are "regarded as lacking in the moral and spiritual qualities desired at the top level of national leaders."

Instead of showing their good side, or seeking to better understand the problem, many corporate executives continue to remain behind stone walls in their top management towers. Cochran asserted, "There are few democratic procedures in business by which opinion from below can effectively influence the major actions of those on top." The simple fact is that companies must learn to accommodate internal criticism and debate in order to learn, and accept the truth about themselves and their corporate actions. The acceptance of this truth will allow the company to be candid about it. Then, the company will be able to communicate more readily to, and interact with, the public.

Recognizing a need to be candid within itself, in order to interact with the public, however, does not, as I tried to indicate in the first part of this introduction, guarantee the right attitude by the executives leading the companies. It is always difficult to be candid; but the best companies try.

Public relations should not be an attempt to create an illusion any more than sound management is the creation of an illusion. It is the recognition of the possible, and good public relations is its explanation. The best experts always caution against obvious promotion, inviting, as it does, obvious attack. David Finn advised,

> Self-promotion cannot take precedence over the natural processes by which society corrects and improves itself in a dynamic culture. The main instrument of those natural processes is free and independent crit-

icism, the very institution which public relations so often seems bent on destroying. It is not the job of public relations to secure public support for a cause any more than its function is to mold or evolve public opinion. Its purpose instead is to make management's opinion public and present the case for the causes that managers believe in.

The Philosophic Base

Forging a good program depends on a managerial acceptance of a philosophic base for that program. It cannot present a false case, or an illusory one, to the public listeners. In the end, the illusion will evaporate, and the truth will almost always come out. Good public relations does not depend on manipulation of public opinion, rather it accepts the public and works with it.

The executive will know whether a program is sufficiently candid if it subjects the rationale for its public relations effort to internal scrutiny. Consideration of the potential criticisms of a proposed action, and then construction of fair response, will almost always result in a better outcome. Good public relations, like anything else, does not simply respond to criticism but generates the kind of corporate action that will defuse criticism.

That takes a great deal of time and effort, and moves the plane of public relations from ad hoc response to a position in long-term strategy. To do that, the company must reflect a corporate identity or public face that dovetails with reality and the company's achievements along with its struggle to contain reverses. Public relations cannot slip into a statement of business ideology, with which the public is more than familiar. It cannot stonewall, nor pander to the public.

Along the way, executives learn to take a positive and not a negative stance in dealings with the outside world. This 180° turn from traditional beliefs will benefit practically everyone. Alfred Chandler has pointed out that, before the end of the nineteenth century, business enjoyed a positive position with its public. Executives were respected and moved back and forth easily between community and corporate duties.

But they took too much for granted, and excesses led to the muckrakers, and the end of the positive position. Now, executives are still convinced that everyone (whether it's stockholders, customers, consumers, or the government) are out to attack their every move. As Ted Levitt explained in "Why business always loses," this naturally negative attitude is "rooted in the fact that [executives] are trying to do the best job they can and keep to a minimum the uncertainties with which they must deal." Ministering to the opinons of the public is fraught with such uncertainty. But if executives will recognize what business has in common with the public, they might stop trying to second-guess the public to avoid uncertainty, or spending too much time using PR to create a smokescreen between themselves and public opinion.

They've got to get rid of the smokescreen. Often it takes the form of a simple denial of all accusations. Such denials never work; they only lead to more inquiries. Executives say that being straight with the public doesn't work. But they're wrong. Those companies that react positively enjoy positive reactions in return. Philip Morris's quiet program of cultural activities, or Shell's "Answer Man" brochures do not obscure their corporate mistakes, but they add a positive side against which the negatives can be properly gauged.

For example, during the controversy surrounding the activities of the multinational corporation in the late 1960s and early 1970s, companies simply replied "no" to every criticism (such as the assertion that an MNC exercised too much economic power in less-developed countries.) But their actions did nothing to calm anyone. Instead, the controversy continued and grew. At the time, John Kenneth Galbraith (by all accounts no lover of the larger company) advised that they must concede the enormity of their power and stress that "it has been deployed, on balance, for socially useful ends; that where it has not, it must expect to be restrained by the nation state."

In most cases, a calm, positive approach may often mean that the best public relations program is the one pitched at the lowest key. Mobil, after all, spends a great deal of money on promoting cultural activities. But it trumpets everything at full volume, and the stridency of its position on public issues obscures whatever good it's doing through other activities.

In discussing the problems of companies in the late 1940s, John Welcker suggested that companies had not been able to relate to their public because the pattern of these relations at various levels is too intricate. The complexity means that there is no simple standard or solution. A good image with the public is based on perceptions that are, by nature, intangible and constantly in flux. He suggested that thoughtful interaction with the community at the plant level is the best kind of PR, and the kind that the public will not perceive cynically.

Throughout the articles on public relations, these kinds of basic themes are sounded again and again. Business must understand its own identity before it can hope to interact effectively with the public; it must listen to internal criticism and respond effectively to that criticism, and in doing so, it will learn to respond to the public; if it takes a positive attitude toward itself it will be easy to have one with the public; companies must balance any programs; they shouldn't ignore the public nor become unduly fond of pleasing it. The main idea behind public relations should not be for the company to set up mechanisms to diffuse negative public incidents in order to contain their potential damage, but rather to tell the corporate story candidly, and regularly over many years, in order to build up the kind of solid reputation that can withstand any kind of storm.

It Can Be Managed

Each of the articles in this collection spends a great deal of time providing a rationale for the right kind of public relations; I think that's an important first step, and one that is often ignored. In addition, however, they also advise managers on the best ways to forge a public relations program. It may contain diverse elements, from media to investor relations, from defining a corporate identity to creating links between corporate executives and the public. But each good program will start out with a strong definition of purpose that is not far beyond the company's central strategy.

This connection is essential because "too often management accepts the need for public relations before adequately appreciating what public relations does that is different and worth the price. . . . [Too often] 'good public relations' is supported as a matter of policy while management proceeds to violate sound public relations practice at every turn."

Public relations becomes an adjunct to other management functions. The best program is straightforward, and comfortable with a wide variety of approaches. Each must be tailored for the specific audience.

Most important, the company must always remember that public relations is not advertising. An organization cannot simply pay for a good reputation. Public relations firms often oversell their capabilities, and companies buy the sales pitch because they have unrealistic assumptions. No matter what professionals say, they are putting your corporate story in the hands of independent judges, who may or may not use it, and in the way that you might like.

To be effective, the best public relations program is carried out by motivated and knowledgeable personnel working for the organization, with the right kind of power base, and knowledge about strategy and the company's history, culture, and future prospects. Despite all the publicity given to public relations, companies ask their public relations managers to do unrealistic things, at the same time they give them little or no power. They relegate professionals to menial tasks, writing annual reports, sending out press releases on every new product introduction or investment, or simply searching for ways to give the CEO more press coverage. Good PR does not have as its aim the creation of celebrity status for a CEO, or even for the company itself.

Good public relations has as its goal the development and maintenance of a solid corporate reputation. It requires a staff that understands the company and its story, that is capable of monitoring the various publics with which the company interacts, and that will be able to judge whether small trends, which anyone can notice, will in fact blow up into problems that might interfere with the company's operations. The idea is to develop a long-term program, not an ad hoc response to every chance that the company might have to get a "good story" into the papers.

This requires a group of professionals that understands that they have responsibility to make the right kinds of input. But that public relations should never be far away from what the company produces, and should be part of the program for the best kind of production (whether of goods or services.) Professionals should have the authority to release, as well as obtain, information.

Experiences here at *HBR* reveal the negative, as well as positive, side of public relations. One bank has been working on a story that will advise companies on a range of financing possibilities in a particular area. Seems straightforward enough, but the story has been shuffled back and forth between both public relations people who are assigned to "pull it off" and top management who keeps robbing it of any significance by taking out the details that are important to our readers, getting anything out of it.

On the opposite end, many top managers have sent in articles that are straightforward, and tell their story well. They don't stint on details or hide positions. You can argue with what they say, but they subject their ideas to the court of public opinion without trying to obfuscate them.

Public relations must be managed well. It's difficult because, unlike advertising, the impact of public relations cannot be measured quickly. It takes time and dedication to corporate excellence on all fronts that will translate into an excellent image with the public. Public relations should not be the only thing a company thinks about; no company should be obsessed with image over substance. Attention must be paid to a straightforward, low-key approach. PR professionals, who know and understand the company, should be given the responsibility and access to do the job well. Above all, executives need to understand the reality of public relations—what it can, and can't, do well.

PART ONE
SHOULD A COMPANY CARE WHAT THE PUBLIC THINKS?
AN OVERVIEW

Before a company can logically decide to what extent and in what form it needs, and how to manage, a comprehensive program of public relations, it must decide the rationale behind it. What place does the company in particular, and business and general, have in society? Does the company consider that it has a responsibility to the public? Or simply to the stockholders? To its employees? Or to the government?

The articles in this section cover the debate on business responsibility to the public as it has evolved since the Second World War. They will give managers the best kind of philosophic discussion to mull over. In "Business and the Democratic Tradition," the historian Thomas Cochran throws down the gauntlet by charging business with neglecting to operate within the harmony, tradition, and ideals of a democracy. By not affirming a belief in the equality of man, business does not, in short, place itself squarely in line with the democratic tradition, and, because of that, is not able to "sell" its side of the case very well to the public. Companies today, who continually fight this attitude, should not wonder why the media and the public give more attention to a group of workers buying back their outmoded plant, than to a corporate investment that will presumably create jobs. Cochran states that only an internal change of attitude will allow a company hope to benefit from the praise of the democratic society of which it is undeniably a part. Rather than patronizing the public—or damning it—business must learn to reflect the strengths of democracy. Such internal adjustment will undeniably lead to external recognition.

The varying opinions among Alfred Chandler, John Dunlop, George Shultz, and Irving Shapiro, chronicled in "Business and Public Policy," bring the debate up to date, with each of the four mapping out a position on the role of business in public policy. It is obvious, according to Shapiro, for example, that business can no longer ignore the public, just as it is obvious to the historian Chandler that it must end its adversary relation with the government. John Welcker's "The Community-Relations Problem of Industrial Companies," talks about particular problems within individual communities, the smallest piece of the democracy, and recommends more close interaction on that level.

In "Why Business Always Loses," Ted Levitt agrees with Chandler that companies must take a different stance toward the public and the government, recognizing that changes in the marketplace can spell opportunity and not danger. Most important, when business locks horns with the public, it almost inevitably comes up short. Peter Berger's "New Attack on the Legitimacy of Business" describes the origins of the latest attacks on business as stemming from the rise of a new class of government employees, lawyers, and the media, as well as academics, and suggests that a company can help restore public confidence with a more democratic and less adversarial treatment of its various constituencies, always emphasizing the bond between capitalism and democracy.

David Finn strikes at the difficulty of achieving this goal in "The Price of Corporate Vanity." Recognizing that companies prefer easy solutions, such as simplistic corporate "dress up" programs, to thoughtful interaction with both the public and private world, Finn nevertheless calls on companies to accept and even welcome criticism from without and within, recognizing that the strongest institutions benefit from critical debate, survive, and even prosper from it. In the same way, John Kenneth Galbraith calls on companies to make a better "Defense for the Multinational Corporation," not by masquerading but by conceding that they do wield great power, but that it is deployed for socially good ends and in a politically constructive fashion.

Robert Ackerman is less philosophical and more operational in "How Companies Respond to Social Demands," but his point is fundamental to the debate. Despite the best intentions of top management to foster the right kind of dialogue and interaction with the public, the company's ideals will not bear constructive fruit unless operations management is won over to them, and helps implement the programs at the lower levels of the corporation.

Finally in this section, William L. Safire's satiric "Financial Adventure of James Debenture," shows how a public relations campaign can go haywire, if based on and mired in the wrong philosophy.

1

Business and the Democratic Tradition

THOMAS C. COCHRAN

If business is to be truly representative of American culture and meet the challenge of its new role of leadership at home and abroad, it will have to make some very tough adjustments.

In the eyes of the rest of the world, a dynamic system of production and distribution is the outstanding characteristic of American culture. Even here at home business is probably now regarded as the most vital force in a rapidly changing society. But beyond this general belief relatively little attention has been given to just what part business actually has played and is playing in shaping American culture. For example, could Charles Wilson's unfortunate statement about the country and General Motors be properly rephrased as "What happens in General Motors is representative of American thought and action"?

The answer to that question should throw considerable light on two of the most important problems which baffle industrial leaders today: (1) the negative reactions of so many Americans, reflected every day in newspapers, novels, public opinion surveys, and the like, to the values and objectives of industrial leaders; (2) the resistance of peoples elsewhere in the world to the American way of life, in competition with the ideology of communism.

Lessons of History

To answer this question of whether American business firms collectively are representative of the main elements of American culture, we must begin by considering some of the history of the interplay of business ideas and more general beliefs. The first half of the twentieth century has embraced such

15

sweeping change in practically all areas of life that it is often difficult to decide what is basic and what is superficial, what is cause and what is effect. Nevertheless, we can identify some of the trends leading to the cultural relationships which prevail today.

"The Good Old Days"

Up to 1929, businessmen shared an increasing confidence in the future of America as they conceived it. While they had been under attack in the early part of the century from socialist groups and from progressives in both major parties, the criticism had spent itself and subsided. Meanwhile, business successfully weathered the panic of 1907, and was raised by war orders from the depression of 1914. "Back to normalcy" in 1920 meant to businessmen a return to the ideas of McKinley with the approval of the American people.

The very backbone of business thinking in "the good old days" was the idea of a self-regulating economy—an economy which, if left alone by government and other "noneconomic" power groups such as labor unions, would always tend toward a position of equilibrium where all the many day-to-day decisions made on the basis of immediate self-advantage would some-how have the cumulative effect of full employment and equitable distribution of income. This doctrine, taught in schools and colleges for many genera-tions, was believed in by so many people outside the business group that it came to be in fact one of the major elements of American culture of that earlier period.

Prosperity after World War I, except for a short sharp depression in 1921, re-enforced the concept of the self-regulating economy. At the same time, new business ideas were emerging regarding the role of leadership in managing the system. Walter Gifford, president of American Telephone and Telegraph, wrote in 1926:

> New conditions have called a new type of man to lead the new kind of business organization. . . . These men must take a long view ahead. They cannot decide questions merely on the basis of immediate advantage, because their company is going to be in business long after they are dead.[1]

The basic contradiction between this idea of leadership and the concept of self-regulation was not immediately evident. The 1920s were a period of buoyant optimism for business leaders, and government administrators were friendly to business. The effects of a better financial system and big cor-porations were thought to have brought a new stability to economic life.

Faith in the future of the economy was bolstered by the belief which many intellectual leaders had in inevitable social evolution. Herbert Spen-cer's idea that Darwin's theory of biological advance through competitive struggle applied also to the social system was still in good standing. While beneficent evolution might be questioned by economists trained in the Ger-man tenet that "economic laws" depend on the social aims of the system involved or in the new American philosophy of William James and John Dewey that truth is what works, these doubters appear to have been a small minority. As for the businessman, social Darwinism was simply another way of stating the "law of nature" that assured success to an able, hard-working man in a competitive society.

The evolutionary idea readily lent itself to elaboration in a doctrine of a national elite of successful businessmen. From a study of statements of men speaking for the National Association of Manufacturers (NAM) and the U. S. Chamber of Commerce in the 1920s, James W. Prothero has worked out six interrelated articles of belief:

1   The business elite are superior to other men in ability.
2   The test of ability is competitive earnings.
3   Material or economic progress is the important goal.
4   Social stability is necessary.
5   Popular or majority control is dangerous.
6   Individualism must be preserved.[2]

Granted that these views were expressed by the level of businessmen chosen to head a then inactive NAM and a Chamber of Commerce that faced few issues, yet they do indicate a tendency present in other business thought in this decade of great confidence. They also represent the continuing dilemma of business—standing for technological and scientific advance at the same time it wants social and political conservatism.

Shock of Depression

But the business ideas of "the good old days" were to meet severe opposition. And the cause was not so much social and political change outside of business as the failure to maintain material or economic progress on the part of business itself.

While the late 1920s had produced increasingly high income for the top tenth of the population, there were no important gains for the lower income groups and no rate of real capital formation that could insure against collapse and stagnation. Fundamentally, America's businessmen, lulled by confidence in automatic economic adjustment, were running an industrial machine whose intricacies they did not understand. As a matter of fact, neither businessmen themselves, nor the government administrators and economists, had any real appreciation of such crucial economic relationships as those between worker morale and productivity, government spending and consumer demand, private saving and stimulation of investment, administered prices and economic rigidity.

Perhaps adversity is the only teacher. At any rate business had to learn the precariousness of its cultural position through bitter experience. Popular confidence in the satisfactory progress of a self-regulating economy was broken in the depression of the 1930s—and at the same time Darwinism gave way to a biological theory of mutation, or inexplicable alterations rather than gradual evolution by the competitive process.

To many Americans it appeared that with the frontier gone and with a "mature" industrial plant the economy would stagnate unless government provided new incentives and opportunities. Capitalism appeared to have lost its dynamics; a higher and higher standard of living no longer seemed assured as the automatic result of the quest for personal wealth. With a declining birthrate, Robert E. Wood, chairman of the board of Sears Roebuck, warned:

> A decline in population must inevitably result in a lower rather than higher standard of living. . . . the sun has passed its zenith and the shadows of afternoon have begun to fall.[3]

It may be hard for younger men of the present day to realize the degree to which business confidence and prestige were shaken by the events of 1931 to 1933. As a result business leaders lacked morale to oppose the idea that the government aid to business offered by the Hoover administration was necessary, or the subsequent idea, reluctantly accepted even by its political advocates at the time, that government must assume responsibility for the economic welfare and security of its citizens. A radically new conception of the use of federal power was beginning to develop, implying not only relief and social security, but also government investment and subsidy to stimulate purchasing power and employment.

Not that businessmen as a whole agreed with these views; they blamed the Depression either on the upsetting effects of World War I or on the frailty of individuals, and criticized the spending policies of Congress in the Hoover administration. In 1932, for example, Alfred P. Sloan, Jr., president of General Motors, said: "The trouble at Washington is that large sums have been voted for post offices, pensions and bonuses not justified."[4]

By the mid-1930s many businessmen were saying that government had already intruded so far that the economy was no longer self-regulating. Possibly, they conceded, the new economy, because it was a mixture of government and private enterprise, needed certain government incentives to avoid the danger of stagnation; but the more state aid it received, the more mixed it tended to become and hence the more aid it would need in the future—and so on and on until the private sector might vanish altogether. Thus did businessmen get caught in the dilemma which to this day they have not been able to resolve completely.

Rise of Bureaucracy

Loss of confidence in the theory of self-regulation was bound to lead to a reassessment of business ideas and new conceptions of the place of business in American society. This painful struggle for readjustment must be seen in relation to another major change in society, the rise of bureaucracy.

Judged by the standards of 1800, American society in 1900 was already bureaucratic, but apparently this fact did not bother anyone at the time.

Congressional debates and serious writing were concerned with the struggles of little business against big business and of individuals against the "laws of nature," but not with the struggles of individuals against collective bureaucracy. Not until the rise of collectivist governments of both right and left in Europe after 1917 were Americans alerted to this issue. The further growth of enormous business companies in the 1920s led intellectuals to extend the scope of their questioning, and the New Deal at last made bureaucracy a major concern.

Although the growth of big government first called general attention to it, the bureaucratic system was actually a response to industrial mass production. Big plants required big management, and the social and economic problems growing from concentration of working population necessitated more and more government. Since the company big enough to have a true bureaucracy—that is, a broad layer of middle management which neither initiated policies nor directly carried them out—would normally be run by professional executives, the rise of bureaucracy also went hand in hand with that of managerial enterprise.

Evaluation at Mid-Century

By mid-century a large part of the individual's contacts were with representatives of various large organizations. Social scientists and artists tended increasingly to see both government and business bureaucracy as parts of the larger problem of the individual in a highly organized impersonal society. Writers such as Frederic Wakeman (*The Hucksters*) and John P. Marquand (*Point of No Return*) turned out penetrating satires of the business bureaucracy with the implicit admonition that the individual should rebel and find some way of asserting his right to a unique human role.

Decline of Individualism

Just as Americans in general had long cherished an image of the individual on the model of the independent, courageous, self-reliant frontiersman, business philosophy in particular had dwelt upon the ruggedly individualistic element in the American national character. It was the existence of thousands of these centers of independent enterprise that made the self-regulating economy work. But with the depression, the resultant increase in government supervision and regulation, and the concurrent growth of organizational complexity, the individual seemed to account for less and less. People still clung to the idea of individual worth, but it was clear the concept needed rethinking and redefinition.

Business leaders did not usually see their own companies, with their hierarchical bureaucracies, welfare politics, and demands for loyalty, as playing a part in the redefinition of individualism. But there were others who could recognize and point out a new order. Thus, *Life* editor John K. Jessup pointed out: "For economic purposes the organization is more important than what it owns, or who works for it. It has a life of its own. It began as a mere legal person. It has acquired a social personality."[5] Management's devotion to the welfare of the corporate unit necessarily emphasized loyalty, trusteeship, self-sacrificing service, planning, and security, and de-emphasized personal acquisition. This shift in emphasis in the society was gradual, as with all cultural change, and was in an early stage by 1950.

Whether one looked at government, as did most business leaders when they lamented the loss of concern for the individual, or at big business, as did novelists and some small businessmen, the conclusion was inescapable that individualism, as traditionally conceived, was declining. Fewer men were left in impersonal relations to markets where their personal eccentricities did not count, and where individual cleverness might win immediate cash rewards. More men had to try to please their organizational associates by some degree of conformity. Businessmen were voluntarily surrendering individual freedom in order to get ahead in a bureaucratic society.

Decline of Wealth

While the traditional business beliefs in individualism, competitive survival, and freedom from governmental interference were being undermined, the social prestige of great wealth was also declining under the influences of mass production and the managerial system.

Luxury articles became increasingly standardized and within reach of practically all consumers. As late as 1930 a Ford and a Lincoln represented vastly different levels of motoring pleasure and appearance, but by 1955 many people could not tell which was which. The large house, in 1900 the chief symbol of wealth, was becoming rare; there was no longer a depressed immigrant or agricultural labor group to provide cheap servants, and the mobility of corporate executives was such that they hesitated to invest more in any one location than could be easily recovered through a sale. Sociologist David Riesman wrote on the new trend of the upper group toward "inconspicuous consumption."[6]

Re-enforcing these trends was the increasing equality of income after taxes. Taxes appeared destined to remain high and to be progressive against larger incomes on both the state and national levels. Aside from preparation for war, the industrial system needed streets, highways, schools, colleges, hospitals, and other collective facilities on a scale never thought of by earlier generations, and the money, of course, had to come from taxes. During the nearly continuous boom from 1940 on, elastic business expense accounts and tax savings on capital gains did encourage a good deal of lavish consumption, but any prolonged halt in increasing business activity and the rising value of equities would greatly narrow the range of spending.

Corporate Giving

In the field of social welfare and philanthropy, bureaucratic action was superseding the individual decisions of successful businessmen. Since the government allowed corporations to contribute a part of their income to charitable or educational institutions before paying taxes, there was a large saving in having such gifts made directly by the companies rather than by the receivers of already taxed dividends. This led to the setting up of general foundations such as The Ford Foundation, and to direct corporate support of higher education. Explaining his participation in this movement, Chairman Frank W. Abrams of the Standard Oil Company of New Jersey said:

> I know I can't take any credit for this. I'm just an ordinary business guy that got shoved into something. It's like being thrown into a Billy Sunday meeting, I suppose, and getting converted. You didn't want to go in, but somebody pushed you—they thought you needed it. And it has been rather overwhelming, and highly satisfying.[7]

The importance of this shift is probably not in its influence on the character of education or welfare agencies. It may be easy to imagine that higher education, perhaps the most influential conditioner of the political and social ideas of future leaders, will fall under the control of business, and a few businessmen have added to these fears by writing of the obligation of the colleges to teach the free-enterprise system. However, private education has always been supported by men who have made their money in business. Donors seem no more likely to interfere with academic freedom as corporate executives than they did as private citizens.

The real significance of corporate giving is the way it marks the emergence of the big company as a quasi-public institution with social and political responsibilities. But while this can be interpreted as a fresh source of democracy to counteract the increased influence of centralized government, it is a very impersonal kind of democracy—it is the democracy of big units rather than the democracy of individuals.

The Problem of Democracy

There still exists the problem that has beset the corporate form of organization since its beginnings in the early nineteenth century—the inability to achieve a democratic system of operation *within the company*.

The spirit of business has always been efficient exercise of authority from the top down. But business is the leading institution in a social system called democracy; to be truly representative it too must be democratic. And democracy works from the bottom up. This means more than equality of opportunity for those qualified to rise, more than democratic manners that allow a worker to call the president by his first name. It means policy formation on a participative basis and an increased business willingness to study and respond to the problems and values of American society. As Sir George Schuster, a British business leader, put it:

> If we try, as many of us do who hold managerial responsibilities, to set out a list of ideals which we are to aim at, or which we think are good

for people for whose employment we are responsible, then I think we are doomed to disaster. *We have to work with an intelligent population.*[8]

Nonmaterial Values

One unmistakable clash between the democratic and the business traditions has been the old assumption that workers are purely "economic men," interested only in material satisfactions. This assumption came under attack as a result of Elton Mayo's study at the Hawthorne plant of General Electric in the late 1920s, and his book, *The Human Problems of an Industrial Civilization*.[9] But the results of this advanced thinking have been slow to spread, and there has been a tendency to apply so-called human relations formulas as gimmicks or manipulative devices rather than sincerely seeking participation.

As late as 1952, *Time* ran a special two-page section, "Human Relations: A New Art Brings a Revolution in Industry." One of the illustrative cases concerned a change in the method of pajama making:

> One group was simply told of the change, another was told of the necessity for it and permitted to work out for itself the necessary revisions in quotas and rates. Result: the second group's production quickly passed the old average of 60 hourly units per worker, and reached more than 80. The first group barely exceeded 50 units, and 17 percent of its members shortly quit.

The article ends with a quotation from Clarence Francis, chairman of the board of General Foods:

> It is ironic that Americans—the most advanced people technically, mechanically, and industrially—should have waited until a comparatively recent period to inquire into the most promising single source of productivity: namely the human will to work. It is hopeful on the other hand that the search is now underway.[10]

Despite many articles and books since then, there still exists "a great demand for guidance and enlightenment on the part of . . . businessmen, who apparently feel all of a sudden that they are deficient in the practice of human relations."[11] Such a feeling of the need to do something in this area is evidence of the persistence of the problem as well as of some progress.

A weakness in the search for what creates the will to work is failure to recognize the wholeness of human personality. The will to work depends not only on good working conditions and respect for the dignity of the worker, but also on the employee's approval of the company, its policies, and its role in society. The talk of businessmen and labor leaders alike is still too much in terms of material wants and satisfactions. Eric Larabee, an editor of *Harper's*, noted at the Corning Glass Works' conference of businessmen and scholars that there was a tendency on both sides to "speak of 'human values' as distinct entities, almost as though they had similar qualities to goods and services."[12]

Seldom does business discussion rise to the level of searching for new positive nonmaterial values that could make business a world-wide standard-bearer of democracy. The fact that a magazine like this one, which is read by top business executives, should have received a citation in 1955 from The Laymen's Movement for a Christian World for a series of five articles providing "insight concerning spiritual values in business,"[13] as if that were something unique, is simply a sign of the rarity of business thinking about the nonmaterial aspects of organization.

Conflict of Ideals

Lack of democracy is certainly not a failing peculiar to American business. On the contrary, American business is probably more democratic than business anywhere else in the world. The trouble is that in the course of its growth from small shop to great corporation it has failed to embody in its structure and operation some basic ideals of American culture.

Defining specific ideals in a complex culture like that of the United States is a difficult task, avoided by most scholars of a scientific bent, and done only impressionistically by visiting literary men or journalistic pundits. Such playing with abstractions is clearly not a game for active business leaders. Yet there have been some cultural common denominators which few Americans would question; they find expression in sayings and beliefs passed on to children by generations of parents and re-enforced by repetition in millions of schoolbooks.

Some of these, such as the belief that rational effort counts, that change is generally good, that active mastery of a problem rather than fatalistic acceptance is the American way, or that interest in the external world of things is better than inner contemplation, have re-enforced the attitudes of businessmen. But other themes that emphasize the American democratic and religious heritage, such as the need for justification of behavior in terms of Christian morality, the strong belief in equality as a law of nature or the "cult of the common man," and the right of every adult to have an equal voice in making decisions affecting the common welfare, have often conflicted with business action.[14] These latter are basic ideals, however, that underlie the operation of most social organizations, of almost all Protestant religions, and of all American governments.

The average businessman, whether of 1850 or 1950, would probably subscribe to these latter ideals in principle, but he would admit, when pressed on the subject, that often they do not appear immediately applicable in business. Business, he might argue, has to have a system of ideals of its own, such as physical efficiency, substantial rewards for unusual ability, and clear lines of authority based on the sanction of ownership. Insofar as the coexistence of these two systems is reconcilable, it is on the basis that business is a special part of the nation's activity which justifies its deviations from the precepts of the Bible and the Declaration of Independence by a flood of products that make a better life possible in all other spheres. From

the sacrifice of certain ideals on the economic altar comes their richer fulfillment in the life of the nation.

Ambiguous Attitude

This rift between business ideals and those of the common people helps to
explain the ambiguous popular attitude toward business leaders. They are
respected for their material success, their control over jobs, and their ability
to supply capital or credit, but regarded as lacking in the moral and spiritual
qualities desired in the top level of national leaders. In American folklore
the farmer's values and attitudes are virtues, while those of the businessman
foster such vices as covetousness and vanity. The upbringing of the poor
country boy was idealized and regarded as a guarantee that, even if he later
achieved economic success, his basic ideas would be moral in the Protestant
religious sense, and they would be democratic in the common people's sense.

Businessmen are seriously troubled by public distrust only when it
takes the form of regulatory legislation. The almost unchallenged position
of business executives as decision makers in their own sphere of action over
many generations gives them the feeling that their ideas are right and that
the public should conform to them. Businessmen tend to regard other types
of leaders as unreliable or incompetent. The motives of politicians are suspect
as corrupt and insincere. Professors, ministers, and literary men are held to
be impractical and likely to have theories dangerous to social stability.

This anti-intellectual attitude has been strong ever since the later nineteenth century. Merle E. Curti, a leading scholar of American thought, notes
that "American respect for business, and the businessman's inadequate
appreciation of the intellectual have, by tradition, been pretty generally taken
for granted."[15] Thus the businessman has been able to a degree to live in
his part of the culture by his own precepts, regarding other beliefs as unimportant to the main task at hand: the material improvement of the nation.

That the tacit assumption of superior business understanding still persists is illustrated by an interesting example:

> In 1950 Edward Bernays, one of the most prescient and philosophical of
> public relations men, promoter of the concept that public relations was
> a two-way street down which ideas came from the public to business,
> nevertheless delivered a speech in Boston on "How American Business
> Can Sell the American Way of Life to the American People."[16] One
> wonders if a small voice at the other end of the two-way street replied:
> "How Can the American People Sell the American Way of Life to
> Business?"

Actually, this instance is somewhat unfair to both Bernays and to
advanced business thought, but it illustrates the unfortunate if more or less
unconscious historic assumption that society should conform to what managers deem best for business.

Often serving as the justification for business dogmatism has been the idea that business decisions are squarely based on the requirements of the market. No doubt in the old days of small business, low mechanization, and weak market controls the businessman struggling for survival in a competitive situation had little leeway. But the big companies of today, the ones that set the tone of business thinking, do have considerable control over prices in the market. And, as already noted, such companies have already gone far in the support of community services, education, and welfare plans for workers.

The fact remains that the *decisions* to do these good deeds have not generally been participated in by their beneficiaries. Aside from dealings with organized labor, there are few democratic procedures in business by which opinion from below can effectively influence the major actions of those on top, or by which changes in policy can be opened to advance discussions. The practical difficulties in the way are great, though not as great as they once were. But if business is to be truly democratic, then the challenge is to find some way to overcome them.

The World Mission

The challenge is all the greater because of the effect upon the rest of the world. In the past the heterogeneous, loosely knit institutions and organizations constituting business never faced the need for a "theology" that would sell the faith to the rest of the world. Now there is an extra reason for business to emphasize qualities that have always been presumed to lie outside its immediate concerns. That this is asking a great deal of business is obvious, but the importance is obvious too.

The aftermath of World War II has placed the American business system in an international spotlight. The United States emerged in the late 1940s as the only Western nation strong enough to undertake world leadership, and she led from a position of strength based primarily on the success of her economic system. Thus, for better or for worse, American business has become a key protagonist in the physical struggle with world communism.

However, the contest is not only a matter of material superiority, and the fight for world influence cannot be won by economic means alone. If such were the case, America would triumph, and American businessmen, as the directors of these economic forces, would be the world's natural leaders. But the United States is battling for men's minds—their hopes, aims, and allegiance—and it is increasingly evident that success depends on a spiritual and intellectual appeal rather than on mere respect for economic power. Approval must be voluntary and cannot be commanded. And although America has had little difficulty selling the products of her fields and factories overseas—her industrial machinery, agricultural implements, petroleum products, grain and crude cotton, automotive equipment—she has not yet sold the rest of the world on the soundness of the American experience.

Because the contacts of the mass of the people with things American are to such a large extent with businessmen and their products, the representatives of U.S. economic power must assume a significant role in this winning of social approval. Thus the very success of American business has placed it in a position for which it never consciously prepared, and for which it is not especially fitted.

I do not mean to say that the businessman will have to take up the whole burden. Political leaders, religious bodies, writers, artists, students— all these groups must help define and sell America to the rest of the world. America is *not* just a business system; it is many things and must have many and various representatives. But since this article is addressed primarily to a business audience, I shall concentrate on the part business must play.

Necessary Adjustments

For this purpose two adjustments are required of business: (1) to fit physically and economically into a state of military strength; (2) to find its particular role in the attitudes and beliefs associated with the American world mission.

It is significant that American industry, whose strength so largely gave rise to this world mission, found its traditional policies thrown into confusion when the need for action developed. Business was swept progressively into a new military order of subsidies to foreign nations, massive government investment, stockpiling of scarce materials, and armament manufacture. Should executives resist the advance of peacetime government foreign aid and arms expenditures at the risk of turning the world over to fascism or communism, or should they accept the administration program at the risk of never again being free from the need of government aid? For a hundred years American private enterprise had prepared its defense against socialist revolution, but it had given little thought to the danger of simply being absorbed by a "capitalist" state.

True choice has scarcely been possible since cooperation with government is the road to profits for the stockholders, and such is the traditional aim of management. For those companies with government contracts, and this includes most of the giants, it is clearly advantageous to cultivate close relations with government officials, particularly in the defense department. For this purpose retired generals, admirals, and high-level civilian officials have made valuable business executives. While quantitatively this movement is small, it does raise fears in some minds of a union of undemocratic forces in business and government—this at a time when the need seems to be for business to give assurances in the opposite direction.

Role of Leadership

The challenge to business to play its necessary role in American intellectual and spiritual world leadership is far more difficult to meet than the adjustment to government contracting.

In the confident days of 1900, evolution, Christianity, the Anglo-Saxon character, and the virtues of democracy appeared to promise the eventual world supremacy of the American way. But now the struggle for supremacy is no longer some unforeseeable situation of the future. And much of the spiritual equipment counted on in 1900 is relatively ineffective. The ways of evolution have become a mystery; conventional Christianity, while strong at home, seems a weak weapon against communism; the strength of Anglo-Saxon character no longer controls the people of backward areas; and the political institutions of the Anglo-American tradition are easily misunderstood and often not immediately applicable to people differently trained.

The one aspect of American life that the whole world continues to respect is its material success. Indeed, the American business system is now the strongest card the United States and her allies hold in the contest with world communism. If the rest of the world can be shown that our business principles are an integral part of a larger value system beneficial to them and possible of adoption, they may be won over.

Our business system cannot be transplanted complete and full-grown on other cultures, any more than our political order, our legal and ethical codes, or our moral precepts and beliefs could be. But there is an essence in our social, political, and economic way of life which can be transmitted, and the task of the businessman is to seek out that essence as related to our economic system, make sure it conforms with the best in our total way of life, and demonstrate it to the satisfaction of the millions who are still on the fence.

Conclusion

On balance, the chronicle of the changes in business ideology since 1900 augurs well for the future. Business has modified its ideas and adapted itself to the inevitable changes in the social and political complexion of the country. Granted that the adjustments were often made grudgingly, and sometimes incompletely, yet they were made. From a philosophy of the self-regulating economy presided over by an elite group who could take care of themselves and who had no responsibility for the welfare of others, businessmen as a whole have come to a realization that bigness necessitates certain governmental controls over the economy; they accept the fact that with their position of great influence in the nation must go some accountability for the general well-being.

Nevertheless, business is far from ready to assume the missionary task which has been thrust on it. It must certainly work at making its own internal operations reflect more adequately the democratic ideals we want to communicate abroad. A more basic problem, perhaps—the same one which confronts all other segments of American society—is the need for reanalysis and rearticulation of the ideals and values we want the rest of the world to accept.

Need for Clarification

In spite of the widely held view that the United States is a "business society," the great majority of the people who work for salaries or wages do not regard themselves as businessmen. Regardless of prosperity, better public relations, and more independent business enterprisers in relation to the rest of the population, a feeling of unity with the aims of business leadership seems lacking. People apparently respect but do not trust business leaders. Corporations may in truth be becoming guardians of the common welfare, but the public is not yet convinced. In May 1949, according to a Roper poll:

> A majority of the people . . . believe that very few businessmen have
> the good of the nation in mind when they make their important decisions.
> . . . They think, therefore, that government should keep a sharp eye on
> business.[17]

American businessmen, for all their important position in society today, do not epitomize America as did the independent farmers of an earlier era. This is as it should be. For any single institution to be representative of the diverse American culture of the mid-twentieth century is impossible. Indeed, the very strength and vitality of this nation lie in its diversity; business, for instance, has its particular rationale and could not hope to succeed in any attempt to mirror the total value structure of the society.

Yet that does not lessen the need for clarification of the various traditions and beliefs which America desires to communicate to the rest of the world. Philosophers and anthropologists point to the confusion and conflict in American values; religionists question especially some of business's ethical precepts, asking "whether the secular functions of society, each existing of itself and for itself, can be relied on to serve human destiny."[18]

If the "image of America" has failed to win the unreserved approval and support of the people we need on our side, it is no doubt largely because we ourselves are not quite clear in our minds what America does and should represent—no wonder that foreigners are so often confused and uncertain about the American way.[19] Businessmen—and other representatives of our nation—have tried to talk in terms of democracy, individualism, inalienable rights, opportunity for all, and so forth; these concepts are, unfortunately, all but meaningless and will never serve to unite the Free World around American leadership until they are given validity, until we are sure what we mean by them, and until the facts of American culture are aligned with our ideas about it.

Need for Realignment

Much of the conflict, much of the apparent lack of unity and purpose in our national life, comes from our failure so far to reconcile business attitudes and aims—such as the pursuit of an ever higher standard of living—with the other fundamental values stemming from American religious and democratic traditions. If business could stand off and take a long look at itself, analyze its values, and try to realign them with those broader ideals of the good society, it could help more than any other force in the country to make stronger and more valid America's message to an uncertain world.

Some 50 years ago the famous public lecturer, Episcopal Bishop Henry C. Potter, told an audience of Yale students: "The supreme vice of commercialism is that it is without an ideal."[20] It is clear that if business is to assume its representative function in America, it must have ideals beyond profit or prestige, and must obviously attempt to live up to them. It is safe to assume that what is good for society is good for business in the long run, while Charles Wilson's converse that "what is good for General Motors is good for the nation" is only true on occasion.

At the stage of technology now present in the United States, greater productivity results from treating the employee as a human being who should be attached to his work by intellectual approval and a sense of "belonging" at the job as well as by the need of the paycheck. The management that adopts the gospel of the democratic custodianship of economic opportunity is going to have improved morale from top to bottom.

Big business, as we have seen, is beginning to move in this direction. Small and medium-size business is still highly competitive, is often inadequately financed, and has less leeway to take nonmaterial considerations into account; hence progress will probably be a matter not of years but of decades. From the standpoint of public relations at home, this is discouraging, since most Americans work for small or medium-size business. The image of our society presented abroad, however, may change more rapidly. Almost all foreign contacts are with the agencies or products of sizable American companies—organizations that are large enough at least to be conscious of their place in a new business order and to be capable of providing leadership in that direction if they want to.

To hope for moral or spiritual inspiration from any size of business is asking for new functions from an institution originally designed to supply only material wants. But the modern corporation has inevitably become more than an economic institution, and its managers have more than material responsibilities. In the words of Meyer Kestenbaum, president of Hart, Shaffner, and Marx:

> We need now some people to tell us how to convert industrialism, which has great power, into the force for good in our own country and elsewhere that it can be. If we meet that challenge, I will say again that we are on the verge of a golden age.[21]

Notes

1. *World's Week*, June 1926, quoted from Hermann Krooss, "Business Opinion Between Two Wars," unpublished Ph.D. thesis (New York University, 1947), p. 22.

2. James W. Prothero, *The Dollar Decade, Business Ideas in the 1920's* (Baton Rouge, Louisiana State University Press, 1954), pp. 209, 210.

3. Hermann Krooss, op. cit., p. 149.

4. *New York Times*, June 7, 1932, quoted from Hermann Krooss, op. cit., p. 121.

5. John K. Jessup, "A Political Role for the Corporation," *Fortune*, August 1952, p. 113.

6. David Riesman, *From Conspicuous Consumption to Conspicuous Production* (Glencoe, Illinois, The Free Press, 1954), pp. 224–225.

7. A. R. Raskin, "The Corporation on the Campus," *New York Times Magazine*, April 17, 1955, p. 63.

8. Eugene Staley, Editor, *Creating an Industrial Civilization: A Report of the Corning Conference* (New York, Harper & Brothers, 1952), pp. 204–205.

9. Boston, Division of Research, Harvard Business School, reprinted 1946.

10. *Time*, April 14, 1952, p. 97.

11. Edward C. Bursk, "Introduction," *Human Relations for Management* (New York, Harper & Brothers, a collection of articles from *HBR*, 1950–1955.

12. Eugene Staley, op. cit., p. 204.

13. See page 136 of this issue, *HBR*.

14. These values or beliefs have been suggested by the analyses of anthropologists and sociologists. While no formal consensus has been attempted, I have never come across basic opposition to the formulations given here. See Clyde Kluckhohn, *Mirror for Man: The Relation of Anthropology to Modern Life* (New York, Whittlesey House, 1949), p. 232; Robin W. Williams, Jr., *American Society: A Sociological Interpretation* (New York, Alfred A. Knopf, Inc., 1951), pp. 441–442; and F. L. K. Hau, "Culture Factors," *Factors in Economic Development: Principles and Patterns,* edited by H. F. Williamson and John A. Buttrick (New York, Prentice-Hall, Inc., 1954), pp. 340–341.

15. Merle E. Curti, "Intellectuals and Other People," *American Historical Review*, January 1955, p. 265.

16. Edward Bernays, *Public Relations* (Norman, University of Oklahoma Press, 1949), Chapter 33.

17. *Fortune*, May 1949; see also Elmo Roper, "The Public Looks at Business," *HBR* March 1949, p. 165.

18. Marquis W. Childs and Douglas Cater, *Ethics in a Business Society* (New York, New American Library of World's Literature, 1954), p. 176.

19. See Max Ascoli, "The Hidden America," *The Reporter*, December 1, 1955, p. 11.

20. Henry C. Potter, *The Citizen in His Relation to the Industrial Situation* (New Haven, Yale University Press, 1902), p. 162.

21. Eugene Staley, op. cit., p. 174.

2
Business and Public Policy

JOHN T. DUNLOP, ALFRED D. CHANDLER, JR., GEORGE P. SHULTZ, and IRVING S. SHAPIRO

On May 9, 1979, a short symposium on business and government was held at the School of Government and the Business School of Harvard University to encourage joint programs that focus on (a) business decisions in the complex environment of new government roles and on (b) business strategies in the process of public policymaking. The symposium attracted a senior group of business leaders and academicians of national and international stature.

In this four-part article, which is adapted from papers presented at the symposium, John T. Dunlop leads off with discussion of the central concerns of business and public policy; he is followed sequentially by Alfred D. Chandler, Jr., who explores why business and government so often appear as adversaries in this country; George P. Shultz, who examines the abrasions of the public-private interface; and Irving S. Shapiro, who focuses on business and the public policy process.

The Concerns

By John T. Dunlop

The past decade has seen a vast expansion in the scope and detail of government regulation of business decisions, beyond those of the New Deal era, beyond regulating public utility industries, and beyond temporary periods of wage and price controls. It is ironic, and yet indicative of the basic character of these developments, that a flood of new legislation emerged in eight years of Republican administration. The cluster of regulations growing around environmental protection, health and safety, pension plans, energy development and utilization, and consumer protection are all illustrative of a qualitatively different business environment.

Older agencies have also penetrated much farther into internal business decisions, as in the cases of disclosure rules of the Securities and Exchange

Commission, the Federal Trade Commission's quest for data, and the emergence of goals and timetables in affirmative action programs. Even private price and wage decisions in some sectors are under continuing and systematic scrutiny.

But more pervasive rules and regulations of administrative agencies are not the only measure of the extent to which private business decisions are now open to public scrutiny and review. The courts have raised the risks of damages in many new areas, and public interest law groups have broadened the range of policy litigation and have to a considerable measure become an independent means of public policy determination. I refer also to the role of congressional committees—with their enlarged staffs—and of the press and other media in shaping the agenda and the climate for many business decisions.

This new and perplexing setting for business enterprises raises larger questions of the future relationship of the business community as a whole to government and to society. Business interests in America do not have an effective mechanism or procedure to reconcile their internal conflicting interests on a wide range of public policy issues. The business views that receive public attention are often only the extreme, antisocial practices of a few enterprises or sectors that adversely reflect on all business.

And while many people recognize that our business community, in its relationships to government and among enterprises, is very different from that of Japan or Germany (e.g., antitrust laws), there are serious consequences arising from the independence and separateness of businesses in the United States and from the absence of business consensus on emerging issues. Stanley Marcus, a thoughtful business leader, said it well:

> Who among the business community today would seriously propose that Congress repeal our child labor laws—or the Sherman Antitrust Act? The Federal Reserve Act? The Security Exchange Act? Or Workman's Compensation? Or Social Security? Or Minimum Wage? Or Medicare? Or civil rights legislation? All of us today recognize that such legislation is an integral part of our system; that it has made us a stronger, more prosperous nation—and, in the long run, has been good for business.
>
> But we can take precious little credit for any of the social legislation now on the books, for business vigorously opposed most of this legislation—and we get precious little credit from the people . . . .[1]

The absence of effective leadership for the business community on many public policy questions—in consensus building and in dealing with other groups and governments—means that business enterprises forfeit almost entirely to politicians. The rapid expansion of government regulations in recent years and specifically government's penchant for rigid, bureaucratic "command and control" regulations, even when ineffective or counterproductive, have arisen in part from a lack of coherence and consensus within the business community about more constructive choices for achieving social purposes.

Thus, in the individual business enterprise and in the business community as a whole, there is a new and more complex setting for dealing with government and the society. The significance of these elements may be expected to grow and to put new demands on business executives and leaders.

The American society, contrary to some views, does basically respect and have confidence in the ability of business executives. In wartime, mobilization of large segments of economic resources has been assigned to business executives. In the fiscal crisis of New York City, business leaders were asked to take over major functions and to resolve tough issues that politicians had avoided or postponed—to the brink of bankruptcy. In some metropolitan localities, the business sector has played a major role in economic development, urban renewal, and racial integration of schools. Increasingly, at local and national levels, the government is calling on the skills and qualities of business executives in many areas of the public sector.

This new setting raises serious problems for government administrators and program officers no less than for business executives. Both groups are thrown much in contact with each other, typically in sharply adversary positions and usually with legal staffs. They have different backgrounds, approach issues with different time horizons, see the press and other media in quite different roles, and they have quite different institutional objectives and—at times—different personal values.

Furthermore, each group sees the role of the law in society in substantially different ways—government, to change; business, largely to preserve. The business executive's perspective often tends to be international, while the government administrator's is much more narrowly national. The two groups are also separated often by a gap in age and experience.

In short, it is little wonder that business executives and government officials do not find it easy to communicate with one another, let alone agree about difficult substantive issues and values.

In the education of both business executives and public administrators, there is a critical need, particularly in executive-level programs. The need is for each to understand not merely the substantive issues of these new areas of government activity and joint decision making but also for each to appreciate the setting, constraints, and personal context in which the opposition operates.

The career patterns of business executives and government administrators warrant review and adjustment: personnel and compensation policies could facilitate development of more sensitive, perceptive business leaders and government officials. It would be helpful if more business enterprises could plan to provide a period of time, such as two to four years, for executives to work in government as a normal part of their development.

Similarly, government executives should be encouraged to spend comparable periods in private industry. A greater degree of two-way mobility across the public-private line would in time make a major contribution to the issues of isolation and parochialism raised earlier. Significant changes in our present conflict of interest concepts, as they are applied, would be required. Even within the present framework of attitudes, more could be done to enhance interchange through recruitment policies, particularly in the government.

The Adversaries

By Alfred D. Chandler, Jr.

Why is it, in the United States. that government and business have so often appeared as adversaries? Why have there not been more of the working relationships that characterize other advanced industrial nations? As one businessman, Crawford Greenwalt (former chairman of the board at Du Pont), phrased the question:

"Why is it that my American colleagues and I are being constantly taken to court—made to stand trial—for activities that our counterparts in Britain and other parts of Europe are knighted or given peerages or comparable honors for?"[2]

Lords McGowan and Melchett, the senior executives of Britain's giant Imperial Chemical Industries (ICI), asked the same question about the American scene when, to their astonishment, the attorney general of the United States brought suit against them and their company early in 1944 for violating the Sherman Antitrust Act. And that was at a time when they did almost no business in the United States.

These questions, asked often by businesspeople and government officials, are ones that intrigue the historian. Why, indeed, did not other countries develop antitrust and regulatory policies similar to those that helped to create an adversary relationship between business and government in the United States?

The question just posed is particularly intriguing because such a relationship between business and government did not always exist in the United States. It came only with the sudden appearance of large-scale business enterprise in the last decade of the nineteenth century. .Until the Civil War, business leaders remained involved in government at both local and national levels, and politicians were able businessmen.

Textile manufacturers like Nathan Appleton and ironmakers like Erastus Corning served as mayors and congressmen as well as local party leaders. The famed Albany Regency that ran the Democratic party in New York State for years in the antebellum period included some of New York's most energetic business entrepreneurs. As was true of Southern planters and Western farmers, businessmen of that day had the time and the interest to take an active part in government.

Antecedents of Alienation

The separation between business and government came, almost inevitably, as both business enterprise and government offices grew in size and complexity in response to the opportunities and needs of a rapidly industrializing and urbanizing nation. With the coming of large-scale business enterprise—first the railroads and then industry—a new class of businessmen appeared. They were the full-time salaried managers who made a lifetime career of working up the managerial ladder. Comparable adminstrative hierarchies came later in local and state governments. They came first in the new cities to meet the needs for mass education and for urban services.

At the federal level, the number of public administrators remained small until the coming of the Great Depression pushed the government into taking an active role in restoring the nation's economic health. Then, with World War II and the continuing cold war, the number of government workers and administrators rose at an unprecedented rate. In no other country, however, were large managerial business hierarchies created before the formation of an extensive government civil service.

Numbers illustrate this point. In the 1840s, there were only a handful of transportation and industrial enterprises that hired more than a single salaried manager. At the beginning of that decade, the total number of civilian employees (not managers) in all government departments working in Washington totaled 1,014. By the 1890s, the railroads had already become giants and the industrials were not far behind, but the federal establishment remained tiny. In 1890, when at least a dozen railroads employed over 100,000 workers, the civilian working force in Washington numbered just over 20,000 and the nation's total military force—army, navy, and marines—just under 40,000.

By 1929, there were 68,000 civilians employed by the government in Washington, and the total number of government employees came to just over 500,000 (of which 300,000 were post office workers, the large majority of whom were being paid for political services rendered). In 1929, therefore, the government's working force in Washington was still a good bit smaller than that at United States Steel, General Motors, or Standard Oil (New Jersey).[3] Then the change began. By 1940, a million civilians worked for the federal government; by 1970, nearly three million did.

Because two sets of administrative hierarchies grew at different periods of time for different reasons to carry out different functions with different objectives, two quite different cultures appeared. The work, attitudes, and perspectives of the business manager and the civil servant became and remained almost as distinct and separate as those of the humanist and the scientist—the two cultures C. P. Snow delineated many years ago.

Nevertheless, the existence of two administrative cultures—one private and one public—can hardly account for the adversary relationship that grew up between them. The same two sets of administrators, the same two administrative cultures, appeared in Europe and Japan, but the relationship between them remained close. One underlying reason for this difference rests, I believe, on the fact that in the United States the role, and with it the attitude, of much of the federal government toward business was defined before the creation of a professional class of public administrators.

Rise of Regulation

In the United States, the coming of the large railroads and then industrial enterprises, with their extensive managerial hierarchies, brought government regulation. The passage of the Interstate Commerce Act in 1887, the Sherman Antitrust Act in 1890, and then the more precise Clayton and Federal Trade Commission Acts of 1914 provided the legislative framework for such regulation. In neither Europe nor Japan did a comparable response occur. Why not?

One answer seems to be that in the United States the growth of big business appeared to threaten the well-being of other businessmen, but in Europe and Japan it did not. In the United States, the railroad and the telegraph played a more central role in the nation's transportation and communication network than they did abroad, where existing roads, canals, and coastal shipping continued to carry a larger share of freight, passenger, and mail traffic.

Moreover, by the 1880s, the American railroads—by far the largest business enterprises in the world—had come to be operated by professional managers whose primary objective was to keep their enterprises profitable. Managers set their rates according to costs and not to meet local or regional needs. Large shippers received lower rates than smaller ones, for the increased costs of carrying the larger shipment involved only those of adding a car or two. Similarly, the cost of carrying freight from one major commercial center to another was often less than that of carrying it to many points not directly on the through route.

Such discrimination between shipper and place, understandable in terms of railroad economics, often determined the success or failure—even the economic life or death—of business enterprises and whole communities. The threatened smaller shippers and the less-favored communities protested vigorously, and they had the numbers that assured them the political power to bring Congress to pass a law creating a regulatory commission to determine just and reasonable rates.

As Lee Benson and other scholars have pointed out, it was not the farmers but the merchants and shippers who pressed for railroad regulation.[4] With the passage of the Hepburn Act of 1906, which gave the Interstate Commerce Commission real power, major rate changes were decided in the courts by adversary procedures between the railroad and the commission.

Much the same type of businessmen—the older general merchants and the newer specialized wholesalers—provided similar pressures that led to the enforcement of the Sherman Act in the early years of the twentieth century and the passage of the Clayton and Federal Trade Commission Acts in 1914. Even more than small manufacturers, these middlemen felt themselves threatened by the rise of large-scale industrial enterprise in the 1880s and 1890s. This was because manufacturing companies grew large by integrating forward in marketing and backward into purchasing and by obtaining their own raw materials. In so doing, they replaced the wholesaler with their own salesmen and buyers, who sold directly to the retailers and bought directly from farmers, processors, and producers.

Such new giants as American Cotton Seed Oil, National Linseed Oil, Distillers-Securities, American Sugar Refining, American Tobacco, Quaker Oats, and Corn Products; such flourmakers as Pillsbury and Washburn; such canners as Borden, Heinz, and Campbell Soup; such meatpackers as Armour and Swift; such brewers as Anheuser-Busch and Pabst—all sold consumer goods directly to retailers in the national and international markets and purchased their materials from agricultural exchanges or the farmers themselves. Others such as Standard Oil in kerosene, Procter & Gamble and Colgate in soap, Sherwin-Williams in paint, and Parke-Davis in drugs also sold branded consumer goods in the national and world markets.

In every case, these new managerial hierarchies replaced the wholesalers by their own salaried employees and managers. At the same time, these middlemen were reeling from the impact of the new giant retailers—the department store, the mail order houses such as Sears and Montgomery Ward, and the new chain stores like A&P and Woolworth. Under this onslaught the proportion of goods distributed by wholesalers (the most influential businessmen in hundreds of small American towns and cities) was cut in half between 1889 and 1929.[5]

Politics of Protest

So powerful was the resulting protest that the regulation of business became the paramount domestic issue in American politics in the early twentieth century. In 1912—one of the rare national elections where there were four, rather than two, major candidates—all four promised in somewhat different ways to regulate and control business. Moreover, by *business* all four meant *big* business operated through managerial hierarchies, not small personal enterprise. The hostility toward large companies lessened during the prosperous years of the 1920s but returned in full force in the 1930s when big business took the blame for the economic woes of the Depression.

Then, in the 1960s and 1970s, business—particularly big business—was quickly blamed for the depletion of resources and the pollution that resulted, almost inevitably, from the enormously increased output of our huge industrial economy. By then, the standard American response to complex economic problems was to pass laws creating regulatory commissions to monitor the activities of the businesses involved.

Elsewhere, the Reverse

Why did other nations not adopt similar laws and create comparable regulating commissions? One reason, as I have already suggested, was that the rise of large-scale enterprise in Europe and Japan did not adversely affect the fortunes of any business group. In Western Europe, the railroads were fitted into an already efficient network of roads, canals, rivers, and coastal shipping. There, because distances were much shorter and communities already established, economies of railroad rate making brought less discrimination between persons and places.

On the Continent, the railroads were built and operated by existing public administrative hierarchies. The railroad system in France, for example, became and remains the creation and creature of the Corps des ponts et chasseurs. Civil servants operating these noncompetitive enterprises were under much less pressure to base rates on costs and to discriminate between shippers and communities in order to maintain profits or to get business from competitors. And they were under more pressure to meet the needs of shippers and communities in the regions which they served.

In Britain, where the railroads were built and operated privately, the merchants and industrialists who promoted them kept a closer control over their affairs than did those in the United States. As early as the 1850s, they had worked out schemes for pooling traffic that eliminated the competitive pressures and discriminations that plagued American railroads until the Interstate Commerce Commission took over rate making and rate enforcing.

Of more importance, the new giant industrial enterprises did not replace existing wholesalers. In Germany and France, very few large companies appeared in the consumer goods industries. There were no giant food, tobacco, canned goods, corn products, whiskey, soap, paint, or drug companies until well after World War II. The large enterprises came instead in the producers' goods industries—in metals, chemicals, machinery, and other industries whose products were not sold in volume to thousands of retailers through the wholesaler network.

In Britain, the first industrial nation (and therefore the first to import food and other materials on a massive scale), large consumer goods enterprises did appear. However, because the domestic market was geographically small (nearly every part of the United Kingdom could be reached in a day), because there existed a well-established marketing and distribution network before the coming of the railroad, and because the existing industrial families disliked weakening the control of their enterprise by hiring managers—for these three reasons—the new and large food, drink, soap, and drug companies continued to rely on the existing wholesalers and other middlemen to distribute their products and to obtain their raw materials.

Only in the 1920s and 1930s did those large companies begin to build organizations for buying and marketing similar to those created by American enterprises 40 to 50 years earlier. As these producers relied heavily on overseas markets and supplies, they did set up branch sales and buying offices, particularly in the Commonwealth nations. That expansion, however, did not affect the middleman in the home country.

As a result, even though there was a strong antimonopoly strain in the economic thought of the British middle class, no group felt the urgency to put pressure on the government to provide instruments to control and regulate concentrated economic power. In Britain, protest resulting from industrial changes also dominated domestic politics in the early twentieth century; however, the protest came not from the middle class but from workingmen, who—unlike their American counterparts—formed political parties to battle for higher wages and better conditions of work and life.

If the growth of the large-scale enterprise in consumer goods did not create pressures, as it did in the United States, for government to regulate business, its growth in producers' goods positively encouraged a closer relationship between the two. In Europe and Japan, where public hierarchies had been established long before private ones, makers of chemicals, metals, and machinery were far more dependent on foreign markets than were American producers.

Therefore, the producers in those countries quickly looked to public officials to help them win and hold overseas trade. The civil servants were willing to oblige by permitting cooperation and cartelization at home and by using diplomacy and even force abroad to keep open markets and sources of supply. They did so because they believed that economic strength abroad enhanced the nation's position in international diplomacy and politics. Cartels at home did indeed help the German and French to expand abroad.

Even in laissez-faire Britain, the Board of Trade encouraged, before World War I, government participation in the corporation that would become British Petroleum. During the war the government sponsored the British Dyestuff Corporation. Then, in 1926, it encouraged the giant merger that became Imperial Chemical Industries. For the creation of that near monopoly, Sir Harry McGowan and Sir Alfred Mond (Lord Melchett) were rewarded by being given peerages. As Crawford Greenwalt complained, a comparable merger in the United States would have instantly brought an antitrust case. Indeed, as soon as the success of American arms began to encourage exporting the American way of life, the Justice Department did bring the two lords and their imperial company into court.

Redefinition of Relationship

Here, then, is a historian's answer to Crawford Greenwalt's question I quoted earlier. In the United States, business hierarchies appeared before public ones. In Europe, the reverse was true. When the large government bureaucracies did appear in this country, the basic adversary role of government toward business had already been defined; that definition had developed largely as a response of an influential segment of the business community to the rise of modern big business. Such a response did not occur abroad. There, on the one hand, big business grew without seriously threatening the prosperity of small business. On the other hand, both public and private administrators saw mutual advantages in cooperating to expand overseas trade.

The adversary relationship that developed in the United States had its benefits. Cooperation and cartelization, for example, did hold back technological innovation. As an ICI executive visiting Wilmington, Delaware in 1937 observed: "The most striking difference between Du Pont's business

and ours arises from the existence of free competition in America.''[6] By
that he meant that Du Pont's research was not held back by cartel-like
agreements (not only with other companies but even with other divisions
within the company). But such an adversary relationship certainly had its
cost, as both George Shultz and Irving Shapiro will make very clear in the
accompanying parts of this article.

Lessons can be learned from history. The lesson of the tale you have
just read is not that the past determines the future but rather that a study
of the past can suggest ways to redefine the relationship between business
executives and government administrators so that the nation can receive
benefits without paying unnecessary costs. I believe that by embarking on
a public policy program the Harvard schools of government and business
are taking a major step toward that redefinition.

The Abrasive Interface

By George P. Shultz
Common talk these days around the board and conference tables of business
is about the overbearing omnipresence of government in every aspect of
business operations. Government is no longer just Robin Hood but some
combination of Louella Parsons and Edward G. Robinson. The business
executive, trying to conduct operations in a reasonably efficient way, is
increasingly joining Jimmy Durante's lament, ''Everybody wants to get into
the act.''

Speaking as a businessman for about five years now, I can vouch for
the fact that there is plenty to complain about. Government seems to be an
opponent, not a friend or even a neutral referee. Nevertheless, I reflect that
during my years in government the situation looked a little different. These
contrasts in my business and government experience embolden me to set
out here suggestions how each party might better approach the abrasive
business-government interface and what areas might better be eliminated
from it.

While in the government, I tried to see all comers insofar as time
allowed, and I found great variety among those who visited me from business. An important dimension of variability involved the homework done
by the visiting businesspeople. Many came in very poorly prepared, with
only a bitch and a groan and without real substance to back up their points
or practical suggestions for dealing with them. Diplomatic and polite though
I am by nature, many of these petitioners went away feeling that I was
unresponsive and unsympathetic.

Increasingly, however, it seemed to me that businesspeople were learning that homework pays off. This is not simply a matter of being factually
informed and reasonably objective in presentation. It also means looking
beyond the very narrow interests of the individual company or industry and

offering some connection between what the business leader wants and the broader public interest.

Sometimes this contrast between the poorly informed, narrow interest and the well-informed connection to a broader interest is emphasized by reliance of the former on a naked reference to political clout. As a person who spent about a decade in Mayor Daley's Chicago, I know that clout can be for real. But I can also think of many sights I would rather see unadorned and which would not produce the same skepticism and resentment.

Effective Business Efforts

Examples of effective business efforts are increasingly easy to come by. Take the difficult issues posed by legislation dealing with the Arab boycott of Israel. Their complexities—rationalizing conflicting national laws into rules of conduct for international commerce—are immense, the stakes are high, and the associated passions intense.

With skillful and creative leadership from Irving Shapiro, the Business Roundtable tackled these issues in a sophisticated and professional manner. Through discussions with leading representatives of various Jewish groups, a legal task force was set up through which private negotiations on the issues took place. Congressional and executive branch groups were kept apprised of these negotiations, and the agreements reached were accepted by them (I believe with considerable relief) and embodied into the law on a word-for-word basis. Here the businesspeople involved did have high stakes of their own on the table, but they went at the task cognizant of the broader interests involved and with the help of thoroughly professional people.

Another type of effective business action is illustrated by a recent study undertaken by the Business Roundtable of the costs of government regulation. Here again, businesspeople conducted a careful and professionally managed research effort. The results show that certain categories of costs can be identified and measured and that they are substantial and growing. The study also takes due notice of the additional large, though unmeasurable, costs of regulatory uncertainty—a real wild card in investment decisions.

This Roundtable study, which has been widely circulated in Washington, should, unless I miss my guess, contribute not only to constructive discussion of this hot topic but also to the impact of statements made by business leaders about regulatory overkill. Let us hope so. The pace of capital formation and productivity is at stake. Attention from top business leaders, speaking with credibility, must be joined to important, substantive proposals in an effective combination.

Still another example is the debate over and now ratification of the agreements concluding the Tokyo Round of trade negotiations. There is no subject as domestic as international trade. Nowhere is the conflict between the general benefits derived from more open trade and the difficulties for certain special interests more starkly portrayed than in this field. The temptation will always be there to move from making a speech about the evils of government intervention in business affairs to arguing in a congressional office for government protection of a special and vulnerable interest.

These are important trade agreements, and the business reaction to them made a real difference in their acceptability to Congress. Business leaders were on the spot to do their homework and to pursue their interests in an enlightened manner. Fortunately, the agreements have now been ratified, with the support and understanding of business.

On a different topic, consider the problem of blame and responsibility, as illustrated by the question of inflation, what causes it, and how it can be cured. Without belaboring the whole gamut of budget, tax, monetary, regulatory, and other government actions that raise costs, I simply assert that the causes of inflation, including our current roaring version, are rooted in government policy and behavior.

However broad the agreement about this observation, even in occasional presidential statements, practical outcome seems to be—almost as though drawn to it by a magnet—some form of wage and price controls. In fact, today's version of controls seems like a rerun of an old movie. I didn't like wage and price controls in the early 1970s, when I was charged with administering them as chairman of the Cost of Living Council, and I don't like them any better now. This is one old movie we should keep in the can.

As these controls move into center stage, unwillingness to conform with them becomes conveniently tagged as the reason for inflation, and those unwilling to conform are tagged the villains. Maybe such scapegoating is good politics, but it is certainly lousy economics, and it contributes to the abrasive interface in a predictable manner.

We can all recall times when a president or his spokesman has lashed out at "inflationary" price increases in some major industry. Lately, to the discomfort of purists like me, some major businesses have been taking the view that they are not going to be put into a no-win political corner. On the contrary, they have said to the president, "We will help you beat on everybody in sight, including labor." In the process, labor emerges as the bad guy, ironically, for upholding the principles of freedom of institutions and markets and the sanctity of private contracts—along with its own interests. More abrasion, but with an added dimension.

At any rate, scapegoating by government at the expense of business and labor has certainly helped to poison the atmosphere. By contrast, John Dunlop, along with some others, has tried and does keep trying to create that conversation among the parties that will increase understanding and bring good politics closer to good economics. Lines of worthwhile inquiry go beyond the *substance* of blame/responsibility type issues—Why inflation? Why energy problems?—into *processes* that may help reduce the abrasive outcome.

For example, how do we hold private discussions between government and labor-management representatives? It is really extraordinary that we have managed to legislate, in this country, a virtual prohibition on regular meetings between top labor, top management, and top government officials. You can't do it. Now nobody stood up and said, "Let's have a law that they can't talk." The situation was blind-sided by a law that says, if you have such a meeting, it has to be open to the general public. And anybody who has ever participated in things like this knows that, if you can't have a private meeting, you can't have a candid discussion. So there's no point in having a meeting. The net result of all this: a law that prohibits constructive discussion.

Who Should Do What?

Basic differences in the structure of authority in business and government add to the potential abrasiveness of the interface. And reflection on these differences raises questions about the comparative advantage of business and government for various important tasks.

I think of government as having a deliberately flat organization structure, stemming from the very concept of checks and balances. The resulting disposition to delay has been compounded in recent years with action-stopping power widely distributed in Congress and in the executive branch. Government action is crablike at best, with an overwhelming emphasis on policy formulation as opposed to execution. Though, as Will Rogers put it, we may "be thankful we're not getting all the government we're paying for," we may still be getting more than we need.

By contrast, the pyramidal structure of organization found in most textbooks does reasonably resemble the reality of business. A "doing" organization must be set up to force the decisiveness that gets action. One of the first lessons I learned in moving from government to business is that in business you must be very careful when you tell someone who is working for you to do something, because the probability is high that he or she will do it. In government, no way! Among other things, he doesn't necessarily consider himself to be working for you in the first place.

Perhaps these variations in the structure of authority can be appropriately thought of in terms of different incentive systems in these two worlds. In government and politics, recognition and, therefore, incentives go to those who formulate policy and maneuver legislative compromise. By sharp contrast, the kudos and incentives in business go to the person who can get something done. It is execution that counts. Who can get the plant built, who can bring home the sales contract, who can carry out the financing, and so on.

This contrast between "debating" and "criticizing" organizations, with their disposition to delay, and "doing" organizations, with their spirit of action, adds to the abrasiveness of the business-government interface. People just have a hard time understanding each other. The well-publicized events surrounding Sohio's effort to move oil from the West Coast inland by pipeline show how frustrating, let alone costly, the processes of debate and criticism can be, and they also show that business may be led simply to throw up its hands and walk away.

In January 1975, Sohio began the process of securing necessary permits and government approvals: a total of approximately 700 permits were required from about 140 local, state, federal, or private agencies. On March 13, 1979, fifty months later, the decision was reached to abandon the project. In the interim, Sohio had spent $50 million and managed to secure only 250 of the 700 permits. When the oil company abandoned the project, it was spending at a rate of $1 million per month in the approval procedures. What's left is government regulating a project that doesn't exist.

The volume of permits and government bodies before whom Sohio had to appear suggests another aspect of the problem. Adam Smith once remarked that specialization increases with the size of the market. Well, perversely, the vast increase in regulation in recent years has been accomplished by a form of specialization that amounts to a balkanization of problems. A whole host of federal, state, and local agencies regulate various aspects of what to a business is one problem.

The legitimate concern is not just a matter of the time involved to go to so many different places for answers. Action can be completely hung up by differences of view among those who represent regulatory interests that are deliberately insulated from each other by statute. A friend of mine once remarked that "whatever is not prohibited nowadays is required." I am forced to amend his statement to "whatever is prohibited may *also* be required."

All this leads me to a central tension that exists in our system of political economy, pulling and hauling at the institutions of business and government—a tension between the essential goals of economic efficiency and of political equity. If better understood and handled, this tension could be a creative force and could help us thread our way to a better division of labor between business and government.

Within the private sector, competition forces efficiency on business executives and financiers whether they like it or not. Indeed, one can say that those in public or private life who have resources placed in their hands must—almost as a matter of trust on behalf of society—see that those resources are used as productively as possible. So the business and financial system marches to the drummer of efficiency.

But not the political system. Most politicians will nod to efficiency, but it is usually little more than a nod. The drummer that the politician marches to is equity. When a problem comes up, economic thinking says, "What is the efficient solution?" Political thinking says, "What is the equitable solution?" In any exercise in political economy, these two distinct patterns of thought are interacting, and the task at hand is to see how they can be meshed where they *must be* but sought separately where they *can be*.

"Crisis of Competence"

Renewed emphasis on the idea of competence can help. We need to recognize that a given organization or aggregation of people cannot do everything. Competence is important and it demands specialization. The more any organization attempts, the more the limits of its competence will become apparent. The widely advertised "crisis of confidence" may more truly be a "crisis of competence."

In business, the bottom line is pretty obvious. Business graveyards are full of companies that tried to do things they didn't know how to do and were shot down by the competitive system. The point is as true of governments, but the bottom line, no less present, is more elusive. As politicization of more and more of our economic and private life has extended the reach of government, it has led government officials more and more into areas with which they are fundamentally unfamiliar. Exhibitions of incompetence bring a general lack of confidence, one of the driving forces behind the 1978 widespread tax revolt, an instance of government's bottom line.

The field of energy today illustrates in spades the problems raised for efficiency by the use of price controls imposed in the name of equity, as well as the results of an inappropriate division of labor between regulation and the marketplace.

The difference between what the federal government has said about energy and what it has done is truly amazing. Unfortunately for our country, this is not just a minor inconsistency; it is an exercise in energy doublespeak with potential consequences of vast proportions both at home and abroad.

The government has suppressed the price of domestically produced oil and gas, and in one masterstroke it has produced these results:

☐ A subsidy for imported oil, thereby encouraging its use and generating a level of demand that helps sustain world oil prices.

☐ A reduction in the incentives to find and produce more oil and gas in the United States.

☐ An incentive to consumption of these and other forms of energy by keeping the price below what is paid in most other consuming countries.

Beyond these direct effects, the suppression of oil and gas prices makes necessary the allocation of supplies by an exceedingly complex set of regulations administered by a large and growing bureaucracy. These regulations and arbitrary changes in them face any investor with substantial political risks, which in turn simply raise the rate of return necessary to justify a new venture. And, as a result of government doublespeak on energy, in the six years that have elapsed since the 1973 Arab oil embargo, our dependence on foreign oil has increased dramatically.

So we turn to coal. We have supplies of coal within the United States, we keep telling ourselves, that can last us for centuries. All we have to do, we keep telling ourselves, is mine it and burn it, thereby converting coal into that versatile and essential underpinning of our economy, electrical energy. Here again, regulations abound at all stages of this process, and they become more severe with each legislative session and issue of the Federal Register.

For example, the Environmental Protection Agency recently proposed new air pollution rules that would have precluded the use of virtually all of the high-sulfur midwestern coal, even after coal washing and flue-gas scrubbing. Though the proposal has since been modified, the uncertainties of the process make mining an ever more risky business, as the burning of coal becomes less and less possible even in parts of the country that are not heavily populated. Once again, doublespeak: bursts of rhetoric encouraging the use of coal accompanied by regulations that make it unnecessarily expensive, sometimes prohibitively so.

Why not let the system of markets and enterprise go to work on the energy problem, in the name of an efficient solution to a problem of central importance to our country? We can find better ways to serve the goal of equity than piggybacking on the rhetoric of poverty and failing to price ourselves *into* development of our own indigenous sources of energy.

Reducing the Abrasion

Coping with the abrasive interface comes down to using a few simple ideas:

☐ Return to the concept of limited-purpose organizations, where government as well as business, universities, and other organizations undertake the responsibilities of their comparative advantage and tread lightly, if at all, elsewhere.

☐ Recognize that running major industries or enterprises, either directly or indirectly, through detailed regulation dictating how to get the work done is not the government's bag.

☐ Recognize as business leaders that attention to homework is really a necessary condition for getting your point of view considered by government and, for that matter, the general public.

☐ Stay away—both government and business—from recourse to scapegoating, which leads people to lose sight of the merits of issues, subverting reality into political posturing.

Let me add a final note. Our society looks to universities for the ideas, the objectivity, and the analysis that will help us think through such problems as how to handle the abrasive business-government interface. Business and government both have developed greater capacity for research and understanding than in earlier days. If they bring more to the party, however, they need more than ever the perspective of genuine scholarship. The interaction in universities of centers for business and government study augurs well for the future. I have no doubt that great centers of learning, with their habit of inquiry, can help us find a better way.

The Process

By Irving S. Shapiro

The dual test of an organization is how well it performs its chosen functions and how well it matches the values of the society that charters it. If it is competent but hostile to the mores of society, or acceptable in that regard but incompetent in its delivery of goods and services, then it forfeits its legitimacy.

Business and government, two of the giants of contemporary society, have not been winning very high marks on this test in recent years. Each has tried to improve its standing with the public, with no great success.

The focal points of public discontent are familiar. Government is seen as overgrown and inefficient, given to the protection of its own bureaucratic legions, corrupted by special interest groups, and unresponsive to the needs of its citizens who are forced to pay for good government without getting it.

Business, particularly big business, is seen as an uncontrolled power that bends the political process to its will and is not sincerely concerned with the quality of its products or the safety of the people whose lives it affects—which is to say, just about everybody.

It is not my purpose to go into any detail on the sad decline of institutional reputations. You have heard all the conventional rejoinders and explanations. I would like to push beyond these to some observations about business leaders and public policymakers, specifically to make the point that, if the American society is be served, leaders in both camps must understand their missions differently and act differently in the future.

In the fall of 1978, John Dunlop presented a paper making the following three-part point:

First, there has been a fundamental change in the political process due to the "massive new penetration [by government] into all manner of heretofore private economic activity."

Second, neither the leaders of business nor those of government have adapted to this state of affairs by learning to live and work with each other.

Third, their failure to do so has potentially disastrous consequences.[7]

I agree with that and want to expand on it. What is needed is not just a little better perspective all around or a little more communication. What is needed is a basic change in the way leaders define their jobs and operate in the public policy area.

What is needed is an understanding in both business and government that these institutions are merely means to an end in our society. Neither is ordained by Holy Writ. Both have to show that they are doing what society wishes, not just what they themselves might wish.

What is also needed is a new premise about the right and proper relationship between business and government. For a long time the two have been circling around each other like gladiators in combat, blocking and parrying each other's moves. That may amuse some of the spectators, but too often it results in poor government policies and lousy business decisions. We get programs grounded in vindictiveness rather than in practicality, and all the while enormous amounts of energy are being put into adversarial politicking that could more properly be used to resolve the nation's real problems.

It is healthy to keep business and government at arm's length, with each behaving in such a way that neither would mind the facts being reported in the newspapers. However, an arm's length relationship doesn't require the kind of hostility that we have seen in recent years.

What the nation needs from business and government is an understanding that neither one of those institutions has a monopoly on intelligence or probity, or the wisdom to prescribe all by itself for the public welfare. I know of no way to build such understanding except through education and experience.

There is a lot more involved here than simply being competent at one's craft. People heading for careers in government and those turning toward business need exposure to each other's theology. As some university programs have recognized, there is a need for people in government to understand the dynamics of economic processes and to have some feeling for the workings of the business organizations that fulfill so many of our nation's economic functions. That logic can be flipped over to apply to businesspeople's need to understand government.

"Common Law" Partners

It is artificial to think of business education as separate from education in government. The outside world no longer tolerates such a split. Like it or not, business and government are "common law" partners—for better, I hope, than worse.

Dunlop's proposition had three parts. Mine has only two:

First, the role of the business executive in America, and certainly the role of the chief executive officer of any sizable enterprise, has changed to such a degree that we are now bringing forward a new breed of manager.

Second, business executives are learning to live with their common law partner. They are taking a few bruises in the bargain, but that is a small price to pay for an on-the-job education in how the public policy process works and how to figure out what is practical and what is not. The central fact is that executives now see this as something they have to learn to run their businesses properly and to make the American system work better— as much a duty for a business executive as for anyone else.

There is a lot of rhetoric about the "tides of change" in our country, but that metaphor does not apply here. Tides come in and go out again. The tide I am talking about came in and is staying.

The only practical course is to regard as essentially permanent the system that has evolved. Call it what you will—"quasi-public," "half-free enterprise," "the mixed economy." By any name, it is a system in which heavy government involvement will remain a fact of life for business. At Du Pont, for instance, we can expect government to continue to tell us whether we can build a plant at a chosen location. General Motors and Ford can expect the government to continue to help them design cars. All business-people can expect government to continue to tell us what fuel to burn in the furnace, what sort of affirmative action we should take in hiring and pro-motion, and how many pounds, if not tons, of reports we shall submit.

Without suggesting for a minute that the private sector ought to take all this lying down, I must admit that some of the government's involvement is desirable and another piece of it is probably inevitable, at least over the short term. The job is to live with that situation even as we try to improve it, and the basic lesson to learn is that business and government operate in different environments: what makes a convincing case for the one seems almost irrelevant to the other.

Washington columnist David Broder has written that government is a process of struggle and accommodation, not an exercise in applied theology. On a given day, politics may outweigh economic and technological facts; at another time, or with the issue handled differently, the facts might carry the day. It follows that forecasts based on economic efficiency or scientific probabilities alone have limited predictive power in government. A busi-nessperson trained in the classical way finds this baffling and illogical.

There has been a pronounced trait in government toward "one issue thinking"—that is, toward focusing on singular problems without much con-cern about related ones. This is a luxury that most leaders in society simply cannot afford. University presidents have to think about multiple consti-tuencies: faculty, students, alumni, the neighbors in the local community, the fund givers in the foundations, and the grant givers in Washington, not to mention the regulatory agencies. Business leaders in jobs like mine have similar sets of constituencies and overlapping concerns. We have to try to balance them all.

It would be nice to report that people in political life are also bound to think about problems in the round. They may be so inclined, but the plain fact is that in practice they often go with a single-issue decision. Maybe it is because they think that otherwise they will be licked at the polls. Perhaps the law as it is written gives them no other choice. Or possibly they are listening to pressure groups that are deliberately trying to narrow the issues on the ground that a wider debate will only weaken their case.

Whatever the reason, it is a mistake to assume that an overall balanced view is going to surface on its own within the government. It is most surely a mistake to assume that your own point of view, based on whatever supporting evidence you have, is going to be given due emphasis—or even noticed at all—unless your team makes an effort to sell it.

Maybe that will happen, and maybe not. An example of the negative view was offered by Hubert Humphrey shortly before his death. Reminiscing with regret about the days when the Congress was considering the creation of the Occupational Safety and Health Administration, Senator Humphrey said that the key decisions were made without much talk about what it all would cost. Nor was much attention given, I think, to the possibility that equal or better results on safety might have been gained in other ways than through another new federal agency. OSHA had been proposed, and OSHA was what we got.

Leaders in business are learning to look realistically at the government climate and to learn from their own mistakes. They are becoming personally involved, not standing on the sidelines saying "I couldn't make any difference, anyway," and not relying exclusively on their paid lobbyists and trade associations.

Executives are realizing that the day is gone when the spot at the top of an organization chart permitted a private life-style. A generation or two in the past, you could get by in business by following four rules: stick to business, stay out of trouble, join the right clubs, and don't talk to reporters. Some business leaders may yearn for that bygone era, but we have to take life as it comes—and today's executive is more often in the midst of the fray. CEOs are now to be found tramping through the corridors in Washington and the state capitols, testifying, talking with elected representatives and administrative aides, pleading cases in the agency offices and occasionally in the White House. Reporters are learning the names of business executives and finding that many more of them have their doors open.

Business leaders are beginning to understand the territory. They have learned, for instance, that to understand tax policy they have to understand Russell Long as well as what is written in the tax code. They also have learned that there often is a difference between what is said politically and what is meant—which tells them there may be room for compromise behind the rhetoric.

Executives are learning to leave their personal politics at home, and work with people in government on both sides of the aisle, looking at issues on the merits and not along party lines. Businesspeople gain nothing in government by making "enemies" lists or by talking only to representatives or senators of comfortable ideology. Washington leaders who may oppose business on one issue may, on another issue, join in a coalition in business's favor.

For example, the vote in Congress that killed the bill that would have set up a new independent consumer protection agency was not made just by the certified friends of business; that bill went under because people with a lot of different political leanings came to the conclusion it was not the solution. Congress realized that, if the several dozen existing agencies were not protecting consumers enough, the logical course of action was to make those agencies function better, not to add on another layer of bureaucracy.

A case in which I have personal involvement is Senator Howard Metzenbaum's effort to change the patterns of corporate governance. I am totally at odds with the senator's proposals, yet I sat with his advisory committee and tried to be an effective minority voice. I probably did not convert anybody, but the theory is that you have zero chance of scoring points unless you get into the game, and it is just possible that you might learn something from other points of view.

One other bit of territorial savvy is that, by its structure, government places a great deal of power in the hands of some people who are relatively little known, who have little experience, and who may not be in the same job or committee slot very long. To ignore such individuals, to try to deal instead only with the stars of first magnitude, is a great mistake. Those lesser lights are probably intelligent, energetic, and the true authors of the bill some senator will present to his peers tomorrow morning.

Central Observations

Out of all the hits and misses and new-found points of contact, what basically do chief executives need to know about government to do their jobs and make the system work better? It seems to me that the business leaders most successful in working with government, those who best represent the new breed, share several traits.

First, they arm themselves with facts. They put significant corporate resources into this effort plus a big chunk of their own time. When the job has been done well and the documentation has been made nearly bulletproof, an interesting thing has happened: people in government have displayed a new attitude toward businesspeople. The government people have concluded that these folks might just know what they are talking about and that they can be trusted.

That sword, of course, has two edges. If a business executive abuses that trust, if the facts don't hold up and the government people are left out on a limb, that executive will be long into retirement before he is trusted again. Simply having the facts, even presenting them in person and effectively, is no guarantee of an acceptable outcome, but it works remarkably well at times; the alternative of not having the facts is usually fatal.

Second, the leaders in the forefront have the common trait of willingness to try new approaches. When the Arab nations announced their boycott of companies doing business with Israel, people in business as well as government, together with leaders of interested Jewish organizations, were able to arrive at a compromise policy recommendation. And it was from this support base that the House and Senate enacted a law to deal with the problem. The law was not a perfect solution by any means, but it was far better than the moves that would otherwise have been taken.

An encouraging note from that example: people in government showed that they, too, were willing to look for a new approach.

Third, successful business leaders recognize that, to work effectively with government, they must come up with positive, not just negative, alternatives. In view of the decades of opposition by some business representatives to almost every step government administrators decided to take—decades in which the final score was like Charlie Brown's baseball team's 50-0, for them—it ought to be clear that knee-jerk opposition is at best a delaying tactic.

The objective is not to win delays but to improve the outcome, and to that end business leaders must come forward with positives. By the time a congressional committee is laboring over a bill, it has long since been decided that (a) there is a problem and (b) government ought to be doing something about it. The decision may be in error on both counts, but opponents face an uphill battle to prove that. Experience shows that the best action is to offer other steps to be taken by the people under pressure, steps they can take back to their constituents and defend in a practical way.

The fourth quality of the new breed I have put last because it is the most general, and it takes me back to my opening point about having to match up to the values of society. The new breed has staying power, I believe, because the people involved see their objectives broadly. It is, of course, partly self-serving to look for ways to work better with government. Business leaders do that to make their companies run better and thereby make more profit. The corollary purpose, though, is to help the government work better and thereby make for a better society.

Thus there are chief executives today working with government on matters far removed from their own corporate interest—for example, the Panama Canal treaty, or the program to reform the Civil Service system, or the problems of minority unemployment in urban centers, even where their corporations do not have any plants.

Where do business executives draw the line? Unless they are careful, they can get sucked into controversial areas where they don't have any particular competence, and in extreme cases their efforts to help could amount to unwarranted meddling. Yet at the same time, executives cannot walk away from national and community problems on the ground that they don't have all the answers. Who does?

Those of us in business management and those who will come into these jobs in the future have an obligation to help the public policy process where possible—recognizing our own limitations, but realizing too that we can go a long way toward improving the climate between business and government and ending the ancient, mutually destructive, and unproductive animosity that has too long discolored the American political and economic environment.

Notes

1. Stanley Marcus, "Can Free Enterprise Survive Success?" a speech presented at the University of Nebraska at Omaha, November 18, 1975.

2. Greenwalt's statement was made to me when I discussed with him background information for the chapter on Du Pont in my book, *Strategy and Structure* (Cambridge, Mass.: MIT Press, 1962). For the Justice Department's antitrust suit against ICI, see W. J. Reader, *Imperial Chemical Industries: A History*, Vol. II, Chs 24–25, especially pp. 428–429.

3. U.S. Bureau of the Census, *Historical Statistics of the United States, Colonial Times to 1970* (Washington, D.C.: U.S. Government Printing Office, 1975), pp. 1102–1103, 1142; also my book, *The Visible Hand*, pp. 204–205. For employment at General Motors and Standard Oil, see *Strategy and Structure*, p. 50, and for U.S. Steel, its annual reports for the 1920s.

4. Lee Benson, *Merchants, Farmers and Railroads: Railroad Regulation and New York Politics* (Cambridge, Mass.: Russell, 1955).

5. Harold Barger, *Distribution's Place in the American Economy since 1869* (Princeton, N.J.: Princeton University Press, 1955), p. 69.

6. Reader, *Imperial Chemical Industries*, Vol. II, p. 93.

7. "Growth, Unemployment and Inflation," in *Economic Growth*, 26th Congress, International Chamber of Commerce, Paris, France, September 1978.

③

The Community-Relations Problem of Industrial Companies

JOHN W. WELCKER

Today executives in many large corporations are considering what policies and procedures would be most helpful to their companies in maintaining favorable community relations. One reason for this concern is the general belief that management-labor relations are improved when a company's community relations are favorable. Another is the thought that the public's acceptance of private enterprise is probably determined in large measure by the attitudes of individual men and women toward the companies with which they have daily contact—as customers, employees, or plant neighbors. In addition, some industrial leaders believe that corporate executives have a real responsibility to participate in community affairs. Clearly, all these views warrant the consideration of business leaders.

What is the principal factor influencing a company's standing in a plant community? In what ways can management itself influence the "grass-roots" acceptance of a company? What basic forces influencing community relations should management consider when formulating a realistic program? What policies and procedures are most helpful in maintaining favorable community relations? These questions and others were considered by the author in a recent study of community relations of manufacturing plants.

The study included a year of field research which can be briefly described as follows: First an intensive study of community relations in several localities was undertaken to determine the grass-roots attitudes of residents toward local factories in their vicinity. Civic leaders, merchants, and local labor representatives were interviewed, in addition to management personnel. In one city a direct mail questionnaire was used (1) to obtain data on the relative standing of manufacturing concerns in the area, and (2) to determine what aspects of community relations were regarded as important by local residents. This investigation of local conditions was followed by interviews with national corporate executives who were responsible for the operation of plants in every section of the nation.

Realistic Approach

The very nature of the subject being investigated, at least as it turned out in the author's experience, made it impossible to develop statistical findings that would have any validity. Indeed, the only really documented conclusions that could be drawn from this particular study are of this kind:

1.   The pattern of community relations is an exceedingly intricate one, involving public relations, management-labor relations, and human relations, all of which directly relate to management's policies and day-to-day actions.

2.   No simple standard is suitable for judging a complex subject such as a company's community-relations standing. The basic criterion is how men and women *feel* about plants in their own vicinity, and this is at best intangible.

3.   Each company's community-relations standing must be appraised on an individual plant basis, for there are many factors which seem to influence a plant's standing and they vary from plant to plant. To name three—(a) the size of the community; (b) the size of the factory within a community as compared to other plants in the same locality; and (c) employee relations—is merely to select those which stand out most clearly.

By way of illustration, a large industrial corporation operating branch plants in several states was regarded quite highly in Community A, and just the opposite in Community B. In the one, local civic leaders commented favorably upon the plant and the local management; its labor-management relations also were good. In the other, residents complained that the management had little interest in their community or in its employees; likewise, the plant's labor relations were strained. Yet both factories operated under policies established by the same top-management group.

Investigation indicated that two important considerations contributed to these divergent attitudes toward different branches of the same company. (1) Plant A was not a dominant employer in its locality; Plant B was. As a consequence, residents in Community A were less familiar with the company's operations than were residents in Community B. (2) The plant manager in Community A made a greater effort to participate in local community affairs, and his activities in doing so were regarded with high favor by civic leaders.

This is only one case—and every other case studied showed different ramifications of intraplant relations, different degrees of feeling, different combinations of external factors. The attitudes of workers to the content of their jobs and the influence of union leaders among the rank and file also affected conditions in the various cases differently—although, it should be noted, generally in much less degree than might have been expected.

Another difficult aspect of the subject of community relations, which deserves consideration in its own right as a phenomenon that is probably typical of many kinds of complex "social" problems, is the wide gap, in both thinking and action, between the extremes of a very general approach to the problem and a very specific application of techniques.

This dichotomy was quite apparent in what most of the management representatives interviewed had to say. Some regarded the whole matter as nothing but "good management." For example, one vice president maintained that if a company operated successfully and dealt with its employees equitably, the company would also enjoy favorable community relations. In contrast, others were primarily concerned with the various techniques to be used in community relations, such as a plant paper, company advertising, and open houses for employees and their families. Several management representatives said they anticipated no serious problems in community relations if these techniques were properly applied.

Of course both these views are true in their own ways. Techniques mean nothing if they do not add up to good management, if they are not utilized with that in mind rather than for their own sake. And good management *is* the nub of the problem in a very real sense, but it is not enough simply to be in favor of it, as we all are; it must be carried out through techniques. The author's own feeling is that the techniques will "fall in line" if attention is focused on the fundamental elements of good management involved in the particular situations. In any event, it is on that basis that the results of the research have been interpreted here.

Importance of Employee Relations

The cases studied indicated that the principal factor influencing community relations is employee relations. Thus, the standing of a plant in a community is largely a reflection of what its own employees think about their employer. This generalization seems to apply equally well to large cities and to small towns.

Few individuals in a city are likely to have personal contact with every firm in their locality. Workers, however, spend about one third of their time while awake in their places of employment. Naturally any and all events or gossip that appear either disturbing or interesting to an individual employee are noted and frequently are mentioned to family or friends. Some of these comments are repeated to others and cannot help but influence local opinion toward a plant.

Replies received to the direct mail survey mentioned previously support this point. Nearly every man who returned a questionnaire explained that members of his family or friends had provided him with knowledge about local concerns. Only in a few instances did men show a lack of familiarity with any one of the companies located in the vicinity of the city where the survey was conducted.

Even more significant, however, was the high standing of those companies which residents considered had good employee relations. One company in particular, a branch plant of a large corporation, was most favorably mentioned; the general belief was expressed that its management had sought to provide satisfying work relationships and to maintain employee security. (Specifically, a disability benefit plan, group insurance, and retirement annuities were available for all employees who desired to participate.) This high standing was as true among those who did not work for the company as among those who were so employed.

The impact of unfavorable employee relations upon a company's standing in a community is also of significance. One concern, a locally managed enterprise in the city where the direct mail survey was conducted, had an exceedingly low standing in the replies. This firm unquestionably suffered from the publicity associated with a 13 weeks' strike which had taken place some eight months previously. The imprint of a strike record apparently lingers on in the public's mind for a considerable period of time after settlement of the strike itself. Businesspeople might well conclude that protracted strikes are just about disastrous to a plant's community relations.

In a Small Town

The importance of employee relations upon community relations was particularly well illustrated by the situation in a small town of 4,500 persons. By 1949 about 95% of the town's annual payroll was paid by a single employer. This plant had grown through the years from a small locally owned factory to become a division office of a large nationally recognized corporation. The community depended practically entirely upon the plant for its economic welfare.

The company took a very active part in assisting many local organizations. Substantial contributions were made each year to local charitable groups such as the Community Chest, Boy Scouts, and Girl Scouts. The management also contributed toward the operating expenses of a hospital in a nearby town which served the surrounding localities. Local executives of the company participated in many community activities. For instance, various church groups and service clubs had one or more persons in responsible positions who were also employed at the plant; these individuals, moreover, sought to avoid possible criticism that they were trying to control these organizations.

Yet the community's attitude toward the company was well described by one discerning resident as "lukewarm." Among other reasons was the simple fact that employee relations were strained. A CIO union in 1946 had obtained a favorable vote—by a narrow margin—to represent the company's employees; management-union relations thereafter were far from satisfactory. For instance, the settlement of grievances frequently extended over a period of six months. In 1948 the management had sought to dismiss the chief steward of the union and replace him with a young engineer. Many union members condemned the move as an attempt to undermine the union and were not completely reassured even when the chief steward was transferred to another job.

These difficulties with the union more than offset the efforts of the company and its local executives to maintain favorable community relations. Certainly management understood how completely the economic and social structure of the town was dependent upon the company's plant; indeed executives had made every effort to meet their responsibilities to the community. Yet unfavorable employee relations had seriously interfered with the fulfillment of this endeavor.

The brief but representative examples mentioned above emphasize the fact that, no matter what objectives or policies management may establish, a corporation cannot hope to maintain a favorable standing in a plant community unless its employees are satisfied and speak well of it.

Management's Role

In what ways can management itself influence the grass-roots acceptance of a company? Several suggestions can be drawn from the cases studied. First and foremost is the maintenance of favorable working conditions in each plant, for, as just discussed, employee relations seem clearly to be the principal factor influencing community relations, and favorable working conditions will strengthen employee relations.

Related to this, and almost as important, is the need for company policies to be fully understood and accepted by both supervisory personnel and the rank and file of workers. A letter to the author from a worker in one city which he visited focuses attention on this need. The letter, which summarizes many of the comments made by other workers, follows:

> Thank you for asking me to join in your survey. I have worked in industrial plants for eight years and am firmly convinced that much can be done on the subject of community relations.
>
> There are a few things I would like to add to your survey. These opinions express my feelings and the feelings of men I have talked with in various plants throughout the city.
>
> 1 There is a distinct lack of cooperation between management and labor.
> 2 Management should present its problems clearly to labor. Let the men know where they stand and eliminate the lack of security the men feel.

3   An arrangement should be made where advancement is
    made by ability and not by joining a certain club, etc.
4   Cooperation between a foreman and his help.

I believe a round table discussion between management and its foremen
should be held at least once a month. Most foremen are put in the position
of passing on orders which aren't explained to them.

Management and union should also meet at frequent round table
discussions.

Too many bosses. I know of an example where there is a supervisor, a
general foreman, a foreman, and an assistant foreman in charge of four
men, and yet the company complains about high overhead.

I have been waiting to talk to someone and express my feelings about
these situations and you have given me an opportunity. . . .

This letter because of its obvious sincerity deserves thoughtful consideration. The views of this man are undoubtedly shared by other employees. Particular attention should be given to two points: (1) Although workers
in the city have definite feelings about community relations, no method
apparently is available to convey their view to management, (2) Both foremen
and workers lack an adequate understanding of shop problems confronting
management. Clearly, effective two-way communication between top executives and the rank and file of workers is essential for both these purposes.

Participation in Community Activities

Another way in which management personnel influence community relations
is by active participation in local activities. If a company seeks to become
a "good neighbor," residents in the plant community are likely to recognize
the fact and to reflect their approval in comments to others in the vicinity.
Such favorable comments help to influence the local climate for a company.
The morale and effectiveness of an employee is generally improved when
his neighbors speak well of the place in which he works.

A striking example of this point was observed in one eastern city. The
president of one of the largest companies in the city was extremely active
in civic affairs; representatives of business generally referred to him as one
of the outstanding leaders in the community. Perhaps more significant, many
workers in the plant indicated a high regard for the company's chief executive—a real sense of pride in his community standing. Although it is difficult
in such a case to judge exactly how much influence the workers' respect
exerted upon overall employee relations, the net result was definitely beneficial.

A further illustration of the influence of a chief executive upon a company's employee and community relations was noted in another locality.
Business leaders, labor leaders, and shop employees were all familiar with
his activities in local organizations. Here too an important reason for the
high standing of the company in the area was the workers' respect for its

president; they regarded him as a socially minded individual, sincerely interested in the welfare of others. In addition, they heard their president mentioned by friends and neighbors with approval. Thus, these employees were also influenced by the attitude of others toward the chief executive. Should we not conclude that employee and community relations may be both directly and indirectly influenced by the local activities of management personnel?

The fact that many companies conduct operations in several communities makes this point even more significant. If the branch plant manager does not mix informally and socially with townspeople, the local residents are liable to consider him "stuck up" and "too good" for the town. What may be even worse, his attitude influences others within the organization. Because he takes little personal interest in civic activities, others in the management group are less likely to join in community affairs. On the other hand, if the local manager takes a genuine interest in community activities and seeks to gain recognition as a good neighbor, others in the management group follow suit, and the public relations position of the company in a community is generally raised appreciably. Top executives in a corporation, it would seem, should encourage local management personnel to participate wholeheartedly in community affairs. Indeed this sort of activity seems important enough to serve as one criterion in the selection of personnel for advancement in an organization.

Steady Employment

A third method by which management can influence the grass-roots attitude toward a company is by understanding and seeking to meet the evolving social responsibilities which most workers expect industry to bear. Obviously space in this article does not permit a complete discussion of this subject, but one phase merits attention: the maintenance of local plant employment. The case studies indicated that this topic is a matter of the utmost community interest—particularly when layoffs or rumors of layoffs are prevalent.

The greatest fear among residents of a community dependent in large measure upon absentee-owned plants is the possibility of either a sharp reduction in employment or the transfer of the local factory to another locality. This concern was well illustrated in one locality when the principal employer dismissed several hundred workers in the spring of 1949 because of the slump in business. Immediately several local bankers and merchants became alarmed and sharply limited credit to their customers. Needless to say, the whole community suffered from a state of "jitters." Many residents condemned the management of the company and felt it had no interest in the community or its problems. This incident completely offset the company's efforts to maintain favorable community relations; management's action in dismissing employees appeared far more significant to local residents than earlier newspaper advertisements and statements by management representatives.

Obviously, a company must sometimes make moves which run counter to the maintenance of steady employment. The question is not whether such moves are justified or not, but rather what can be done to minimize their effect. From the standpoint of community relations, at least, the fact is that the residents of a community do not mention, or seem to care, where a company is to obtain the funds to meet its "obligation" to the community on this score. They leave that responsibility to the company, and it is a necessary part of any realistic community-relations program that such a fact be recognized for what it is.

That the people of this country feel it is an obligation of management to provide high-level employment—witness the passage of the Full Employment Act of 1946—stems from the basic social and economic changes which have taken place during the past 50 years. Management interviews indicated that these changes are often overlooked in appraising community-relations programs, yet they would seem to merit attention because they serve as external forces influencing the climate or setting within which such programs must be carried out.

Employee Security

Another manifestation of the same basic social and economic changes which give rise to the widespread interest in high-level employment is the emphasis on the need for greater personal security on the part of workers. Clear evidence of the sincere desire among the rank and file of employees for greater security was revealed in the direct mail study discussed previously. A large number of men specifically mentioned pensions and other employee benefit plans as primary considerations for their preferring to work in particular plants. One concern in particular was very strongly commended because of the steps taken by its management to provide workers with greater security than was available in most plants in the vicinity.

This illustration gives added emphasis—if any is needed—to the unions' demands for additional pensions and other welfare benefits. Executives cannot dismiss the 1949 union demands as simply a current bargaining matter; they reflect a genuine and deep-rooted interest of workers. The admittedly inadequate federal social security benefits have led organized labor leaders to one conclusion: welfare benefits, pensions, and social insurance must be provided in large measure by industry. And such a demand has the full support of the rank and file of workers, if the results of this study have any meaning at all.

What causes workers to feel such need of greater security? For one thing there has been a shift in occupational status, drawing people from the farms where they were largely self-sufficient and increasing the numbers in jobs where they are completely dependent on others for their livelihood; the net result has been a growing sense of insecurity. The effects of the introduction and widespread application of mass-production techniques constitute another consideration. The emergence of community relations as a problem may well be, in a very real sense, as much a symptom of such deeper problems as it is a problem itself.

That the effect of such forces on community relations is sometimes quite direct shows up particularly clearly in the matter of mass-production techniques. The application of new manufacturing techniques and mass-production methods has permitted substantial cost and price reductions in many lines. Over the years these savings have placed the products of industry within the reach of millions of additional customers. At the same time, individual workers have experienced enormous changes in their shop assignments. Machinery rather than a worker's proficiency frequently determines the rate of output. Skilled and unskilled jobs are often combined or so related to one another as to cause a layman difficulty in discerning between them. As a consequence, many workers feel they have lost any personal recognition for their individual performance; others have no real sense of personal accomplishment.

A typical example of the impact of mass-production techniques upon the attitude of employees was observed in one community. Individual workers there were disturbed by job changes even though the company had introduced them only after the completion of careful time and motion studies. They were particularly critical when they were expected to handle more pieces per day, yet the physical work involved was no more arduous. Job simplification was interpreted by some workers as simply a "speed-up" device imposed by management.

Again, when the company undertook volume production of a new product after World War II and, needing technical "know-how" for its design and manufacture, hired a number of trained engineers from outside, many employees appeared disturbed. This reaction is by no means unusual. Engineers are frequently regarded with hostility by the rank and file of workers.

This antagonism of workers toward engineers is common enough to warrant a little elaboration. Workers expect engineers to introduce new machinery or to suggest modifications in shop procedures. They are naturally apprehensive about possible changes in their jobs, and any persons responsible for possible shifts in production methods are regarded somewhat critically.

Another factor is that engineers are frequently placed in charge of employees having considerable tenure. The experienced workers thus situated usually lack the formal training or personal qualifications necessary for their own advancement. Indeed, constant technical advances have served to make promotions into the ranks of management increasingly difficult for those employees who lack either special training or who are unable to demonstrate unusual capabilities. Thus, modern technology has indirectly resulted in placing a ceiling over the heads of large numbers of industrial workers. Many employees feel this limitation on their possible advancement, and they resent those individuals who are able to obtain promotions.

In other words, mass production is viewed by many in the rank and file of labor as requiring a constant struggle to maintain their status in an environment where technical advancement never ceases. Such are the underlying reasons that increasing numbers of persons now seek security to protect themselves in their existing circumstances—whatever these may be. Clearly, one strong appeal of the union movement today is the emphasis placed upon seniority provisions in most union-contract agreements.

We might pause here to note that one of the most fundamental questions in our society is raised by this widespread desire on the part of persons in all walks of life to secure greater personal security. How can our sort of economy provide such security without stifling further advances in the nation's standard of living? Somehow a balance between individual security and industrial progress must be found.

The experience of this study confirms the fact that the desire for security does not represent a general lack of initiative or laziness. Rather in most instances it reflects a *fear* that the impact of further work changes will be to eliminate existing jobs or to remove opportunities for individual advancement. As a nation we all welcome technical advances which permit greater efficiency, lower manufacturing costs, and savings to the customers. Individual workers, however, generally resist shop practices which result in the elimination of existing jobs or the necessity of learning new techniques.

Every management needs to understand the high place security now holds in the minds of many workers, and on this score to give particular consideration to the effects of technical developments upon employee security whenever they consider the introduction of new machines or processes in a factory. Here is a situation where what is done is less important than the spirit in which it is done, for the basic problem is out of the control of management. Yet sincere concern will help to achieve more understanding of the employees' point of view; and by contributing to more favorable employee relations, it will also strengthen community relations.

A Community-Relations Program

The preceding sections of this article have referred to several factors which a corporate executive needs to consider in the formulation of a community-relations program—for instance, good management, favorable employee relations, and participation of plant executives in community activities. The following outline presents a fuller synthesis of the suggestions drawn from the study—not as a master plan to be followed completely, but rather as a listing of the major elements a responsible management might want to examine in reviewing its community-relations problem.

I. The first step is a determination by management of its immediate and long-term objectives with respect to community relations. In general these aims are:

    A. To demonstrate that the company has a genuine concern for the welfare of its employees and of the communities in which it operates, as shown by:

        1. The attitude and behavior of local management representatives.

        2. A sincere effort to provide employees with employment security and job satisfactions.

    B. To consider the long-term interests of employees and the community when examining situations or changes which offer substantial short-run profits for stockholders.

    C. To secure an understanding of management's philosophy and policies on the part of its employees and plant neighbors.

    D. To encourage criticisms or comments about the company's policies or actions from the residents of communities in which factories are operated.

II. Implementation of the above objectives by management involves the following steps:

    A. Scrutiny of company relationships in each plant community by such methods as:

        1. The use of independent polls to ascertain local opinion toward the company;

        2. Interviews with community leaders such as newspaper editors, ministers, union officers, municipal officials, and merchants.

    B. Designation of executives responsible for the community-relations program, including:

        1. Selection of a top executive to administer the company's whole program.

        2. Assignment of local management personnel to carry out the program in each plant community.

        3. Communication of company's plans with respect to community relations, through:

            a. Discussion with plant managers of alternative procedures for implementing policies;

            b. Agreement as to desirable procedures for each plant to follow.

    C. Selection of procedures or techniques for implementing the program, such as some or all of the following:

        1. A management-training program for all supervisory personnel with emphasis on community-relations problems of the company:

            a. An initial program for plant managers;

b. A somewhat longer program for foremen and other supervisory employees.

2. Distribution of detailed information with respect to local plant operations, with emphasis on operations, employment trends, and overall company progress:

a. Periodic meetings with foremen; an opportunity for them to raise questions as well as to obtain information;

b. Publication of a plant "house organ";

c. Mailing of material about the company directly to workers' homes;

d. Release of news of local interest to the press and radio.

3. Meetings with local "thought" leaders and publicity about the company's operations:

a. Group meetings with plant executives at which those attending can raise questions about local factory operations;

b. Mailing of literature about the company to a selected list of community leaders;

c. Periodic advertisements in local newspapers.

4. Invitations to attend a plant "open house" at least once a year:

a. Families of employees invited to visit and see where their relatives work;

b. Invitations to selected individuals in the community to see actual plant working conditions; an opportunity for an informal meeting and a question period is most desirable.

5. Participation of local plant executives in community activities:

a. Active leadership in desirable projects for civic betterment;

b. Contributions of corporate funds for charitable campaigns.

III. A periodic reappraisal of the community-relations situation of the whole business community and of the individual company is also needed, covering:

A. Modification of established community-relations program, if necessary, in keeping with such a reappraisal.

B. Adaptation of new procedures, if necessary, to deal with changes in company's community-relations problems.

Clearly, individual applications of the community-relations program outlined above will differ substantially. Each management group will want to prepare a company-wide program which will meet its own particular situation. After all, the ultimate standard for measuring the success of any such program *is* the reputation a company acquires in the local community. Corporate executives have an important role in adopting and administering a community relations program.

Summary

Employee relations are of the utmost importance in community relations. If a company's workers feel that their working conditions are favorable, both its employee and community relations will benefit. Thus, management's policies and procedures strongly influence a plant's standing in its community.

This study indicates that those executives who maintain good community relations for their companies do so by (1) demonstrating a genuine concern for the welfare of the company's employees and the communities in which operations are conducted; (2) maintaining a two-way communication about the company's progress and problems between top-management personnel and local employees and local plant neighbors; and (3) participating in plant community activities and helping to provide leadership in community affairs.

A management group which is thus successful in maintaining good community relations not only improves the company's internal operations but also strengthens the reputation of industry as a whole, thereby assisting private enterprise throughout the nation.

4

Why Business Always Loses

THEODORE LEVITT

American business, the author says, "has placed itself in the unedifying role of contending against legislation which the general public has viewed as liberating, progressive, and necessary." He offers several reasons for business's typically Pavlovian response to what it considers provocations from Washington and suggests that its attitude is based not on ideological grounds, but on inability to grasp the significance for the corporation and the public of changes in the external environment. The prospect for improvement in this situation, the author contends, is "dismal," but "not hopeless," and he explains why he thinks so.

Ever since 1887, when American business had its first important experience with government regulation in the form of the Interstate Commerce Act, business has been a persistent and predictable loser in all its major legislative confrontations with government and with the voting public.

Business has vigorously resisted; but in spite of its enormous economic powers and sophisticated persuasive skills, whether exercised in Washington, D.C., or Washington Court House, Ohio, it has suffered defeats with a monotonously repetitive style. It has placed itself in the unedifying role of contending against legislation which the general public has viewed as liberating, progressive, and necessary. Business has been the perpetual ogre, the bad guy who is against good things.

Business has generally blamed its problems on so-called opportunistic politicians, rapacious bureaucrats, misinformed do-gooders, and a duped public. The fault is always with "them," not "us." But there is a chance that Cassius was right: "The fault, dear Brutus, is not in our stars, but in ourselves." Consider what would be the reaction of a corporation president faced with a division manager who habitually blamed his repeated losses on the actions of his competitors. The president would surely think such a chronic loser must have only himself to blame. "Early retirement" would be his early fate.

It is my thesis that the blame for the chronic defeats of business lies as much with business as with its "competitors," that perhaps business has made the mistake, not of fighting its competition poorly (it is too well practiced in the arts of competition), but of fighting competition when it should more frequently have joined it. And I have for all this a "marketing" explanation.

Losing Record

Let us first take a quick introspective look at history.

It is not necessary to recount in detail the dismal record of American business's endless series of lost causes. Whether we talk about the Sherman Antitrust Act or the Federal Reserve Act, of the Federal Trade Commission Act or the National Park Service Acts, of the Child Labor Acts or the Securities Exchange Act, of the Wagner Act or the Fair Labor Standards Act of 1938, of the Old Age and Survivors Insurance Benefits Act or the Federal Housing Acts, of the Marshall Plan or Aid to Dependent Children Act, of the Federal Education Act, the Poverty Program, or Medicare— business as a rule fought these programs and lost. Often it fought them with such gruesome predictions of awful consequences to our private enterprise system that one wonders how the foretellers of such doom can now face themselves in the mirror each morning and still believe themselves competent to make important decisions on major matters in their own companies.

Business has not really won or had its way in connection with even a single piece of proposed regulatory or social legislation in the last three quarters of a century. The only exceptions are the Smoot-Hawley Act (1924) and the Taft-Hartley Act (1948). Significantly, these were also the only statutes during this extended period which business did not oppose. In short, it has won only in those instances where it *favored*, not opposed, a bill in Congress.

Sometimes it has taken time to lose, so that at any given time business may have confidently felt itself the victor, such as when President Truman first proposed national health insurance in 1947. But it was a transient victory, for today we have Medicare and Medicaid. And what we have is only the beginning; we are also in the process of getting a systematic overhaul of our entire environment—highway beautification, urban cleanup, air and water cleanup, and probably advertising cleanup.

Thoughtful and fair-minded readers will grant the difficulty of proving that the legislation business opposed has in any way seriously damaged our economy. Indeed, I believe they will find it easier to show it has been for the good of our society and for the good of business:

☐ Business is far better off with the Sherman Act's final dissolution of the giant trusts. For example, instead of having one huge oil monopoly in the form of the old Standard Oil Company, we have now, as a result of the Supreme Court's 1911 decree, five vigorously competitive and effective progeny—Standard Oil of New Jersey, Standard Oil of Ohio, Standard Oil of California, Standard Oil of Indiana, and the Mobil Oil Corporation.

☐ Clearly business is better off with national parks that provide their employees with low-cost, noncommercial vacations where they can refresh themselves and strengthen their family ties and commitments.

☐ Clearly business is better off with the elimination of child labor, so that children can grow into healthy, educated, productive, and amply consuming adults and parents.

☐ Clearly business is better off with legitimate and respectable labor unions—unions that increasingly bargain as responsible institutions, help enforce work rules, and produce sensible grievance procedures—than it would be if it were dealing with loose bands of dissatisfied and even embittered workers.

☐ Clearly business is better off with the disclosure requirement and regulatory activities of the Securities Exchange Act than it was back in the dark days of sharpshooting exploitation and mistrust.

☐ Clearly business is better off with the Pure Food and Drug Act, which brings all competitors under the same civilized rules, rather than with a situation where Gresham's Law poisons both competition and consumer.

☐ Clearly business will be better off with highway and urban beautification than with the present messy sprawl—for which business must accept major blame, but about which no company acting alone can easily do anything, without perhaps sacrificing profits and competitive effectiveness.

Executive Blinders

But if all these measures, on which business has repeatedly lost, have been so clearly in business's own interest, why has business so consistently opposed them? Why has business not taken the long view of where its own interests lie—or even the short view, as in the case of trustbusting?

American business executives are proud that they run their businesses on facts, not sentiment. They do what needs to and can be done. They constantly shed obsolete practices, produce new organizational charts, scrap inefficient plants, move to new cities, and usually hesitate only briefly to fire old colleagues who no longer carry their own weight. They are always looking for new ideas, new opportunities, new ways of doing things. Gone is the old greeting, "How's business?" It is now, "What's new?" Newness is what today's executive works with and welcomes.

Yet with all their calculating pragmatism, all their unsentimental zeal to junk what is old and decaying, and all their eagerness to find and adopt new things for their businesses, modern executives act in a contradictory manner when it comes to new ideas about social reform and relations between business and government. They welcome new things in their businesses, but not in the relationship of their businesses to government and society.

Nor has business's historic negativism been altered particularly by its headline identification with Great Society reforms such as the Poverty Program, Head Start, and urban reconstruction. Business's active involvement in these activities is, as a proportion of the business population, so microscopic as to be almost invisible. Headlines have whipped a thimbleful of soap into a hogshead of lather. Moreover, most of the involvement is strictly commercial—running Job Corps projects for cold cash, not for charity or service. Finally, business never took the lead either in the creation of any Great Society legislation or in any of the early implementing efforts. At first, business generally fought the Great Society. It joined, reluctantly, only as the result of President Johnson's direct private overtures to the upper executives of what John Kenneth Galbraith calls the "technostructure."

While I myself have argued that American business, during Johnson's tenure, has undergone a felicitous liberalization in its attitude toward government,[1] I believe nonetheless that history will show that business's current association with Great Society activities has been largely episodic. It is an incident in time, not an element of a trend. To see where business really stands, one needs only to wait for the next piece of specific regulatory or control legislation to be proposed, or to wait for the next new ideas in social service or regulations to redistribute resources and social power. The moment these are suggested, the old negative instincts will surely materialize, the old clichés will surely be pressed into vigorous service, and the nation will surely be lectured once again on the enormous folly of what it is about to do.

Readers perhaps can recall their own reactions the last time they heard suggested a new idea for government's involvement in the external environment. It is a safe bet that the old negative instincts took over with almost electronic speed. The computer is programmed to cry wolf.

Reasons for Resistance

There are, I believe, four explanations for business's obvious opposition to new things in the social and what may be called the government "guidelines" area of the environment.

1. *Fear of higher taxes.* Some business leaders fear that new social programs (such as the Poverty Program) will result in new taxes, and higher

taxes mean higher costs. Yet since these taxes would presumably hit all companies pretty much equally, none would suffer a relative disadvantage. So, logically, one would expect opposition to be moderate, if taxes were the only reason for it.

2. *Fear of a "bigger" Washington.*   Here is where nonrational considerations are more evident. In the Truman days a lot of opposition to expanding state activity was based on what may be called the *slippery road psychosis.* It will be recalled that this was a time of vigorous ideological and economic competition between East and West. France and Italy were torn with communist-inspired strikes. England was nationalizing steel and inland shipping. Russia was taking over in the East European countries. Understandably, communism and socialism were feared not only as institutions but as ideas.

In this atmosphere of fear, threat, and dislocation, things that proved distasteful at home were often tagged with the threatening labels of communism and socialism. Hence Truman's proposed Compulsory National Health Insurance program was quickly labeled "socialized medicine." Jackson Pollock's wildly nonrepresentational paintings became "socialist art." Few people seriously considered these as being of themselves purely socialist ventures; rather, they were viewed as the intrusive beginnings of socialistic ideas and practices. To adopt National Health Insurance or embark on any other activity that broadened Washington's base was viewed as descending a slippery, one-way road to inevitable socialism.

Today, this deterministic notion of how the world works is no longer as strong as it once was; but it has always been strong in one fashion or another—the most extreme form being the ringing declaration, "That government which governs least, governs best." Big government continues to be perceived as bad government. The uncertain and unpredictable consequences of power lurk in our minds.

So business—which perceives itself as having most at stake—has always tended to resist the expansion of government, even when it was in business's best interests, because of the uncertainty of where this would lead in terms of administration of both the legislation under consideration and succeeding legislation.

Since its advent in the Soviet Union, socialism has been promoted as the teleological consequence of an expanding government. As a result, U.S. business's fearful uncertainty about the outcome of specific new social or control ventures was replaced by an even more fearful certainty—the certainty of socialism. Hence, this argument says, business has typically opposed state-sponsored goodness because that kind of goodness automatically leads to badness.

3. *Associated interests of business.*   A third possible reason for business's opposition to the expansion of government stems from business's feeling of "associated interests." Its notion is that when a proposed government expansion appears to threaten the unrestricted freedom of certain

businesses, it threatens all of business. It follows naturally that other businesses come to the defense of their oppressed brethren.

The Pure Food and Drug Act is a good example. When the food and drug industries were clearly threatened with regulation, the machine tool industry was easily persuaded to denounce it. It felt an associated interest, or a communality of interest, with other businesses threatened by the government. When "truth in packaging" was proposed and viewed as cramping the food processors, one might have expected the insurance industry to come to their defense.

In short, when it comes to looking at what Washington does or proposes, most business executives, regardless of industry, consider themselves as being in the same boat. Washington is "them." Everybody else is transformed into a cohesive and sometimes alarmist "us."

4. *Discomforts of change.* What I believe is the most persuasive explanation of business's chronic hostility toward Washington, even in cases where the proposals are obviously necessary, sensible, and wanted by the public, is that business simply abhors change.

That may sound odd in view of the fact that change is the most palpable of all facts that business deals with. Indeed, business is a great and constant creator of change, a constant reactor to change, and, generally speaking, a master at dealing with change. Yet is is crucial to note that the changes which business regularly deals with are of a very special and limited nature. These are the day-to-day changes in business's accustomed "internal environment"—the routine and almost automatic changes in customer and competitive behavior, not the massively organized man-made and planned changes produced by powerful governments.

It is precisely because the day-to-day competitive and consumer changes which business is organized to deal with are such a constant condition of the business world that businesspeople so constantly fear and resist this different kind of change emanating from Washington. They already have their hands full and want merely to avoid more trouble. The more the external environment can be kept from changing, the more time there is available for effectively dealing with the constant changes in the internal environment that so relentlessly bombard executives each day.

Poor Pragmatists

What so often looks like a conservative ideology, to critics and students of business leaders' posture in public affairs, is nothing of the sort. It is pure pragmatism of an understandably distorted variety, a simple and primitive consequence of their short-run preoccupation with trying to master the job of running their businesses. And the fact that this posture is consistent and almost predictable does not make it ideological.

The people who write for publication and make analysis of society their profession are specialists in words and ideas. It is therefore not surprising that they so frequently interpret events and individuals' actions in ideological rather than pragmatic terms. They say that if the measures business has always opposed have actually been in its long-term interest to support, then a reasonably thoughtful pragmatist would have realized this and therefore supported what he in fact opposed. Then the only remaining explanation of his continued resistance must be that it has indeed been ideologically motivated. In sum, he opposes things that are in his own best interest because they violate a hardened ideological commitment.

But a more realistic answer is that in a good many things businesspeople are very poor pragmatists. When it comes to the regulation of business, government expansion, social welfare measures, and other matters in the external environment, it may be that they are simply poorly equipped to see and understand exactly what is going on, why, and whether what is happening is good or bad for them.

When they step out of their own metier, they, like most of us, are surprisingly inept—a fact that does not prevent any of us from freely opinionating about affairs outside our accustomed sphere. Even in areas remote from their normal affairs, few people hesitate to speak, and generally do speak with unabashed self-confidence. Enormously uninformed people regularly make vigorous attacks on nonobjective art, on psychoanalysis, on rioting students at Berkeley, on General de Gaulle, on African nationalists, on atonal music, on civil rights marchers—in fact, on anything and anybody who is making change, who challenges old, familiar, and accustomed ways.

Insulated World. The more successful the large corporation executive is as professional manager and the higher his rank, the more he is asked to take a public stand on matters outside the area of his experience. It is, however, the unhappy irony of a world whose work increasingly gets done by specialists that the more successful a person is as a manager and the higher up he is in his organization, the less he is equipped to understand proposed changes in the external environment, particularly in regard to their impact on his own business.

For, say, 30 years, he has diligently dedicated his life to mastering the task of managing the internal environment of his company, but in the process he has automatically insulated himself from the world around him. While he believes himself informed, he often in fact has little more than a headline familiarity with the complexity of the constantly changing external environment. When he has read the newspapers during these years, rarely has he given the front page as much time as the financial page. When he has read a magazine, it usually has been a trade journal or a general business magazine, not a public affairs journal. When he has read a public affairs journal, it generally has been a popularized oversimplification, read hurriedly. When he has read lengthier public affairs articles, all too often he has read them in a business journal whose chauvinistic patter told him what the editors thought he wanted to hear. And when he has read a book, it usually has been a "how to" manual, and if not that, a relaxing murder mystery.

Every business person knows how she spends her time—and undoubtedly none will be flattered by this version of how she gets information about the world or about its adequacy. But even *Time,* not a magazine that often departs from establishment patter, agrees that the typical pattern of job devotion has created in America "eighty-hour-a-week executives" who don't even take time for their families, let alone for understanding the world. "Making a living is important, but selling soap should not destroy the process of raising sons," *Time* chided recently. American executives, the magazine went on to suggest, need perhaps to recast their values and change their lives.[2]

It is almost impossible to exaggerate the importance of good information in assessing the factors that condition our attitudes toward the world around us. One of the most distressing facts about so many highly intelligent business leaders I know—men whom I respect and admire—is how poorly informed they are about matters on which they have strong views. A weekly inside-dope newsletter from Washington, speeches by like-minded sycophants at association meetings and luncheon clubs, and the business press are generally very inadequate for a person's continued education about the realities of our world. Yet the high-level executive makes decisions each day about the future shape and direction of his world based on information so flimsy and often so inaccurate that if his subordinates used the same inadequate standards in connection with such lesser decisions as the layout of a proposed production line or the particulars of a new pension plan, he would not hesitate to fire them on the spot.

Indeed, most business executives who reach high positions have never really wanted to study and understand the "external environment." If they had, they would not have devoted themselves so sedulously to their companies' problems and hence would not have risen to such managerial eminence. There are, of course, exceptions to all this; but for the greater proportion of successful executives, what I have outlined is anything but a caricature.

It is no surprise therefore that the usual executives are poor pragmatists when it comes to the externals. They simply lack the equipment. Preoccupied with internal change and uncertainty, they generally denounce any external changes being proposed. And so they get tagged, as most of American industry is tagged, as being systematically and ideologically opposed to what the public has over the years clearly felt was good for society.

Some Who Began at the Top
Significantly, a more liberal posture is characteristic mostly of high-level business executives who reached their positions in *other* ways than the slow and arduous, 30-year, promotion-by-promotion path:

☐ All the Rockefeller brothers are, by most standards, politically liberal and receptive to (indeed, creators of) radical changes in the external environment. All of them have been associated with large business enterprise, but none of them clawed his way arduously to the top. They were born there. (Interestingly, they are also great connoisseurs of art—Nelson Rockefeller particularly of nonobjective art.)

☐ Norton Simon, another art fancier, while starting with a reasonable legacy, forged by himself the diversified empire he now leads. From the beginning he was a boss in business, never really a subordinate.

☐ Charles Percy, the senator from Illinois, was singled out as the protégé of his benefactor at Bell & Howell when still in college and was pulled into its presidency before he was 30.

☐ Henry Ford II was suddenly elevated to high rank in the Ford Motor Company when he was almost fresh out of Yale and his father, Edsel, died unexpectedly. Interestingly, many people believe that in his early years, before the implacable requirements of running a business had monopolized his attention, he held much more "liberal" views than he does today.

☐ Arnold Maremont, the socially and politically active liberal head of Chicago's Maremont Industries, essentially inherited the business which he has expanded.

☐ The same pattern of youthful inheritance of big business stewardship is true of other men often thought of as business liberals: Joseph Block of Inland Steel, who sided with President Kennedy on the famous steel industry price increase controversy; Edgar Kaiser, under whose leadership Kaiser Aluminum developed the famous comprehensive medical-center plan for its workers and their families, and who pioneered in large companies the idea of profit sharing for hourly employees; Thomas Watson, Jr., of IBM; the Reynolds brothers of Reynolds Metals; Gardner Cowles of Cowles Communications; and Irwin Miller of Cummins Engine.

The younger a person is when he reaches the top, or the less dependent his accession is on a generation of selected screening and dedicated commitment to a restricted purpose, the more likely he will see that his company's interests lie in supporting changes coming from outside. He will have escaped the disciplining and narrowing process regarding the external environment that tends to distort his vision. He will be more flexible, more tolerant of diversity, more understanding of the necessity and virtue of man-made change.

Other Conditioners. The character of the industry in which executives operate also affects their attitudes toward these changes. While bankers are usually thought to be especially conservative politically, this is not true of certain segments of the banking business. It is no accident that the top officers of large banks with a long history of intense international business involvement are often liberal on domestic issues—excessively so, in the view of their more insular colleagues in banking and in other businesses. Constant contact with different cultures and different institutions in foreign lands quickly makes them see that to do effective business abroad requires flexibility of viewpoints and tolerance for the ways of different institutions and cultures. They observe how business in other lands can live very well indeed with a great variety of governments and public controls. The resulting attitudes spill over into their ways of thinking about affairs at home.

An executive's religious or ethnic background also can endow her with a broader perspective on the forces at work today. One reason American Jews and Catholics in business are, by and large, less hostile (or more hospitable) to external change is simply that the minority antecedent conditions of their lives have automatically made them more aware of the world around them. Conscious awareness of their environment leads them to seek more information and more understanding. And these lead to a more open attitude toward suggestions for its improvement, without paranoid fear of injury to their businesses.

All this discussion is, of course, somewhat of a grand simplification of the dynamics of our world and of how people's views and actions are shaped. But to simplify does not mean to miss the basic point, or to fail to catch the central reasons for its existence. It means only that the point and its reasons are highlighted in order to amplify the picture, as an artist amplifies by modifying perspective and intensifying or moderating colors.

In sum, business's chronic negativism is rooted in the admirable fact that the businesspeople are merely trying to do the best job they can and keep to a minimum the uncertainties with which they must deal. Their negativism is not ideological; it is a consequence of keeping their noses to the operating grindstone. It is only the businesspeople who have had the luxury of not having had to claw their way to the top or to keep so close to the grindstone who have more generous views about external change.

Widening Gap

While we may understand and appreciate the work-oriented cause of business's hostility to external change, we need not automatically condone it. Indeed, we do not condone companies whose single-minded preoccupation with their own production and internal financial problems makes them insensitive to their customers. It is now commonly suggested in business circles that unless narrowly product-oriented companies get market-oriented and do what the market, rather than the assembly line, requires, they will meet the awful fate of the dodo and the dinosaur. They may end up producing excellent buggy whips.

This same currently popular view of business realities can also be used to suggest that the Pavlovian resistance of business to proposed changes in the external environment, no matter how commendably professional the reasons, is a form of narrow product orientation that can cause the entire business society to become competitively impotent in the political market. It can even be suicidal.

If the general public which makes up part of the external environment usually seems to favor things that business, because of its narrow orientation, so predictably opposes, one of these days this public may well begin actively to oppose business. Instead of merely favoring regulatory measures or meliorative legislation on a case-by-case basis, it may begin to develop hardened antibusiness attitudes that will envelop business in an oppressive wave of very unpleasant legislation. A 1966 study for *Newsweek* magazine indicated that already well over one half of the population favors continued and even more stringent government regulation of "big business."

As business becomes more complex and demanding internally, it will have even less time for its maturing top executives to develop the skills and viewpoints that would enable them to discover more easily and generously what the political market's needs and values really are and what is really good for the whole society. It is reasonable then to expect a widening gap between the public's aspirations and the business community's appreciation of the intensity and perhaps even good sense of these aspirations. And as the gap widens, so may the hostility. It is a dismal prospect.

Can anything be done to close the gap, particularly as it applies to mature executives? The fashionable answer is to suggest educational retooling or, in the educator's professional rhetoric, "continuing education for leadership." I suspect this will help very little. Mature executives may be retoolable on technical matters that directly apply to their internal environments, but their ideas about externals are likely by this time to be too firmly set to be successfully remolded.

What is needed is proper tooling from the beginning, before men go into business, and continuing tooling while young executives mature and grow in their organizations.

Forces Bringing Change

But while things are dismal, they are not hopeless. There are forces at work within business today that may almost automatically liberalize the business posture on public issues. Here are some of them:

☐ The ever increasing internationalization of business will expose more and more executives to the variable nature of the external world, to the necessity for understanding and accommodation, to the legitimacy and feasibility of diversity, to the broad view of the corporate self-interest. If these businesspeople are exposed to the international scene early and constantly enough, the fallout value for American business's attitudes at home may be considerable.

☐   A second force is the increasing use of more systematic consumer information in internal operations. This reflects business's recognition of the need to see the world from the consumer's viewpoint, not the producer's. Business has not only abandoned the primitive idea that "they can have any color car as long as it's black," but it is vigorously embracing via consumer research a doctrine it has in the past merely preached—consumer sovereignty.

☐   Only recently, however, has the notion of consumer research been extended to the probing of consumer motivations and values. Today it is largely confined to product development and advertising. But it is likely that in time it will spill over into regulatory and public issues as well. (Indeed, some research organizations are already doing this for business.) As companies do more monitoring of the consumer and his environment, and do it more effectively and routinely, businesspeople will be faced with certain implacable facts of the real world, not the filtered facts from their country clubs. They will face a reality which they will see cannot be fought as naively and wastefully as they have so often fought it.

☐   The civil rights turmoil is another fact of our existence that makes the future encouraging. The economic pressures produced by Negro militancy, combined with the exploding Negro population, has forced business not only to open its doors to Negroes, but to open its mind to the spectrum of social problems in its environment.

☐   After a large national company's Los Angeles plant was virtually destroyed during the Watts riots, the president told a small gathering of industry executives, "Suddenly I saw we could close our eyes to this issue no longer. I went out and saw the ghetto, not because I had never been there, but because circumstances forced me to really *look* at what before I had only seen. It was appalling. If we do not straighten this matter out, we will be in an awful mess. We are going to get on board of the civil rights thing—and seriously. I will be the first to admit that we have been blind to the Negro problem in our company. It is because *I* have been blind. Well, that is over. We are going to do our part. If we do not, we will all go under."

☐   For this executive a powerful transformation had obviously begun. Never again will he be blinded by the pressing requisites of the internal environment. He had begun to see things he had never before seen, and as a consequence he will get "on board" many more public issues than civil rights. Never again will he be narrowly "product-oriented."

☐   Perhaps the most powerful impetus for change in the business posture on major public issues is the widening use of long-range company planning. This practice, like the computer, obliges business to state explicitly its assumptions regarding the future. In its more sophisticated uses, it has forced a searching inquiry about future conditions in the external environment. One national consulting firm now offers a "search service" in precisely this area.

Hence, notions about the future will be subjected to more careful scrutiny, with documentation to substantiate the probabilities of certain events. Such substantiation will require research and facts—and they will be chastening. No amount of personal preference will be able to assuage the reality which economic and sociological calculations will examine and clarify.

But the most important consequence of long-range planning will come in another fashion. Long-range planning is less an attempt to predict the future than to deal with it. Prediction, by emphasizing the operational and strategic consequences of the uncertainties it is designed to reduce, makes the executive more willing to face that future. And if it is his abhorrence of more uncertainty that accounts for the executive's historic opposition to proposed changes in the external environment, then more systematic (if not necessarily better) prediction of the probability, direction, and scope of such changes will moderate his opposition. Once this moderation sets in, he is likely also to be less paranoid, more understanding, and more congenial and responsive to the broader aspirations of the voters who are also his customers.

It is then, and only then, that business will be fully in the mainstream of American aspirations. With this felicitous liberalization of the business ethic, everyone will benefit, and business perhaps more than anybody.

Notes

1. See my article, "The Johnson Treatment," *HBR*, January–February 1967, p. 114.

2. "On Being an American Parent," *Time*, December 15, 1967, p. 31.

5

New Attack on the Legitimacy of Business

PETER L. BERGER

When people genuinely believe in the "rightness" of certain social arrangements, those arrangements are experienced as proper and worthy of support—that is, as legitimate. And when institutions like the modern business corporation are seen as legitimate, they not only function more smoothly but are also better able to help realize a society's most cherished goals. American business once enjoyed this kind of implicit social charter. It does not today.

The question is, What happened? And perhaps more important, What does it matter? The author responds by citing the interests and needs of the "new class," that confederation of knowledge workers not directly concerned with the production of material goods, who therefore oppose in spirit—and as a matter of policy—those individuals who are. The author also suggests possible strategies for dealing with the unprecedented challenge to the place of commerce in American life.

Most people in the business community greeted the outcome of the 1980 elections with relief. This relief is no cause for surprise, since the returns gave powerful evidence that, after years of increasing hostility, many voters outside that community now agreed with views long held within it. Agreement surfaced, for example, on the responsibility of government for inflation, the excesses of regulation, and the tax system's discouragement of capital formation.

The election also signaled the defection of a sizable portion of the working class from the liberal ranks to the "side" of business. Were those groups with a stake in a productive economy—blue-collar and white-collar alike—finally joining against those interested primarily in the redistribution of wealth? If so, the recent political isolation of business might be at an end, and with its passing American society might come again to understand the value of its capitalist heritage.

Various pundits to the contrary, it is much too early to say whether these political events will indeed lead to a favorable reevaluation of the place of business in American life. But it is surely not too early to ask why the business community became so isolated, so ill regarded, in the first place.

From Harmony to Discord

As recently as the early 1960s, both the friends and foes of business still thought that American society was deeply hospitable to capitalist endeavor. To be sure, ever since the New Deal business had been conscious of adversary forces in society. Businesspeople had, however, adapted themselves with remarkable flexibility to the institutions created by those forces—the apparatus of organized labor and the alphabet soup of government agencies. Through labor and government frequently opposed certain private interests, at no time did either question the overall legitimacy of business enterprise.

In fact, their mutual reluctance to do so infuriated the few genuinely radical critics of the time, who viewed even the limitations of business power brought about by the New Deal as but another means of strengthening America's character as a capitalist society.

During the 1970s, however, very different conditions prevailed. The business community found not only this or that interest contested; it found the general climate of opinion exceedingly hostile. The greatest animus came not from organized labor, long the sharpest critic of business, but from the once-friendly pillars of establishment culture—the elite universities, the intelligentsia, and the national media.

Conventional wisdom on the most prestigious campuses pronounced capitalism a cosmic evil, America a sick society precisely to the degree that it was capitalist, and every businessperson a rapacious oppressor. National television eagerly gave air time to reports about major companies that despoiled the environment and endangered public health and safety in the mad pursuit of profits. And when not portrayed as villainous polluters, America's corporate giants were shown to be allied to corruption at home and tyranny abroad.

Whatever the lasting influence of this antibusiness sentiment on public opinion, it certainly had the immediate effect of putting businesspeople on the defensive. But this was not all. Angered and puzzled by the altered cultural climate outside their organizations, they discovered an even more disconcerting change within—not, of course, the overt hostility just described but a lessening of commitment and dedication among their younger colleagues. The reliable "organization men," whom William Whyte had criticized so sharply some 20 years before, had become rather hard to find.

Managers were not alone in perceiving the chill in the atmosphere. Observers of the business community, both friendly and hostile, noticed it too. But the most thoughtful of them—for example, Daniel Bell, the noted American sociologist commonly counted among the "neoconservatives," and Juergen Habermas, a leading European neo-Marxist—went further. More than just a passing chill in the air, these cultural changes represented in their opinion a crisis of legitimacy for the business community. America's managers were not simply imagining things.

Then as now, this diagnosis has a comforting ring of authority: the problem may be severe, but at least we know what it is. Or do we? What, after all, does it mean to speak of a crisis of legitimacy? For that matter, what do we mean by legitimacy in the first place?

The Concept of Legitimacy . . .

Sociologists have attained well-deserved notoriety for coining terms that insult the English language. In this case, though, they are innocent. When sociologists speak of *legitimacy,* they use the term pretty much as it is used in ordinary language—that is, to refer to the belief in the rightness of an institution.

During most of European history, for example, the authority of rulers was legitimated by the notion of divine right. Only when people began seriously to question that notion did the rightness of kingly authority lose its hold on their hearts and minds. The old order in Europe did not suddenly collapse when Louis XVI lost his head under the guillotine; the dramatic events of the French Revolution merely ratified a loss of legitimacy that had already taken place.

. . . Is Empirical

Legitimacy, therefore, refers to a real state of affairs in the real world and not to some dark mystery one can only speculate about. People either believe or do not believe in the rightness of a particular institution, and their beliefs can be known. Bringing them to light may be more or less difficult, depending on the circumstances, but in principle any statement about legitimacy is open to empirical investigation.

Legitimacy, then, concerns neither ethics nor legality. A tyrant may exercise power in a manner both technically unlawful and ethically scandalous; but his power is nonetheless legitimate as long as the people over whom it is exercised accept it as rightful. It is their acceptance, not value judgments imposed from the outside, that matters. Thus, despite the many long-standing pronouncements of moral philosophers and legal scholars, if the American people no longer believe in the rightness of business, the private sector faces a crisis of legitimacy.

. . . Is Normative

To speak of the rightness of an institution is also to speak normatively—that is, to talk about what *ought* to be. It is important to note, however, that every such statement involves a prior assumption about what *is*.

No cultural norm—say an incest taboo against marriage with a close relative—makes sense unless the society in question recognizes the reality to which the norm applies. A normative prohibition against marrying one's fifth cousin is useless if an individual has no idea what a fifth cousin is.

In other words, every functioning norm presupposes a cognitive "map" of social reality, a vision of how the world really is. Though some managers believe differently, most critics of the legitimacy of business today act not in response to abstract moral principles but in response to what they believe business to be or do in the actual world. The normative dispute concerns empirical facts.

Indeed, many advocates of business would, of course, promptly change their position if they believed that business really is what its critics purport. This insight, depending on how one looks at it, is either bad news or good news: *bad* in that cognitive maps are often deeply engraved in the mind and not easily changed; *good* in that beliefs about the empirical world are open to rational discussion.

Let's say you believe, as a matter of unshakable moral principle, that people who mistreat their pets should be subject to capital punishment. Although I may have a very hard time dissuading you from your belief, I have at least a fighting chance to prove that I, at any rate, am not mistreating *my* pets. So, too, with the current attack on the legitimacy of business. Whatever the critics' normative prejudices, the empirical facts are there for all to examine.

. . . Is Plausible

Because human beings are social beings in what they think as in what they do, all items of belief are plausible to the people who hold them only within a given social context. This context provides the belief's plausibility structure. The need for such structures applies to norms as well as cognitive maps and certainly to beliefs about legitimacy. Deprived of its accustomed plausibility structure, any received notion will undergo predictable forms of change.

Tibetan Buddhism, for example, is an eminently plausible belief system to a person who has spent his entire life in a remote Tibetan village in which everyone else is a Buddhist and in which alternative views of the world exist, if at all, as tales of far-away places. But take someone from this village and transplant him to a small community in the American Midwest populated by sturdy Protestants and amiable agnostics. In a very short time his beliefs will seem much less plausible; at the very least, they will have lost their taken-for-granted certitude. Of course, the reverse will occur if a small-town midwestern businessperson is suddenly stranded, all by himself, in a Tibetan village—or even in the faculty club of one of America's elite universities.

. . . Is Artificial

Legitimacy does not just happen. It is something constructed and maintained, for belief in the rightness of an institution depends on the ongoing acts of belief by countless individuals.

As with a theatrical performance, if all the actors behave as if they believe in their roles, the play will appear plausible and its universe legitimate. If several of the cast can no longer keep up that quality of performance, the play will quite rapidly fall apart for actors and audience both.

Because legitimacy is an artifice, it is also relative. As beliefs change, so does the legitimacy of an institution. What is legitimate in one place may not be legitimate in another, and what was legitimate yesterday may not be legitimate today. These changes may take a long period to emerge or, as with modern opinions of business, they may happen quickly. Especially in a media-conscious age, a climate of opinion can change overnight.

. . . Is "Interested"

Business executives know that vested interests affect beliefs—even belief in the legitimacy of business. If there is a notion abroad in the world that bananas cure miscellaneous ailments from leprosy to the common cold, it will come as no big surprise that it is especially popular among banana merchants. Marxists, of course, have made a general theory out of this worldly insight, maintaining that *all* human beliefs are thus grounded in vested interests. Their theory is simplistic, for the linkage between beliefs and vested interests is not always immediate or obvious. If, for example, most banana merchants are Buddhists and if Buddhism has no particular views about the curative power of bananas, then the inevitable Marxist effort to tie religious faith to economic interest explains little.

Still, all of modern social science is indebted to Marx for having shown the importance of economic motives in the shaping of beliefs. But people are not motivated by economics alone. They have other interests as well, and their different sets of interests often conflict. Some people even act contrary to their economic self-interest—out of religious or moral convictions, for considerations of status, or for emotional reasons not easily analyzed.

Most sociologists (unless they are Marxists) view the relation between beliefs and vested interests as reciprocal. Vested interests clearly do affect beliefs, but the way in which people understand their own interests is in turn influenced *by* their beliefs. As a rule of thumb, however, it is probably wisest to begin by looking at the vested interests in play, keeping in mind that people are far more complex and far less rational than economists usually assume.

Business Legitimacy and Social Class

Not so long ago—certainly not further back than the 1950s—the American class system, whatever its tensions and conflicts, did not pose a threat to the business community. As sociologists then taught, that system was a roughly diamond-shaped affair with a big bulge in the middle containing the lower middle class and the "respectable" sector of the working class, including organized labor.

Above that central bulge was the upper middle class and a mysterious stratum known as the upper class (mysterious, in part, because sociologists rarely gained access to it). Below the working class was an agglomeration of poor people (variously identified as the lower class, the underclass, or even the proletariat), which served as the major target of welfare-state programs.

From nowhere in the system arose an important challenge to business legitimacy, a fact regularly bemoaned by the radical critics of American society who, except during the 1930s, were confined to small and generally ineffective coteries of intellectuals. All levels of the middle class recognized business as a legitimate institution.

The upper class, in America a plutocracy rather than an aristocracy, enjoyed positions of authority in the business community. The working class, though locked into an adversary relationship with business through the activity of labor unions, was far more interested in extracting benefits than in challenging business's right to exist. And at the lowest reaches of the class diamond, what dissatisfactions there were—and there were plenty—did not coalesce into a revolutionary antagonism to the business community as such but to this or that inequity, this or that excess.

In other words, during this earlier period American society as a whole served as a plausibility structure for business. Today only certain portions of it do. No mysterious change has come over the belief system of Americans, but what has changed is the constellation of vested interests in the society. To put the point bluntly, if many Americans today challenge the legitimacy of business, more than likely they are getting something out of it. And what might that be?

The Rise of the "New Class"

Only a tentative explanation is possible. To make sense of the new pattern of vested interests in America, a number of analysts, Irving Kristol best known among them, have developed a theory of the so-called new class. This theory, while still hotly debated in its implications, is based on empirical data that nobody doubts. A significant shift in the makeup of the American labor force has indisputably taken place—a movement of workers to the service sector caused by the reduced need for labor in the production and distribution of material goods.

The sociologists' notion of service occupations, however, is broad—embracing such diverse groups as hairdressers, psychoanalysts, and professors of musicology. A narrower, more useful concept is that of the "knowledge industry," a term first devised by the economist Fritz Machlup in the 1960s with roughly the same meaning as John Kenneth Galbraith's "technostructure." The knowledge industry includes all those who engage in the production and distribution of what passes for knowledge in a society.

But even this narrower concept, as Machlup knew, refers to millions of people in America. Sociologically it is still too broad, for it lumps together nuclear engineers and purveyors of Maoist ideology, corporation managers and recreational counselors.

In both the service sector and the knowledge industry, however, there is a smaller group of people engaged not just with any form of knowledge but with knowledge that is not itself concerned with the production or distribution of material goods. These people constitute the new class, or knowledge class. Unlike nuclear engineers and corporation managers, new-class knowledge workers concern themselves, directly or symbolically, with things other than material goods or techniques—that is, with all those things that have to do with the quality of life.

Membership in the new class is not restricted to intellectuals, although intellectuals do occupy its most prestigious positions. Just as the old middle class was divided within itself (the upper-middle stratum as against the petty bourgeoisie, for instance), so the new class is internally stratified. It includes not only professors at the elite universities but also masses of lesser pedagogues (indeed, the bulk of the educational establishment), the nonbusiness and nontechnical professionals in the media, members of the "helping professions" whose "help" is essentially nonmaterial (recreational counselors, but not dentists), and government bureaucrats with jurisdiction over quality-of-life issues.

The dividing line often runs through certain professions, separating, say, corporate lawyers from public interest lawyers, rural clergy from campus ministers, and civil servants in the Department of Commerce from those in the Environmental Protection Agency. The dividing line does not, however, run according to income categories, which has made some analysts reluctant to use the term *class* at all. An elite intellectual may enjoy an income similar to that of a second-echelon corporate manager, but his views on most issues will differ sharply from those of the latter.

Because of the noncorrelation with income, sociological data on the new class are as yet sparse. Finer distinctions remain to be made. But clearly the old middle class has split in half. Where previously there was *one* middle class (stratified within itself), there now are *two* (both internally stratified). People bent on moving out of the lower classes now have two distinct, though not mutually exclusive, career ladders to choose from. No matter which is chosen, the ensuing social mobility will involve fundamental changes in personal beliefs and values.

Class Culture

Social classes differ from each other not only in the material goods of life but in values, tastes, and life-styles. Studies dating back to the 1920s show that middle-class and working-class people in America differ in their religious affiliations, their moral codes, their notions of beauty and proper manners, and even in their sexual practices.

A sociologist who knows only that an individual is a member of an evangelical Protestant church, strongly disapproves of marijuana, prefers popular to classical music, takes his hat off while riding in an elevator with women, and prefers to make love in the dark will be confident that his subject is from the working class. To be sure, there are always exceptions, and any *one* of the above data is not decisive; but the aggregate of such cultural indicators holds for the great majority of people. This should not be surprising. Humans are social beings and derive their cultural traits from the group to which they belong.

Put simply, there is such a thing as class culture, and it provides the best means of identifying the members of the new, or knowledge, class. An individual about whom nothing is known except that he engages in transcendental meditation, prefers marijuana to alcohol, likes nonobjective painting, believes fervently in the Equal Rights Amendment, and engages in more or less daring sexual experimentation is far more likely than his evangelical brother to belong to the new class.

Class Politics

As there is class culture, so there is class politics. Class interests vary; and though people are not motivated by such interests alone, a good deal of political behavior begins to make sense when one asks who gets what out of a specific political position. Indeed, much of the political history of the United States since the mid-1960s is inexplicable unless seen in light of the rising new class.

For reasons grounded in class culture, the two most dynamic political developments of the 1960s—the civil rights and the antiwar movements—served as rallying points for the new class. Just as the latter movement and the "new politics" that institutionalized it marked the arrival of the new class as an identifiable political force, its capture of the Democratic party in 1972 showed its influence at flood tide. The defeat of George McGovern in 1972 was above all a defeat of the new class; the aftermath of Watergate, a temporarily successful effort to reverse that defeat. It remains to be seen whether the victorious coalition in the 1980 election represents a durable realignment of class forces in American politics.

Class Business

In interest, culture, and politics the new class in America tends to be antagonistic to business and a threat to its legitimacy. Whether that legitimacy survives—and, if so, in what form—hinges on the outcome of new-class efforts to augment its power in American society. But why has this antagonism developed in the first place? No simple answer is possible. Not all attitudes and beliefs are the product of vested class interests. Yet it is clear that the new class has its own interests, that these directly affect its beliefs, and that both pose a challenge to the business community.

Do not forget that a high proportion (almost certainly the majority) of the new class is either publicly employed or heavily dependent on public subsidies. No wonder, then, that the new class is generally disposed to a "statist" orientation which, in the context of American society, necessarily implies antagonism to private, market-oriented business interests.

Take a very clear case: the ongoing debate over the environment. Environmentalism is a virtually pure instance of a new-class movement, and its beachheads within the government bureaucracy—the EPA in particular—are largely held by new-class individuals. It is, obviously, in the interest of these people to allege that business, if left alone, would do terrible harm to the environment because the allegation directly legitimates their own activities.

Class Future

Neither the new class nor its vested interests will disappear overnight. Its place in the structure of the economy is far too secure, and its stake in an interventionist state is far too high. Nor is its challenge to the legitimacy of business likely to evaporate. The beliefs and values of a class culture have enormous staying power. The new class has long taken its cultural cues from the upper crust of elite intellectuals, who—as part of what Lionel Trilling spoke of as the "adversary culture" in America—have been contemptuous of business and all its works for at least a century.

But at least some change is in the air. For one thing, a substantial portion of the new class is not employed in the public sector and thus has economic interests that may converge with those of business. For another, members of the new class are also taxpayers and citizens and thus have suffered from class-supported social experiments even while sympathizing with their underlying ideology. Then, too, in recent years many in the intellectual community have rediscovered an affection for the ideas and institutions of democratic capitalism.[1] And finally, political success—as in the 1980 elections—attracts, and sometimes converts, people even if they started out on the other side.

Roughly speaking, the current alignment in American politics is between those who have a vested interest in economic growth as against those whose interest is in the redistribution of wealth. Almost until the fall of 1980, business stood alone with many in the working class against the new class and those groups—notably among the racial minorities—whose needs were allegedly served by new-class "helpers." Now, however, sentiment is growing among black and Hispanic leaders that much of this alleged help has aided primarily the new class and much less so the intended beneficiaries. If this sentiment takes root, it will leave the new class in a dangerously exposed position, since much of its legitimacy derives from its identification with the aspirations of America's racial minorities.

A Strategy for Business

What can the business community do to meet the challenge of the new class? Simply repudiating the charges levied against it is not enough. Nor is re-iterating its history of efficient economic performance. To argue that capitalism builds more and better mousetraps will not convince those people who do not like mousetraps to begin with.

New-class constituencies do have their vested interests, however, and business can try to make a deal with them. Two groups in particular suggest themselves—the more important being, as the 1980 elections showed dramatically, the working class as represented by organized labor.

The American labor movement is distinct in that it continues to follow a hard-nosed, pragmatic, nonideological tradition, which was classically expressed in Samuel Gompers's reply to a question about what labor wanted: "*More!*" Although this tradition implies an adversary stance toward management, it accepts the principles of a business-run economy. As labor has a strong class interest in a productive, growing economy and much to lose from the redistributionist policies of the new class, business must recognize labor as an important ally in the defense of free enterprise.

The second group includes both the poor and the disadvantaged minorities, whose poverty bestows legitimacy on the new-class professionals who devise the policies and man the programs to serve the disadvantaged. Virtually without exception, every increase in the power of the new class has been legitimated in terms of the welfare of the poor. And the poor, especially the black poor, have consistently given political support to the new class in its various redistributionist policies, and they have indeed benefited from them. But as an increasing number of black intellectuals have recognized, these benefits come at a high price.

The price is dependency—dependency on government and especially on the new-class bureaucrats and professionals who administer the redistributionist machinery of the welfare state. Although business cannot credibly argue against these welfare benefits, it can show that lasting improvements—meaningful jobs, substantial property formation, real changes in self-image—come from economic independence and not from political dependency and redistribution.

Deals are also possible between business and at least some members of the new class, especially those who offer their services in the marketplace. Sharp conflicts of vested interest will, of course, continue: the new class clearly stands to gain from more government; business, from less.

But business does have a strong, even an inspirational, case to make at the level of cultural values about the empirical linkage between capitalism and freedom. It is no accident, as Marxists like to say, that no democratic society in the world is not capitalist and no truly socialist society is democratic—although there are, to be sure, nondemocratic capitalist societies, notably in the Third World. Here lies a promise of common ground with even the most committed new-class advocates.

Its legitimacy seriously challenged, the American business community need not lack a workable strategy for action. Opponents have vested interests that can be understood and a system of beliefs that can be called into question. Restoration of legitimacy will depend as much on successful competition over ideas as on successful performance in the market. From a sociological point of view, business must learn to speak a new language. It knows economics and politics; now it must address meaning and value.

Notes

1. For a discussion of this development, see Norman Podhoretz, "The New Defenders of Capitalism," *HBR*, March–April 1980, p. 96.

6

The Price
of Corporate Vanity

DAVID FINN

Here is a PR man who believes the PR mirror should show the true image of business.

The experience of American business in recent decades has clearly established the fruitfulness of making a good corporate impression. But it has also become clear that corporations (and perhaps governments and other human institutions) can go overboard in the effort to make other people like them and that this can do considerable harm. The exaggerated prominence which the word "image" has achieved in our vocabulary suggests that we may be going too far in our practical concern for external appearances and that sound business considerations (as well as human, moral, and cultural considerations) warrant a re-evaluation of the basic approach to public relations as practiced in our society.

Dangers Created

I believe that three types of danger may result from an overweening interest in one's corporate image:

    1.   When facing business reverses, management can deceive itself about its real weaknesses by believing that the only thing wrong is a bad public image. This deception has emerged as a national tendency in government and has provoked criticism from those who feel that we should be less concerned about whether we "project *an image* of vitality" to the world and more concerned with making a straightforward examination of just what our vitality as a people and as a culture actually is.

    Some economists are similarly upset by the idea that a business recession can be reversed by slogans aimed at building positive attitudes rather than by concrete measures to alleviate the sources of economic distress. As one journalist said recently, we are beginning to behave like fat old ladies primping ourselves in front of the mirror. We are attracted by the idea that we can look beautiful at all times whether we really are beautiful or not.

2.   We are also misled if we define wisdom as that policy which wins the widest approval rather than that policy which creates the highest values. Such a view holds that management should do things because they are popular, not because they are right. This can make us a people without principle, without morality, without faith in ourselves—a people whose primary gratification is an approving pat on the back. Businesspeople become, then, not a force for progress in society, but a mirror reflecting existing tastes and deflecting any effort to work toward a better world.

3.   Our passion to establish a good public posture may lead us into a third danger. We may destroy the process of free public debate, which is both the most prized characteristic of a democratic society and the essential mechanism by which a competitive business economy can work and prosper. A free press is one in which editors may write as they please and criticize even the most powerful groups in society. To the extent that business interests seek a favorable press through special pressures or inducements, they deny themselves the value of constructive public criticism of their affairs. What is more, are not scientific research, educational policy, and theological judgments most fruitful when they are directed by the experts in the field rather than by vested interests seeking third-party endorsement for their points of view? How much do we damage the foundations for our long-term success as a culture by seeking the immediate public support we believe necessary for the success of our individual enterprises?

These three areas of risk necessitate a careful re-examination of the means by which public relations practitioners are trying to help corporations deal with their public images. It is important to learn in what ways these efforts may be harmful or helpful.

The Fallacious Image

On the face of it, the basic notion of public relations image making does not seem potentially dangerous to the corporation. To the contrary, it seems plausible that the idea should be a great help in making it easier to do business with the multiplicity of companies operating in a mass society. The reasoning goes as follows:

1   By definition, images are impressions and mental pictures about things.
2   If management has publicly stated its corporate philosophy and expressed a consistent point of view in its trademark, its advertising,

and its public service works, the public will have the feeling that it knows what the company stands for.

3   If people like what the company stands for, then they may choose to do business with it rather than its competitors.

4   This seems particularly true when it is impossible to know at first-hand the management running a company or the manner in which its products are made; impressions or images are useful substitutes for concrete knowledge.

Significantly, no one individual claims to have originated the phrase "corporate image." Industrial designers introduced the idea of "corporate identity" programs just a few years ago. At the same time, opinion researchers were working on "image studies," and public relations practitioners were trying to cope with the problems of what they called "faceless corporations." When the phrase "corporate image" appeared, it was quickly adopted as describing exactly what they all had in mind. The need for some unified approach to developing company reputation seemed to have been answered by the coining of a phrase.

Has the need really been answered? Or have we just deluded ourselves?

Mixing-Bowl Approach

Some executives believe a corporate image can be created for anybody who wants one by mixing together a standard set of ingredients without regard to what any particular company really is like. Such executives will ask their public relations adviser to recommend a good image and then get to work to create it. The inexperienced or insensitive practitioner proceeds to do so "by the numbers." He produces a trademark that may not express the corporate personality at all, yet which is thought to qualify because it is a compelling design by an outstanding artist. He produces articles and speeches which tend to sound alike because they are ghostwritten by the same person, but which are excused if they have some kind of theme and get exposure. One public relations program can look frighteningly like any other, and images may differ only in the extent of the "treatment" that companies have received.

But here is the rub. If an image fails to be individual and distinctive, it will have no relation to reality, that is, the actual corporate personality. It will be only a fabrication. As such, it negates one major premise of its existence—that an offered image can make up for the public's lack of first-hand knowledge of the corporation. It exploits, rather than compensates for, the public's lack of direct contact and represents an attempt to make people think what the corporation wants them to think, rather than to give them a grasp of what the corporation actually is like.

More basic still, how valid is the notion that there *is* such a thing as an actual corporate personality? While certain characteristics may be attributed to present and past managements, it is a grave mistake to view a corporation as a monolithic entity. All its employees do not think alike about any issue. The idea that a single pattern of thought differentiates one entire company from another is an unforgivable presumption. It suggests that a corporation is, or can be made, an amalgam of stereotyped human beings, and does not consist of a group of individuals thinking for themselves.

Finally, as this corporate haberdashery mushrooms, one must ask: Is the whole idea of image-making nonsense? Can any kind of public relations activity really create or change images in people's minds? The research done to date on this question is inconclusive, and much of it suggests that efforts to persuade the mass only reinforce the opinions of those already persuaded. Most opinions, it seems, are formed out of a multiplicity of influences, and no one image-making scheme can be so powerful as to overcome all contrary opinions just by the sheer brilliance of its technical virtuosity. The best one can do (practically, as well as idealistically) may be to get the truth as one sees it on public record and let images be hanged!

Impulse to Disguise

Recently a professor of philosophy at a large university reviewed the work that was done by a public relations firm for one of its clients over three years. He examined all correspondence as well as other written material produced as part of the program. Then he led a series of discussions with ten members of the staff who had worked for this client. He attempted to determine if there was any difference between what everybody thought they had been doing and what they actually had been doing.

The stated goals of the campaign were: (a) to establish a nonprofit educational foundation through which an industry association could attempt to combat negative attitudes toward its product and, through this effort, (b) prevent restrictive legislation, and (c) help build sales. In the course of the discussions, the group became aware that:

☐   The client actually did not represent the industry but only a few individual members of the industry who happened to be especially sensitive to public opinion.

☐   There was no evidence that the public's opinion was negative, or at least negative in such a way as to affect sales or legislation; anxiety about public opinion seemed to be entirely subjective.

☐   The foundation was not truly educational and, while it did not make money, its true purpose was the profit of the industry. The program could have served its purpose just as well by using a perfectly straightforward commercial name like "association" instead of assuming an educational guise.

☐   Legislative interest seemed to be based on a technical evaluation of the tax levies imposed on the product. This was a question which deserved legitimate public debate. Everybody in the public relations firm assumed uncritically that the client's arguments were valid, and no real effort was made to check the facts presented by the opposition.

☐ Published comments on the fine values of the product were made in the press as if they were the opinion of the editors, when actually the stories were written by the public relations specialists in the employ of the companies making the product. The comments would have been just as effective if their source had been openly identified.

☐ Nobody really believed that the program could succeed in changing attitudes.

☐ Everybody agreed that the real, though unspoken, value of the program probably was to provide the client companies with the subjective satisfaction of seeing a positive evaluation of their products made in public.

Thus, this campaign was carried out through a technique of disguise which might have made sense in terms of the supposed goals but was silly and unnecessary in terms of the real goals. The activities of the client, the PR practitioners, and the press were all characterized by a series of disguises which were both misleading and unnecessary. This made the whole campaign one of play acting rather than truthtelling, when telling the truth seemed to be the real objective of the campaign.

Placebos for Mismanagement

When business is bad, or at least does not live up to expectations, management tries to do everything it can to find the cause of the trouble and provide the remedy. On such occasions, however, many executives seem to have a weakness for patent medicines. They tend to look for ready-made solutions as described in the latest issues of the "how to" trade publications. These cures often work, partly because of the mental therapy involved in taking any medicine, and partly because the formulas contain some ingredients which are of real value. But sometimes they can do great harm. If the ailment is serious, something drastic may be required to save the business; and wasting time on faddist measures may prove fatal.

Image making can be one of the more dangerous types of management panaceas. It gives the false impression that a fundamental change is being made, for creating a new image of oneself seems deceptively like creating a new self. This looks like the ultimate step in solving the most difficult of management problems—the deficiency of management itself. And yet, of course, it is not. Management needs to do more than change its image to change itself. Recognizing its blind spots and learning useful new skills are essentials.

Trying to project a new or improved face for oneself in such situations is like undergoing plastic surgery to correct a basic personality disorder. For a while everything seems beautiful, but the remedy is only skin-deep. A Pagliacci suffers behind the smiling mask.

Business executives are particularly inclined to mask their shortcomings. They tend to measure their achievements (to the extent that they can measure them at all) in terms of the popular notions of success. Since the purposes of business are served by promoting and catering to mass appeals, it is natural for the businessperson to respond to them in her own life. And then, when something goes wrong, she may feel she can cope with it if she keeps up the appearance of success. From this it is a short step to believing that the appearance of success *is* success.

There are several classic situations in which this tendency shows itself, and most experienced public relations practitioners have encountered conditions similar to those that follow.

Incompetence at the Helm

First and most common, there is the case of the inadequate company president who thinks himself better than he really is. Inadequate leadership radiates from this kind of top executive like spokes in a wheel.

If the hub is weak, the company's public relations will be weak and no amount of professional ingenuity can make it otherwise. But if, in addition, the president considers himself a really dynamic manager and thinks the fault is elsewhere, he is prone to believe that public relations can solve his problems. He suspects that the only thing wrong is the "spirit" of the company or its "look" to others, and that the arts of persuasion can change all this. The more strongly he believes this, the less likely he is to face the truth. If he is lucky (and his company unlucky), he can go on for years believing that in the long run and with the right kind of public relations, his fate will change.

Is it an exaggeration to suggest that public relations is ill-used or harmful in such a case? If the practitioner is at all sensitive, he feels, at best, that his tactics are diversionary and, at worst, that he is perpetuating a lie. A sensitive PR person realizes that the president who purrs at the minor acclaim he receives should instead be mourning his failures. There is no future in such a publicity assignment or in any firm that employs public relations under such conditions.

Imaginary Team

A contrasting case is that of the strong company president who wants to build public confidence in his second- and third-level management because too many people believe he is running a one-man company. Usually people believe this because it is true, but the president once again does not want to see the truth. He hires good executives to work under him to disprove these accusations and asks his public relations specialists to spotlight the depth of the management team.

The appointment of the executives is itself a public relations move, calculated more to influence opinion than to strengthen management. What the president does not do, of course, is actually delegate authority, so the public relations effort turns out to be unavailing. A continuous turnover of executives is proof that the president does not take the idea of management in depth seriously, and that he is trying to use public relations as a cover-up for a weakness that he will never overcome. All this is bad not only because the public relations does not work but also because everybody involved is clearly making a fool of himself in acting out the farce.

The Dying Product

What is perhaps even more serious is the use of public relations to create fanfare for a product that is losing its market because of basic deficiencies in design, quality, pricing, or marketing. PR people know that their skills cannot be of value unless the product has *natural appeal* (a quality that no one knows quite how to analyze, but that is clearly a necessary ingredient for success), can stand up to competition, and has an effective selling machinery behind it.

Many industries have run into major problems because of a deterioration of, say, their dealer setup through uncontrollable price cutting, the inroads of other more profitable items, or lack of effective sales help from manufacturers. But too often management decides to sponsor a public relations program to reintroduce the element of glamor in the product instead of correcting the structural defects. Everybody works hard and perhaps some glamor does get created, but sales continue to slump. Those who realize what is happening get the feeling that the industry "is fiddling while Rome burns"—making lovely images while the market is falling apart instead of spending its energy first to put out the fire. If the situation is not calamitous, both can be done simultaneously. However, to consider public relations alone as a cure for so basic an illness is self-deception.

The Failing Company

Another classic situation is the case of the company which has a bad financial record and counts on public relations to make it look good. But if the record is bad, can any amount of hullabaloo change it? To be sure, there are frequently special circumstances which may put the failures in a better light, and it is perfectly legitimate to attempt to highlight these circumstances. Yet sometimes companies go much further than this. They convince themselves that because of their great dreams for the future, the record should be virtually ignored. The public relations assignment then is to try to make the dreams look real. This, unfortunately, may succeed, and then management, the stockholders, and the business community all believe what is actually no more than a fairy tale. When the truth comes out, the company may be too far gone to save.

In all such cases as those mentioned, the conscientious public relations practitioner abhors the sense of working on a mask rather than on reality.

He knows that management is dealing with mirages, not images, and that this cannot do any good. He feels obliged to help the executives look inward rather than outward and see what is really wrong, rather than try to create the impression that everything is right. If he is successful, he finds himself acting like a consultant to management on management rather than on public relations; his hope is that self-knowledge and self-improvement will take place so that a more natural and positive form of public relations can evolve.

Mirrors Instead of Ideas

Even when business is good, too much concern for a company's public image can sap the company's energy, weaken its leadership, and ultimately destroy its capacity for self-generation of new ideas and new directions. Most executives who expose themselves to this danger are unaware of what they are doing; they feel that they are sensibly examining their profiles in a mirror and making adjustments which can further improve their business. But it is unfortunately too easy to step over the line and begin to run a company as one thinks others want it run rather than following one's own best judgments as a manager.

Courage or Popularity?

Philosophers and critics in many fields have for some time been complaining about the excessive desire to be liked which seems to characterize many adminstrative tendencies of our time. One prominent educator has maintained for several years that public relations specialists should be kept out of all board meetings of universities lest the courage to support unpopular ideas be undermined. His favorite comment is that any new idea which immediately wins majority support is years behind its time. Good administrators must dare to be wrong, and the willingness to be unpopular is a test of this strength.

Again, statesmen have become increasingly concerned with government officials who are preoccupied with the image they project. Americans have been told many times that they have the wrong idea of public relations when they point out the negative attitudes that a particular move might provoke. Action should be based on inner conviction, not on a concern for public sentiment.

In marketing, the battle has raged even more fiercely. Should automobiles be designed according to public taste or according to principles of safety and good engineering? Should TV programming give the people what they want (the programs that get the highest rating) or what is good in terms of deeper cultural values? Should foods be sold which are flavored and colored to appeal to the largest number of people, or which have the best natural taste and highest nutritional value?

Similar dilemmas face management in other areas of decision making. To mention a few:

☐   How should humanitarian interests in employees and the community be balanced against high production costs when a particular plant becomes unprofitable?

☐   Should a generous community relations program be maintained because of public pressure in spite of poor business conditions?

☐   Should a missile be fired in a way that will gain the most public applause or in a way that can most advance the state of knowledge—especially when the latter choice might result in what would publicly be called a failture?

A Reasonable Balance

The wisest approach to these questions involves striking a balance between conflicting interests. Making products that will not sell, broadcasting programs no one will listen to, or firing missiles in a way that loses public confidence and congressional appropriations is impractical. On the other hand, concentrating exclusively on the most popular products, programs, and missile shots can also lead to public stagnation.

Long-range values (e.g., possibilities for sales tomorrow as well as for today) and the satisfaction of personal ideas (e.g., producing a product one can be proud) are needs which cannot be met with popularity ratings. Seeing ourselves in the mirror may at times help us work toward these goals, but we must not worry too much about outward appearances. Albert Einstein never chose to dress up, even for the most formal occasions, and there are corporations which are also successful even though they don't particularly care about their public image. What we look like is important only when it expresses how we feel and what we are.

The "dress up" programs of corporations can well be evaluated on this basis: Do they represent what management feels is most important or are they slick masquerades designed only to entice public interest? This standard should be applied, I believe, across the board—to the architectural design of company offices and of plants; to the graphic design of trademarks, letterheads, and packages; to the design of products; to speeches of top executives; to company house organs; to advertisements; and, finally, to corporate policy.

The Ultimate Conceit

It has long been argued that healthy, vigorous criticism is an important spur to creativity. The personal histories of many artists bear this out. Critics train themselves to be brutally honest in their reactions rather than to be tactful and politely complimentary. It is a widely held proposition that criticism is often a more effective means of provoking creative effort than applause, and that failure and frustration often breed success.

A corollary to this proposition is that success breeds failure. An artist who achieves acclaim and recognition may find the spark which drives her to greatness extinguished by the pleasures of flattery. Accomplishment in life seems to be a product of inner tension, and circumstances that make one self-satisfied can easily dissolve the basis for initiative, drive, and, above all, the daring to be original.

This is hardly a universal truth, but it applies quite widely, I think, to businesspeople as well as to artists (though the criteria are quite different for judging if success has taken its toll). For the executive, the test is not in the works, as with the artist, but in the manner and the attitude with which work *is done*. Also, the businessperson may not suffer personally from an overdose of success, but almost certainly the firm, and society, will have to bear the burden of any conceit that comes with this power.

In the world of art, the critic is ever present. Thus, the too-successful artist can be cut down to size when the quality of his work diminishes. But the businessperson has no such watchdog. If he loses touch with reality through an overinflated ego, no one is there to cut *him* down to size. His employees and business associates may bewail his exaggerated sense of importance and his pretension to infallibility, but there is little they can do about it.

Can the business press serve the business executive as the critic serves the artist? Management fights this possibility with all its strength. In fact, as I have suggested, the assignment of the public relations specialist often is to see to it that negative criticism is kept out of the press, thus warding off the jolt that would bring the executive to her senses. Management's *ultimate* conceit is to imagine that it should be above public criticism, that its power and self-sufficiency give it the right to utilize a technique which is designed to banish unpleasant controversy from executive life.

This self-destructive conceit operates on many levels. Let us look at some examples now.

Self-Glorification

A legitimate function of public relations is to help an executive take a position in his industry or in public life which is in keeping with his background, his ability, and his ambitions. The same is true about helping companies become better known for achievements of which they can be justly proud. But too often the public relations approach to such an undertaking is out of proportion to the facts. The business executive is encouraged to look at his achievements as events unequaled in human history and to feel that his public realtions goals will be reached only when the rest of the world looks at his success with equal reverence.

Fortunately, most businesspeople have better sense than to believe that all the praise that comes their way is entirely justified. But there *are* those who insist on looking at themselves as Horatio Algers. And there *are* public relations practitioners who think it is part of their job to encourage this hallucination, or even (in some cases) to foist it on an executive who would otherwise have better sense. And there are *many* who, while not so extreme in their views, are sometimes influenced by these attitudes.

It is unfortuante for the business community, and, in the long run, even for the public relations practitioner and her client, that such programs are ever launched. Few people are as impressed with personal glorification as the subject of it, and the sad truth—as every experienced public relations specialist knows—is that the impression doesn't last very long. The executive is pleased momentarily, but then he discovers that he is the same person he always was and is disappointed. If he has the "bug," as the saying goes, he wants to feel a little more than mortal through his public relations program. Thus he always wants more, hoping that the next honor he gets will do the trick. And, in the process, his delusion gets greater, his capacity to manage the business wisely and with a sense of balance diminishes, and, sooner or later, he becomes frustrated.

Self-Righteousness

Occasionally in the life of any corporation something happens which leads the press to report unfavorably on something dear to the heart of management. This may be in connection with labor problems, selling methods, a proxy fight, product failures, or the successes of a competitive product. If it is bad enough, the public relations specialist may get a spanking for letting such a "distortion of the facts" get into print. The battalions then are brought out (advertising pressure, meetings with publishers, counterattacks against "the other side," etc.) to turn back the tide.

How amazing it is that management cannot realize the self-deception involved in the notion that it alone has "all the facts;" and that if reporters would only learn to "get their facts straight," the problem of an unfavorable press would be solved. Unhappily the sad truth is that sometimes management is wrong and deserves to be brought to account by a responsible press. There is no reason why this should be done with kid gloves. The press has a right (some think an obligation) to speak its mind if it has the damning facts. These facts admittedly may not be enough for a final judgment. However, the purpose of a critical press is not to assess corporate values for the "Good Book," but rather to be an instrument by which an alert society can make progress more rapidly and fruitfully.

A sturdy, self-confident management responds to critisism with action, not with public relations, when it is under attack. This does not mean that the public relations specialist is not consulted, but it does mean that her job is to help management learn and respond to criticism rather than fight like a bully or hide behind a smoke screen.

Self-Perpetuation

Many exeuctives have a keen interest in public affiars and feel rewarded in their public relations efforts if they gain the opportunity to express their opinions forcefully or even play a strategic part in obtaining social action which they support. There is no reason to hide the connection between one's business interests and the social, economic, or political position one publicly supports. The integrated individual who holds the same beliefs in both his business and his private life is certainly better off than the individual who leads a double life. Expressing one's convictions effectively and working toward a better society as a businessperson and as a citizen lead to personal fulfillment.

But this impulse can go awry if an executive loses the capacity to look at opposing opinions as being just as worthy of a public hearing as his own. If he denies that public argument should be a fair battle between competitive ideas and may the best man win, he finds himself waging a no-holds-barred crusade in which he believes management's point of view is a holy cause. All ideas which serve to perpetuate the business are right; all values which may be in conflict with these ideas must be sacrificed.

This, of course, is shameful and entirely inconsistent with the principles of democracy. People are entitled to think that peace is more important than the perpetuation of business, that public health is more important than the perpetuation of business, and that freedom of opportunity is more important than the perpetuation of business. I do not mean that business interests are opposed to these worthy causes, but the fact is that they *may* be (or that harried managers may *think* they are).

To discover the truth, the marketplace must provide a free and effective exchange of *all* points of view. Every time business interests become intolerant of the opposition and, through public relations efforts, fight a secret or underhanded battle to stifle public expression of contrary convictions, they strike a blow at the foundations of the system which permits their own enterprises to thrive. At a time when the system of free enterprise is facing its most serious challenge, this is indeed a dangerous course to follow.

Conclusion

Now, more than two decades after the dragmatic definition of public relations as " the engineering of consent" was conceived[1]—and subsequently discredited—the time has come for the self-destructive, antisocial tendencies of public relations to be separated from the constructive and useful contributions it can make.

PR practitioners know that mass persuasion through some elaborate form of brainwashing is an illusion, primarily for the reasons Abraham Lincoln made famous and which still hold true. But practitioners also have learned that self-promotion has important limitations; it cannot take precedence over the natural processes by which society corrects and improves itself in a dynamic culture. The main instrument of those natural processes is free and independent criticism, the very institution which public relations so often seems bent on destroying. It is not the job of public relations to secure public support for a cause any more than its function is to mold or evolve public opinion. Its purpose instead is to make management's opinion public and to present the case for causes that the managers believe in.

Constructive Promotion

The destructive tendencies of public relations are a product of vanity in business. This conceit leads to false images which deceive no one, but dissipate the energy and dull the talent to manage well. Public relations has no business promoting illusions. Its business should be to help the businessperson gain the kind of personal satisfaction from his work that stimulates the drive to greater achievement.

Artificiality, disguise, subterfuge, pressuring, manipulation—all these can play a part in public relations if it is employed by business executives whose power and success have gone to their heads. How can these tendencies be checked? Not by moralizing, for this leads people in the business to think that "our" kind of public relations is always right, and that the transgressions are only committed by "the rascals," whoever they may be! And not by self-restraint, for this is not in the nature of those with strong promotional instincts.

What *is* vitally needed is a strengthening of all those institutions which have a potential for criticizing business or even for fighting actively against destructive business interests. These critics include editors who sometimes find it difficult to cope with pressures from the companies which they write about, scientists and scholars who may feel impelled to tread carefully on subjects of interest to their industrial sponsors, and government officials and legislators who are always conscious of the commercial interests of their constituents. If these groups were stronger, the job of the public relations practitioners would be to make straightforward appeals to the independent judgment of "third parties," and to help businesspeople themselves respond constructively to critical opinion. What I am saying, in other words, is that the constructive role of public relations cannot be secured by goodwill, but only by the effective workings of a healthy democratic society.

Developing Criticism

The best way in which a strong institution of criticism can be developed is through education in the specialized schools which train the critics (particularly the journalists), the businesspeople, and the public relations practitioners. Cooperative efforts by these schools can help clarify what the most effective relationships should be among those in each field. There is need for workshops in which students practice reacting to opposition, and seminars which explore mutual responsibilities in a world of conflicting ideas and interests.

Since many successful people in these fields do not graduate from the schools of their speciality, some means should also be found to create a mature and sophisticated understanding of business-community relationships in general colleges and universities. The primitive concept of "the public" as a receptacle for all sentimental notions about life must be dispelled. Every educated individual must learn that whenever he expresses an opinion in public, he *is* the public. His primary obligation as a citizen is to make sure he is expressing his own opinion and not that of some others who are trying to use him for their own purposes. If he decides to support their cause, fine; if not, he must have the courage to speak out against them. And all those who accept the democratic idea must learn to hold this independence inviolable.

Most important, business leaders must accept the fact that free, vigorous, constructive criticism helps improve the course of human enterprise. They must recognize that the job of public relations should be to further this process, not impede it. Only in this way can the professional practice of public relations avoid becoming a corrupting influence in our society and instead become a force for continuous social betterment by performing the useful task of giving public expression to dynamic leadership.

Notes

1.   Edward L. Bernays, "The Engineering of Consent," *The Annals of the American Academy of Political and Social Science: Communication and Social Action*, March 1947, p. 113.

7
The Defense of the Multinational Corporation

JOHN KENNETH GALBRAITH

Multinational corporations have been indicting themselves in the courts of world opinion. Their spokespeople deny that they exercise great power and even concede that it would be inappropriate to exercise such power. The companies guiltily seek to give themselves a low profile, as if to conceal their foreign origins. They identify themselves with American management prowess. These and other efforts are designed to defend the multinational, writes the author, yet they have the opposite effect. The countries in which they operate see that their defense is spurious; it is apparent that they *do* use power, that they *are* controlled from another country, that their management prowess is *not* uniquely American. It would be far better if the multinationals built their defense on the truth, holding that their economic and political power is necessary, conceding the realities of their control, and making no claim to proprietary management skills.

In the past 30 years no economic institution has so intruded itself on the economic landscape as the multinational corporation. None has provoked so much discussion or been the subject of such obsessive concern—and almost every reference has in it a note of anxiety.

In the autumn of 1976, a friend, fellow liberal, and onetime government colleague of mine, Theodore Sorensen, was nominated for a high public post in Washington, D.C. There was conservative objection, as might be expected. But liberals also expressed concern. He had been a counsel in private law practice for a number of large multinational corporations. He was being proposed for the directorship of the Central Intelligence Agency. Any association between the CIA and the multinationals was automatically suspect.

But even in the absence of such association, references to the multinational enterprise have a pejorative, even sinister connotation. Executives of these companies, when they gather for conferences or other corporate festivals, are regularly told by visiting professors on modest fee of the anxieties they arouse.

In my television series and book *The Age of Uncertainty,*[1] I allowed myself some amiable references to multinational corporations, especially as they diminish nationalism and the importance of national boundaries and contribute to economic development. No other reference brought such indignant criticism.

Such hostility, the existence of which no corporate executive will deny, rests, most executives will plead, on public misunderstanding. They look at themselves, their colleagues, their hours of work, their service to customers and tax collectors, and at their families, churches, charities, and largely innocent recreations, and ask if they are really wicked men. Their answer, quite rightly in the main, is no.

But no executive of a multinational corporation should be in doubt about who is responsible for the misunderstanding. He is misunderstood because, usually after some deliberation and often with some passion, he insists on misunderstanding himself. He puts forward an explanation of himself and his company that is based on outworn economic theory with a strong aspect of theology. It is, in consequence, almost wholly implausible. No man, to quote Keynes, is so much a slave of defunct economists.

There are difficulties with a defense of the multinational corporation that is based on reality. They arise because it must concede what for so long was so indignantly denied. Nonetheless the time has come when a realistic defense is not only wiser but even, I would judge, inevitable.

I've lived most of my life in close professional association with the large modern corporation. I have come to accept its inevitability. Among other things, it combines energies, experience, engineering, scientific and other specialities for results far beyond the abilities or, on occasion perhaps, even the conceptual reach of any individual. The collective character of this achievement, like so much else, is in the sharpest contrast to the economic, social, and political case that it makes for itself.

I would like in this article to look first at the circumstances that explain the rise of the multinational corporation; next at the exceptionally primitive ideas which now guide its defense; then at the case as it might be made; and, finally, at the cautionary management behavior that this defense requires.

Rise and Reaction

The multinational corporation—the company that extends its business operations under one guiding direction to two or more countries—intruded itself upon public attention in the 30 years following World War II. During these years it moved heavily into industrial operations—into the manufacturing or processing of goods, their marketing, and their sales.

It had, however, three antecedents in nonmanufacturing fields, all of them exceedingly ancient. These had something, in fact much, to do with the reputation of, and the reaction to, the industrial corporation when it became the dominant corporate form operating across national frontiers.

Ill-Chosen Parents

First, since the rise of the modern national state, banking operations have been carried on across national frontiers, partly to finance international trade, more significantly for present purposes to take capital from countries of relative abundance to those of relative scarcity and consequent higher return. Second, the resource industries, mining in particular, have long been multinational. These industries have gone, as a matter of course, to develop operations where the ore, naural products, or, latterly, the oil were available. Third, the multinational trading corporation has long brought the products of the industrial countries to the economically more backward lands.

In each of these antecedent forms there was a major element of adverse reputation which became part of the legacy of the modern multinational:

The international banker had a notably sinister reputation; his concern for his capital transcended national interest and caused him on occasion to consort with the enemies of his sovereign. He was invariably richer than the borrower; and he was thought to exploit the profligacy or unwisdom of the latter, or, in any case, was celebrated for doing so. In the absence of any other ill fame, anti-Semitism could be evoked.

Resource industries, inevitably, were believed to be robbing the countries where they operated of their patrimony—natural wealth. They were thought, no doubt justly, to exploit local labor, which usually had an even lower opportunity cost, and to bend weak local governments to their purposes.

In India, Indonesia, and Indo-China the trading corporations were intimately linked with colonialism and in China with foreign penetration and domination. Socialists still celebrate them as the *compradors*.

Thus, like so many children, the multinational industrial corporation was unwise in the choice of its parents and is visited with their sins.

New Realities

The case for the modern multinational begins with its considerable differences from its three antecedents, something which has been but rarely noticed although it should be added the antecedents have themselves changed. The older multinationals mostly traded between the rich countries and the poor. They bridged the gap between those countries with more capital than they needed and those with less, those with manufacturing industries and those that could supply only raw materials and agricultural products, those with finished products to sell and those which, being devoid of modern industry, could only buy.

International banking continues but operations between the rich countries and the poor are not what now evokes the modern image of the multinational banking corporation. Much of its operation—and to a singular degree its better recent fortune, as the big New York banks will affirm—has been between the industrial countries. Raw materials and some tropical food products come from the poor countries to the rich. But the greatest suppliers of wheat, feed grains, coal, wood and wood pulp, and cotton fiber are the two North American countries—the United States and Canada. If to be part of the Third World is to be a hewer of wood and a supplier of food and natural products, the United States and Canada are, by a wide margin, the first of the Third World countries and should vote accordingly in the United Nations. The trading corporation has, of course, receded greatly in relative importance.

Thus even the older forms of multinational operations are now mainly, though of course not exclusively, between the developed countries. This, however, is most strongly the case with the burgeoning area of multinational operations—manufacturing—and for a very special and much neglected reason. The multinational corporation is the nearly inescapable accommodation to international trade in modern capital and consumer goods. One must emphasize this central point.

The products principally traded in past times—foodstuffs, cotton, cotton textiles, wool, coal, steel rails—required no connection or communication between producer and consumer. They could be and were shipped and sold through intermediaries; the producer never saw the user. Products were also sold at the market, and, very often, the market price was unknown when the goods were shipped. Before 1914, grain ships aproaching Land's End from North America regularly received a signal as to where they should proceed in Europe for the best price. Until then even the destination was unknown. For this trade, and similarly for simple unbranded products like cotton greige goods, there was no role for a multinational enterprise, and we need scarcely remind ourselves that the original producers were, in the vast majority of cases, very small.

To a greater extent than one likes to think, this view of international trade still rules in the economics courses and textbooks. It is one of the several reasons that formal economics has had difficulty in digesting the multinational corporation.

The modern industrial enterprise, in contrast, has products that must be marketed. Only in the economics textbooks is the consumer left to his or her sovereign decision. There also must be control over final prices; it is elementary that General Motors and Volkswagen do not ship their vehicles for sale, in the manner of wheat, for what the market will bring. Both the merchandising and the market regulation require a well-controlled sales organization, as also do the instruction, repair, and service that many modern products require and often receive.

Need for Power

The modern industrial enterprise has, as well, numerous needs from the government of the country in which its products are sold—far more things than the conventional and mindless litany of private enterprise admits. The government is an important customer. Also, the nation-state is the source of the airports, airways, highways, television channels, telephone communications, and weapons orders without which many, perhaps most, modern industrial products cannot be sold. It is the source as well of a wide and increasing range of permissions and restrictions governing the sale and use of products.

So the modern manufacturing corporation has an intimate relationship, that is, dependent, symbiotic, and sometimes suborning, with the modern government. It must, in short, have influence and power in its own markets— over its prices, costs, and means of consumer persuasion. Similarly, it is impelled to seek influence and power in the modern state.

Power is a word that, in deference to conventional economics and its more general public influence, every business executive seeks to avoid. There is something exceptionally improper about its possession. But power, all know, is indispensable to the operations of the modern large corporation. It must have power over its prices; its planning operations could not possibly survive the kind of price instability that characterizes most small entrepreneurial industry. It must have a measure of control over its earnings; these are a vital source of capital, as all accept. It has a long production period involving heavy investment; it must, accordingly, be able to persuade the consumer to want the product that eventually emerges. It lives with the consent of, and by the support of, the state; so living, it seeks to influence the decisions of the government.

This exercise of power is not a matter of choice but of necessity. It is true of the multinational corporation. And it is wholly and equally true of the large national corporation.

Dynamics of Multinationality

We have here, along with the omnipresent impulse for growth, the prime impulse for multinationality. A corporation in New York or Grand Rapids and confined in its operations to that location cannot bring power to bear in France to protect its prices in French markets, to defend or advance its position with the French consumer, or to protect or advance its position with the French government. Yet it will need to do so, denials in conventional economic theory and official corporate doctrine notwithstanding. It follows that if the corporation is to do business in France, it must have a base or presence there for the exercise of the market power and the public power needed to develop and protect its market position and its public position. The extent of the influence and power so exercised will be in very rough proportion to the scale of the national presence.

Such facts explain the corporate tendency to go on from a sales and marketing mode to a more fully integrated national development. The broad dynamic of multinational development is the required form and consequence of modern international trade. This dynamic is reinforced by further factors.

Where advanced technology is involved, multinational operations realize the economics of scale—the returns on one development cost are realized in several or numerous national markets. Multinational intrusion by the corporations of one country also forces reciprocal action by those intruded upon. If there is no such response, markets are lost with no chance of compensatory gain. Such riposte may also be necessary to preserve what economists call the "oligopolistic equilibrium," meaning that the intruding corporation will not cut prices for, if it does so, it will be vulnerable to the same action in reciprocal form in its own home country.

The forces just adumbrated are not transitory or casual. They will continue, and so, accordingly, will the development of multinational enterprise. This development will proceed with considerably more security if those involved learn to defend the multinational with some semblance of plausibility and good sense. To the present defense I now turn.

Defenses: Self-Contradictory Implausible

Not seeing that the multinational corporation is the necessary manifestation of international trade in manufactured products, business spokespeople rarely make this point. Failing to see that power is an essential aspect of corporate development, they urge with great implausibility that none is exercised. They suggest that the foreign corporation—a guest in the house—would be most cautious about influencing the habits, tastes, markets, or public opinion of the host country and much less the actions of its government.

The denial that the corporation has power derives from neoclassical economics, the accepted basis of modern economic and business theology. It holds that markets are made by numerous entrepreneurs and all are ruled by the market. All accept and should accept the instruction of the sovereign consumer. Anything else is monopoly or oligopoly or monopolistic competition—market imperfections—and thus an aberration. And as market power is absent, so also is public power. The classic corporation, like the citizen, can petition the state; any further exercise of power is irregular and improper. Its association is "with words like free-trade and free-enterprise and laissez-faire, [which] holds that business is politically neutral, existing only to satisfy the economic desires of the world's people."[2] To concede that a corporation has market or public power in the neoclassical economic tradition is to confess to impropriety or antisocial behavior.

Then, having taken the position that they have no power, the executives must exercise power in the most visible possible fashion. The reality of modern economic structure is not of industries composed of numerous entrepreneurial companies. It is a bimodal structure that divides business production more or less equally between a relatively few large corporations that are infinitely large and many small companies, that are infinitely numerous.

This bimodal pattern is strongly characteristic of manufacturing, the expanding area of multinational operations. In 1974, the 200 largest manufacturing enterprises in the United States supplied about 60% of all manufacturing employment.[3] A handful apart, all are multinational enterprises. For the reasons noted, they could not be otherwise if they are to engage in international trade. In this half of the economy—that of General Motors, General Electric, Exxon, IBM, and so on—prices are set. Customers are persuaded. Cultural patterns are altered. Governments are persuaded.

An increasingly attentive public sees these facts, and thus the ridiculous aspect of the corporate defense. The executive of the multinational corporation, having denied that she exercises power, having conceded that her possession of such power is improper, and having conceded its special inappropriateness for a foreign-based enterprise, then proceeds with the utmost reliability to convict herself in the public eye by her own actions. The day after she disavows market power, explains that her corporation is wholly subordinate to the market, and denies any thought of interfering with the government, the company announces a price increase, launches a major advertising campaign to alter consumer preference or taste, and is revealed to have brought public pressure in Washington or some other capital against some regulation, or in favor of some regulation, or on behalf of some new weapon, or to have contributed substantially to some domestic or foreign politician, not purely as an act of philanthropy.

The only reasonable defense of the multinational corporation is now the truth. That it has power must be conceded. The only durable defense is to hold that such exercise of power is inevitable and, if subject to proper guidance and restraint, socially useful.

The "Low Profile"

The second conventional line of defense of the multinational is to seek to conceal or deny its own foreign base and origin. The literature of multinational operations stresses this point ad nauseam; so presumably do the internal manuals, handbooks and lectures. The corporation operating in a foreign country should always keep what executives with a less than original gift for language unite in calling a "low profile." It should also make maximum use of local technical and managerial personnel—the number of people from the country of origin should be kept to a minimum. It must always be a good local citizen.

This defense is also implausible and self-defeating as well. No one worth persuading is ever likely to believe that General Motors in its origins is anything but American, BP anything but British, Fiat other than Italian. Persuasion is possible but not against elementary common sense.

However, there is also the question why, in an adult industrial world, there should be apology for this kind of iternational development. International trade always had to be defended against those who saw only its costs, never its advantages; who saw only the intrusion of foreign competitors, never the resulting efficiency in supply or products or the reciprocal gains from greater exports. The multinational corporation comes into existence when international trade consists of modern technical, specialized, or uniquely styled manufactured products. Accordingly, it should be defended, as international trade was defended, for its contribution to efficiency in production and marketing, to living standards, and to reciprocal opportunities in other lands for the enterprises of the host country.

This affirmative defense is excluded if a negative defense concedes, in effect, that there is something wrong with being a foreign corporation. And this, precisely, is what talk about a low profile or minimizing the foreign presence concedes. It would be a poor defense of foreign trade to pretend that French wines in the United States, or American cotton in Britain, were really domestic products or somehow not foreign. This tactic would concede that there was something wrong with iternational trade in these commodities. The low-profile strategy of the multinational corporation is on all fours.

Superiority Complexes

A third defense of the multinational corporation, more often implicit than explicit, has been that it reflects special aptitude in the development of management skills. It is said that this aptitude is peculiarly American; the multinational reflects the extension of this peculiarly American skill to the other industrial countries of the world. It is greatly to their advantage.

This defense lurks strongly in the consciousness of many American executives, but it also owes something to the flattery, genuine or contrived, of their foreign colleagues in the business world. In the prose of one British leader, the "track record of the United States—in business as well as in government—makes legitimate your leadership of the rest of us in tackling the world's economic problems."[4] The multinational corporation, so viewed, is the natural expression of American economic leadership, the natural expression of a basic American skill, the natural flowering of the American economic system.

However, the recent pattern and history of multinational development refute this conclusion. It is certain that American companies give more prestige to business managers than do other countries. Also, no other country is so deferentially frightened of anything that is thought to be damaging to business confidence, while agreeing that what has been best for business confidence, notably the presidencies of a Herbert Hoover, Richard Nixon, and Gerald Ford, has almost always been bad for business. We can certainly take credit for pioneering in the field of business education and in the theory and practice of management.

But it is nonsense to suppose that there is an American managerial genius, that there is anything known to anyone from Illinois or California that cannot equally be learned by anyone from England, Switzerland, or

Sweden. Conceivably, in some aspects of multinational operations there is an American inferiority complex based, as in the case of the Japanese, on our congenital inadequacy in languages.

However rewarding to national or corporate vanity, the notion that the multinational corporation reflects American achievement or leadership is uniquely poisonous. Those who take credit for it as an American achievement must then defend it against the counterpart charge that it is an instrument of American economic, cultural, or military imperialism.

A Convincing—and Valid—Case

Let me now turn to the affirmative arguments—the case that, with candor and a modest exercise of practical intelligence, could be made.

This approach requires, first of all, that the power of the multinational corporation be conceded. The point to be stressed is that this power has been deployed, on balance, for socially useful ends; that where it has not, it must expect to be restrained by the nation-state. The achievements of the international corporation are then open to mention. The supply of automobiles, chemicals, computers, television sets, tobacco, alcohol, and other products of multinational origin is rarely a source of complaint about quantity or cost. Other achievements involve international trade, the creation of an international civil service, and managerial autonomy.

Lessening of Tariffs

Business enterprises, large and small, have never been indifferent to government policy on international trade. They have not hesitated to use their power to influence such policy. It has rarely been noticed or urged that, as the multinational manufacturing corporation has grown in importance, the importance of tariff barriers has greatly receded. The barriers are not needed by the multinational company; for integrating and rationalizing operations between plants in different countries, they are a nuisance. Foreign competition also diminishes in terror when a company owns the competitor.

So power that was once deployed on behalf of tariffs is no longer exercised. On balance, it is deployed against them. The European Economic Community did not come into existence because of a sudden access of Smithian economic enlightenment after World War II; it came into existence because modern corporate and multinational organizations had made the old boundaries and barriers obsolete. European farmers, with their different and earlier and essentially classical economic structure, would never have created the Common Market. They are now the source of most of its disputes, nearly all of its crises, and all of its unfavorable notices.

Pacifying Influence

The great reduction, except in agriculture and a few other national industries of the importance of tariffs has, in turn, removed or reduced an important source of international friction. This reduction is one accomplishment of the multinational corporation, and it has made a yet more profound contribution to international amity. The absence of economic conflict, like peace in general, is so unobtrusive that we often do not notice it.

In the last century national industries, notably in steel, coal, shipbuilding and machine manufacturing, were the natural allies of national governments in the development of armaments. They had an economic interest in fostering international tension, as Marxists rightly emphasized (even if they may have overemphasized it in relation to ordinary public chauvinism and military insanity). That there is still an economic interest in arms and their development no candid person can deny.

But no multinational corporation can be suspected of promoting tension between the governments of countries in which it operates. IBM cannot be associated with any suspicion of stirring up trouble between France and Germany in order to sell computers, or ICI in order to sell chemicals. And it is persuasive that such suspicion in a suspicious world does not even arise. We should wish that there were more multinational operations between the Soviet Union and the West.

The multinational corporation also brings into existence the world's first truly effective international civil service—men and women who have a nominal loyalty to their country of origin, a rhetorical commitment to the country in which they serve, and a primary loyalty to Shell, DuPont, Philip, Nestlé, or whatever other company employs them. In a world which has suffered so much from national chauvinism, especially in this century, this development is a small pacifying influence in the world, a civilized step up from narrow, militant nationalism. But in the corporate rhetoric this dividend goes almost completely unmentioned.

Local Management Power

A wholly reliable tendency in the modern, very large corporation, national or multinational, is for authority to pass from the stockholders or owners to the management. This means that it matters less and less and eventually not at all who ultimately owns the corporation, or where it is owned, for the owners are without power.

As power passes to the management of the multinational company, it passes in part to the management of its various national entities. They have and, as a matter of course, must have a voice in the operations in which they are directly involved. While ownership of a multinational can be concentrated in the originating country, management by its nature must always be partly local.

This defense also is very rarely used. Failure of imagination may again be a factor. Many managements are still unwilling to abandon the ridiculous fiction that their stockholders have power. All know that in the great multinational they are dispersed and passive, vote their proxies automatically for the management slate, are never otherwise heard from.

But there remains the strong desire to keep alive the myth that the owners are still somehow important. The principal corporate folkrites, the stockholders' and directors' meetings, are carefully scripted to give the impression that the owners are somehow a force in the affairs of the corporation.

In consequence, Canadians are not allowed to notice that the Canadian management of a U.S. company has, and must have, an extensive say in its Canadian operations. They are allowed to see only that its shares are held mostly in the United States and to believe that this is the fact of importance. They are never persuaded to the view that, since those stockholders are totally without power, it does not make any difference whether the shares are held by Canadians, Americans, or in trust for Micronesians.

Once again the approved mythology is damaging to multinational corporations; the truth is favorable. Nor would this truth be costly. Most stockholders know they are without power. To say and keep saying that the real power lies with management, that ownership is irrelevant, and that extensive managerial autonomy must be granted to national entities as a matter of simple necessity would combine truth and plausibility with the calming of national fears.

Economic Stimulus

Finally, critics allege that the multinational corporation exports jobs, capital, and technology. This is one of the few matters on which the multinational enterprise has developed a defense. It holds that, in one way or another, it cares most about its home country and labor force—these are its primary interests. It should hold more often than it does that, as it goes abroad, others from abroad come in. The aggregate result is a more rapid spread of technology, a better international division of labor, greater productivity, greater aggregate employment. This is the old case for international trade.

It is an indication of the poverty of thought brought to these matters that even this traditional defense is so imperfectly made.

Danger Zones

No one should assume from the foregoing that the multinational enterprise is without capacity for antisocial action. And its opportunities for such action are important, for they mark out the zones of danger which the leadership of any sensibly run enterprise will avoid.

Threats, Bribes, Dirt

The first of these zones of danger lies in the peculiar advantage held by the multinational enterprise in its relationship to the nation-state. The large corporation, national or multinational in its nature, has power in the state— a point I again emphasize. As a general rule, the foreign-based company brings its power to bear more tactfully than the domestically based multinational. Volkswagen could not risk the kind of lobbying in Washington on emission standards that is done for General Motors. General Motors in Canada would not dream of instructing Ottawa as to its needs with the arrogance that Canadian Pacific once considered appropriate to its corporate dignity.

Though the multinational must speak and work for its needs, some things it must not do: in the face of unwanted regulation, environmental constraints, or labor relations, it must not threaten to move operations to another country. This threat exploits a particular advantage of multinationality; it will always, and reasonably, be considered an unfair exercise of multinational advantage.

A second zone of danger, now obvious, lies in the area of bribery. This danger is great even though such payments are an accepted source of political revenue or personal income in the country in question. There is, in all countries, something peculiarly pejorative about being in foreign pay. Bribery is especially unwise for an American multinational, for to be paid by Americans who are thought to be rich and powerful is especially indiscreet. And only the hopelessly obtuse can now be unaware of the first truth concerning the United States, which is that there are no secrets in the American republic, only varying lengths of time until all is revealed.

Currency Speculation

The third zone of danger lies in the area of international finance. The multinational company should probably always avoid currency speculation; it must, at a minimum, be extremely cautious about moving large funds in anticipation of the fall in a national currency or its appreciation. Such action also exploits an advantage peculiar to multinationality, and it helps precipitate the depreciation or appreciation against which the speculative action is taken. In an age of currency instability, such action by large multinationals is certain to provoke attack.

Perhaps eventually, since injunctions to virtue are not often compelling in such matters, large international movements of funds by the multinationals will bring some kind of international registration and regulation. This I would welcome, as should all multinational executives whose primary concern is with less damaging ways of making money.

Insensitivity to Environment

A fourth zone of danger may well be in the area of the environment. There is no reason to suppose that the foreign intruder is likely to be more damaging to ambient air, water, landscape, or the tranquility of life than the native enterprises. Industrial progress has, with rare exceptions, involved a movement from dirty processes to cleaner ones—from coal to oil and gas and from the filthy steam engine to the internal combustion engine and the electric motor. The modern problem of pollution arises not from the fact that processes have become dirtier but from the fact that, though cleaner, so much more is produced and consumed. Local industries, being generally older, wil often be dirtier than the newer arrival from abroad with the newer process or product.

But no one should doubt that foreign dirt is worse than domestic dirt, and also that a little new dirt (or noise or damage to the landscape) is worse than old dirt (or noise or damage) to which the senses have become adjusted. The multinational corporation must be acutely sensitive to community feelings on environmental issues. It should rarely if ever seek to override them. It should be scrupulous in conforming to existing laws and regulations and be the last to object to valid or seemingly valid new constraints. It should lose no opportunity to improve voluntarily on present practice. None of this is to get its executives a reward in heaven. It is to maximize their hope for peace on earth.

The Arms Trade

The fifth and final zone of danger has to do with weapons and the arms trade. It cannot have escaped anyone's notice that over the last several years weapons producers, along with the oil multinationals, have attracted an overwhelming share of the criticism that has been directed at the international operations of the corporation. All have suffered for the errors and absurdities of Lockheed and Northrup.

By its nature the weapons business will always be regarded with unease, and it is well that this is so. No sensitive person can look with equanimity on investment in the instruments of mass death; in recent times much of this business has been with countries that have other and pressing needs for their resources. Arms have absorbed money that could and should have gone to other and better purposes. And the fact that this business is all with governments and politicians (as much of the oil business also is) adds appreciably to the likelihood of scandal. Politicians are bribed. The same payments, when made to other businesspeople, are a finder's fee or commission.

It is evident that anyone making the case for the multinational enterprise should urge it to steer clear of the arms trade (though without much hope of that advice being taken if the company is already in it). But most multinationals are not in this trade. Also, it must be stressed that Lockheed and Northrup and the weapons companies generally are not, in the strict sense, multinational corporations—exceptionally, for organizations of their size, they do not have a substantial overseas presence. (The fact that they were operating through footloose sales and commission men explains, perhaps, some of the idiocies to which they exposed themselves.)

In the recent scandals civilian manufacturing multinationals have not been much involved. A habitual but misguided clubbiness between business executives has kept the civilian companies from emphasizing this fact. One way to avoid guilt by association is to make clear that there is no association.

There are other matters on which the multinational enterprise, because it is in conflict with never completely latent national suspicion, must be cautious. The recently agreed guidelines of the Organization for Economic Cooperation and Development (OECD) provide some further suggestions, most of them impressively bland as to content.[5]

Conclusion

The literature of the multinational enterprise is vast, and volume has been notably a substitute for perception. This is dramatically so of the case which the multinational enterprise makes for itself. That case denies the exercise of the power that is evident to all seeing eyes. Indeed, if one accepts the present defense, it can logically be shown that the multinational enterprise should not exist.

I would like to urge a defense which affirms the existence of power, accepts that it must be responsibily employed, and notes that there have been substantial advantages from such employment of power in the past. I would also urge that all concede the existence of opportunity for the exercise of power and associated practices which are socially damaging. It should be part of the defense that the prohibition of such power by governments, where this is possible, is affirmatively welcomed.

All this will require thought—a scarce and ill-regarded commodity in this area, as we have amply seen. I urge it, nonetheless, not out of compassion, not out of fear for the future of the multinational enterprise, not even from any especial warmth of friendship, but rather out of a sense of offended art. Great organizations that are so skilled in so many other matters and pride themselves on their performance should not be so outrageously clumsy in the case they make for themselves.

Notes

1.   Boston, Houghton Mifflin Co., 1977.

2.   "People, Politics, and Productivity: The World Corporation in the 1980s," address by Walter B. Wriston, London, September 15, 1976.

3.   William N. Leonard, "Mergers, Industrial Concentration, and Antitrust Policy," *Journal of Economic Issues,* June 1976, p. 356.

4.   Sir Reay Geddes (chairman of Dunlop, Ltd.) in "The Future Role of Business in Society," A Special Report of Conference Proceedings from The Conference Board, edited by Lillian W. Kay (New York, The Conference Board, Inc., 1977), p. 17.

5.   See "The OECD Guidelines in Brief," *Business International, June 11, 1976.*

How Companies Respond to Social Demands

ROBERT W. ACKERMAN

As concerns of society such as clean air, fair employment, and honesty in packaging are thrust on U.S. business with growing intensity and frequency, corporations are finding it very difficult to integrate responses to these demands into their regular operating procedures. This is especially true of the large, decentralized companies, whose profit-center managers are reluctant to change their procedures as long as they are judged on their bottom-line performance. This article is based on a year of intensive study of a number of large companies that are wrestling with this problem. The author analyzes the painful response process that starts with futile attempts from the top to accomplish change and ends (if the organization is adaptive) with the institutionalization of the new corporate policy at the operating level.

The president of a consumer goods company and the manager of one of its divisions were confronted recently with different but equally uncomfortable problems.

The former had been an early supporter of fair employment, especially in respect to minority hiring and training. He devoted much time to federal and state commissions locating job opportunities for minorities in the business community. The company from time to time had assisted minority enterprises in various ways and, on his initiative, had accepted a government contract to operate a job training center.

The president had communicated in strong terms his commitment to a policy of equal employment at all levels in his organization, and he had received general support for it. Despite these efforts, he felt that the company's record in hiring blacks and other minority group members and advancing them into management positions left much to be desired.

He pondered how to close the gap between his public statements and the indications he received of actual performance. He also worried about the impact—tangible and intangible—of stricter government enforcement.

The division manager's problem was in some respects more difficult. He managed one of seven operating units in the company and was responsible for six plants, several dozen sales offices, and 2,200 employees. Each year, he and his management group assembled a plan that included a financial projection supported by an environmental analysis and a strategy for achieving the goals. After negotiations, top management and division management agreed on somewhat revised figures as the division's performance commitment for the coming year. Although the division manager took pains to keep the president and others on the corporate staff alerted to major strategic developments or changes in the forecasts, he was expected to take responsibility for managing the business.

The division manager understood and agreed with the president's position on equal employment. In view of the diversity of attitudes and values in his organization, he became convinced that the only way of implementing the president's policy was to agree on minority hiring and advancement targets with each of his manufacturing, sales, and administrative managers, and to hold them accountable for the results.

He had not, however, taken this step. He rationalized that the plants operated against very tight budgets; as long as a plant performed well on this measure, the plant manager knew he would win praise, earn pay raises, and preserve his relative autonomy. For several reasons the division manager was unwilling to disturb this arrangement by appearing to put limits on the plant managers' autonomy in choosing their subordinates. He was equally reluctant to insist on the hiring of minority salespeople, thus risking damage to the sales managers' commitment to meeting volume targets. At least for the time being, the task of establishing standards and getting action was left to government enforcement agencies.

This familiar illustration is not unique to this company or issue. By rearranging the situation, I could present comparable cases for other organizations struggling with pollution control, occupational health and safety, consumerism, and so forth.

The U.S. corporation is faced with a twofold dilemma:

☐   The organizational innovations enabling it to manage growing product diversity and to adopt to technological, economic, and competitive change may inhibit effective responses to societal concerns.

☐   The need or desire to absorb a growing array of societal demands into its operations—affecting product design and marketing policy, to name just two—may reduce its effectiveness as a producer of goods and services.

When a company falls victim to either of these dangers, the cause, in my view, lies in the difficulty of the management tasks involved, rather than moral or ideological intransigence. In the long run, the more successful corporations will be those that can achieve both social responsiveness and good economic performance.

In the remainder of this article, I shall first sharpen the issue by providing a framework for thinking about the managerial problems created by social responsiveness. Then I shall describe the response patterns I observed during a year of field research in corporations attempting to implement programs covering a variety of social concerns. Finally, I shall offer suggestions for improving the management of this difficult process.

My primary concern will be with the large U.S. corporation. This is not because small enterprises are lacking in social or economic impact, but because the concentration of resources in large companies and the prominence of their chief executives often endow them with positions of leadership and make them inviting targets for critics. Moreover, for larger companies the internal dilemmas are the most acute.

A Poor Fit

Periodically in our history, the scope of corporate accountability has been extended. The rapid expansion of the labor movement in the 1930s is one obvious example among many manifestations of social change that businesses had to assimilate during the Depression years. So, if the responsive corporation managed to adapt to them without serious damage, is not our problem today merely one of relearning the solutions to old problems? I think the answer is no—not so much because of the intensity of public expectations as because of the radically changed configuration of today's large corporation.

According to recent studies, the divisionalized organization has rapidly replaced the functionalized organization as the dominant formal structure among the largest U.S. industrial corporations.[1] Exhibit 1 shows the dramatic shift.

Exhibit 1. Structure of the Fortune "500" Companies in Three Time Periods

Organization structure	Estimated percentage of companies		
	1949	1959	1969
Functional	62.7%	36.3%	11.2%
Functional with subsidiaries	13.4	12.6	9.4
Product division	19.8	47.6	75.5
Geographic division	.4	2.1	1.5
Holding company	3.7	1.4	2.4
Total	100.0%	100.0%	100.0%

The adoption of the divisionalized structure, a result of the sharp swing toward diversification, has been accompanied by important modifications in the internal dynamics of the corporation and in the assignment of responsibilities for responding to environmental change.[2]

But the results have not always been satisfactory. A prime reason is the poor fit of social responsivness into the modus operandi of the decentralized company. In its attempt to fashion flexible and creative responses to changing social demands, top management faces three main problems. I have summarized these in Exhibit 2 and shall explain them in some detail:

1. *The separation of corporate and division responsibilities is threatened.* In the illustration cited at the beginning of this article, the barriers between corporate and division offices had been built on mutual consent. The division manager, in exchange for the opportunity to run his own show and the promise of rewards if he did it well, had shouldered the responsibility for achieving agreed-on results. The president was then relieved of the task of formulating and implementing strategy in a number of (possibly unfamiliar) businesses and devoted his attention to matters of companywide interest.

However, as a result of the president's public statements and actions concerning equal employment, the world assumed he was responsible for seeing that it was accomplished in his organization. Successes or failures anywhere in the corporation reflected on him. Yet performance in employment opportunity—as in most areas of social concern—was closely related to operating decisions that had been delegated to managers down the line.

How can any president ensure an effective corporatewide response without interfering with his division managers? Should he choose to use the influence of his office, what effect would it have on the commitments he could expect for the achievement of corporate financial goals? Sharing the responsibility for social responsiveness may entail making traditional responsibilities more ambiguous. That is a result which most managers naturally want to avoid.

2. *The financial reporting system is inadequate.* Divisionalized companies rely heavily on sophisticated financial reporting systems to monitor the performance of operating units. Indeed, the flow of plans, budgets, and accounting reports often constitutes the primary dialogue between corporate and division offices.

However reliable the reporting system may be in measuring operating unit performance against financial goals, not only is it ineffective in measuring social responsiveness, but by and large it is irrelevant. Analysis of a division's financial statements provides little indication of its effectiveness (however that may be judged) in controlling waste emissions, providing safe working conditions, or manufacturing safe products.

Aggregation of the direct cost of programs related to social commitments is getting increased attention. For instance, one large packaging company isolates the projected expenditures for pollution control equipment in

Exhibit 2.   Critical Aspects of Managing Corporate Responses to Social Demands in a Decentralized Company

Existing management patterns	Problems in responding to social issues
Allocation of responsibilities Corporate level: secures division performance commitments and monitors the results, while fostering operating autonomy. Divisional level: formulates strategy for the division's business and accepts responsibility for achieving the results.	A corporatewide responsibility is implied, with the demand or desire for a corporatewide response. But that response involves operations, and implementation is possible only at divisional levels.
Management through systems Division performance is monitored by financial reporting systems that are: related to division commitments amenable to corporatewide aggregation reasonably simple to communicate and understand	Social costs and benefits are often not amenable to financial measures or planning. Current expenditures are real; long-run benefits are uncertain. Benefits may be general and not related to the spending unit.
Executive performance evaluation Performance of assigned responsibilities—often measured through the financial reporting system—is reinforced by incentive compensation and is the determinant of career paths in the organization.	Benefits of social responsiveness may appear in time frames longer than the manager's tenure in his job. Current expenditures of time and money may penalize the financial performance to which the organization is committed. Trade-offs are required which involve values and judgments on which managers may reasonably differ.

the capital budget (though the associated operating costs are not reflected in the projected income statement). A bank keeps track of expenses associated with its community relations program. The results, however, are at best incomplete, even on the cost side, and little progress has been made in the measurement of social benefits. Nor are substantial breakthroughs to be expected in the near future.[3]

The obvious alternative is to create new measures of social responsiveness for each area of concern. Aside from whatever methodological problems such an attempt might pose, the result would be an enormous increase in the complexity of managing the organization—assuming that each reporting system was taken seriously. That, again, is a result most managers would prefer to avoid.

3. *The executive performance, evaluation, and reward process is challenged.* This dilemma is in part an outgrowth of the first two and is perhaps the most difficult to resolve.

In the case of the company whose situation was described at the beginning of this article, the division manager participated in setting the standards to be used in evaluating the performance of his unit, and he secured commitments of support from his subordinates. He was not assuming that their behavior was predicated solely on the desire to meet the budget; their needs and satisfactions were defined in much broader and subtler ways. So he did not evaluate their performance solely in terms of the bottom line. Yet financial appraisal was an important tool for securing the subordinates' support in the pursuit of the division's strategy. The division manager was reluctant to insist on minority hiring and advancement quotas which he felt would introduce new restrictions, ambiguities, and, possibly, discord into the process of evaluating his managers.

How can an organization obtain its middle managers' support for social responsiveness if their careers do not in some explicit way depend on it? A division manager in a large electronics company made the point to me very clearly: "Look, let's start with the idea that I don't need pollution control equipment or minorities to run my business. If the company wants me to do these things, they'll have to make it worth my while."

Pattern of Response

There is an argument that appears to justify ignoring the administrative implications of managing corporate responsiveness. It holds that social expectations for business's behavior become legitimate only when the government requires compliance, and to the extent that governmental regulations exact penalties, a social issue is converted into an economic one and so can be managed just like any other business problem. The fallacy in this reasoning lies in the premise that corporate *action* on social issues is either voluntary or required. In fact, during the period when responsiveness is most important, it is neither.

For every issue there is a time period before it becomes a matter of social concern, and espousing the issue may even arouse economic and social sanctions. There is also a time when its acceptance is so widespread that adherence is an unquestioned part of doing business. (Child labor laws create little anxiety in 1973.)

Between those two points there is a period of uncertainty as to the strength and durability of public support for the issue, standards of socially acceptable behavior, timing of desired conformity, and the technologies or resources available for complying. This period might be called a zone of discretion, in which the signals the company receives from the environment are unclear. It cannot avoid responding in some way, but it still has discretion in the timing and strength of the response.

The history of federal air pollution control legislation is one current example. The first national standards and enforcement provisions appeared in the 1963 Clean Air Act; it was another four years before the Air Quality Act strengthened them; and three more before nationwide ambient air standards were established, to be fully effective in 1975. Regulations have also been imposed at the state and local levels, frequently permitting variances for those facilities with the "latest available technology"—itself a changing standard. So for many years, while the federal legislation was evolving, corporations were engaged in activities affecting air quality and had choices whether to alter them.

A number of social issues have progressed so far through the zone of discretion that their final dimensions are beginning to take shape. Equal employment and ecology are two examples, although even in these instances great uncertainty remains as to the intensity of enforcement and the ultimate standards to be applied. Other issues are much less well defined.

Based on intensive observations in several companies that have been recognized as leaders in managing those social issues of particular relevance to their businesses, I think a common response pattern is developing. (The nature of these particular issues creates differences, but the similarities are far more noticeable.) There are three phases to this response process, spanning a period of at least six to eight years. The first two phases are necessary but insufficient in themselves for an effective response. I shall discuss each in turn.

A Policy Matter

First, the chief executive recognizes the issue to be important. He may rationalize his interest as a matter of corporate responsibility or as farsighted self-interest. Either way, it coincides with his recent experience, often outside his business milieu. One chief executive I know became concerned about minority opportunities during the widespread urban disturbances in the mid-1960s, when a riot took place near the company's headquarters. Several years earlier, some personnel managers had tried to generate his interest in the issue, but they had gotten nowhere.

The chief executive's involvement is marked by several activities. Initially, he begins to speak out on the issue at meetings of industry associations, stockholders, and civic groups. He becomes active in organizations and committees involved in studying the issue or influencing opinion on it. He may also commit corporate resources to special projects, such as ghetto businesses, waste recovery plants, and training centers.

Soon he perceives the need for an up-to-date company policy, which he takes pains to communicate to all managers in the organization. Responsibility for implementing the policy is assigned as a matter of course to the operating units as part of the customary tasks performed in running the business.

The directives from top management, couched in terms of appeals to long-term benefits and corporate responsibility, fail to provoke acceptable action or achievement. Heads nod in agreement, but the chief executive's wishes are largely ignored. Managers in the operating units lack evidence of the corporation's commitment to the cause; responsibilities are unclear, scorecards are lacking, and rewards for successes or penalties for failures are absent. The managers view as foolhardy any attempt to implement the policy at the risk of sacrificing financial and operating performance.

Onus on the Specialist

The first phase may last for months or even years. The key event heralding the beginning of a new phase is the president's appointment of a staff executive reporting to him or one of his senior staff to coordinate the corporation's activities in the area of concern, help the chief executive perform his public duties, and, in general, "make it happen." The new manager, often a specialist in her field, carries one of a variety of titles that have recently appeared on organization charts: vice president or director of urban affairs, environmental affairs, minority relations, consumer affairs, and so on.

The vice president of urban affairs views the problem as essentially a technical one that can be attacked by isolating it and applying specialized skills and knowledge to it. She begins to gather more systematic information on the company's activities in the area and matches these data with her assessment of environmental demands. If her responsibility includes minority relations, she gets personnel statistics from the operating divisions and attempts to pinpoint where problems exist in minority representation. During the audit process, she also develops methods for systematically collecting information, which she plans to use as a control device in the future. Finally, she mediates between operating divisions and external organizations, including government agencies, that are pressing for action.

But these efforts, while not without impact or merit, do not elicit the response envisaged in the corporate policy. The staff manager's attempts to force action are so alien to the decentralized mode of decision making that he becomes overburdened with conflict and crisis-by-crisis involvement. The only arrows in his quiver, aside from his own powers of persuasion, are the corporate policy and the demands of outsiders. But line managers may consider neither one credible. One environmental control director commented to me:

"We find ourselves in a 'damned if you do, damned if you don't' situation a lot of the time. We get accused by the regulators of backsliding when we argue that the company is doing the best it can. Then when we argue for a program inside the company, we get accused of giving money away. The operating managers fail to see that if they don't take steps now, the cost in the long run could be a lot greater. They hear the wolves howling out there, but they only notice the ones that get in and not the ones we're keeping outside."

Consequently, if staff proposals interfere with its operations, middle management stands aside and lets the staff take responsibility (or blame) for the results. Faced with a choice between supporting his senior line executives (who have major operating responsibilities and probably a long history of sound judgments) and his new urban affairs vice president, the chief executive usually backs up the former.

Nevertheless, the job done by the corporate specialist is essential for the eventual implementation of the policy. She crystallizes the issue for top management. She also unearths and collects a great deal of information that serves to clarify what will be expected of the corporation in the future and the techniques or technologies that will be available to fulfill those expectations.

Organizational Involvement

The chief executive recognizes at this juncture that responsiveness entails a willingness to choose among multiple objectives and uses of resources. Fundamentally, such judgments are a general management responsibility. Top management sees the organizational rigidities to be more serious than previously acknowledged; they cannot be waved away with a policy statement nor can they be flanked by a specialist.

Instead, the whole organizational apparatus has to become involved. In this third phase, the chief executive attempts to make the achievement of policy a problem for all his managers. That is accomplished by institutionalizing policy, which I take up next.

Institutionalized Purpose

In the cases I have observed, the chief executive's problem was not winning acceptance of the new company policy; in numerous instances, managers down the line were found who, from a personal standpoint, wished the policy had been stronger. Rather, the problem was in the institutionalization of the policy—that is, working it into the process through which resources were allocated and ultimately careers decided.

A well-known characteristic of large organizations is that, unless somehow provoked to do otherwise, they tend to approach today's problems in the same way that worked yesterday, even though the context in which the new problems arise may be different. A study of the Cuban missile crisis ascribed this phenomenon to "standard operating procedures" that are enormously useful in simplifying complex problems and organizational interaction.[4]

To illustrate, companies with strong unions and a long history of successful labor-management relationships develop routines for processing employee grievances that grow out of the union experience. If a complaint arises alleging plantwide discrimination, both union and management try to rephrase it in traditional terms; then they can handle it in their usual fashion.

However, the minority employees may feel that their situation will not receive the special attention they believe it warrants if they rely on a decision-making process that has failed to satisfy their needs in the past. Consequently, they avoid the union and attempt to communicate directly with executives many levels above those managers normally responsible for employee grievances. The normal reaction in such instances is to rule the employees' tactic inadmissible and insist that they "play by the rules."

This phenomenon helps to explain the stability (stated negatively, the unresponsiveness) of most large organizations. For the chief executive of the decentralized corporation, the problem of securing responsiveness to social issues is compounded by the rules governing the interrelationships between corporate and division levels. The rules state that while the chief executive is obtaining and evaluating divisional results, he is not to meddle in the divisions' standard operating procedures. If he wants to change those procedures to coincide with the spirit of the new corporate policy, he presumably must attempt it indirectly by changing the standards for judging performance.

The chief executive does indeed try to play by the rules. This letter, written by one president to his subordinates, is a graphic illustration:

> The most significant change this year—the one that is basic to all others— is to place responsibility for achieving equal opportunity objectives where it rightfully belongs: with operating management, with each of us. Achieving these objectives is as important as meeting *any other* traditional business responsibility.
>
> It follows, of course, that a key element in each manager's overall performance appraisal will be his progress in this important area. No manager should expect a satisfactory appraisal if he meets other objectives, but fails here.

If one talks with operating managers shortly after such an announcement has been made, one finds interest in the policy but considerable skepticism about the corporation's will to enforce it. They detect gaps between pronouncement and performance:

> ☐ Since reporting on implementation of, say, a minority hiring quota cannot be integrated directly into the financial control system, it must be communicated separately. Consequently, it must compete for attention with the regular reporting system. In view of the technical problems likely to be encountered with the new procedure and the central position and historic importance of the old one, the competition may be very one-sided.
>
> ☐ It is doubtful that managers who have met their economic targets

will be criticized, let alone severely punished, for failure to perform adequately in the area of social concern. The president may be uttering strong words on appraisal, but it is the manager's immediate boss several layers down, not the president, who does the appraisals.

Creative Function of Trauma

In due course, a test case is encountered, though at the time it may not appear to be particularly significant. The institutionalization of purpose may hinge on the creative use of trauma. The trauma results not from the problem posed in the test case, but from the organizational dynamics through which the problem is resolved. Top-level executives suspend the rules governing their relationship with the operating divisions. For a brief period, division executives lose control of their operations: their decisions are countermanded and staff managers reporting to their superiors exercise inordinate influence in directing the outcome.

The whole affair is very unsettling for the divisions. Worst of all, questions are raised in the operating executives' minds about who really is responsible for managing the divisions' response and what the consequences may be if it is not them.

For instance, shortly after the letter quoted earlier had been sent, a smoldering controversy about minority relations erupted in a small service unit four levels down in a division. Eventually, no fewer than seven levels of line management, from the first-line supervisor to the president, were involved with their associated staffs in attempting to settle it. For a two-week period, the normal chain of command was tenuously observed. Then, the president intervened directly by issuing a decision that overturned the one announced by his subordinates. By his own forceful action, he dramatically illustrated the quality of management he expected in response to employee problems.

Intervention from the top level may not have been executed effectively in the test case, but that is not the issue. The experience has had two very beneficial results:

1.   The managers in the division realized that to prevent such a fracas from recurring, they must be responsive to the issue in the future. That may mean incorporating action programs related to the issue into the division's strategy and modifying the process of evaluating the managers who are positioned to influence responsiveness directly.

2.   The company has provided clues to the new standard operating procedures that it wants adopted to establish the policy in the operating units. The policy has been tested and a precedent established that can serve as a guide for its implementation throughout the corporation.

The response patterns I have described may appear to be chaotic, and, in fact, they were often characterized as such by the managers involved. Yet there is underlying order and logic to the process.

Exhibit 3 illustrates how a policy problem is converted into a managerial problem through the process of institutionalization. During these three phases of involvement of the organization, concern for responding to the social issue spreads from the chief executive to middle-level managers. The awareness of a social need that produced the policy is enriched by the infusion of new skills and finally matures into a willingness on the part of middle-level managers to commit resources and reputations to responsible action.

The process receives strong impetus from the changing and increasingly demanding environmental conditions that often parallel the response pattern in this manner:

☐ *Phase 1.* Social concerns exist but are not specifically directed at the corporation.

☐ *Phase 2.* Broad implications for the corporation become clear but enforcement is weak or even nonexistent.

Exhibit 3.   Conversion of Social Responsiveness from Policy to Action

Organizational level	Phases of organizational involvement					
	Phase 1		Phase 2		Phase 3	
Chief executive	Issue:	Corporate obligation	Obtain knowledge		Obtain	organizational commitment
	Action:	Write and communicate policy	Add staff specialists		Change	performance expectations
	Outcome:	Enriched purpose, increased awareness				
Staff specialists			Issue:	Technical problem	Provoke response	from operating units
			Action:	Design data system and interpret environment	Apply data system	to performance measurement
			Outcome:	Technical and informational groundwork		
Division management					Issue:	Management problem
					Action:	Commit resources and modify procedures
					Outcome:	Increased responsiveness

☐ *Phase 3.*   Expectations for corporate action become more specific and sanctions (governmental or otherwise) become plausible threats.

Undesirable Consequences

While the particular response pattern may eventually produce acceptable results, it is often inefficient and entails some undesirable side effects:

1.   If the six to eight-year cycle that I have observed in relatively successful instances is typical, the elapsed time required may be excessive. Unless social issues can be processed with reasonable speed, they may pile up and ultimately put the company in a position where it cannot function effectively in its traditional role as a producer of goods and services.

2.   Until the final phase, operating managers are not intimately concerned with the issue; specialists direct the responses. The legal staff and the environmental control director work out compliance schedules for pollution control, the minority relations specialist communicates with factory personnel managers about affirmative action programs, and so forth.

But without middle-level management commitment, it is likely that the specialists will interfere with operating activities, misapply resources, or be ineffective in securing results. That is, in the two examples I just cited, compliance schedules do not mesh with planned capital spending programs, and minority relations seminars are taken lightly. Deservedly or not, the specialist often shoulders the blame.

3.   Performance evaluation is usually skewed to distributing penalties for failures rather than rewards for successes. Moreover, the process is very unsystematic; it relates not so much to consistent performance against objectives as it does to poor handling of particular conspicuous situations. The manager cited for polluting a stream or charged with discrimination may find his career badly tarnished. His counterpart, who fails to construct and implement an effective environmental program or meet her hiring and advancement goals—but is not guilty of an overt action—may escape sanctions.

The excuse normally given is, "We needed an example for the rest of the organization." Perhaps so, but it is unfortunate that such sacrifices must be made when the entire organization is trying to learn how to respond effectively to a new set of problems.

Needed: Response Process

Issues of social concern are generally recognized as certain unrealted environmental phenomena demanding substantive corporate responses of some kind. Product safety, equal employment, ecology, and work safety each require a particular set of activities that change over time and are dealt with separately. A more sophisticated concept calls for a systems approach to the environment through which the interrelationships among issues are explored and the likely trends and impacts predicted.[5]

A third way of viewing corporate responsiveness focuses on organizational requirements. Social issues arise not as discrete events but as a flow of events which may or may not be closely related, but which share a call on corporate attention.

They are at different stages in the zone of discretion. The outlines of some, such as air pollution control, have been well described; while the shape of others, such as "the new work force," is still murky. For example, referring to the evolving regulations covering noise levels, an experienced engineer charged with applying federal environmental standards in his company commented to me, "If the company gave me $10 million to spend on getting noise levels down to 90 decibels, I wouldn't know how to spend it." He had neither the technology nor the directions for using it.

Guidelines for Strategy

From an organizational standpoint, the need is for a response process through which issues can be recognized and formed into policy, implications and possible solutions explored, and, finally, plans generated to govern action. The challenge for management is to facilitate a means of organizational learning and adaptation that will permit flexible and creative responses to social issues as they arise. In the divisionalized organization, that assignment will not be easy; some preliminary suggestions on the nature of such a process follow.

Do Not Overload the Response Process.   The process for responding to social demands described in this article is a reasonable way of approaching a difficult managerial problem. There is, however, a real danger of overloading the process. The time and energy of the chief executive are limited. So are the tolerance and capacity of the organization for wrestling with the environmental uncertainties that accrue to the ones who take forceful action. Top management should balance the numerous social demands pressing on the organization and the social goals it seeks. It should give priority to those areas that are most likely to have an impact on the company's business and should try to maintain a low profile on the others.

To ease the problems of implementation, top management must anticipate the transition from one phase to the next and clearly communicate to middle-level management the ground rules for managing the new phase.

Use Specialists Effectively.   New skills and knowledge are particularly necessary in the formative stages of the company's response. It must scan an unfamiliar environment, master new technologies, and collect and analyze a vast amount of information, both internally and externally. The staff specialists have the difficult task of developing approaches to this environment and designing systems to permit the planning and evaluation of programs for adapting to its needs. Although the specialists' role as an agent of change is vital, there are two dangers to be considered:

☐ Operating managers often resist or even ignore the specialists' advice. This is predictable; after all, they are usually the purveyors of bad tidings. Furthermore, since this is a new field, they may be new to the organization and therefore lack the mutual trust built up over time with the operating executives. Worse, they are both highly visible and largely void of influence other than having the proverbial "boss's ear," which can be seldom used and then only with caution. Clearly, the specialists are vulnerable and needs support from the top if they are to be successful.

☐ The specialist may keep her hand in the issue too long. Her vantage point at the corporate level and her inclination to tackle the job herself may impede the assumption of responsibility and commitment by operating managers. Independent responses at the middle levels are essential for effective action.

The staff specialists' role in implementation of new policy should be temporary. Top management support during the critical second phase is necessary, but as soon as responsibility and accountability have been lodged with operating managers, the staff specialist's involvement should be limited to providing technical advice as requested.

But he has a crucial, broader role in the organization. If he has managed his relationships in the organization well, he will be immensely useful in equipping it to respond to the next social issue. For instance, the specialist who has been concerned with air and water pollution has skills in engineering, environmental analysis, and government relations that may prove to be very useful in working with, say, the occupational health and safety issue. He can become a multipurpose corporate change agent.

Formulate Response Strategies.   To plan a rational sequence of activities in support of goals in areas of social concern, a response strategy is necessary. Placing the responsibility for formulating these strategies with middle-level managers who also set operating strategy exploits, rather than subverts, the organizational strengths of the decentralized company. The procedure of goal setting and strategy evaluation is second nature for both corporate-level and operating managers.

Insisting on a direct parallel between social response strategies and the more familiar business strategy yields three benefits:

1   The response becomes anticipatory and not merely reactive.
2   The response demands a level of analysis that is too often lacking when resources are allocated to social problems. It may not be

possible, or in the long run even worthwhile, to measure social costs and benefits in economic terms; however, requiring rigorous justification for the action to be taken makes the best use of the information and analytical tools available.

3 The articulation of a strategy provides the basis for subsequent measurement and evaluation.

Complicate the Evaluation Process.   This final suggestion is, in my judgment, the most important but the least likely to happen of the four. It is commonplace to hear managers describe their jobs as being more complicated now than in the past. One division vice president summed it up this way: "Business used to be fun. But now there are so damn many people around demanding this and that, I just don't enjoy it anymore."

Ironically, while the job of managers—especially those in the middle levels—has been growing more complex, the basis on which their performances are evaluated has often become simpler. The reason, of course, lies in the need for a lowest common denominator that can be used for allocating resources and making comparisons among units operating in different businesses and geographical environments. The financial plan serves these purposes admirably.

If the corporation is to be socially responsive, however, this divergence may have to be arrested. Top management may have to tolerate a greater degree of complexity in the measures it uses to evaluate the performance of middle-level executives. The path need not lead to more subjective or less results-oriented evaluations. Indeed, if attention has been paid to setting strategy in areas of social concern, the power of the results orientation may actually increase over a procedure that does not subject social programs to planning and analysis. Economic performance no doubt will always remain the dominant yardstick (and with good reason), but it should be augmented to reflect the greater complexity and scope of middle management's responsibilities.

In Conclusion

There are hopeful signs that large corporations in this country are developing processes for converting the rhetoric of corporate responsibility into meaningful action. The burden for implementing corporate policy on social issues is ultimately placed on middle-level managers, the same managers who are primarily responsible for planning and directing the operations of the business. Through the creative and persistent leadership of top management, the barriers to incorporating social change in the decentralized company can be overcome.

The response to social demands is not without human cost. Managers' careers have been tarnished by the bad luck of getting caught up in conspicuous incidents that may be learning experiences for the organization, but at their expense. Does somebody have to get hurt? Unfortunately, the answer all too often is *yes*. An urgent challenge for the top managements of large corporations is to make their organizations more understanding of the human costs of change as well as the demands of society.

Notes

1. Richard P. Rummolt, *Strategy, Structure, and Economic Performance* (unpublished D.B.A. dissertation, Harvard Business School, 1972).

2. For a discussion of this transition, see Bruce R. Scott, "The Industrial State: Old Myths and New Realities," *HBR*, March–April 1973, p. 133.

3. See Raymond A. Bauer and Dan H. Fenn, Jr., "What *Is* a Corporate Social Audit?" *HBR*, January–February 1973, p. 37.

4. Graham Allison, *The Essence of Decision: Explaining the Cuban Missile Crisis* (Boston, Little Brown, 1972).

5. Herman Kahn and B. Bruce Biggs, *Things to Come: Thinking about the 70's and 80's* (New York, Macmillan, 1972), Chapter 1.

9

Financial Adventure of James Debenture

A Parody with a Moral

WILLIAM L. SAFIRE

Those who have read Ian Fleming's novels about supersleuth James Bond—*Goldfinger, Dr. No, From Russia With Love,* and the rest—will immediately recognize the elements of the parody that follows. Familiar trappings in the Fleming novels, such as *Smersh, M,* and, of course, *James Bond* himself, are matched here by *Pubdam, C,* and *James Debenture.* The story is more than a parody, however. The author uses it to communicate two serious themes: (1) the true rationale for the social responsibility of corporations, as he sees it, and (2) the dangers already inherent, in his opinion, in the trend toward more government control of business.

Can a company be allowed to exist, even if it operates within the law, if it does not recognize its social responsibility?

That was the issue placed before Sorespa, the Social Responsibility Protection Agency, on a balmy Sunday afternoon in Washington. Sorespa's board meets only on Sunday, because, officially, the agency does not exist, and meetings held on weekdays would necessitate an elaborate set of excuses for the participants, who come from over a dozen federal and private agencies.

Unlike other clandestine operations, there has never been any difficulty in keeping Sorespa totally secret; no substantial budget needs to be buried—forestalling the congressional watchdogs and prying reporters that plague CIA and AEC. Sorespa's budget is infinitesimal because it is the only federal agency with a working staff of just three people—a single agent, a coordinator, and a secretary. There has never been a need for another agent.

Sorespa's coordinator—a scholarly, pipe-smoking gentleman who hardly gives the impression of a man who cornered the world market in manganese early in World War II—sits at a clean desk with a white telephone and a red "destruct" button. His informal Sunday gatherings are never called meetings.

"These are simply informal gatherings over a pleasant julep," the co-ordinator, called simply C, once told the board. "We are all interested in the same objective, and perhaps I can help provide a kind of clearinghouse in difficult situations." Attendance, never statutory or mandatory, has been good. Nobody has ever missed one of these "informal gatherings."

C was assigned his job one embarrassing day when both the Justice Department and the SEC subpoenaed corporate records that had already been impounded by Internal Revenue. Blunt instructions were issued: "This tripping over each other will stop forthwith; it does not encourage social responsibility, and it's giving us an antibusiness image."

From its rudimentary start as a clearinghouse for Justice, Treasury, and SEC, Sorespa soon grew to encompass all federal regulatory agencies, key state attorneys general, local better business bureaus in six cities, several national consumers' groups, and to draw on some specialties of the FBI and USIA.

"The problem before us today," began C, "concerns Silvertoe Fabrics." There were slapping noises, almost like applause, as a dozen manila folders labeled "Silvertoe" were hurriedly laid on the conference table.

A consumer frauds official of the state in which Silvertoe's far-flung enterprises were headquartered reviewed the background. "The products made by this company are uniformly inferior. They copy—but never quite infringe on—patents of their competitors, coming out with a shoddy line of fabrics which they then effectively market. Sales up 20%, profits before depreciation up 30%. Fantastic example of undeserved success."

"Allow me to be the devil's advocate," said C. "Surely, their aggressive competition forces industry prices down, ultimately benefiting the consumer."

"That's the damnedest part," interjected the Federal Trade Commission man. "Their prices are higher for their inferior products. And still they sell. We've had their advertising agency in and out of court all year. Our delay ratio is over 6:1—it takes them six months now before they can get into print or on television with one commercial. We can never pin them down with a really false claim. They keep hammering away with a fuzzy, archaic 'For Over One Hundred Years Silvertoe Has Meant Quality.' How can you fight that?"

"Have you tried," C asked acidly, "pointing out that the company is six years old?"

"Sure, you make it sound easy—but they bought out a little shoemaker who also had the name of 'Silvertoe,' and his great-grandfather opened a shoe store in the Civil War. Court upheld the slogan."

C shifted in his chair. "It can be argued that a company partially meets its social responsibility by serving an economic function, making profits which can then be taxed and the taxes used for public good."

The Internal Revenue man made short work of that. "First of all, Silvertoe took over a shell with a whopping tax-loss carry-forward. Then the company merged with a real estate outfit whose property depreciation, for tax purposes, gives it a shelter against payment of income taxes for as far ahead as I can see. On top of that, Silvertoe pulls inventory write-downs every year. We keep auditing them, and all the executives personally, for harassment purposes, as you suggested at our last gathering, but it's costing us a bundle in agents' time. And we'll never see a nickel from that oufit."

"Employment," said C. "Silvertoe must provide wages and purchasing power for thousands of individuals, thereby contributing to the nation's economic growth."

"I guess that's my area," volunteered the NLRB representative. "At the last attempt at unionization of Silvertoe plants, we were especially alert to possible threats of firing by the company if the employees joined the union. That's an unfair practice, as you know. But just before the vote, the first token shipment of automated equipment arrived at each plant. It had been ordered six months before. Neither Silvertoe nor any executive had to say a word. No union. No paternalism, even—lowest wage scale in its industry, dragging the rest down. My interest is in protecting a fair election, but I can tell you that Silvertoe plants are a blight on the labor picture wherever they operate."

"Higher prices, lower wages, no taxes," murmured C. "That must mean a bonanza for the 13,000 stockholders, who, after all, are mostly little people—"

"Some bonanza," said the SEC man. "Never a dividend. No capital appreciation, either; as soon as the stock starts to go up, Silvertoe, who owns a load, dumps thousands of shares and that depresses the market. Of course, whenever there is a flurry of activity, we hit the outfit with a 100% margin requirement, and the Exchange cooperates by suspending trading every now and then. But that only makes the present stockholders unhappy, by keeping the price down. Only one stockholder has made real money on Silvertoe stock—that's Silvertoe."

C dropped his devil's advocacy, and his eyes grew cold. He turned to the chief counsel of a Senate investigating committee: "Have your efforts borne fruit?"

"Sir, we've had Silvertoe's entire management team before the committee in public hearings for the better part of a year. Full treatment—television coverage, leaks on the next day's testimony to catch the early editions of the morning newspapers, sometimes three Senators present. If any company should be thoroughly discredited, that's it."

"But the net effect," broke in the FTC man, riffling through the company's ads for the next year, "has been a sales rise through increased identification. Look what the outfit is planning next, to capitalize on the open hearings: 'Silvertoe—the company everybody is talking about.'"

"That's known as the 'sleeper effect,'" explained the bespectacled representative of the U.S. Information Agency. "Hovland of Yale has shown that, after a two-week lapse, the propaganda target tends to remember the message and reject any memory of the source, resulting in—"

"Resulting in Sorespa's first failure," snapped C. "Or perhaps I should amend that—the first failure of this group assembled here since social responsibility coordination was begun. The Agency itself, you are aware, has not yet acted."

The Justice Department man bridled. "I don't see how your Agency, consisting of you and one lone agent, can hope to stop Silvertoe when the aggregate power of federal, state, and private social responsibility enforcement agencies has failed."

"That, my dear sir, is because you are afflicted with the Cult of the Team. Sometimes, one lone agent acting individually can be more effective."

"But we've used every *legal* means . . ."

C posed the question no one else dared to ask: "Can a company be allowed to exist, even if it operates within the law, if it does not recognize its social responsibility?"

Silence in the room. "I needn't burden your consciences, gentlemen," said C. "That is for me to decide. And for my agent to carry out."

James Debenture's Social Security number is 446-7703-007. This makes him the only employee of the United States Government permitted at his own discretion to assassinate a corporation.

The exploits of other double-O agents in other countries have been widely publicized, but their activities are limited to individuals. Debenture's deadly discretion extends far beyond a gangland-style "hit"; when the situation requires it, James Debenture is authorized to subvert, raid, sabotage, take over, bankrupt, or liquidate a multimillion-dollar corporate entity. Skillfully sewn into the lining of his natural-shoulder suit is a form for a Chapter II Petition in Bankruptcy and an S-9 declaration of intent to solicit proxies.

"James, I have a familiar assignment for you."

Debenture remained respectfully silent—whenever C called him by his first name, it meant that a powerful organization known as Pubdam was involved.

"Remember that Pittsburgh job a couple of years ago?"

Debenture nodded. Same crowd. The code word for their insidious organization stood for "The Public Be Damned." Long ago, they had ruled the economic world. Driven underground by the ascendent trustbusters, their ranks decimated by defectors to the new breed of business leaders with "corporate conscience," Pubdam had regrouped in recent years and was now threatening to impose its alien philosophy on an unsuspecting populace.

"The name of the company is Silvertoe Fabrics, James. My secretary will give you the dossier. I shall sell short." C's short sales of the stocks of companies to be ruined by James Debenture were the main source of Sorespa's income, saving the taxpayers many thousands of dollars and removing the requirement for a place in the federal budget.

Debenture's flannel-gray eyes turned to slits at the mention of the company's name. Added to the assignment was a personal score; his own natural-shoulder suit was made of a Silvertoe fabric, and it had shrunk, tightening the bankruptcy petition in the lining across his back.

"And why in the world, Mr. Debenture," said R. G. Silvertoe "would I need the services of a public relations consultant?"

Momentarily taken aback when he first met Silvertoe—the fabric executive's striking, silver-haired appearance had not been what Debenture expected at all—the protector of the public interest quickly recovered. With a cover identity as President of Universal Public Relations, the ostensible purpose of his visit to Silvertoe's office was to solicit the fabric company's account.

"For the headquarters of a $200 million firm," Debenture countered, "this is a pretty sleazy-looking office." The agent had rehearsed his cover identity well; he knew that the first remark in a new-business solicitation had to be (1) unresponsive, thus not defensive, and (2) attention-grabbing.

"There's no carpet on the floor," Silvertoe readily admitted, "and the one window looks out on a brick wall. My secretary is just one of the girls in the typing pool, and I don't have a key to the executive washroom. You know why?"

"Sure, I know why," snapped Debenture, stepping on Silvertoe's point. "You've got some kind of mental thing about rejecting status symbols. You think the amenities of executive life would make you seem weak. You're not fooling anybody."

Silvertoe relaxed, and touched a button under the desk that rolled rosewood paneling along the walls, flopped down a throw rug, flickered on indirect lighting, and removed the false brick wall blocking the view from the fortieth floor. "I like your attitude, Debenture. But you haven't answered my question."

"Public relations can do a great deal for your company."

"How?"

"First of all, public relations can create a climate of goodwill around the corporate name, thereby helping the sale of products."

"No sale," said Silvertoe. "There's a certain tawdry aura around our name now which exactly suits our needs. Our consumer public feels guilty when it buys our competitors' products—they're long-wearing. When our stuff wears out quickly, the consumer can buy new things, with no guilt at all about discarding a perfectly good article. The consumer has faith in our shoddiness, and we don't let him down; but go put that in writing, and he'll kill you. No, lay off the climate of goodwill—it could only hurt. What else?"

"Your dealer-supplier publics—"

"They hate us. Because they hate us, they fear us, and that makes them do business with us. Wouldn't change it."

"Let's get a little closer to home, then, Silvertoe. Financial public relations could be helpful to your price-earnings ratio, within the proper limits of full and prompt disclosure of all—"

"You mean tout the stock? I've already dumped a load—I don't want the price up this year. The only other reason for a jiggle is to use our stock for acquisitions, but the way we're set up on cash flow, I'd rather use cash. You sell anything else?"

"Community relations?" Debenture suggested weakly. "Plant tours, open houses, Little Leagues, Good Citizenship awards—"

"When you come right down to it, doesn't that really waste a lot of time?" When Debenture didn't answer right away, Silvertoe continued. "I see two reasons for what you call community relations: to cut down employee turnover, which would save training money, or to effect legislation about taxes and zoning. We put our plants where the labor market can't push us around, and we hire good lobbyists. Saves both time and money, and there are no kids' baseballs to break any windows. You about finished?"

Debenture leaned forward, taking a sincerity tack. "You don't seem to realize that business is no longer done in a vacuum. Today, a powerful concept exists—known as the social responsibility of corporations. The days are long gone when a corporation could abdicate a conscience; now, the human element must enter into every business decision." There was a fine cadence to Debenture's pitch, his resonant voice rising and falling on the waves of public welfare.

"Employee morale," he pressed on, "the rights of stockholders, and the responsibility toward the consumer are all part of the warp and woof of the new way business is done. Moreover, modern business managers are coming to realize that a corporation must make a contribution to the entire socioeconomic network in which it operates."

"Says who?" demanded Silvertoe.

"Says every modern executive—"

"Not quite." Silvertoe's smile was charming. "It's true that's what the Commerce Department spokespeople say, and what the editors of our leading business magazines say, and what the professors of business schools say, and it's what the entire humanist establishment has been saying for years. And a lot of businesspeople parrot it, especially after they've made a killing and want respectability. I'll even grant that a lot of executives believe it with all their hearts, especially those in the middle echelon of huge publicly held corporations.

"But," Silvertoe continued, "there are a few still, small voices that can occasionally be heard from those who wonder if all this social responsibility stuff is not just a cover-up for inadequacy and inefficiency and guilt. These voices say that a business is not a human being, that a corporation's responsibility is to itself—to be successful and profitable. Social responsibility is the concern of individuals and philanthropies and governments—and not of businesses."

Debenture sighed and played his trump. "I can get the United States Government off your back."

Silvertoe grinned. "So that's what your brand of public relations comes down to in the end, eh? Fixing the Feds."

"When was the last time you could look anything up in your files?"

"Let me tell you about those files. Our files, all six years' worth, used to take up 5,500 feet of floor space. At $5 a foot, that's $27,500 a year. Ever since Washington began subpoenaing our files, we've had the use of that space for office workers. As soon as we fill up a file, off it goes to Internal Revenue or the U.S. Senate, or wherever. They pay the storage, and when anybody sues us for something that requires records, we just send him to Washington; it's not our responsibility anymore. As for my own personal files—" Silvertoe smiled. "They're in my head."

"Come on now," James Debenture said. "You'd love the heat off, and you know it. Think of it—no Federal Trade Commission delaying your commercials, no personal tax audits, no Labor Relations Board snoopers around whenever there's an attempt made to organize your plants, no more antimonopoly suits—"

Silvertoe softened slightly. "I might buy, if you really could deliver."

Debenture was noncommittal. "It may take a few days."

He rose and took a last, hard look at R. G. Silvertoe. She was the most beautiful woman he had ever seen. Silver-blue hair, silver-gray eyes, silvery fabric clinging to her long body.

"When you lie awake in bed at night," Debenture said before he left, "don't you ever get to worrying about your responsibility to the public?"

"The public?" Silvertoe laughed, tossing back her straight, glinting hair. "The public be damned!" Debenture smiled back. The opposition organization was clearly identified.

Debenture winged back to Washington on a Silvertoe expense account. Facing C, he gave his assessment, "She has the body of a seventeenth-century courtesan, and the mind of a nineteenth-century robber baron."

"I would never presume to disagree with you about a woman's physical characteristics," C observed, looking out over steepled fingers, "but you misjudge her mind. The modern Pubdam is no mere throwback to an earlier era. Madame Silvertoe is distinctly a product of our times."

"But a public-be-damned attitude dates back to William Vandergilt—"

"True enough, but the robber barons denied the existence of the rights of the public. Silvertoe recognizes those rights, including the public's right to delude itself and to become impatient with the dullness of long-lasting products. Since the public feels guilty about discarding the still useful, Silvertoe caters to that anxiety by providing something quickly useless. Indeed, she may have a twenty-first-century mind."

Debenture shrugged off this hairsplitting, eyeing the red destruct button on C's desk.

The Old Man felt it necessary to drive home his point: "The philosophy of the modern Pubdam organization and of Madame Silvertoe, my dear James, is to recognize the rights of the public established by law, but to reject all responsibility for social concerns beyond those limits."

"But that's clearly out of step, sir. Social responsibility has proved itself to be good business, especially in the long run—"

"Ah, the long run." C seemed suddenly pleased with James Debenture. "You are justifying a corporation's social responsibility by calling it 'good business in the long run.' You are trying to give an *economic* justification to a clearly *un*economic action, to a purely *social* action. That's what most business leaders are trying to do today—and more and more of them are beginning to realize that it doesn't add up. Pure altruism on the part of a corporation, what we call social responsibility—acts that do not even indirectly redound to a company's benefit—are a big fat waste of corporate assets."

Debenture frowned. "Which side are we on, sir?"

"The side of the angels, James! We're *for* social responsibility of corporations—remember that, it's your job—but *not* because it's 'good business' for any individual company. Most of the time, that's a phony rationalization. I am going to tell you the *real* reason we must defend the social responsibility of corporations, and why our Agency has the unique power to assassinate at its own discretion.

"If individual businesses do not assume responsibility for social welfare, then that responsibility will devolve to Big Government or Big Labor. And they'll take complete charge, leaving all business mumbling that it serves an economic function, with nobody listening because the public is primarily interested in its own welfare. The only way for Big Business to stay a powerful force in our society is for each individual executive to leap on the social responsibility bandwagon."

"That means," Debenture said solemnly, "that the future of business—of the free enterprise system—depends on you and me." Mainly, he added to himself, on me.

"It has finally penetrated your marvelously hard cranium," C said wearily. "That is why no company, even if it operates within the law, can be allowed to exist if it does not accept social responsibility. Whenever a company says, 'But social responsibility is really not good business for us in the long run,' we must destroy it—for the good of the free enterprise system, and for all business."

Coldly, C reached his hand over the red destruct button and mashed his thumb down on it. C's symbolic destruct button did not so much as sound a buzzer on a secretary's desk—it was connected to nothing—but it provided a dramatic outlet for the Agency chief and meant that James Debenture's visit was nearing an end.

With the destruct button pushed, James Debenture knew that his arsenal was sharply limited. There was no time for a prolonged proxy fight. He considered pouring acid in a vat of fabric dye, delivering obviously defective goods and swamping the company in lawsuits, but the litigation would drag on for months. A swift garroting of Silvertoe herself would do the trick, but Debenture's authority for assassination covered corporations, not individuals, and the limitation on liability covered every silken hair of Silvertoe's head.

"I need to gain her complete confidence, Chief. Call off the committee."

The governmental heat was suddenly taken off Silvertoe Fabrics. The harassment vanished. Revenue agents left the premises, pickets left the front gate, delisting procedures were halted, antimonopoly suits were not pursued; a hush fell over corporate headquarters. Silvertoe herself was ungracious about having to find space for the truckloads of returning files, but secretly she was pleased.

Debenture moved into an office next to Silvertoe's. To the gleaming feminine executive, James was a lean, hard public relations man who delivered on promises. Naturally, the annual report—due in ten days, requiring a crash printing job—fell in Debenture's bailiwick.

With no time for real finesse—a salad oil drain-off or a fertilizer storage-tank pyramid would have been more his style, and Debenture much preferred cushion-shot corporate assassinations—the Sorespa agent was reduced to planning a direct bludgeoning.

"On the night the annual reports begin their press run," he informed C on the scrambler telephone, "I'll switch the figures to show a whopping loss and insert a paragraph in the President's letter indicating there'll be losses for years to come. I'll wire the phony figures to the financial news services as the next business day opens, and then I'll short-circuit the company's telephone switchboard."

"That allows about three hours for a panic," C mused, "before the reporters show up in person at the company to get a denial."

"You'll have to make sure the Exchange doesn't suspend trading," Debenture said. "The stock specialist will be ruined, but we can't look out for everybody. When the shares go through the floor, a couple of your friends with social responsibility should be able to pick up enough for control. The SEC boys can nab Silvertoe for fraud, and I'll check into our Brazil office for awhile."

"The whole coup lacks subtlety," C muttered, "but we mustn't indulge in delicious deviousness on a rush job. We'll take care of this end. You be certain Silvertoe is incommunicado during the crucial three hours."

Debenture's plan started off without a hitch. With the false reports in the mail and the phony news on the wires, he shorted out the company's switchboard. An ominous lull descended on corporate headquarters.

"The phone people say they'll have it fixed in a little while," James said lazily, strolling into Silvertoe's office and stretching out on the couch. "Why don't we use this little interlude to get to know each other better?"

The long, lithe woman swung out of the chair behind her desk, picked up a silver cigarette holder and a silver lighter, and perched on the edge of the couch, crossing her silvery-stockinged limbs. "I suppose a break every now and then is good for me in the long run, James."

A little bell rang in Debenture's mind. "The long run? I didn't think those words were in your vocabulary. Isn't social responsibility supposed to be good for a company in the long run?"

Her laugh tinkled like silver bells. "That's what the goody-goody types say, when they're trying to give some economic justification to a waste of corporate assets. Oh, don't get me wrong—I've bought my share of tickets to the Policeman's Ball, when I wanted to cozy up to the local cops. But throwing good money away and then saying it's good for business in the long run—thanks, I'm no hypocrite."

That seals your doom, Silvertoe, thought Debenture. Don't say I didn't give you a last chance. Pubdam philosophy means that social responsibility winds up the exclusive province of Big Government and Big Labor, and the free enterprise system is shot. Lucky for business that C sees the big picture, and lucky for C that he has me. Right this minute, this delectable woman's stock is collapsing, and C's friends are standing by to pick up the marbles.

Another little bell rang, and this time it was neither in James Debenture's mind nor in Silvertoe's throat.

"That's my private phone," she said, crushing out her cigarette and starting up. "Only my broker has the number."

"Wait a minute."

Debenture's entire operation hung in the balance. There was still time for Silvertoe to deny the false figures, turn the stock around on a dime, keep control, and drive the shorts into a corner. Sorespa would look idiotic, all of C's friends would be personally bankrupt, and James Debenture, expendable and convertible, would not even have a friend at a nonchartered airline.

He leaned forward and extended his arms. "What's another phone call, in the long run?"

Silvertoe smiled and moved toward James Debenture, suddenly oblivious to the futile ringing of a phone on a desk a million miles away. She may have been devoid of social responsibility, but hardly lacked social response.

10

The Case of the Suspicious Scientist

ROY AMARA and GREGORY SCHMID

"But we did everything right," complains the president of Advanced Electronics when he learns that an environmental water report has ballooned into a potential challenge to his plant's existence. This case, based on a real but disguised company's situation, explores a problem that is becoming increasingly common—the detection of a carcinogen in the environment that may or may not be due to a plant's operation. In this case, the company had made careful efforts to head off such potential difficulties. At the end of the case, five managers who have experienced this type of problem give us their comments.

George Thompson, president of Advanced Electronics, had driven to his company's Roseville plant from his headquarters in the San Francisco Bay area. The four-year-old plant manufactures integrated circuits in a rapidly growing community in the Sierra foothills that is quickly becoming a second Silicon Valley.

Thompson had been alerted to a serious "public relations problem" the day before and had decided to look into it himself. He brought Larry Sperling, the company's legal counsel, with him. On arrival, they went immediately to Tom Sedgwick, the 48-year-old engineer who heads the Roseville plant. He had with him Laura Young, an environmental engineer in her mid-thirties who had been brought into the company to monitor health and safety concerns, and John McGuire, the company's director of public affairs, who had spent the preceding week in Roseville.

Thompson had made it to the presidency of Advanced Electronics because of his ability to identify a critical problem early and his single-mindedness in sticking to that problem until it was resolved. With his usual directness, he turned immediately to Sedgwick for an explanation of why he hadn't been told of this problem 10 days before, when he had last visited headquarters. Sedgwick explained that the problem had been minor until a week before, when it had escalated into a major community challenge to the company's operation in Roseville.

"Community challenge!" Thompson exploded. "But we did everything right. How can that be? Five years ago this company made a commitment to be a leader in dealing with the public and the government. We worked actively with the EPA and OSHA in establishing rules and standards. I kept in regular touch with congressmen, governors, and agency personnel at the expense of a lot of my time. We contributed funds to national and state candidates. We supported our industry associations. We moved into Rose- ville early and grew with the community. We contributed to schools, Little League, and arts councils. We have a public affairs department. We have always carefully tracked possible environmental impacts."

He paused for breath, then said quietly: "We've done everything, and here we are treated like a steel mill in the 1970s that's dropping untreated sludge into the reservoir. I thought we acted to prevent this type of difficulty. I want to know how we got into the problem, what went wrong, and what we can do about it!"

What Went Wrong?

Sedgwick shrugged. "Maybe the best thing to do is to review this problem from the beginning," he said. "Last August the state water resource board made a routine inspection in the Roseville area. They used some new so- phisticated measuring devices that gave a report on water quality that was much more detailed than usual. Isn't that right, Laura?"

"It was an experimental system developed at one of the universities," Young answered. "With new technology, measuring capabilities have im- proved immensely over the last few years. They're now far beyond the slower standard-setting procedures.

"Anyway, the water met all of the government standards. But a young analyst from the board noticed that the asbestos content of the water sample was much higher than that of other communities in the foothills. Asbestos is a carcinogen; he thought he saw a potentially serious community health problem. Then he made a big jump. He knew that the area has a lot of serpentine rock that can harbor deposits with high asbestos content. He connected the asbestos in the water supply with the leaching action of the acidic effluents from the electronics industry treatment plants.

"His conclusions don't have much hard support in the literature, al- though I admit the hypothesis makes some sense. We do know two things, though: one is that the asbestos content is still within the safe range, and the other is that lowering the acidic content of our effluents beneath the standards we now have would be extremely costly.''

John McGuire interrupted: "What really matters is the political reaction. The local newspapers picked up the story, and after that a small ad hoc committee that called itself COMSOW [the Committee to Save Our Water] was formed. I think the group started from one of the local co-ops in Carmichael. They asked us about our effluents, and we told them what we thought: the asbestos level comes from the local terrain, it has always been there, and now it can be detected by better instruments. We assured them we'd cooperate with the government to make sure we don't contribute to any community health problem.

"COMSOW went to the local water commission and asked for a public hearing on the health matter. The commission agreed, set a date, and invited a spokesman to state the industry's position. We agreed to coordinate our position under the leadership of the Roseville Electronics Group.''

Thompson broke in, "Why did we do that?''

"Well,'' said McGuire, "that was probably a mistake. The electronics group really miscalculated COMSOW's intentions, which were supposed to get a public response. Ten days before the hearing, COMSOW asked for the local public-access cable-television channel to televise the proceedings. That station is desperate for something to broadcast, so they were happy to agree, and so was the commission. Then, in the next week, COMSOW got out word through the co-ops, the churches, and the schools about how important it was that each household in the area watch the show.

"At the meeting, we gave the water commission a professional discussion of how we more than meet all government standards. But COMSOW put on a real show, not for the water commission but for the TV audience. They had a biology professor from the university and a representative from an environmental group talk about the long-term dangers of asbestos to community health. Then they showed an animated film on the links between acidic effluents and asbestos. They even had a movie star, a politician, and a couple of local citizens. Later, we found out that the presentation had been put together by a public interest group that specializes in safety and health problems in the electronics industry and by a PR firm.

"I think our more technical discussion went over well. At the end of the meeting, COMSOW commended the industry for its treatment record and agreed to rule on the public health aspect later.''

Misjudging the Public

"So then, what's the problem?'' Larry Sperling interjected.

McGuire sighed. "The meeting was a success all right, but we sure missed with the public. Within five days, COMSOW had sent packets to the 25,000 households that had seen the hearings. They asked people to join the group, send donations, and contact local government officials. The cable TV people could give COMSOW exact profiles and addresses of households tuned into the program.''

Thompson was becoming quite restive. He broke in: "So what has come of all this?''

McGuire answered: "Well, their follow-up campaign was extremely successful. Now they have almost 5,000 members and $250,000 in their treasury. Roseville officials and some of the surrounding county boards of supervisors tell me they have been swamped with phone calls demanding immediate controls on our effluents.''

Sperling added: "In fact, the Placer County Health Board has called for what sounds like a major series of hearings on the impact of all electronic industry effluents on local water. COMSOW has commissioned an environmental health study, and they will use it at those hearings. I understand they are going to ask for a restraining order on the further dumping of effluents until the Placer board grants formal approval. The chances of the court going along aren't great, but if they do, that could virtually shut down our Roseville operations.''

Thompson had a puzzled look. "Didn't we get any advance warning of this? We've spent a lot of time and effort working with OSHA, NIOSH, and the EPA. Aren't they in the best position to set acceptable standards?''

"Times have changed,'' said McGuire. "The activists now are different from those of the 1970s. Washington agencies don't have the budgets to be the unquestioned leaders anymore. Standards are coming out of many different places, and interests and issues have become more localized.''

"OK,'' said Thompson, "I can see what got us into this mess. We're darned lucky that the San Francisco papers haven't picked it up yet. Let's look at our options. First, what happens if we do nothing and the courts do nothing?''

"I'm afraid if the courts don't act, the county board of health will,'' McGuire answered. "The board is under a lot of pressure from local groups, and that ad hoc coalition seems to be gaining public support. All that suburban, middle-class pressure will make it pretty tough for a local government board to resist. If we do nothing, we could find ourselves suddenly having to reduce the levels of acidity in our effluents, and that would cost us a lot of money.''

Thompson was indignant. "Well, I'm on my way back to Washington tomorrow. I was going to spend three full days talking to congressmen and other people in government about trade, taxes, and R&D incentives to fight Japanese competition. Instead, I think I should draw on our political capital to plead for federal intervention here.''

"The administration is very understanding. But I don't think they can do a thing,'' Young interjected. "These are state and local standards we're talking about.''

Sperling had a suggestion: "Well, why don't we use our local influence?

Roseville needs the jobs from our industry. We've put up a lot of our PAC money, and employees, merchants, and suppliers depend on us. Let's call in our markers and get these people behind us. We can pressure the local politicians. Tell them to get us off the hook—or else.''

Sedgwick was dubious. ''Anything you do in this community is an open book. If we start strong-arming, people will yell like banshees about undue corporate influence over the government. Don't forget that most of the local residents are state employees from Sacramento, and they have no love for the private sector.''

''What about our own employees and their impact on the community?'' Thompson asked.

''We can get some real positive support out of them,'' Sperling responded, ''but the picture is not all good. There have been two inquiries from our employees to Cal-OSHA about possible disability benefits. Also, our ombudsman reports that 10 members of the professional staff have asked what we're going to do to clean up the mess. They're feeling a lot of pressure from families and the community. Anything we do has to take account of those concerns.''

McGuire suggested an aggressive public education program. ''We could lay out the benefits of the electronics industry to the area, the small likelihood that industry effluents could be a serious problem according to the best scientific literature, and the risk-reward relationships based on government standards.''

Young wasn't enamored of that idea. ''People are frightened by carcinogens, and they're especially frightened by threats to their water supply,'' she said. ''I'm afraid bringing this up for public debate is not going to do anything but scare a lot of people who aren't even involved now.''

''Then maybe we should sit down quietly with COMSOW and see if we can discuss this issue on its scientific merits,'' said Thompson.

McGuire responded: ''Maybe, but they've already defined the issue and the standards for judging it. Their best bet is to keep the issue before the public.''

There was a pause. Sperling muttered, more to himself than to the group, ''I told you four years ago we should have gone out of state. We wouldn't have these problems in other places.''

Thompson leaned back. He had to make some response to the development at Roseville, but he knew a wrong move might only make things worse. Further, in the crunch of current competition, time and money were limited.

What Should the Company Have Done?

The case of Advanced Electronics raises a number of critical questions. Why was the company so surprised by the public response? What could it have done differently? What is the appropriate response now for the company? At HBR's request, five corporate managers with backgrounds in planning, safety and health, line management, government relations, and environmental engineering give their views on the case. After you have formed your own opinion, you may find it interesting to compare your views with those of our commentators.

Most of the commentators agree that Advanced Electronics made critical errors in its dealings with the community of Roseville and the water problem that developed there.

Ann B. Lazarus of the planning department of Pacific Gas & Electric Company thinks that the major problem at Advanced Electronics was a fundamental misinterpretation of the environment in which it was operating: "The company believes it has followed a strategy of good corporate citizenship and therefore does not deserve this present dilemma. In fact, the company has consistently missed a key audience in its efforts and continues to do so in this present situation. Moreover, the company has already defined the issues and the standards for judging possible responses without a thorough evaluation of its options and their consequences.

"While Advanced Electronics claims to have made a commitment to being a leader in dealing with the public and the government, all actions were directed largely toward government agencies, national and state officials, and industry associations. None of these operates at the local level. The company has failed to practice good leadership that could have a visible and direct effect in the community. Its contributions program and public affairs department were very traditional, cosmetic answers to community relations. Nothing Advanced Electronics did was customized for the town where it was operating. The company's naiveté concerning its real constituents is manifested in the comment: 'We should have gone out of state. We wouldn't have these problems in other places.'"

For Lazarus, this misperception of a company's responsibility to a local community led Advanced Electronics to make a series of mistakes: "The company maintained this attitude during the hearing before the local water commission. First, it took refuge behind the cover of the Roseville Electronics Group. Second, it provided a technical discussion of how Advanced Electronics more than met all government standards. These two actions contributed further to the company's low profile and to an obviously growing sentiment that Advanced did not care about the local community. The company even concedes that while the more technical discussion went over well with the water commission, 'We sure missed with the public.' Again, the company defined the issue in its usual terms—how it should deal with the regulators—and not in terms of the people affected by it. Thus, it is continuing its pattern of internal dialogue, of talking to each other and therefore not hearing what the community is saying. The company doesn't even seem to talk directly to other electronics firms, but rather through the association."

Lawrence Barron, associate director of the safety, health, and environmental affairs department of Union Carbide, agrees that Advanced Electronics misread the entire situation: "This is a classic example of a well-intentioned company underestimating its neighbors' mentality and then misreading the aggressive environmental activism of today. This stronger and broader movement has been gaining momentum at the state and local levels where all signs have clearly indicated greater environmental awareness and opposition to any relaxation of safeguards. A company cannot rest on its laurels of having grown with the community and complied with official technical standards.

"The company is guilty of complacency; it did not stay in touch with its own environment. The qualified staff should have participated more in community and state activities, where specific health concerns and technical advances can be monitored, real contributions made, and adverse situations properly anticipated."

Other commentators stress that Advanced Electronics did have many opportunities to lessen the emotional buildup.

Robert Kennedy, executive vice president of Union Carbide, stresses such opportunities: "There may have been good legal recourse to block the televised public hearing. Failing that, it is clear they went to the hearings unarmed and woefully underestimating the job they had to do to state their case."

John Beckett, director of government relations at Hewlett-Packard, outlines some concrete steps that Advanced Electronics could have taken to avoid a purely emotional popular response: "Advanced Electronics should have used it connections in state government to put some restraints on the process and to get a peer review of the hypothesis proposed by the young water resources board analyst. It should have requested that the local water commission delay any public hearing until it could collect more data to support or disprove the analyst's hypothesis. It could even have agreed to fund such a study."

He adds: "The important element of time to defuse the initial public alarm is very important. The company also needs to look at some technical alternatives to its acidic discharge. To simply sit on a position that treatment is extremely costly does not show a good-faith effort, even if Advanced doesn't believe it is the cause of the asbestos in the water. It also could have communicated the important facts on the issue to its employees."

Further, according to Beckett, "Advanced Electronics can do a better job of anticipating change by treating any study as a potential news story and public issue. Doing its homework before any issue breaks can give the company a better chance to head it off."

What Can It Do Now?

The commentators suggest a variety of courses of action for Advanced Electronics that reflect their own diverse perspectives. One priority is to stop any further escalation in the public protest. Again, Robert Kennedy stresses the usefulness of the law: "Presumably, an appropriate response would be to draw up a legal action plan to forestall precipitative action by either the court or the board of health. This is a country of law, not trial by television."

But the company can take more constructive steps as well.

John Barker, director of environmental engineering at Armco, suggests a new series of objective technical studies to get at the three main issues. "The response of Advanced Electronics must address three underlying questions: Is the drinking water within safe limits? Do the effluents from the electronics industry have any reaction with the granite formations to adversely affect the water supplies? Can the existing production process be economically changed to reduce or eliminate the acidic effluents?

"The first question has to be studied and addressed by a creditable, independent, and objective third party. The company should hire a well-recognized expert, perhaps from the academic, medical, or consulting fields, to do a thorough analysis of the groundwater supplies. The study should include the communities in which the electronics industries are located as well as communities that are situated in the same geological formations but that do not have those industries. The independent expert should use the same analytic techniques as those used by the state water resources board.

"Company management, in conjunction with the outside expert, must then devote the necessary time and resources to holding a series of meetings to explain the results. These meetings need to be carefully planned to inform first the plant employees, then the merchants, suppliers, and community leaders in Roseville, and certainly the local water commission. The company must also be willing to meet with the schools, local civic organizations, and any interested groups to openly, candidly, and freely discuss the facts.

"The second question, regarding the effect the acidic effluents may have on the granite formations and subsequently the groundwater quality, must be addressed in a similar manner. The company should retain an independent, recognized expert trained in groundwater hydrology and geology. The results of this study must then be shared with the same groups, beginning with the employees.

"The third question, which involves changing the production processes, could be handled by the company's own R&D department. Or an outside consultant could do it. In either event, it must be conducted aggressively and simultaneously with the first two studies.

"Should either of the first two studies show a detrimental effect, the company must be prepared to change its production processes or waste treatment practices to reduce or eliminate the problem.

"The three studies must be carefully coordinated. To carry out such a program requires a major commitment by top management. To treat the matter casually, or to delay action, would be courting disaster."

Robert Kennedy of Union Carbide also sees the need for more facts, though he stresses the economic aspect: "The company can hardly respond intelligently without all the economic facts. How much money and how many jobs does the electronics industry put into the community? What is the industry's local tax base? What is the cost of reducing acidic levels in the effluent to some lower level? To what level? Who knows what the 'normal' level is? Is there any way of establishing the preelectronics asbestos level in the water? What really is the competitive threat if the industry incurs greater costs? How would the industry, and jobs, be affected?''

Further studies are only half the problem, for the company must be willing to use the studies to help define a strategy for itself, even if that strategy involves some sacrifice. Ann Lazarus of PG&E thinks that Advanced Electronics ''will have to develop a variety of options for responding, assess each one alone or in combination with others, and define a strategy that is other than the current reactionary one. Simply writing off every option is not going to make the problem improve or disappear.

''Fundamentally, the company must begin to recognize the need for talking directly with the people who feel victimized by it. If it can begin to relate to the individuals in the community rather than government officials, the company can start to create an exchange for developing mutually acceptable solutions. Right now, it is talking about going directly to the public. The company clearly has the tools but doesn't know how to use them. John McGuire comes closest to recognizing the central issue when he says 'public expectations reflect local interests and issues.' If Advanced Electronics can fashion a strategy that incorporates this key idea, it will be able to unravel its problems.''

John Beckett of Hewlett-Packard suggests that studies be used ''to find a technical solution to the acidic discharge and get on with the show. In the long run, Advanced Electronics should support efforts not only to disprove the hypothesis but also to get the public to adopt a reasonable drinking water standard for asbestos.''

Lawrence Barron thinks that objective studies will ''identify any previously unrevealed potential health hazards. The company should then commission specific remedial programs. As soon as the company has gained understanding and cooperation, it can make joint public announcements—with definite dates for reporting progress—to lessen community fears and tensions. And the company should mount simultaneously a public education campaign or, at the very minimum, build one into the public announcements.''

Keeping In Touch

The commentators stress that past problems and future resolutions all depend on Advanced Electronics keeping in direct touch with the local community. Such contact should involve dealing with community members as stakeholders in company activities who have right of access to objective data on such issues as health hazards. But the company must use all of its resources to remove as much of the emotional content of the issue as possible through standard legal processes, reasoned technical studies, and full public education forums.

In the long run, most of the commentators are confident that such efforts will pay off. As Robert Kennedy of Union Carbide summed it up: "The industry has a responsibility to deal openly and honestly with the issues, and that has to be done, now, in the public arena. The local citizens are aroused, but in most cases—given time, honesty, and facts—they are generally fair."

PART TWO
FINDING AND KEEPING THE RIGHT CORPORATE IDENTITY
AN OVERVIEW

A major theme of the best kind of public relations advice is knowing what your company is—and isn't. Without some kind of strong sense of identity, the company cannot hope to have good relations with the public. It will simply exist, without making the right kind of impact on the marketplace.

When faced with this idea, most managers rightly complain that their company cannot hope to come up with a single identity to present to the public, since the company is a huge, diversified organization representing myriad product lines, management styles and personalities. But the major reason for attempting to forge such an identity is to allow the company to present a single image to the public, so that the market won't be confused by all the businesses in which the company operates. Unifying the company's numerous identities not only allows it to project a positive image to the skeptical market, but it also helps it to create a single culture within the organization, allowing the diverse groups to feel as if they are contributing to a single, and very powerful whole.

In "Sharper Focus for the Corporate Image," Pierre Martineau first tries to educate *HBR* readers into the importance of these concepts. That was before the onset of studies into "corporate culture." While Martineau obviously does not use the same words, he is trying to begin to make companies understand the importance of the concepts. It's true that most large companies are all over the industry map, even when they operate in a single business such as telecommunications. But what is also true is that "the human mind can only handle so many complexities . . . the simple symbolic images act as a rough summation or index of a vast complexity of meanings." And Martineau maintains that it makes the company's job easier in dealing with myriad publics, advertisers, and customers if it has a single, positive, and very forceful self-image to project.

Of course, there is a danger in image molding, namely molding the wrong or false image. David Finn's "Ethics in Public Relations" points out that "it is . . . shortsighted to equate public relations with publicity, or with defending management actions . . . it (is) better to consider that one of the major functions of a company's public relations . . . is to help clarify the company's role." This emphasis on clarity, and not obfuscation, is important to the company in molding its image. Any attempt at short-circuiting the truth usually fails, says Finn, and a company should learn to look for the negatives within itself as well as the positives. After dealing with the negative as well as it can, it will be ready to project the right kind of image.

Walter P. Margulies wrote in the late 1970s, "Making the Most of Your Corporate Identity" after looking back at more than 20 years of corporate image-making. While many companies had followed the advice of sages like Finn and Martineau, many others had not. Corporate identity programs are much in vogue, but like many other good ideas, they are often badly practiced. Martineau points out that the program of forging a good image takes good management, and involves much more than changing a name or a trademark. The company must first learn to recognize its true identity, before it can possibly be able to teach all levels of managers what it is, and how to disseminate the message throughout the company.

One of the best ways to find a company's identity is to look back at its history. Two scholars, George David Smith and Laurence E. Steadman advise managers about the "Present Value of Corporate History." They advise companies to look at their past in order to better understand their present. They show that the history can be used in a wide frame of management processes, from molding the right image, to strategy, management development, and marketing. The basic message remains the same as in the first article dealing with image in the 1950s: That the best companies find, understand, and preserve a single, positive image within themselves and toward the public, an image that reflects the realities of the past, not the dream of a public relations executive.

11
Sharper Focus for the Corporate Image

PIERRE MARTINEAU

Ask any schoolchild what the simple cartoon figures of Uncle Sam, John Bull, and the Russian Bear mean, and he or she will correctly identify the United States, Great Britain, and the USSR. When faced with complexities, the human mind tends to oversimplify and abstract a few salient meanings, and the simple symbolic images act as a rough summation of a vast complexity of meanings, feelings, and attitudes.

Can a company which produces a diversified array of products and which deals with a varied group of publics hope to coalesce into a clear, understandable corporate image? Pierre Martineau discusses the problems and the rewards accruing to the company that recognizes the goal of *Sharper Focus for the Corporate Image*.

☐ There has been a lot of talk about something called the "corporate image." Is this just another loose notion—or is the idea an important one?

☐ Many hardheaded business leaders seem to have an uneasy feeling that promoting the corporate image is little more than a vague gesture of public goodwill. Does it *really* make any difference if a company's image is favorable or not?

☐ Does the corporate image have to be focused by hit-or-miss methods and trial and error, or are there right and wrong ways to project

Author's Note. I am indebted to the following consultants for their provocative ideas on the subject of the corporate image: David Cox of Cox and Cox, Leo Shapiro of Leo Shapiro and Associates, Burleigh Gardner of Social Research, Inc., and Ray Winship of *Fortune*.

it effectively? Can one corporate image please all of the people all of
the time?

☐ To what use can advertising be put in creating a clear image? Have
we overlooked one of our most powerful channels of communication
while concentrating on public relations?

The promptness with which management and public relations consultants have adopted the notion of the corporate image would indicate that
the concept fills a very real vacuum. Apparently some such concept is needed
for the sake of completeness in our thinking. If it is important to be concerned
with the psychological overtones and impact on buyer attitudes of the company's individual brands, it also seems important to be concerned with these
factors as they affect the company itself.

In one sense, the idea of a corporate image is certainly not new. Companies have done institutional advertising for many years, and sophisticated
public relations people have long stressed the significance of many kinds of
intelligent effort in building up a general reservoir of goodwill for a firm.
But the concept of a corporate image has given much greater meaning to
these efforts. Against the background of thinking about brand images and
product-area images, it offers something new, distinct, and valuable.

Mirage or Reality?

Because the transition from brand image to corporate image has proceeded
so fast, many of the component parts of the corporate image concept are
still muddy and need to be overhauled in the light of other knowledge and
experience. Businesspeople are doing and saying things that do not make
sense. For instance:

☐ One current estimate of how much United States business spends
each year to make itself better liked is $1 billion. But when average
presidents are asked what impression they are trying to create in the
public mind, they emphasize "selling good products at reasonable
prices."[1] Is this all? Is this the way the public assesses corporations?
Or is this a primitive kind of thinking on the subject of corporate
images?

☐ For many years leading corporations such as American Telephone
& Telegraph and Standard Oil Co. (New Jersey) have conducted public
opinion surveys hoping to learn the climate of public feeling toward
them. Are such studies measuring anything of significance? Are they
measuring what they assert to be measuring? What does it mean when
the index of negative reaction drops—a more favorable (less critical)
image or a weaker (more apathetic) image?

☐ The literature on the subject implies that the task of molding a corporate image is essentially a public relations function. Is it? Is this the most important way for a company to convey meaning about its image?

☐ One study purporting to show the corporate image of the steel manufacturers asked the respondent which company he would recommend as a place for a young executive to start working and which company he would invest $5,000 in if he had $5,000 to invest. In defense of the study, it was asserted that the image of the company as a place to work would be indicative of its future growth possibilities. Is this plausible? Is there any such logical relation between the different aspects of the corporate image?

Company Personality

In order to put the corporate image in perspective as a workable concept, we need to understand where companies are trying to go with it. And what started this line of thinking in the first place?

In a remarkably few years the goals of advertising and marketing in the consumer field have been broadened past the functional stages. Today sophisticated strategy embraces a conscious effort to create a distinctive and, of course, positive brand image. The successful brand invariably has psychological meanings and dimensions which are just as real to the purchaser as are its physical properties, and in many instances the purely subjective attributes play a far more important role in the brand's fortunes than do the functional elements. But in every case the aura of the symbolic dimensions contributes to the value and the public estimate of the brand.

Often the scope of the problem becomes widened to include a whole product area. Furriers want to know why women buy fewer fur coats. Retailers in the men's clothing field are concerned about their decreasing share of the consumer dollar. Trade associations in the beer industry are asking themselves why per capita beer consumption is declining, whereas wine consumption is increasing. Obviously what is involved is essentially not price, not distribution, not the physical products, but the sets of attitudes which are bearing on and directing consumer behavior in a whole area.

To go a step further in the complexity of images, perceptive retailers everywhere are sensing the vital importance of the many nonprice components of their operations which contribute to their store character. Speakers at leading conventions in both the supermarket and the department store fields have urged the development of store personality as a primary objective of retailing today.[2] Theorists readily acknowledge that the decision maker in the department store relies more and more on nonprice factors as a major competitive weapon for building sales volume.[3] In other areas of retailing, management is learning how to "sell the store" as a commodity, just as it learned how to sell products. For example:

☐ The Kroger grocery chain is launched on a major operating and advertising program specifically designed to project a favorable company image.

☐ Jewel Food Stores, though operating in only one market, has become one of the largest grocery chains by marching under the banner of a pleasing store personality. What started out years ago merely as a promotional idea—"Shop at your friendly Jewel Store"—has long since become a religion for management.

The merchant is realizing that unless the prospective customer can consciously or unconsciously see a "fit" between her own self-image and the image of the store, she will not patronize it, no matter what price offerings are made. It is perfectly logical, therefore, for the manufacturer to inquire whether a similar attraction or repulsion may be taking place between the consuming public and the company's personality, which would have tangible bearing on the sale of the products.

Distinction or Extinction

To be sure, the corporate image is complex and diverse. Yet there is considerable logic now for attempting to mold it into a clear, distinctive form. Westinghouse, for instance, has embarked upon an extensive corporate advertising program designed to build a public image of an inventive and friendly company because it believes that this will influence sales by raising company stature.[4] The very considerable institutional advertising beamed at the public by such companies as General Electric, General Motors, Goodyear, Firestone, U. S. Steel, Kaiser, and countless others undoubtedly is inspired by a similar wish to control the company image.

Business magazines in the industrial field—particularly those addressed to top management—carry much corporate advertising that contains no attempt to extol products. Container Corporation of America, the largest manufacturer in the fiber-box container field, uses a very imaginative advertising program which does much to mold an image of the company without ever discussing its products. Indeed, the number of hitherto staid corporations in the industrial field that feature abstract art and symbols in their corporate messages has assumed the proportions of a major shift in advertising style.

Obviously, the aim of such advertising is to impart distinctions and meanings in an area where it is difficult to create distinctions and meanings on a functional basis. There are precious few products that can be sold today on the basis of a demonstrable product superiority, and this is particularly true in the industrial field. We have developed an economy based on mass production, and mass production depends on standardization. Both buyers and sellers have managed to level off any real differences in the products they deal with. There are countless people in the laboratories and at the drawing boards who are trying to build in or design in actual superiorities, yet our competitive system will seldom permit one product to remain superior for long.

Too Much to Focus?

Much of the confusion over the corporate image stems from somewhat conflicting sources. On the one hand, some people are likely to be uneasy over the fact that so little can say so much. On the other hand, a great deal of skepticism exists that such a conglomeration of activities as the modern corporation *can* lend itself to compact expression.

In the strictest sense, every company can be said to have a corporate image. Every bank, every railroad, every manufacturer has a personality or reputation consisting of many facets. The corporate image of American Airlines embraces infinitely more meaning than some airplanes flying in the sky; it symbolically projects associations of waiting rooms, stewardesses, type of equipment, excellence of meals, interior décor of the planes, how fast the baggage is unloaded, the extra fare flights, attitudes toward serving liquor, the company's color scheme and trademark, and so on. The vague generalized image behind the specific is called into mind by some specific facet. Yet it is the vague part, the set of many associations and meanings, which the image really refers to.

But, as if the subtlety of the problem were not enough to bother people, there is also its complexity. For example, I know of one consultant who questions that these complex images even exist. Why? He argues that the manufacturer, if a large one, operates in so many different areas that no one image is possible. The company is a workshop, a research laboratory, a training school for executives, a source of employment for hundreds of workers, a civic institution, a buyer, and, among these many other things, a maker of profit. The point is, he argues, that it has no one single image because it cannot have. It is far too complex.

Or, to use a more concrete illustration, what is the corporate image of the Chicago Tribune Company? It publishes newspapers. But also it operates radio and television stations; it is an office-building landlord in both Chicago and New York; it syndicates comic strips and feature articles to newspapers throughout the country; it operates a fleet of ocean-going boats; it is one of the largest paper manufacturers and one of the largest owners of timberlands; it has built and maintains an entire Canadian city; it has important hydro-electric developments; and it is part owner of a major aluminum-manufacturing project.

The business scene today is characterized by an infinitude of corporations with just such sprawling structures and diverse holdings in many totally unrelated areas. Look, for example, at these two companies:

☐ W. R. Grace, among other things, is a major factor in steamships, airlines, insurance, banking, and outdoor advertising; it is one of the largest manufacturers in South America with an immensity of products;

and in a relatively few years it has become one of the largest chemical manufacturers in this country.

☐ International Harvester has long since become far more than a manufacturer of farm equipment and harvester machinery. Besides its steel mills, it is one of the very largest makers of such diverse products as motor trucks, ball bearings, sisal, and construction equipment, and only recently it withdrew from the fields of home refrigeration and household appliances. Presumably, few of the buyers in these fields would be impressed with the corporate image of a farm equipment manufacturer. The motor trucks carry the insignia "International Trucks," not "International Harvester Trucks."

"Let the Product Speak"

In each particular product area, the buyer would generally be concerned only with the activities of the company as a manufacturer in that field, and give very little thought to the baffling complexities of the corporate image. This is why the particular consultant I have mentioned contends that management thinking should be solely about the product at the point of sale. What is important in organization thinking is what happens at this critical spot, he argues. Naturally he turns a jaundiced eye on institutional advertising. Not only is it ineffective, in his viewpoint, but it might give rise to misunderstandings about the company's motives. "Let the product speak for you," is his advice. If there is such a thing as a corporate personality, he does not feel that it is viable—that it will pass coin from one public to another.

There is still another problem. The multiline company not only has to address a number of buying publics but also many other significant groups that have to be influenced in extremely diverse ways. For example, the labor unions who bargain with International Harvester are surely not impressed with its attractive "I H" design or the excellence of its machinery. And the investing public is probably only concerned with the dividend and earnings record, and the general character of management: whether it is progressive, competitive, and stockholder-oriented. May it not be, then, that there is not only too much for the modern corporation to say but also too many different people to say it to?

Direction and Indirection

In trying to unravel some of the misunderstandings about the corporate image, I must grant at the outset that much or even most institutional effort is ineffective and not communicating what the company hopes it will. It does not follow, however, that these meanings cannot be imparted with a different kind of communication.

I think that if advertising is viewed as a communication process, it will be seen that there are many other ways to convey and mold the corporate image besides the customary platitudinous messages to the effect that the company is visionary, honest, friendly, considerate, dependable, trustworthy, brave, with unbelievable resources, and so on and on. Certainly management should evolve advertising strategy which not only has such rigid meanings but particularly will cause us to like the corporate personality just as we like a person. But it must do so by indirection. To illustrate:

> In the Westinghouse study previously mentioned, readers of strictly corporate advertising stated that Westinghouse is a very stable company, its stock is a good thing to own, it is a leader in research, the company's appliances are good and the new lines are greatly improved, and that Westinghouse is a good place to work. *Yet the advertising said none of these things.* All of these comments were provoked voluntarily by corporate advertising showing six applications of atomic reactors.

While I have deliberately pointed out the difficulties of abstracting one simple symbol for a complex corporate image, nevertheless that is the way the human mind tends to think. To pragmatic persons who say, "Why all of this bother about images? Let's just run our companies," I should like to refer to what is undoubtedly the best book on the subject: *The Image* by Kenneth E. Boulding.[5] The author points out that it is not mere knowledge and information which direct human behavior, but rather it is the images we have—not what is true but what we *believe* to be true. In any situation these patterns of subjective knowledge and value act to mediate between ourselves and the world.

The human mind can only handle so many complexities. It has to oversimplify and abstract a few salient meanings. We bundle up whole nations in simple cartoon figures like Uncle Sam or John Bull. The simple symbolic images act as a rough summation or index of a vast complexity of meanings. We personalize them and like them or dislike them because this is the only way we can interact with things—to endow them with the attributes of people.

Built-In Filters

Business executives cannot afford to scoff at this subject of images because people are acting toward their companies on the basis of them—not on the basis of facts and figures. Once these stereotyped notions are formed in people's minds, they are extremely difficult to change. They serve as emotional filters which are used by everyone in listening and seeing. Facts or no facts, these images cause us to reject what we do not agree with. On the other hand, we allow agreeable material to pour in unchallenged. The good image has a halo effect, so that it gets credit for all sorts of good things which might be quite contrary to truth. To illustrate:

☐ In a study by the *Chicago Tribune,* United Airlines was the only major airline not mentioned in connection with fatal accidents, though actually it had recently been involved in three spectacular plane crashes.

☐ By contrast, when a certain newspaper with the image of being sensational and for lower-status people scored a news scoop of considerable significance to the business community, it sold no extra papers whatever on the newsstands in the financial district. Because the image was negative to the people of this class, they simply refused to believe their senses. The image prevented them from "seeing" the headlines of this paper.

Power of Stereotypes

I have pointed out that the image is a kind of stereotype. It is an oversimplification. In a sense, therefore, it negates the complexity of the modern diversified corporation. But this does not make it less workable as an operational tool. Far from it. In fact, it is the reality that creates the need for the illusion.

The Hidden Perceivers

To begin, I think it would be most fruitful to look a little closer at the notion that the corporation is addressing itself to many different publics, each of which is looking at the corporate image from behind a different set of lenses. Many public relations people who acknowledge this in theory behave in practice as if there were only one public to be addressed.

While it is certainly true that the various publics overlap and are not discrete, they all see the image differently because their perceptions, their expectations, and their wishes differ. Compare the viewpoints of the following groups:

1   Stockholders—sophisticated people who determine the company's access to capital.
2   Consumers—relatively unsophisticated people who buy the company's products for any number of reasons.
3   Potential customers—people who could buy the company's products but do not.

Whereas companies generally address consumers and nonconsumers alike, in our experience at the *Chicago Tribune,* they may be poles apart in their attitudes. Consumers like the products, they are familiar with them, they read the advertising to support their favorable opinions. But nonconsumers very often have negative stereotypes of the company which prevent them from learning anything about the products. Their negative attitudes in some way have to be altered; otherwise they will always act as a barrier to getting information through.

4 Employees—top management, middle management, and the rank and file of production workers.

Here it is worth noting that each group will have very different perceptions of the company as a place to work. The perennial sin of employee publications and employee benefits is that they are conceived and remain embedded in the mental set of top management.

5 Vendors in the distribution system—retailers, wholesalers, manufacturer's agents.

A very large part of so-called consumer advertising is really designed to influence the vendors. In the Antitrust Division's action to prevent the Procter & Gamble Company's merger with Clorox Chemical Company, considerable stress was placed on Procter & Gamble's ability to secure overnight retail distribution for its then-new products, such as Crest Toothpaste and Comet Cleanser. The retailer's image of the salability of Procter & Gamble's products constitutes a very tangible factor in its greater resources.

6 Suppliers—those who furnish credit, services, materials, and prices.

The attitudes they form about a company can be very important. For example, if the bank believes the company will ultimately be successful, it allows much greater credit leeway. Thus, fabricators are (as they should be) deeply concerned with the attitudes of textile mills and steel mills that are their suppliers.

7 Neighbors—the community where the company has plants or general offices.

If a company operates stockyards or quarries or stream-polluting mills, or anything like that, obviously local opinion becomes very important. Local officials assess taxes and pass zoning ordinances. So of course such companies have to make themselves welcome to the communities where otherwise they would be regarded as a nuisance.

In a broader perspective, nearly all companies recognize the importance of a favorable public climate at the local community and plant city levels. Presidents speak at civic occasions, executives are active in local charities, educational scholarships are created, and many corollary activities are undertaken with the purpose of creating an image of a good neighbor and a responsible citizen. I think this aspect of the corporate image is extremely important in dealing with government functionaries. And also in lawsuits. Remember that railroads and public utilities constantly face the problem of excessive and unreasonable verdicts in personal injury cases because the judgment of the typical juror is swayed by personal unfavorable images of these companies.

Between each of these publics and the company are surrogate groups that in reality act for them. For instance, the union is not really a public, but acts for the employees. Investment counselors, bond houses, and stock-brokers are the surrogates for the shareholders, and in most instances it is more important for them to perceive a favorable corporate image than for the shareholders; they are, after all, the "influentials." The retail dealers have wholesalers, distributors, and manufacturer's agents between them and the company. And the retail dealers finally are the ultimate links in the chain of surrogates between the consumer and the company.

"What Everybody Knows"

While it may be true that ordinary consumers do not care about the complex operations of business as such, they clearly pay some heed to the particular units that make or sell the individual products they buy. For example, in our studies of retail advertising, the reader invariably asks herself some question about the goals of the store owner, either consciously or uncon-sciously, before she will allow herself to consider patronizing the store: "Are they dependable? How will they treat me in case I need service? What is their attitude about exchanges? Are they just trying to sell me?" I am con-vinced that the same kinds of questions are asked about the refrigerator manufacturer or the mail-order house.

The consumer may come into contact with only a small part of the manufacturing operations of an organization like Pillsbury, General Electric, Eastman Kodak, Scott Paper, Ford, Revlon, or Borden. What does it matter if typical motorists are in total ignorance of the industrial activities of the Standard Oil Co. (Indiana)? It is entirely sufficient that for them it is just a company selling gasoline, tires, and car accessories. In this buying context they definitely have a corporate image of the company that deeply influences their purchases of motor products. It makes a decisive difference at the point of retail sale whether the product partakes of the Westinghouse aura or is a totally unknown brand.

Here is where I disagree with those who disdain the corporate image. I know, on the basis of research, that at the critical point in time when the product, the buyer, and the manufacturer come together, the buyer generally gives some heed to the character of the maker. The buyer shares the public stereotype—"what everybody knows" about the company. It is always surprising to me how widespread these public stereotypes are—and most have *some* basis in fact. While it is perfectly true that the buyer may not have a sharp and detailed mental picture, he does have access to the broad, general, diffused stereotypes which permit him to make first decisions whether to purchase or not. It is these broad stereotypes which cause him to patronize Montgomery Ward or Marshall Field, to fly Eastern or Delta, to buy Philco or Kelvinator products.

Another reason for respecting the corporate image is that among the subjective elements that constitute a brand image, there generally are some aspects of the corporate image playing an important role. For instance:

> In a study of the sales position and consumer desirability of various packaged meat products in the Chicago and Los Angeles areas, the critical difference was the corporate image of the various packers. Meat is meat. Animals are animals. The consumer *knows* all this. Moreover, Armour and Swift were shown in this research to have communicated all the dutiful and dull virtues of quality, value, and dependability. But the consumers surveyed overwhelmingly preferred the products of a regional packer who had acquired an image of youthfulness, fun, imagination, inventiveness, and sincerity. In umbrella fashion these qualities of the packer's image were held over his meat at the self-service displays in the stores to make it distinctively different and far more desirable. Demonstrably, the corporate image, and only that (because meat is meat), must have been the decisive factor in the economic mix.

Industrial Marketing

I would argue that the same is true of industrial marketing when and if the manufacturer creates a distinctive corporate image with some applicability to the products. I cite the case of one purchasing agent for a manufacturer of heavy industrial equipment. This individual frankly justifies his purchases and his preference for the products of a principal supplier because of the president's reputation for constantly and enthusiastically discussing his company stock with security analysts. In the words of this purchasing agent, he can always justify his buying from this company because he has a feeling of confidence stemming from a corporate image of dependability and progressiveness built by the seemingly unrelated activities of the chief executive.

The buyer very definitely recognizes that people run companies, and it does make a critical difference what kind of people they are. Because they are human, they must have a value system, and it is important to sense how well-intentioned they are toward the buyer. Who dominates the company? Container Corporation, for example, is obviously a style-and-design company because of its executives; it is not just another production company manufacturing containers at a price.

Molding the Image

Let us turn now to the practical question of how to create a clear, persuasive corporate image. Let us consider such aspects of the question as what products the company should identify itself with, how one company can be distinguished from another, and the relative roles of public relations and advertising.

Idealized Identifications

The consumer is always asking: "What do they want me to do? Do they want me to clean my desk? Do I scrub floors, or do I enjoy myself?" As you look at dishwashing compounds, you sense that the company not only wants to sell you something but asks you to do something unpleasant. A vacuum cleaner company is persuading you to perform a nasty, thankless chore. A scouring powder forces you to do hard, dirty work, and the subjective conclusion may be that any maker with such goals does not like you. By contrast, the maker of an electric toaster or a new gas range wants you to be happy and appreciated.

In advertising, therefore, the company has to be careful about which products it appears to "love" and which it just handles. Procter & Gamble just "handles" detergents and scouring powders. But it identifies with Zest and Camay soaps, which have significant emotional connotations as toiletries of beauty and scent, and with Ivory soap, which is identified with child-loving.

Too often companies identify with products they like instead of products that the consumer finds pleasant. It is, of course, important to discern which products the consumer likes and to identify the company with those. It *does* make considerable difference whether the company identifies with products like meat or cosmetics as compared to items that force one to do disagreeable tasks. "Cooking is a chore, but my family will love me, will compliment me, will realize I am indispensable and very capable. Hand lotions, lipsticks, hair sprays will make me attractive. The company wants me to be beautiful. How nice! What a nice company."

The products and services that the consumer identifies a company with have a far more important bearing on the image than all the knowledge of economists and antitrust lawyers who know the "big picture." To illustrate:

☐ I think a primary reason that the government failed to whip up any public feeling toward Atlantic & Pacific stores in its antitrust suit was because people did not see Atlantic & Pacific as some powerfully big corporation—the largest retailer. Rather, people knew individual A & P stores that trimmed lettuce, sold aromatic-smelling coffee, and accommodatingly carried out heavy bundles.

☐ How can the public dislike General Motors? In the public eye, it is not seen as a huge corporation dominating the automobile field. At the point of public contact, the GM image has filtered down to become one of pleasant people making and selling cars at retail, figuring out trades so the prospect can have a car with an AM/FM radio, whitewall tires, and air conditioning. "GM bargains with me; it wants me to be happy with a new car."

□   Jersey Standard is not "the biggest oil company"; rather, it handles Flit and radiator cleaner, just like any small company handling small things. So people can like Jersey. "How can you hate a company that makes Flit?"

□   United States Steel brought itself within public awareness by promoting a "White Christmas"; people like the notion of appliances for Christmas, and therefore U.S. steel is simple and nice.

At the point where the consumer, the public, and the company all meet, the corporate image has to be uncomplicated so that it can be expressed quickly in feeling or logic. The public must accept the various deeds of the manufacturer so that it can fit them together logically or emotionally; if it cannot find a simple motive for some corporate activity, then it is liable to impute a wrong motive. Accordingly, Lever Bros. should not put out vitamins and Schenley should not manufacture penicillin, for these are illogical steps. They do not fit the pattern of the corporate image. But if a company should make a success of some such maverick enterprise, then the public reconstructs its logic to accept the company in this new field.

Common Pitfalls

Molding and shaping the corporate image is a highly positive, constructive job, which needs to be approached with vigor and enthusiasm. There are, however, several problems that management should frankly face up to— and some that it may have to live with.

First there is the problem of "living modern" in times of continuous change. It is quite true that, today as always, there is no substitute for the excellence of a company's products. But we have an economy which has emerged from the production and refinery stage. Unless all products in the marketplace are good in a functional sense, they die an immediate and unlamented death. Now we are in the era of promotion and merchandising, where the fortunes of a company depend far more on its abilities to advertise and mechandise and promote its products, because it is taken for granted that all products will perform their functions. But in my experience there are far too many mental "DPs" at the management level who cannot shift their perspective from the long-gone days when there were distinctive product differences to dramatize.

Take the case of an advertiser selling electric motors. One ½-horsepower motor performs exactly like another. Yet the maker typically has such a dearth of imagination and of communicative skills that his only recourse is to spell out 10 or 12 points of superiority. The buyer knows that ½-horsepower motors are identical. Furthermore, he will recognize that all of the points the manufacturer alludes to are of such miniscule importance as to be valueless. I have heard my wife spontaneously object to dull TV commercials: "What are they telling me such nonsense for? Who cares?"

Generally when it dawns on the executive group that there is such a thing as a corporate image, it fails to distinguish between two general sets of meanings: (1) the functional meanings, which have to do with quality, reliability, service, price, and the like; and (2) the emotive meanings, which have to do with the subjective viewpoints or "feeling tone" of the various publics. In large measure we believe that we wish to believe. Modern communication theory recognizes that our feelings steer our senses.

If a company or a brand is saddled with a negative image, even the most realistic and functional qualities of its products will be colored and altered. We find reasons to reject what we do not like. And at the other extreme, when the feeling tone is favorable to the corporate image, we persistently look for the good side of every experience with this company and its products. This is why any consideration of corporate images has to be concerned with feeling tone and emotive components as well as with the functional and intellectual meanings.

The extreme difficulty of changing a negative image stems from the fact that consumers' attitudes are embedded in a subrational matrix of feeling. They remain immune to logic. In our *Chicago Tribune* studies of nonconsumers in the newspaper field, these groups remained stubbornly oblivious to any changes or improvements in the newspapers they did not like. They will go on for years parroting the same attitudes which long since have ceased to have any basis in fact at all. For example, a newspaper, which had changed its name 13 years ago and had been sold in the meantime, was still associated with the same name and the same ownership as far as these nonconsumers were concerned. Their feelings simply would not let them accept reality.

In the task of molding a favorable corporate image, the public relations people can and should play an important role; there is an infinity of meanings and situations that cannot be approached with direct advertising. Public relations is a tool, however, that is little understood by management. For the most part, its use is still mired in the primitive notions of grinding out news releases or arranging for the president to speak. Public relations itself suffers from a poor image. Too many executives still characterize it as glib press-agentry. They associate it with some company frantically trying to get off the hot seat after particularly bad publicity. Rarely is it thought of as a dynamic on-going program, like the company's advertising, which in its own way can mold public attitudes.

Imaginative Imagery

The most direct, overt way for the company to project its character to the public is by advertising. I do not mean traditional institutional advertising. Much of it, in my opinion, is too stilted, too impersonal, too management oriented, and too much the same to be effective in achieving its goal of creating a favorable climate of public feeling. Certainly, sameness of approach will not build a sense of psychological uniqueness and richness for the corporate image in the public mind—and I think that is necessary. Fortunately, however, neither dullness nor conventionality is necessary. Advertising is a field for originality and imagination.

Let us begin by looking at the meaningful intangibles which advertising can develop. Taking a cue from the increased attention given to abstract symbols in corporate advertising, and from the greatly increased importance of product design and package design, it is worth exploring the nonverbal elements of advertising as significant carriers of meaning. We seem to have the habit of overlooking them.

A European social scientist singles out as an idiosyncrasy of the American mind *our tendency to evaluate all things and actions in objective and quantifiable terms.*[6] This stems from our pioneer heritage, from the settler's need for a simple way to evaluate strangers. As Americans, we have to quantify everything to prove its validity. And with this national tendency, we lose sight of the fact that humans and things can be assessed in many dimensions of meaning which are nonquantifiable, nonobjective, and nonrational. Certainly our relationships with our friends and our relatives are not formed on the basis of quantifiable meanings. Thus, individuality and richness of meaning can be created for the corporate image by approaches other than the quantifiable and rationalistic approaches of traditional institutional advertising.

This is where abstract and esthetic symbols come into the picture. Look at what some companies are doing:

☐   Alcoa pulled together many aspects of corporate meanings when it began using abstract symbols as a sort of trademark.

☐   The Ralston Purina Company no longer believes it necessary to stress the company name on its products; the red checkerboard design has more meaning and identity than does the company name. Many diverse products such as breakfast cereals, crackers, poultry feeds, and insecticides are given family identity by means of the checkerboard square.

☐   The typical corporate advertising of the aircraft manufacturers and engineering consultants should make it irrefutably clear that it is possible to create highly significant character without resorting to the sententious clichés and rudimentary functional claims customarily associated with institutional advertising.

☐   All the rational qualities of the small car have so much social currency today that it is unnecessary for Volkswagen to spell them out; the company symbol and style of advertising are sufficient to evoke all of these associations while still preserving the distinctiveness of Volkswagen.

Tone and Style

The style of advertising—literally how it is done—contributes enormously to brand and corporate images. Olivetti, for example, has used a unique style of abstract advertising to create a very distinctive quality image in the field of office machines. Any competitive manufacturer could duplicate whatever words Olivetti might choose to say about itself, but no one could retrace the corporate image created by this particular style.

The big department store has generally sensed this much better than the manufacturer. The astute store manager knows that all of his or her activities are acting as symbols to project to his or her public the store's inherent character, and therefore they should be expressive, distinctive, and congruent. In the manufacturer's terms, this means that his advertising style, his trademarks, his packaging, his stationery, his reception rooms, his general offices, his reports to stockholders, and his color schemes should be expressive—all saying the same things about the company.

The annual financial reports have become a meaningful and distinct channel of communication—and they say more than the words alone convey. For example, after looking at a Bell & Howell report, it is easy to understand the enthusiasm of investment counselors for the company. The format of the report eloquently conveys that this is a youthful, dynamic, years-ahead organization. All of this is totally apart from the content of the report. By contrast, the report of Pacific Gas & Electric unmistakably relays an image of a staid, old-fashioned management.

The retailer rarely uses straight institutional advertising. Rather, he or she sees every merchandise offering as institutional advertising. At the same time that he or she features timely merchandise, the tone and style of the advertising are proclaiming volumes of meaning about the personality of the store itself. This is why the manufacturer should see his regular product advertising as contributory to the corporate image. Regardless of how little or how much it is conveying about the company as a maker of the product, it is saying *something*.

Conclusion

There is no one corporate personality. There cannot be because every firm has different publics, and the four primary ones—stockholders, employees, vendors, and buyers—will see different aspects of the corporate image.

Creating and selling a corporate image is far more than a task for the public relations staff. Every activity of the company adds some meaning to the public's picture of the management that is running the organization. Regardless of the complexity of the corporate structure, at the point where product and buyer come together the consumer also weighs in the balance some associations about the maker of that particular product. Many corollary meanings emerging from the corporate image can play a role in the actual purchase decision at the moment of sale.

Because any functional and price attributes of the product will be filtered through an emotional lens in the buyer's mind, it is important for the corporate image to be liked. This is why it is so necessary to consider what I call the "feeling tone" and the emotive meanings as well as the functional and rational dimensions of the corporate image.

Many channels of communication by which we humans customarily and believably convey meaning to each other are mostly overlooked by management. These avenues of meaning are particularly important in molding positive brand and corporate images. Creating a spectrum of meaningful intangibles is a dual responsibility. In advertising, for instance, the agency as the creative force has to propose symbols which will communicate successfully to the company's publics. And management has to allow such creative effort instead of holding to narrow rationalistic approaches.

Notes

1. Kenneth Henry, "Creating and Selling Your Corporate Image," *Dun's Review and Modern Industry,* July 1958, p. 32.

2. Pierre Martineau, "The Personality of the Retail Store," *HBR,* January–February 1958, p. 47.

3. Perry Bliss, "Non-Price Competition at the Department Store Level," from *Marketing in Transition,* edited by Alfred L. Seelye (New York, Harper & Brothers, 1958), pp. 161–170.

4. "How Westinghouse Builds an Image," *Printers' Ink,* July 4, 1958, p. 40.

5. Ann Arbor, University of Michigan Press, 1956.

6. Jurgen Ruesch, "American Perspectives," *Communication—The Social Matrix of Psychiatry,* edited by Jurgen Ruesch and Gregory Bateson (New York, W. W. Norton & Co., 1951).

12

Make the Most of Your Corporate Identity

WALTER P. MARGULIES

The challenges in projecting an effective image of corporate identity have become more intense than ever. This author maintains that corporate identity, far from being intangible, is a specific asset that must be managed at the highest level. He gives examples of how an orderly approach can reposition a company so as to improve its ability to obtain financing, attract new customers, protect it against tender offers, and help in its executive recruitment—all in addition to serving as a marketing stimulus.

Corporate identity programs are thrust into the limelight every now and then when some large company changes its name or displays its old name or nickname in a strikingly new fashion. Everybody seems to have an opinion about the new look or name, and there is usually much discussion about the good taste, or lack of it, on the part of the executives who made the choice.

This process may seem to involve simply putting one's best foot forward. For a small business such as a single neighborhood store, this could well be so. But for the large corporation with diverse product lines and a national or international scope, putting one's best foot forward in a manner that is compatible with overall capabilities and goals can be a difficult, intricate, time-consuming, and highly rewarding task.

In the somewhat specialized language of the field, *identity* means the sum of all the ways a company chooses to identify itself to all its publics—the community, customers, employees, the press, present and potential stockholders, security analysts, and investment bankers. *Image,* on the other hand, is the perception of the company by these publics.

A corporation influences its image by the way it manages its corporate identity and has a much greater capacity to change the public perception—for better or worse—than many executives realize.

To begin with, let's look at a hypothetical company whose mistakes are typical of several real companies and who succeeded spectacularly in transforming their weak images into *worse* ones by misidentifying their corporate identity needs.

The symptoms, fairly common ones that trouble many companies, were well defined. The diversified manufacturer made high-quality products that were among the best in the industry. Its sales had grown steadily, if not spectacularly, and its earnings performance was about average for the industry with which it was grouped (incorrectly) by security analysts. But its price-earnings ratio was the lowest of the group. Because of the low stock price, the company had difficulty in raising capital for expansion and feared it might become a victim of a takeover bid as well. In addition, it was having difficulty keeping its top sales representatives and engineers and recruiting new ones.

The name of the 115-year-old company, the executives reasoned, was too closely identified with the past. It decided therefore that it needed a zippy new name and a sleek new look. The art department came up with a crisp rendition of the company's initials, and the new name was born. The company redesigned its stationery and began replacing the old name with the initials on its packages, a few products at a time, as the supply of old materials ran out.

But things got worse. It turned out that the old name had actually been the strongest element in the corporation's identity. The public—both consumers and the financial community—continued to refer to it by the old name, as did many of its own salespeople.

The only element (the old name) that unified its many products now coexisted, often on the same shelf, with the new initials. Lacking specific instructions as to how to implement the name change locally, many divisions and individual plants never did make the change to the new initials or adopt the new stationery, which further compounded the confusion.

Let's discuss what the company did right and then all the things it either did wrong or failed to do in addressing its identity problem.

First, the company recognized that it had a corporate identity problem. So much for what it did *right*. Now for the failures:

1   The company failed to study its needs in detail.
2   It failed to diagnose its product identity problem—too many products were not identifiable either with each other or with the corporation because of a confusing coexistence of names and designs.
3   It then disposed of its strongest corporate identity asset, the old name, for lack of adequate information.

4 It added to the confusion by failing to coordinate the introduction of the new name on a companywide basis.

5 It did nothing to clarify to security analysts the industry group to which it correctly belonged or to otherwise improve its standing in the financial community. In fact, its inept handling of the new name had quite the opposite effect.

To sum up, the company had attempted to solve deep problems with cosmetics.

How to Get Started

A successful corporate identity program certainly requires the involvement and support of the company's chief executive officer. The CEO will, of course, ask many tough questions before endorsing a program. A big one, expressed in the popular catchphrase, is likely to be "What's the bottom line?"

It is, unfortunately, the wrong question.

If this seems heretical, let me hasten to point out that investors are willing to pay far more for the bottom line of some companies than for others; that is, the price-earnings ratios of even highly similar companies can differ dramatically. A major factor in such discrepancies is the way companies are perceived by present or potential investors and their advisers.

A classic example arose a few years ago, when conglomerates were in disfavor with the financial community. Two giant, nationally known companies were both involved in electronics, EDP, aerospace, aircraft, communications, military supplies, chemicals, marine products, education, transportation, and consumer products. One company, perceived as a conglomerate, had a price-earnings ratio of 6, while the other was not regarded as a conglomerate and had a multiple of 32. In other words, one company's bottom line was worth more than five times as much to the investor, largely as a result of public perception of its performance and prospects. The "conglomerate," incidentally, was LTV; the other company was General Electric.

The argument over conglomerates has since faded, and the price-earnings gap between LTV and GE has narrowed somewhat. But even at present, when sky-high multiples have virtually disappeared, examples of striking discrepancies in the relative market prices of similar stocks are abundant.

The point is that investor perceptions, correct and incorrect, influence a company's ability to perform in the financial marketplace. But, as we have seen, investors are only *one* of the many publics whose perceptions affect corporate success. For many companies, final approval of the sale of their product or service may involve the opinions of a customer's board members about the seller's overall corporate capabilities.

A corporation that is doing a good job of marketing its products effectively could still have difficulty obtaining financing for expansion because the financial community perceives the company as sedentary. It may not be able to recruit the brightest business school graduates; or it may find itself an easy target for a takeover bid because its stockholders have negative sentiments about its management.

It should be remembered that different companies require different financial relations strategies. A company with a small stock float and a company whose shares are widely held by large institutional investors cannot always benefit from the same program. Some case histories of successful corporate identity efforts involving some of the same problems faced by our composite company may serve to demonstrate the techniques that the specialized communications field uses today.

When the Name Doesn't Fit

A decision to change a well-established identity cannot be taken lightly. It would seem foolhardy, as our composite example shows, for a large corporation to substitute an unknown name for one that has become highly esteemed by the public and by the business and financial communities.

Yet U.S. Rubber reached just such a decision and made a highly successful name change to Uniroyal, initially chosen as a cohesive, communicative name and eventually adopted as its new legal name. But the name change, unlike that of our mythical company, was only one result of a corporate identity program that addressed itself to the peculiar difficulties that can arise as a corporation grows and diversifies its operations.

The problem with the old name was twofold: neither "U.S." nor "rubber" correctly described the company's activities. It had become a multinational company with more sales abroad than in the United States, and its product line had come to include chemicals, plastics, fibers, and many other products, in addition to rubber.

The large number of products was a problem in itself. More than 400 brand names were used for the company's thousands of products produced by plants in 23 countries. A company official summarized the problem in these words: "Everywhere, U.S. Rubber seems to be doing business as a small local company. Nobody gets the idea that it is a worldwide corporation."

The search for a new name was begun. It had to be suitable for almost all potential markets; without geographic or cultural restrictions; applicable to all products, divisions, and affiliates; free of embarrassing meanings in major foreign languages; and it should relate, if possible, to major brand franchises. The name also had to be brief, adaptable to visual presentation, unique, and legally available. And, of course, it had to project desirable attributes.

Thousands of possible names were generated by a computer and screened before the name Uniroyal was chosen. This name proved highly suitable to an integrated international enterprise. It expresses the company's international stature, binds together its many parts, and contains nothing to offend nationalistic feelings. It also retains the equity the company had in its largest selling tire, U.S. Royal.

But the corporate identity program did not begin with a new name and certainly could not end at that point. Exploiting the Uniroyal mark required a threefold program of graphics, nomenclature, and application. Research had already shown the graphic versatility of the name. The role of nomenclature was to wed the symbol to the generic names of divisions and affiliates so as to identify every part and function of the company in a uniform way.

Successful performance in these two fields created the opportunity to embrace all potential uses. But application involved an even more extensive effort, which included these steps:

☐   Preparing a corporate identity manual to ensure uniform application of the symbol's various forms in all possible situations.

☐   Meeting with company managers and department heads to explain the identity system.

☐   Indoctrinating all divisional sales executives.

☐   Discussing the new communications philosophy with union leaders.

☐   Addressing financial audiences to clearly explain the new name.

☐   Communicating the change and the rationale behind the name change to the company's shareholders.

☐   Preparing advertisements for media throughout the world.

☐   Mailing announcement brochures to 60,000 employees and letters to twice as many major customers.

The public announcement of the new corporate name and logotype, its accompanying internal communications efforts, and the resulting external publicity made the initiation of the new symbol an international event. But the hard work of the week-in, week-out advertising of brand name products, which will eventually have the greatest impact worldwide, is necessarily a continuing activity, as is promoting the name under which the stock is sold.

Humana, Inc. is typical of the many companies that have solved a number of problems with a well-executed identity program. Humana was originally called Extendicare, and in the mid-1960s was a large operator of nursing homes. In the late 1960s, it changed its focus to management of health-care institutions and operation of hospitals. The nursing home scandals of other companies rubbed off on Extendicare, and its stock slumped. Research showed that brokers were routing customers away from Extendicare simply because of the industry it was in. After it undertook a corporate identity program, changing its name to Humana and overhauling all its corporate and financial communications, its market position improved considerably.

Another recent example of the same kind of problem encountered by U.S. Rubber and Extendicare was United Aircraft's case of mistaken identity. While it was and is engaged in designing and building aircraft products, for many years the company had been extending its aerospace-based technological know-how to a wide variety of other fields, including electrical power generation and transmission, industrial processes, electronics, communications, marine propulsion, appliance and automotive systems, laser technology, and automotive diagnostics and controls.

Yet the company was less known than many of its subsidiaries, despite the fact that it was among the famous Dow-Jones "30 industrials." It continued to be identified principally with aircraft manufacture, when it was not confused with United Air Lines. Since the security analysts who followed the company were usually those who followed the airframe companies, United tended to share the relatively low price-earnings characteristics of that volatile and cyclical industry dependent on defense contracts. This severely limited its growth potential and its proper recognition.

What all of United's activities had in common was their high technology. A study of the company's communications needs led not only to a new name, United Technologies, but to a clarification and strengthening of the corporation's sense of its own future, as well as a plan for compatible acquisitions.

One immediate result has been that Wall Street interest in United Technologies is no longer confined to analysts who follow the airframe manufacturing group. Its price-earnings ratio has improved. The company now has applied its high-technology capabilities to consumer products and has grown impressively in recent years.

Establishing an Identity

Not all corporate identity programs are therapeutic, that is, a response to specific ills. When introduction of a new product or service creates an entirely new business for an established company, an identity program can help the company through the difficult first stages as well as provide a solid base for continuing operation. Such was the case with First Federal Savings & Loan of Lincoln, Nebraska.

Electronic transfer of funds, the computer-based system that enables customers to deposit, withdraw, or transfer money at any location equipped with a special computer terminal, is revolutionary. All the customer needs is a coded plastic card. The implications are immense. The spread of such systems could dramatically change the way people handle their money. But these implications do not translate into an automatic marketing success.

One of the earliest institutions to market the systems was First Federal and its subsidiary, TMS Corporation of America. Computer terminals have been installed in a number of Nebraska supermarkets, and TMS is now licensing the operation in other regions of the country.

TMS quickly recognized the need for a strong identity program. Their efforts began with a series of attitudinal surveys among savings and loan executives nationwide to discover how other institutions felt about electronic funds transfer. The results led to the development of specific marketing strategies, among which was a complete graphics system, including a plastic card designed to accommodate individual signatures of participating institutions.

The card was part of a marketing package called "The Money Service," which included point-of-purchase displays, decals, countertop posters, booklets, stationery, and business forms. But the identity program did not stop there; it also encompassed a broadcast and newspaper advertising campaign.

Thus the program was a far cry from the mere design of a logotype, and it was rewarded with nationwide success and public recognition of the TMS service.

Going Beyond the Name

For Hardee's Food Systems, anticipation of corporate-identity needs helped to head off potential marketing problems and also served as an immediate stimulus to sales. Hardee's is a highly successful operator and franchiser of more than 1,000 restaurants in 34 states and one of the largest fast-food operations in the country.

Hardee's had to project sales appeal to potential franchisees and investors as well as to its customers, but, in doing so, it had to avoid a hard sell promotional look that many communities were finding objectionable.

A comprehensive communications, marketing, and design audit was conducted. All facets of restaurant operation and appearance were investigated, including signs, menus, roadside visibility, restaurant surfaces, and packaging and paper products. The shape and style of the facilities were also considered. The 12-week audit provided a foundation for Hardee's overall repositioning in the marketplace as a nationally known fast-food restaurant.

A prototype restaurant featuring an environmentally compatible design served as a model for new units and for remodeling of existing restaurants. It avoided the hard sell appearance that often disturbs zoning boards and was designed to meet requirements for both sales potential and cost control.

The prototype featured a distinctive mansard roof and floor-to-ceiling windows that allowed potential customers a clear view of the restaurant sales area. Specifications for construction materials were flexible, permitting the local businesspeople to select the roofing and siding that best fitted the site and community standards. Although the size of outside signs was reduced by about half, they were made more visible from a distance. Also, the new signs cost 45% less to make and about half as much to illuminate.

Sales gains averaging 35% have been registered by newly remodeled units, demonstrating that a corporate identity program can be designed to be compatible both with business and with environmental requirements.

In July 1976, shareholders learned that the company had received consent from its long-term lenders to begin a $10.5 million expansion program. The capital probably would not have been available before this effort.

The Hardee's situation is an example of a corporation that did not have a name problem but could and did profit from a program to improve its image in light of environmental considerations.

The Name May Not Be the Problem

Name changes have been a common phenomenon in recent years. But for a successful change, a company must have a clear idea of why it is necessary and of what results the company expects. When this initial assessment shows that a new name will help the company to communicate with its various publics more effectively, development of the new name can begin.

A name change alone will not modify a corporation's identity. Even the most modest identity programs must include extensive preliminary research and extensive implementation efforts for successful corporate repositioning. In some cases, a corporation's problems are so profound that new nomenclature alone is not likely to be effective. In other cases, an overly rigid imposition of the corporate name on subsidiaries would be counterproductive.

RCA Corporation has chosen to keep separate identities for Random House, which seeks to attract top authors, few of whom can identify with the parent company; for NBC, to avoid the appearance of an overly dominant parent-subsidiary relationship because of potential regulatory problems; and for Hertz, to keep the complaints that are an occupational hazard of its business from rubbing off onto the parent.

For FMC Corporation, on the other hand, the high visibility of many divisions proved undesirable because the parent did not have a well-established identity. This is often the case with industrial companies with relatively small advertising budgets. Such names as Link-Belt, John Bean, American Viscose, and Niagara Chemical obscured the image of the parent, FMC.

The repositioning program for FMC involved a study of its marketing capabilities that resulted in a redefinition of its subcorporate nomenclature and a clarification and regrouping of the company's marketing expertise. Most divisions were renamed generically to express their particular expertise, with the FMC logo added for corporate continuity.

Another example of a nonchange of name was Bendix Corporation. Because extensive consumer advertising had established it as a maker of washing machines, it continued to be identified as such long after it went out of the washing machine business. Bendix industrial products were well respected, but because of the small size of industrial advertising budgets, these operations did not have a strong public identity.

The question that had to be answered was "What is the real Bendix?" Top management became involved in what might be described as a search for the corporate essence, and this was the important first step in successfully repositioning Bendix and cementing its well-established skills to its existing name through a companywide communications program reaching customers, the financial community, and the general public.

The principal lesson of these examples is that a new name is only a single, though quite visible, part of a corporate identity program. In some cases it is only a cosmetic change, which would obscure rather than enhance corporate identity.

A single negative example may serve to reinforce this point. When Universal Oil Products changed its name to UOP Corporation, it decided to try to register the initials on the public consciousness by running an advertising campaign that asked the question "What is a UOP?" After all the company's expensive efforts, people are still wondering what a UOP is.

The Benefits

In summation, a corporate identity program is ideally a systems approach to management of a tangible corporate asset. It should begin with research and in-depth analysis to clarify how the company itself perceives its corporate assets.

When this self-perception is measured against the views that are found among the company's various publics, steps can be taken to refocus the public perception and even, when necessary, the corporation's view of itself. Identity programs that accomplish both are remarkably effective and are also long-lasting.

The program may include stronger financial communications planning, a different marketing thrust, redefinition of product uses, and many other activities. In each case, the action involves intensifying and redirecting an existing strength.

An important benefit is emphasis on the corporation as an integral whole—to employees as well as to other publics. Among Wall Street institutional analysts especially, the whole corporation can indeed be greater than the sum of its parts.

To ensure that the graphics system is used effectively, a management guide to the application of the system is invaluable. A transition to the new identification system under the supervision of a staff officer or a specially appointed identity manager is recommended. Like any corporate program, repositioning of identity must be *managed*.

13
Present Value
of Corporate History

GEORGE DAVID SMITH and LAURENCE E. STEADMAN

Corporations, like individuals, have more than skeletons in their closets. They have accumulated ways of doing things. And, like individuals, corporations may benefit from the old ways of doing things but may also become unable to adapt during periods of change. At these times, managers can look at the history of an organization to find ways it adapted in the past.

A history is also useful as a diagnostic tool and as a way of calling up great moments from the past to motivate employees in the present. A company's history contains its heritage and traditions, which managers need to understand if they are to see the present as part of a process rather than as a collection of accidental happenings. Perceiving a company in this way can enhance a manager's ability to plan for the future. Managers need to learn how to develop historical resources and how to put them to use.

Rather than sophisticated planning systems and guidelines, what ultimately gives managers confidence in their decisions is their accumulated knowledge of the way things work—their experience. Out of their own sense of the past, managers necessarily formulate visions of the future. But frequently executives have to consider the experience of the organization, in which their own histories are limited. A more systematic and rigorous approach to the past is crucial if they are to achieve a sense of the corporate past greater than their own peculiar memories of it.

A history of the company is an important though generally unexploited corporate resource. It has many values extending well beyond the celebratory function of the conventional "company history," in either its publicity brochure or anniversay-book form.

Some companies, like Citicorp, AT&T, and Consolidated Edison, have recently commissioned scholarly historical research on strategy, structure, and the decision-making process that is useful to the companies' managers. For the most part, however, the problem with company history, to steal a phrase from Henry Ford, is that too much of it is more or less bunk.

Most histories are self-serving celebrations or sensational exposés, two sides of the same worn coin. And most managers we interviewed regard the histories that their companies have commissioned as amusing but not very useful. They see them as full of apocryphal anecdotes, burdened with pointless routine and detail, or too focused on some particular event to be of value. As H. Peers Brewer, a corporate planning vice president at Manufacturers Hanover Bank and an ardent reader of history, argues: most internally generated histories are "too superficial, too low in thematic content, and too low in their levels of abstraction" to be either useful to managers or trusted by historians.

Most company histories deal with the contents of a corporation's past, rather than with its essence. They should concentrate on the dynamic accumulation of past events and decisions that have abiding significance for the present and the future.

As part of a 10-year planning effort, for example, Citicorp treated its corporate character and long-term success not as static givens but as a historical process. It correctly recognized that the present is a moment in the past's trajectory into the future. Corporate history can be a way of thinking about the company, a way of comprehending why the present is what it is and what might be possible for the future.

Thinking historically about the company does not, however, necessarily result in a company's developing scholarly histories like Citicorp's or AT&T's. We studied several corporations to determine what types of historical investigation are the most useful and legitimate for a company's purposes. Although we mainly investigated large corporations, much of what we discuss applies to smaller companies of more limited resources as well. Once managers recognize the value of the corporate past, they can enhance their ability to diagnose problems, reassess policy, measure performance, and even direct change.

Coping with Change

A little more than a decade ago, a large and successful technology-based company found itself at a strategic crossroad. Since World War II, the company had employed a decentralized management structure and a strategy of product diversification. It had increasingly relied on debt financing. By the late 1960s, for internal as well as environmental reasons, these characteristics had become dysfunctional. Unprofitable lines of business had developed, and the technological heart of the business exerted too little influence.

The company's top managers engaged a business historian to help them understand some of the long-term strategic and structural issues they would face correcting the trends of decentralization and diversification. One of the historian's more important tasks was to develop a corporatewide educational program to acquaint managers with the need for change.

The managers read cases on the company's history replete with stories of changing strategies, organizational innovations, and various management styles. The program presented data on the company's long-term financial policies, research and development, manufacturing output, and sales. The historian took care to distinguish the abiding from the transient characteristics of the business.

Managers learned that the organizational forms and management styles with which they had become familiar and comfortable were really impermanent and had, to a great extent, outlived their usefulness. They were reminded that decisions and structures are not absolute but adjust to changing circumstances. In the company's own pre-World War I corporate organization, they found an instructive analogy for the impending new order.

Business historians undertake several important jobs: first, to understand a company's history in great detail; second, to convey this history to present-day managers; and finally, to act as agents of change. For these functions the historian's training as scholar and teacher is essential. By stretching managers' awareness of the company beyond their immediate experiences, the historian enhances their ability to direct and cope with change.

History as a Diagnostic Tool

Managers at every level of the corporation, from the boardroom to the shop floor, have a need for a history of the company that is larger than their own experience. Indeed, an innovative manufacturer of consumer goods facing a serious labor relations problem in an extremely important plant made one of the most powerful managerial applications of historical thinking we have found. Founded 15 years earlier as a "model environment" for its workers, the plant had (after strong beginnings) suffered serious problems in morale, in relations between superiors and subordinates, and in productivity. According to one company executive, everyone remembered that in the 1960s the plant was well oiled and its employees ambitious and productive. "The intent was good, the structures were good, morale was high—but it went bad." By 1975 no one knew why.

An internal adviser quickly noticed that a certain potent wistfulness crept into people's voices when they spoke about the plant's early years. Suspecting that people were succumbing to the good-old-days syndrome, he thought he should get the facts about what really happened to demythologize the nostalgia. A social scientist who had no ax to grind was hired to construct a history of the plant.

Having little documentary evidence to work with, the social scientist used interviews with all the employees—sometimes singly, sometimes in groups. To thoroughly reconstruct the past and to establish a precise chronology of events, he anchored the employees' accounts on the measurable and verifiable evolution of the plant's technology and its changing output volume. In consultation with the plant's management and hourly employees, he developed an objective account: a common history that was more than the sum of the particular memories of the people who had lived it.

The history revealed that during the years when the company was rapidly upgrading the technology, no one noticed incipient problems in operations. As the plant grew from a small, experimental, collegial shop into a larger, more routinized, hierarchical bureaucracy, it required a different kind of management. As new executives attempted to manage the new standardization and demands for heightened productivity, they made decisions that unwittingly violated hourly employees' long-held work habits and expectations about decision-making processes, standards of conduct, tasks, and relationships among employees on the plant floor.

While management failed to recognize the ways in which it had gradually undermined employee trust and expectations, the hourly employees neither realized the sources of outside pressures on management nor understood them (although they indirectly experienced them). For instance, when division heads pushed for tighter controls to sustain successful operations, hourly employees couldn't see that increasing interdepartmental competition for corporate resources induced the controls.

Eventually it became obvious that the organization and its products had grown old together. As its initial products reached the end of their life cycle, the plant had to compete with newer facilities making new-generation goods. When the plant shifted its operations toward more diverse industrial and commercial applications which required more stringent tolerances and shorter production runs, managers had to adapt existing technology. And as able and ambitious employees transferred to newer operations, it became increasingly difficult for plant managers to hold down unit costs. At the same time, they had little control over product or capital decisions.

Things were so bad that a new plant manager even encountered problems getting labor and management to sit at the same table. When he finally succeeded, they began by studying the corporate history. Learning the plant's common history had a liberating effect on the employees. They began to understand management's problems and to gain a better sense of the economic and organizational realities of the company. Managers, in turn, began to see how employee trust had eroded, and they acknowledged the legitimacy of the employees' sense that their expectations and rights had somehow been violated.

Instead of pointing fingers at each other, people began to ask the basic question, "What happened?" After discussing answers, the parties agreed to work on solutions to their common problems. As a result, labor-management relations have vastly improved, information flows more easily from the top down, and employees more readily respond to work-related requests.

Using the original technology with some modifications, the plant is now a very strong generator of income, producing some of the highest-margin products of the company overall. And (according to one internal account) instead of seeing the plant as a dying organization, people now see it as a testing ground for new ideas and an exporter of talent to the rest of the corporation. A detailed case study of the plant's past has become required reading for new employees. According to one company executive, the understanding the company gained from the experience is being applied to a new overseas operation.

The current plant manager, an employee of the company for over a decade, contends that charting the plant's history gives people a sense of what has happened in "real time"—an experience of the company larger than their own participation in it or perceptions of it. Those involved thus came to understand the significance of events they had lived through, whose underlying meaning they had not sensed at the time.

History as Analogy

While every organization develops its own peculiar history and culture, different organizations often face similar problems. The learning achieved by one is frequently transferable to another. The people in the foregoing example took this to heart, and benefits continue to accrue.

This transferability is, of course, the whole point of teaching business cases: many are often like short histories. But while we all acknowledge the value of business cases in an academic setting (where they become kinds of parables of instruction), not so many see that cases can also serve managers as episodes to illuminate organizational processes.

Corporate histories, especially histories of older companies with continuity in a single industry, often contain analogues to contemporary concerns that can illuminate durable truths and reveal lost lessons about the fundamental nature and operations of particular industries. In a 1955 study of the Singer Sewing Machine Company, for example, Andrew B. Jack noted two contemporary sets of problems that had strong analogues in the company's nineteenth-century experience.

During the 1950s, Singer was using many of the techniques in marketing to certain foreign countries that it had applied a century before to domestic areas with a similar level of economic development. Moreover, certain contemporary problems Singer had in working with modern appliance dealers corresponded, amid strikingly parallel conditions of market growth and product development, to problems it had in th 1850s dealing with franchised agencies.[1]

History, of course, never repeats itself exactly, and it is dangerous to rely uncritically on the past to predict the future. Even so, lessons are there to be learned. Sometimes a history's relevance lies in pointing out the irrelevant. Sometimes finding out why and how watershed decisions were made reveals not only their latent significance or comparative value but also their pertinence to the present.

One company developed a marketing policy very early in its life for reasons that made eminent sense at the time. Over the years the policy assumed an inviolable stature as "the way we do business." On the ground that something inherent in the business demanded continuation of the status quo, managers defensively dismissed challenges to the policy from within the company as well as from customers.

A consideration of the historical context of the original decision revealed that it had been made under conditions—financial, legal, and technological—that no longer existed. The question then shifted to its proper place: not "Did the policy work in the past?" but "Is it relevant now and will it be useful later?"

History as Heritage

Resurgent interest in corporate cultures has led sociologists, anthropologists, and other students of organizational behavior to serious study of the role traditions play in the life of a company. Every company, even a new one, has a heritage and a body of tradition. If the company's heritage is the whole of its discoverable history, then we can define tradition as the selective transmission of that heritage. In other words, tradition can be thought of as the company's surface memory—the folklore, ritual, and symbols that represent the company's sense of its origins, purpose, and identity over time. Company tradition is passed on formally through orientation programs, written histories, tangible symbols, and policies. It is also informally transmitted through stories and routines people accept as standard. All traditions are embedded in the past but alive in the present. For this reason, their history is vital.

As it does in all cultures, tradition plays an important role in maintaining culture. But corporate cultures are more circumscribed, more easily altered, more manageable than the cultures of society. Managers, moreover, have long been aware of the motivational benefits of corporate tradition. In a study of the oral tradition at Hewlett-Packard (a company only a generation old), an authority on corporate folklore explains how the retelling of a story about the "Nine-Day Fortnight" has become an informal but powerful vehicle for boosting employee morale.[2]

Ten years ago Hewlett-Packard avoided a mass layoff during an industrywide financial crisis by having everyone work only nine of every 10 days and take a 10% cut in pay. This episode has become a tale which old-timers tell to ensure newcomers that Hewlett-Packard takes care of its own. Moreover, the attitude the story reflects is now the basis for management's actions during hard times. In an industry short on skilled and experienced people, employee loyalty is one of Hewlett-Packard's prized assets.

But as we have seen, traditions that maintain the status quo can become liabilities when changing times demand new approaches. For example, the historical benevolence of one major retailer toward its work force has evolved in ways that constrain the company's ability to compete. Too often it has retained indifferent workers while insufficiently distinguishing outstanding performers from the pack. According to one report, this traditional paternalism, rooted in an early company manifesto, may have cut into the company's profitability and ability to compete against energetic newcomers in its field.[3]

Understanding how corporate paternalism evolved at this retailer versus how it evolved at Hewlett-Packard might reveal ways in which companies can either build or hurt employee effectiveness.

Times of great change or devastating crisis also call traditions and long-standing habits into question. When corporate traditions are challenged, managers can consult the company's heritage, ask questions, and relate newly discovered or long-forgotten events to contemporary concerns.

A heritage is often broad enough to support multiple traditions, some of which the corporate consciousness brings to the surface or submerges according to changes in circumstance. For example, as AT&T moves from the "age of telephony" into the "age of information," market forces and political pressures have called into question the basic ethos of the company as a public service corporation. Competitive pressures have shaken its tradition of benign bureaucratic management (which had stayed essentially unchanged in a regulated environment for 60 years) to its core. New communication technologies, impending legislation, and changing markets have forced AT&T to develop a new breed of manager—more entrepreneurial, more competitive, and more attuned to the marketplace.

Also, since the mid-1970s AT&T has been reorganizing its structure from a function-oriented to a marketing-oriented organization. The effects of this reorganization are reverberating throughout the Bell System. A recent regulatory decision that AT&T should separate the regulated from the unregulated Bell System businesses and find appropriate organizational forms for each has put immense pressure on AT&T's management to change and adapt.

Speaking recently about the company's reorganization and the attendant shocks to AT&T's traditional value system, Chairman and CEO Charles Brown noted that the attempt to sustain the old service ethic with a "new spirit of venturesomeness . . . carries with it the risk of corporate schizophrenia. For, to put it mildly, not in all respects do compulsions of the marketplace match the public interest obligations of a regulated public utility." But, said Brown, AT&T must reconcile this apparent duality into a single corporate character, using its history and heritage as its "surest guide."

To put it another way, AT&T's problem is to manage the required change with a sense of continuity—a sense of staying true to itself that is especially important to a company with a long history and deep-seated traditions. "Sense of continuity," says Vice President and Assistant to the Chairman Alvin von Auw, "is the strongest influence on the decision-making process at AT&T." When top management formulates policy, it often consciously keys the policy to AT&T's traditions. An internal booklet on policy, replete with writings of AT&T chairmen and presidents, provides a starting-off point for new policy statements.

The historical research on AT&T currently under way confirms what the company's executives intuitively grasp—namely, that the company's heritage supports alternative traditions. As it enters the less regulated, more technologically explosive world of the 1980s, AT&T's managers can look back at the company's risky and entrepreneurial beginnings in an ill-defined market with a novel technology. AT&T managers can learn a lot from previous encounters with heavy competition and the profound strategic and structural transformations that marked the company's history before it took its modern form in the 1920s.

The Discipline of Thinking Historically

In the examples we've discussed, historical thinking was not undertaken in the detached removes of the university library or the scholar's study. It took place in the active life of the business, where managers applied it to practical problems in which they had a real and current stake.

In thinking historically, however, managers should follow *some* formal rules. History is, after all, a discipline and—like economics, psychology, or physics—has its own approaches, methodologies, and constraints. While professional historians concern themselves routinely with methodology as they strive to perfect their craft, we'll simply note a few key attributes of historical thinking that the manager should bear in mind. Studying history entails the ability to:

☐ See and explain the flow of events as a process over time, not just a sequence of isolated happenings.

☐ Approach the past with a sense of surprise—that is, regard events and decisions as uncertain and thus recapture them unaffected by their real outcomes.

☐ Treat any part of the past on its own terms and in ways that would have been comprehensible to people of that period. (Our natural tendency is to distort the past by reading it in light of our own experiences, ideas, and values.)

☐ Understand particular historical problems or episodes in their contemporary social, intellectual, political, and economic contexts.

In order to discriminate between good and bad historical data, it is especially important for managers studying corporate history to have a strong knowledge of contexts. Moreover, the available records may be scarce or idiosyncratic and the most relevant reasons for decisions may not have been recorded at all. Indeed, re-creating the past is often a matter of intelligently plugging the gaps with well-reasoned historical judgment.

Importance of Memory

Historical judgment cannot be applied in a vacuum. Because memory is crucial, the preservation and management of the corporate memory are among the truly important (though often neglected) tasks of the modern corporation.

Every organization has a memory, even if it is little more than the body of anecdotes illustrating something about corporate life that is passed from one generation to the next. Even bureaucratic forms, simple routines of work, standards of dress and protocol, or styles and arrangements of furniture convey impressions of the past, the corporate culture, and the company's identity and purpose.

The best support for the corporate memory remains a well-preserved and easily retrieved record of events and decisions. Some corporations have undermined their ability to make sound decisions through careless destruction of critical records or simply inattention to old data. As Earl F. Cheit, dean of the school of business at Berkeley, recently noted: it is "ironic . . . that at a time when all American institutions are becoming sensitive to the need to think beyond the short run, the very store of knowledge that could contribute most to the development of a longer-term point of view is being weakened."[4] The tendencies toward mergers, acquisitions, and appointments of outside top managers and directors, plus greater reliance on oral communication, have all contributed to a weakening of corporate memory.

Compounding the problem are the "records management" programs that destroy records rather than discriminately preserve them. In their fear of increasing the risk of litigation, some managements have carried the spirit of records destruction to ludicrous extremes.

One large company cited for antitrust violations many years ago found that, during the course of the trial, its position was unexpectedly attacked on the basis of what it had regarded as an insignificant internal memorandum. The corporate response was to defend itself against future legal assaults by taking no minutes of high-level organization meetings.

The result was isolation and confusion. The company did not destroy merely its history of 50, 20, or 2 years past; it destroyed its formal remembrance of yesterday. Managers quickly discovered they could not remember what had been agreed to or why or who had taken what positions on an issue. They lost their ability to reconstruct decisions, all for the sake of obviating unpredictable legal hassles.

Fortunately, many organizations are now systematically preserving significant records in the belief that the benefits outweigh the risks. Wells Fargo, Foremost-McKesson, Chase Manhattan Bank, AT&T, and the New York Stock Exchange are developing sophisticated, high-level archival programs. Wells Fargo, for instance, has a department of history staffed by professional historians, archivists, and curators.

Others, such as International Harvester, General Motors, Ford, CocaCola, and the Bank of America, already have splendid archives. Iron-

however, managers rarely tap archives for practical business applications. The problem, as one public relations executive told us, lies in getting top-level support to take what people ordinarily think of as "just a collection of dusty documents" and turn them into a "living resource."

Creating a living archive is not simply a case of preserving important economic, financial, and legal records or of enshrining formal statements of policy, strategy, and public relations. Correspondence, memoranda, recorded interviews, and even informal notes that might shed light on the decision-making processes of the organization must be available for study and analysis.

Peter Drucker has suggested four areas in which managing for the future requires careful assessment of the past: capital appropriations, personnel decisions, innovation, and analysis of strategies. Archives should be geared to the historical evaluation of the company's management and its ability to move from problems to decisions to desired outcomes.[5]

Applications and Wider Significance

Historical thinking can enhance some concrete corporate tasks (see Exhibit 1). These tasks range from public relations to corporate planning and include market research, legal support, and personnel.

The development of good corporate history has importance for historians as well. Lying at the heart of our technological, social, and economic development, the corporation has become a central institution of contemporary society. Well-researched historical cases would not only broaden the base for business scholarship but also inform public policy. Policy is sometimes weak in historical understanding of the private corporation, its dynamics, and its long-term relationship to, and impact on, society.

At Citibank, historians look forward to preparing historically based arguments about the ways government controls have succeeded or failed in their industry. According to Harvard's Thomas McCraw, an expert on the history of regulation, business executives and regulators have a long way to go in sorting out successful from unsuccessful patterns of business regulation. Rhetoric too often substitutes for understanding.

Thus, at one level, good corporate history contains meaning through which mangers can relate their own experiences and values to the larger life of the company. At another level, it relates the company's long-term role to the larger life of society.

Preserving the Corporate Memory

The story is told that when David Rockefeller was preparing for a trip to China, he asked an assistant to go to the Chase Manhattan archives to find out something about the bank's early dealings in the Far East. When the assistant reported back that there *were* no archives, Rockefeller was astonished. An archival program was promptly begun.

Exhibit 1. Corporate Applications of Historical Research

Focus	Products of research	Purpose
Corporate planning	Studies of the fundamental strategic and structural development of the company	To help avoid irrelevant or misguided trajectories into the future, ensures that assumptions about the past and present are correctly based
	Case studies of corporate successes and failures suggesting effective and ineffective courses of past action and their determinants	
	Studies of specific past policies, strategies, or decisions to determine their relevance in current contexts	
	Studies of the causes and evolution of specific contemporary problems	
	Studies of the abiding and transient features of the corporate culture	
Management development	In-house publications or programs for acculturation of new employees	To provide managers with an experience and knowledge of the company larger than their own
	Case studies for management training programs	
	Resource materials for diagnosing organizational ills and for reorienting managers in times of change	
Marketing	Themes for advertising	To help differentiate the company from its competitors, to authenticate advertising, and to support market-planning efforts

Exhibit 1. *(Continued)*

Focus	Products of research	Purpose
	Development and maintenance of corporate and brand images	
	Analysis of historical market entry into and exit from target communities	
Legal support	Assemblies of primary resources for legal research	To supplement the specialized legal resources of the company with expertise in either more general or more historically arcane research problems.
	Determinations of facts in support of legal claims, positions, or briefs	
	Briefings for attorneys as to the underlying social, political, and economic reasons for past events and decisions together with their specific causes and consequences. Especially valuable for antitrust or regulatory proceedings in which historical patterns and relationships loom large	
Public affairs	Collections of relevant histories or historical data for company officials responsible for dealing with outside agencies and stakeholders (e.g., regulatory bodies, lawmakers, special interest groups)	To provide background and contexts for company policy and behavior to enable more informed public policy

Exhibit 1. (*Continued*)

Focus	Products of research	Purpose
Public relations	Anniversary publications	To enhance public understanding of the company and the business
	Annual reports	
	Publicity pamphlets	
	Corporate histories	
	Exhibits	
	Resources for scholars, museums, historical societies, and so forth	
Archival development	Well-indexed and accessible records concerning key aspects of the corporate history— major events, decisions, policies, strategies, and financial and operating data	To support all of the above

When senior management decides to take stock of the company's historical resources, the first thing to consider is the potentially high value-added uses of the company history:

☐ At Citibank the payoffs are seen as related to the process of corporate planning.

☐ At Consolidated Edison management succession is being aided by a history of the recent period to provide a context for decision making.

☐ At Wells Fargo, which operates in an industry with relatively undifferentiated product offerings or service offerings, the corporate history is a powerful marketing and advertising tool that gives the bank a distinctive character.

☐ At Hewlett-Packard the history has been a vehicle for sustaining employee morale.

☐ At AT&T historical research illuminates organizational issues.

☐ At General Motors the company's history is used to support programs in management education.

☐ At the New York Stock Exchange the corporate history underwrites strong university and public relations programs.

☐ Elsewhere, professional historical research serves as an aid to corporate litigation, policy reviews, and even (as we discussed) labor-management relations.

Whatever applications the company's history may have, identifying and articulating them is the first step in making the company's historical resources coherent. To do this, management needs to ask the following questions:

☐ What is the state of our corporate memory? What records-management policies pertain to it? When did our historical resources and our policies governing them last undergo executive review?

☐ What has been written about the company? By whom? What is the general quality of such work? Does the public history of the company contain serious distortions or omissions?

☐ Does the company have a strong connection with the historical profession? What policies govern the response to legitimate scholarly interest in the company?

☐ Have historical accounts been published in such corporate publications as annual reports, house organs, and publicity pamphlets? How reliable or useful are these accounts?

☐ What historical records or resources do the company's various departments require? How, for example, is historical research for legal purposes conducted?

☐ Does the company have within it or connected to it experts who can organize, tap, and use the company's historical resources? Does the company have a professional archivist or (in smaller companies) professional archival advice? Does it maintain relations with professional historians who know how to find, assemble, and interpret historical data or train others to do these things at a parahistorical level?

Because archival organization and methodology and the contextual problems of dealing with the often scrappy remains of the past are complex and specialized, the last question is especially important.

Managers also need to consider how to preserve high-quality data for use in the future. While corporations have mastered recording of quantitative processes, such as financial reporting and accounting, they find it hard to maintain good records on the processes of management and decision making. Because the electronic age makes it possible to write instantly erasable memos, it is doubly important to have someone on board who thinks about how important problems, events, deliberations, and decisions can be preserved in the corporate memory.

Many companies are undertaking oral interviews with significant people, conducted by an expert who asks focused and probing questions. Perhaps more important, however, is the development of ongoing methods of recording and preserving important facts. Historians can help here.

And, finally, the company could develop programs that use a well-researched history. Some useful questions managers can ask are:

☐ How does the company communicate its history to new employees? What is the historical content of training programs or ongoing management seminars?

☐ Would it be useful for the company to have ongoing public relations activities based on its history? Should the company create a museum or open a library? Should the company create ties to universities, museums, historical societies, or other community agencies that might have an interest in its history?

☐ When major policy changes are debated at the senior level, does the history of existing policy inform that debate? Should histories of policies be prepared for ready access?

☐ Should histories of company strategies and other decisions be developed to assess the past performance of the corporation in qualitative as well as quantitative terms?

☐ Should histories of the company's experience with social and government pressures be prepared to aid responses to public policy debates?

Once a company takes the three basic steps toward making its history useful—establishing the high value-added uses of the company history, identifying and rationalizing its historical resources for current and future use, and developing specific programs and studies—it will find that it has acquired a powerful managerial tool. While we do not imagine that our own enthusiasm alone will convince skeptics or convert ahistorical managers, we can at least suggest that executives take a preliminary look at their corporate histories in terms of costs and benefits. If they do this seriously and conscientiously, they can assess both. We are confident they will find that the benefits dominate.

Notes

1. Andrew B. Jack, "The Channels of Distribution for Innovation; The Sewing Machine Industry in America," *Explorations in Entrepreneurial History,* February 9, 1957, p. 113.

2. See *Dun's Review,* June 1980, p. 96. A working paper by Alan B. Wilkins, "Organizational Stories as Symbols Which Control the Organization," June 1980, provides extended discussion of corporate folklore at Hewlett-Packard.

3. See *Business Week,* October 27, 1980, p. 148.

4. "How Quickly We Forget," *San Francisco Examiner-Chronicle,* November 23, 1980.

5. See Drucker, *Managing in Turbulent Times* (New York: Harper & Row, 1980), pp. 68–71.

14
Struggle for Ethics in Public Relations

DAVID FINN

To what extent should business respect the basic principles of the democratic process and the right of the people to make up their own minds, rather than attempt to engineer consent through whatever techniques seem to work?

☐ How honest a picture of its product should a company present to the public?

☐ What part should the artificial "buildup" play in the field of public relations?

☐ How far should a company go in exploiting its contacts with influential people?

☐ Is a company obligated to be truthful about labor policy, pricing, and other touchy problems?

☐ What role, if any, should ulterior motives play in framing public relations policies?

With the rapid growth of public relations activity on behalf of industry, management is being confronted more and more with the notion that it has a distinct public responsibility and an obligation to serve the public interest in the course of its business activities. Very few executives would consider it wise to repeat today, even behind closed doors, the famous, or rather notorious, words of Commodore Vanderbilt, "The public be damned!"

Whatever the reasons—genuine concern for the welfare of others, or sophisticated self-interest; strengthening of the democratic values in our society, or an increased pressure to conform and be "other-directed"—the climate of business activity has markedly changed.

It seems hard to argue with the real benefits achieved through steadily increasing public relations budgets for scholarships, research grants, art collections, and teaching aids. They suggest convincingly that, at least in some respects, the development of public relations thinking has brought about some improvement in the ethical behavior of corporations in America.

Disturbing Factors

And yet three distinct points of view are becoming increasingly evident that make it difficult to accept too readily this optimistic picture of the social value of public relations:

☐ There is the absence of idealism in management's motives for undertaking public relations activities. Hardheaded business executives look for dollar values, not rewards of altruism. Public relations must pay off somewhere along the line—whether in sales, productivity, stockholder confidence, or government support. If doing good deeds will help achieve these objectives, it can be justified. If not, money can be spent more profitably in other activities. This raises the question whether a company's public relations posture is in the last analysis a sham.

☐ Another conflicting point of view is that put forth by social critics who find the social mores of American capitalism a threat to civilization. To them, the question of sham is less important than the destructive acts committed by vested interests behind the public relations smokescreen. It is not the posture which bothers them so much as the manipulation which goes on while the pose is being struck.

☐ There is concern that public relations often leads to irresponsible and deceitful acts. Publicity stunts, false fronts, the effort to suppress negative facts, and many similar practices have brought forth a mounting chorus of criticism.

These three points of view make the evaluation of public relations a demanding task. Unfortunately, it is a subject not being discussed openly and straightforwardly in business circles, which in itself is not a good sign. Rationalizations, self-righteousness, and platitudes do not get rid of discerning challenges—nor do untalked-about skeletons in the closet make for well-adjusted consciences.

In this article I shall seek to examine the basic issues frankly and describe a new approach to the ethics of public relations for industry.

Sharper Focus

The social responsibility—or lack of it—of what management does public-relations-wise is only one factor in a total behavior pattern which embraces all company activities. Accordingly, I wonder if it is not shortsighted to equate public relations with publicity, or with defending management actions, or with building goodwill.

Would it not be better to consider that one of the major functions of a company's public relations activity is to help clarify the company's role in society? Public relations, in that sense, not only can be a tool of management; it can also have an identity of its own, serving both the public community and private industry. It has been called by some a bridge between the two. Actually, it can be more than that. It can be a method of analysis and activity by which the basic tendency of every company to both serve and exploit the community becomes apparent and is expressed.

The question, therefore, is not whether public relations is "good" or "bad." A company's public relations tends to be more ethical when it has a more positive role to play in the community; it tends to become less ethical when its role is less positive or more destructive.

If a company takes a good, hard look at the ethics of its public relations activities, it can gain an insight into how it is behaving toward the community in general. To the extent that it finds the need to strike an artificial pose when in public view, or to the extent that it finds it necessary to dissemble or keep facts out of the news, it is probably socially destructive; to the extent that it feels free to tell the truth and generate acts in the public interest, it is probably socially constructive. There is a mixture of both tendencies in all companies; learning to face that fact frankly and cope with it can become a vital aid to their health and stability.

Seminars in Ethics

Early in 1957, our public relations firm decided to do some organized thinking about developing an approach to ethics in our public relations work. We initiated a series of seminars among 10 of our top executives to undertake this task. Background information on codes of ethics developed in this country and in England and Australia was presented to the group, and we tried to examine our point of view toward these codes.

The initial spirit of the discussions was one of self-confidence. We were very pleased with ourselves for taking time out to discuss the problem at all, and we were convinced that we were very "ethical" people indeed!

By the time the third session rolled around, however, we found ourselves in the midst of a heated, hair-letting-down bout in which each participant was urging the others to "stop kidding ourselves" and "face reality." How could we in all conscience criticize others for their malpractice when, if we looked at things squarely, we would have to admit that we were guilty of pretty much the same sort of thing? In fact, everybody was guilty. To deny this would be hypocritical. And what was more, if we were going to stay in business, we would have to continue letting our consciences play second fiddle to practical considerations.

We became so involved in this discussion that we simply could not let go of it. To help us think more clearly, we decided to look for some professional help.

Developing Sensitivity

Fortunately, a group of theologians, philosophers, and scientists who had formed The Institute on Ethics expressed interest in our dilemma. This organization (interdenominational and interdisciplinary) was actually a part of a larger undertaking including The Institute for Religious and Social Studies and The Conference of Science, Philosophy and Religion, which had been in existence for 18 years, under the sponsorship of The Jewish Theological Seminary of America. While primarily interested in studying the ethical aspects of the major social issues of our day, the members were also interested in relating theory to action. They were eager to help individual groups of practical people cope with the ethical dimension in their own work.

There followed a series of seminars in which different scholars joined our own staff members to pursue the question of ethics and public relations. The conversations were tremendously exciting. We pulled no punches. In fact, many of our staff members became very aggressive about the fact that they felt we had to lie and do other unethical things in order to remain in business. It was remarkable to see the scholars roll up their sleeves and help us think through these problems, rather than express shock and dismay at the "facts of life" that we were talking about.

We have discovered, of course, that there are no simple answers. While we had apparently passed the first great hurdle when we agreed to talk among ourselves frankly and critically, the job could never be finished. We were involved in a continuing effort to develop an ethical sensitivity in decision making.

Because of this, the seminars never did come to an end. Instead, we decided to continue them indefinitely as part of our regular business procedure.

Finding the Threshold

One of the most important aspects of the problem which has become apparent to us over the years and which was re-emphasized in our discussions is the fact that each company has its own threshold of what it is comfortable in doing from an ethical standpoint.

Most companies would agree on certain obvious extremes to which they would not resort. These widespread agreements are frequently expressed in codes. But the difficulty comes in the gray area in which one person feels comfortable about telling certain kinds of untruths, or making certain kinds of bribes, or engaging in certain kinds of moderately deceitful practices, while another person feels entirely differently about it. However we rationalize these actions, it is clear that each of us has a different breaking point beyond which we would not go because it would make us too uncomfortable, too conscience-stricken. And this is our point of no compromise.

In a corporation, decisions are made continuously by executives on the basis of what they think the company threshold is, as well as their own individual thresholds. The former often exerts a greater influence than the latter. An atmosphere exists in a group in which certain types of irresponsible acts are sanctioned, and one may get the feeling that in business it is all right to have a lower ethical threshold than in private life.

This understanding is usually tacit. There is great value in making it explicit, in bringing out into the open the whole question of what we do or do not feel comfortable in doing. This enables us to examine our corporate ethical threshold in terms of our personal thresholds. If the two can be brought more in line with each other, an important step can be taken in helping individuals to identify with the company and see a value in it to which they can personally respond.

Statement of Policy

Clarification of the company's ethical threshold in public relations is one of the major responsibilities of top management. The top operating executives of a company have to decide how far they want to go in influencing the press, government, schools, public institutions, and the like. If this is left unspecified, management is failing to come to grips with the basic question of the company's role in society.

Ethics is, unfortunately, a bad word to use when executives are sitting around a table struggling with practical problems of the day. Any public relations specialist who has ever had the experience of counseling a client to do something because it is "ethical" knows this to be true. It is considered a *foreign*, if not embarrassingly *naive, word.* Most business executives react more positively to such phrases as "better from a long-range point of view," "sounder business policy," or even "good public relations" than to the idea of doing something because it is "more ethical."

Thus, in a frequently disguised form, public relations performs the role of keeping management itself in line. When functioning well, it acts as the anvil against which management's moral problems can be hammered.

This actually means that when business people apply themselves to establishing a public relations policy for their company, they are really concerned with significant ethical questions—without quite realizing it. The trouble comes when top management feels that these matters can be left in the hands of lower-echelon executives to decide, and thereby unwittingly delegates a key corporate responsibility.

Most middle-management executives seem to be in a very uncertain position when it comes to establishing corporate ethical policy. Their responsibility is clearly operational. They must produce results for the company which are as clearly as possible translatable into profits. They are afraid to think of public good because their job is to think of company good. Or, perhaps more accurately, they would like to be more concerned with the public good, but they feel obliged to suppress their personal inclinations and yield to what they think is the company pattern. Oddly enough, this pressure sometimes leads middle managers to undertake activity that, besides being inconsistent with their own ethical thresholds, is equally embarrassing to the top managers it is supposed to please.

Top management can take a significant and constructive step forward by stating clearly, positively that it is seriously concerned with its responsibility to the community. But this cannot be accomplished by a moralistic injunction to avoid unethical procedures, for this would be dismissed by all as simply putting up an innocent front to hide the dirty work. Instead, management must be prepared to face the issues honestly, letting all executives know that while it recognizes that every business decision involves compromise, it feels that the struggle to fulfill community responsibility must be vigorously pursued. Of especial importance, it should demonstrate that it is not afraid to discuss the ethical question openly, with its own employees and even with the public.

This takes courage, but it is worth it. The very process of discussion leads to a catharsis of aggressions, doubts, and guilt feelings, and ultimately to a healthier, better-adjusted, and socially more useful attitude for all employees of the company—and, of course, a deeper respect from the community.

The Major Issues

The ethical conflict in public relations for industry appears to break down into six major issues, Inevitably, discussion of any one of them boils down to the question of "Where do we draw the line?" Such discussion helps clarify the ethical threshold of the company.

In this article I cannot and shall not try to recommend an ideal ethical threshold which companies ought to develop in relation to any one of these issues. This is an individual corporate task. What follows is intended only to illustrate a method of undertaking such a task. The examples are taken from experience in our own office through the years. They cover a cross section of industry, since when a public relations firm analyzes its own ethical responsibilities, it is in fact reviewing the ethics of all of its different clients.

Artificial Images

To what extent should a company present a frank picture of its business or product, or build a corporate image designed to give the public an invented picture of the business or product, whether it is accurate or not?

There are, of course, many examples illustrating this problem. Tendencies toward artificial image making have appeared to many social critics to be as "Orwellian" as the Soviet habit of rewriting history. It gives one a sense of unreality and makes us (as members of the public) feel that we are living in a hall of mirrors.

On the other hand, public relations professionals feel that their social role can be fulfilled by improving communications in a complicated world. Image making is not supposed to be artificial, but rather clarifying, simplifying, helpful to understanding.

"Independent" Research

To illustrate the temptations, conflicts, and agonizing appraisals that can develop, here is a simple case example:

> *Company A decided to build an image of one of its major products as being purer than its competitors'. This was actually so. However, advertising claims of purity had been used and abused so heavily in the past by other companies that it decided to undertake a public relations program to get the story across. Accordingly, a complicated scheme was invented involving the development of an "independent" research report that was to provide the basis for newspaper and magazine articles.*
>
> *The trouble was that the research was engineered; in fact, it was not even to be paid for unless the publicity appeared in print. To ensure the success of the project, the man who arranged all this had some editors on his payroll as consultants for the research, thus almost guaranteeing eventual publication. It was a neat scheme—effective for the company and profitable for researcher, editor, and middleman.*

The question was: *Is this a responsible method of communicating the image of purity to the public?*

In support of the argument was the fact that the image was accurate; the product was a pure one. The public was not being deceived. It was being told the truth. And there was nothing specifically wrong with the plan. No one was being bribed to do something he should not do. The research was being done by qualified scientists.

Against the plan was the fact that it short-circuited the usual checks and balances which protect the public against deception. Normally, if the product was touted as being pure, the public could have the claim checked by truly independent research. This research could again be checked by truly independent editors, who would publish it only if it seemed valid to them. But if the cooperation of these two intermediaries could be secured by special payments, then the way would be clear to present false images to the public. This could be done simply by confining the research to those areas which would bear proof and by omitting negative areas. An aura of research could be created to prove any point, and a public relations smokescreen could be developed to hide the bad while the good shone forth.

In our discussion, the temptation to endorse the plan was very strong, since there was very little doubt that it would accomplish legitimate public relations objectives. It seemed foolish not to go ahead with it. Did not society in general operate in an atmosphere and environment in which efforts to create such disguises were largely condoned? One of the scholarly consultants at our seminar paraphrased Plato to point out that if we make the choice to live in this world where each person primarily looks out for his own gain, we have to be prepared to find some form of deception everywhere. The only way to escape this would be to retire from the world and become an anchorite.

Weighing the Risks

And yet, after a great deal of analysis, the risk of possible exposure of the whole scheme emerged as the most important consideration of all. If this happened, then the whole claim of purity, which was really based on fact, would be suspect.

Our conclusion was that if research could be conducted on a truly independent basis—and there was no reason to feel that it could not—there would be no danger whatsoever, and results would be just as effective. This was the spirit of the work sponsored by the Tobacco Industry Research Council, where funds were given with no strings attached—from all indications, a fine example of responsible public relations thinking. A prime prerequisite of such an approach, however, is that a company be prepared to face up to the consequences of independent research no matter how the chips fall.

Everybody who participated in the seminar discussion of this case history felt that the conclusion was based upon practical considerations (that is, to avoid the risk of exposure), rather than upon ethical considerations. It was pointed out, however, that Immanuel Kant and other philosophers have argued that one should not concern oneself too much about why these decisions are made, for the pragmatic and categorical imperatives become the same in the long run. Many of our ethical standards today, for example, originated with some very practical decisions made centuries ago.

The Prestige Build-Up

To what extent should a company build its growth on deserved recognition and earned prestige, and eschew the fanfare of artificially stimulated applause?

The accusation that public relations involves an artificial "build-up" is one of the most serious ever leveled at it. This has created concern for business leaders in two ways. On the one hand, some businesspeople expect that when they hire public relations counsel, they will become famous overnight; they even complain when they do not. On the other hand, some executives with a sense of modesty are afraid their public relations counsel will inflate their reputation to a point of embarrassment.

The problem has become particularly sensitive with the introduction of public relations into new fields in which, heretofore, recognition has supposedly resulted from merit alone—into the arts, religion, education, science. Many have wondered whether public relations bastardizes the higher values that people have always striven to maintain in these fields.

Prearranged Award

Here, again, general principles that seem clear enough when stated in the abstract become subject to dispute in the day-to-day conduct of business. To illustrate again from our personal experience:

> *Company B was seeking special recognition for a new variation of a standard product. To highlight the innovation, a new package had been created. The design was particularly striking, and the suggestion was made that somehow a design award should be arranged. Publicizing this award would help impress both salespeople and customers with the company's concern for high quality and, by association, would bring recognition to the new product's features.*

The question was: *Should public relations exploit only means of gaining recognition which would be above influence and partisanship?*

In support of the project was the fact that the design was of high quality and could in all probability command a citation from some authority. The latter would not be asked to give the award unless he really felt the design deserved it; so there was nothing forced about it. Without public relations effort, however, the authorities would probably not see the package design at all, and would have no opportunity to honor it. So there was legitimate reason to arrange to have the package reviewed by as many design experts as possible, with the idea of finding one of them who thought it worthy enough to give it an award.

Against the project was the closeness which this approach came to fixing judges, whether it was for design awards or anything else. To the extent that endorsement from official quarters could be arranged, we, as members of the public, would lose our respect for the standards of the judges and the integrity of their judgment. *Quality* became less meaningful if awards could be secured by able public relations people.

In our discussion, two different approaches to arranging citations were discussed.

1.   One was taken by a manufacturer who paid a fee to an organization whose business it was to give out awards that could be used for advertising purposes. This seemed to be a complete prostitution of the notion of a merited award.

2.   The other was used by a publisher who sent a copy of his product, a new dictionary, to outstanding academicians, as part of his public relations effort. The dictionary was, in fact, a pioneering achievement, and many of the recipients wrote unsolicited letters of praise. These endorsements later became the basis for an effective advertising campaign, which succeeded because the men quoted were obviously above influence.

It appeared to us that making the effort to gain recognition was not wrong. The case of the publisher illustrated this point. His project was a catalytic one in a society grown so complicated that catalysts are necessary. What we felt uncomfortable about was doing something that would undermine the basis for unbiased judgment, which could clearly result in gaining recognition where none was deserved.

Sale of "Influence"

To what extent should a company accept the criticism of editors, government officials, and other public representatives, rather than secure their support through specialists who sell their influence?

A common description of the unsavory aspects of public relations is "influence peddling." Effective public relations is supposed to be a result of knowing the right people. This means knowing the right editors, the right politicians and government officials, the right civic and industrial leaders, the right scientists and artists, and so on. Making a business out of these contacts is supposed to be the shortest road to public relations fame and fortune.

Buying Publicity

At some point, however, this road leads to abuses. For example:

> *Company C was extremely anxious to gain attention at an annual trade show. One way to accomplish this was through the local newspaper in the city in which the show was being held. The competition for publicity in that newspaper was fierce, with every manufacturer at the trade show vying for it.*
>
> *A public relations representative of Company C knew a photographer on the newspaper, and spoke to him about the problem. The photographer developed a cute idea for a specially contrived photograph which might succeed in getting the company mentioned in the newspaper. He said he would set up and take the photograph for a small fee, with the understanding that if the picture was published in the paper, he would get considerably more money.*

The question was: *Should the company exploit this special "in" with the newspaper photographer to help solve an important problem?*

In support of the plan was the argument that other companies represented in the trade show might be using similar opportunities, or would use this same one if it became available to them. It might be that the photographer himself was being unethical in his conduct, which hardly was the company's responsibility. Besides, no one was being paid directly to publish the picture; it would only be used if it was worthy. The newspaper would not be put in a position in which its standards would be compromised.

Against the proposition was the fact that the editor of the newspaper would not know that the photographer was receiving money for taking the picture or, even worse, was getting a substantial payoff if he, the editor, decided to use the photograph.

In discussing the problem, it became clear that the issue was whether or not this constituted bribery. The scholarly consultant suggested that we should all be able to agree that bribery was "wrong." But defining bribery is a difficult task in all aspects of life. It is not always easy to say where "undue" influence begins.

The conclusion we came to was that in the case of Company C the executive would feel a certain amount of pressure not to disclose the details of his arrangement with the photographer. This would mean that if the details were made public, he would feel embarrassed. This disclosure might actually harm the company and its participation in the trade show. Therefore, it would be wisest not to go ahead with the project. This same guide rule might apply in other instances where special influence is sought.

Manipulating Opinion

To what extent should business respect the basic principles of the democratic process and the right of the public to make up its own mind, rather than attempt to engineer consent through whatever techniques seem to work?

This is one of the most flaming issues in the field of public relations and ethics.[1] It involves the building up of false fronts, such as those used in the historic railroad-truck public relations battle. It is also a key question in connection with political campaigns, where candidates spend more energy on lining up support through organized public relations efforts than in making clear their position on questions of policy.

There is no doubt that a primary objective of public relations activity is to gain public support for a product, a political candidate, or any cause. There does not seem to be anything inherently illegitimate about this. On the other hand, what is the meaning of freedom in a democracy if public opinion can really be molded? Many books predict unhappy consequences for society because of the potentially diabolical uses to which effective persuasion can be put—books with belligerent titles like *The Rape of the Mind*,[2] *The Hidden Persuaders*,[3] and *Battle for the Mind*.[4]

Campaign Tactics

To judge from some of the speeches business leaders give, the less they have to do with government, the happier they are. In practice, however, just the opposite may be true. In such cases the nature of the alliance between business executives and politicians can be a controversial one. For example:

> *Campaign D centered around an amendment to a state constitution. Some business interests were directly involved with the campaign. In similar battles in other states, opposing interests on the other side had*

used "dirty tactics" and won victories although the public never really understood what the issues were. A great deal was at stake in this election.

The question was: *Should "our side" attempt to conduct as clean a campaign as possible and stand a chance to lose the election? Or should it pull out all the stops as undoubtedly the "other side" would?*

In favor of the latter course was the fact that the object of the campaign was to win the election. Those who did not sympathize with the cause did not have to work for it. But those who did, and who accepted the job of promoting it, should bend all their energies on succeeding.

The argument against this approach was that if democracy worked, it was because a well-informed electorate had made a wise decision. Our responsibility to the system of government which we endorsed was to help present the facts to the public, and be willing to accept its vote as just. Waging a dirty campaign would hardly fulfill this responsibility.

Our discussion revolved on exactly what was meant by the words "dirty campaign." In some respects, dirty seemed to mean what the other side was doing—particularly if it was winning. One problem was how far to go in the use of slogans and other emotional appeals. We wondered, for instance, about the validity of campaigning against the other side by pointing out who was supporting it—in other words, not discussing so much whether the amendment was good or bad, but suggesting that the voters could see that the other side was wrong by noticing where the money for the campaign came from. The scholarly consultant quoted Spinoza to support the proposition that one cannot persuade by reason alone; he also pointed out that arguing by imputation is legitimate, though it should not be a substitute for campaigning on the issues themselves. He felt that both should be used.

We all agreed that the line should be drawn at anything that might be considered a smear. This could backfire and lose the election, and therefore was, in practicality, bad tactics. It could also destroy people. The smear emerged as the prototype of the kind of technique which marked a program of persuasion as "dirty" or "unethical."

Truths and Untruths

To what extent does a business have a responsibility to tell the truth to the public—about prices, labor policies, and so forth—and to what extent can it afford to dissimulate?

In public relations, truth is a hard word. Businesspeople often make speeches and put their names to articles which have little or nothing to do with their own ideas or words. This has become standard practice. Liberties are often taken when information is given to the public about sales volume, number of employees, cost of products, or size of investments. The result, as in the case of the more general problem of image making, is to give rise to a fairy-tale picture of our times.

And yet, it may be argued, this is part of salesmanship. A certain amount of deviation from the truth is all right because it is comparatively harmless; it is considered a "white lie" in the business world. The problem is where to draw the threshold line. What kind of a compromise, if any, should be made between the practical world and the world of ethics and ideals?

Tempting Deception

The rationalization that a "white lie" is harmless probably had something to do with the development of the following situation:

> *Company E sold its high-quality product to a few scattered discount houses, but claimed it did not sell to any. This was common enough policy. If the truth were told, the company's regular customers would be very angry. And yet the few discount houses it did sell to brought a great deal of business.*

The question was: *Was dissimulation a justified business practice?*

In support of the position was the fact that the violations of its policy were so limited (since, for the most part, the product was kept out of discount houses) that the company was only saying what might be considered true in the broad sense. Against the position was the fact that it led the company to tell a specific untruth when talking to customers or when stating its policy publicly.

The scholarly consultant in our discussion suggested as a "piece of litmus paper" never to do anything you would not want to see published in tomorrow morning's newspaper. He suggested that the case of Company E was an illustration of this point. If key customers discovered the lie, they would seriously consider boycotting the product. He also pointed out that the company has a responsibility, not only in this instance, but whenever it gives out information. If an untruth is told about discount houses, it would hurt its credibility in other matters and therefore ultimately hurt the company's entire reputation.

The more we discussed the problem, the less reason we saw for maintaining the deception. Telling an untruth seemed the easiest way out of this troublesome situation—but by no means the best way. The major market by far for this product consisted of quality stores, and it did not seem worthwhile to jeopardize that market by flirting with discount houses. These practices cannot be hidden from the trade. The attempt to do so would sully the marketing reputation of our client, which in other respects was most highly regarded and trusted by his customers. It should be worth giving up the discount house business to protect that reputation.

Credit for Good Deeds

To what extent should business consider the ancient ethical calling to do good because it is its own reward, rather than doing good for publicity purposes?

It seems almost naive to ask the question. It has become accepted as good business practice that if acting in the public good will win friends for the company, then it is good public relations. And since this type of thinking seems to bring benefits to society, why question it?

Yet this is exactly the fundamental dilemma raised at the beginning of the article. Does it mean that we no longer wish to have as an ideal the genuine person who behaves responsibly because he *really* has a concern for others, or are we willing to accept the idea that all of us are actors, striking a pose of do-goodness to help us better achieve our ulterior ends? In like manner:

> *Company F had developed an ambitious R & D department. Many of the projects undertaken by this department were of a pioneering nature. Management was anxious to capitalize on this work, and repeatedly directed public relations activity to call attention to it. Members of the department, however, were unenthusiastic. They wanted to feel free from publicity considerations in planning their research program.*

The question was: *To what extent should public relations enter into the making of policy; should research be guided by the idea of what has the best chance of winning public recognition or of solving the most significant problem?*

The argument for active public relations participation in policy making was that management should be kept constantly aware of public sentiment in making key decisions. Only in this way could it live up to its social responsibility and ultimately succeed in filling public needs. No function, research included, could operate effectively without sensitivity to public reaction.

The argument on the other side was that public relations people wanted to pay special attention to the kind of research which would get the most publicity. Researchers wanted to do their job well and conscientiously, and then to let publicity follow if it came naturally—rather than have the publicity tail wag the research dog.

In our discussion it became clear that any research projects which might be undertaken with public relations benefits primarily in mind would have a poor chance of long-term success. Publicity on such projects would tend to be of the "flash in the pan" variety. A much more serious public relations contribution could be made by helping the research department verbalize its basic policy, and calling public attention to that overall point of view.

There was a fine line to be drawn between doing research which would win immediate recognition and doing research for the public good. The former might be "gimmicky" and not do the public any good at all, even though it received publicity. The latter would tend to be the kind of research that would do the company the most good, since only if it fulfilled a public need could the company capitalize on it. The conflicts seemed to be among quick publicity, long-term company gain, and public good.

The company good and public good seemed to be synonymous when looked at from the long run. Sound public relations thinking suggested adopting the researchers' point of view and counseling management against trying to force a publicity orientation on the department.

Conclusion

There are no absolutes with which to resolve the basic ethical questions of public relations for industry. There are no clear-cut "do"'s and "don't"'s. And the issues which bother sociological commentators about the "public relations approach to life" are real. We come to grips with them in many aspects of our business life.

It does not help to try to ignore these questions. They are there anyway, and we have to face them whether we discuss them or not.

When they are brought to light, the dilemmas can be viewed in the perspective of age-old questions and the thoughtful observations of philosophers, theologians, and psychologists on the conduct of life. Such discussion dignifies the questions, relieves us of the anxiety of dealing with them privately, and possibly makes us feel better about the decisions we make.

The responsibility for stimulating open discussion on this subject belongs to top management. Only through its help and active participation in the discussion can the ethical threshold of the corporation be clarified. The most effective way to organize such discussions is to talk about specific problems confronting the company, rather than broad issues; the latter become clarified in the course of analysis. This inquiry should be conducted by top management together with middle management. The company's public relations representatives should act as a foil against which introspection and analysis take place. Whenever possible, outside scholars should be included in the discussions.

In examining the ethical threshold of its public relations activity, a company is actually analyzing its social role in the community. It considers what its deeper values are as a social entity. As management sees its way clear to acting more responsibly, it finds its attention focused more on determining the contributions it can make to society rather than on exploiting society to help it meet its own ends.

This process does not serve to repress the aggressions or ambitions of the prime movers in industry. Public relations is still a process by which those drives can be fed—and satisfied. But it accomplishes this end by serving, rather than by destroying; by building, rather than by undermining.

Notes

1. See Raymond A. Bauer, "Limits of Persuasion," *HBR*, September–October 1958, p. 105; also, Edward C. Bursk, "Opportunities for Persuasion," *HBR*, September–October 1958, p. 111.

2. Joost A. M. Meerloo, *The Rape of the Mind* (New York, The World Publishing Company, 1956).

3. Vance Packard, *The Hidden Persuaders* (New York, David McKay Company, Inc., 1957).

4. William Sargant, *Battle for the Mind* (New York, Doubleday & Company, Inc., 1957).

PART THREE
MANAGING PUBLIC RELATIONS
AN OVERVIEW

Putting the rather lofty ideals discussed in the early part of this book into practice is difficult, as any manager who has tried realizes. Thomas Yutzy, in two landmark articles, addresses the real problems with public relations and gives *HBR* readers advice that has stood the test of time.

In "New Perspective on Public Relations," written with Simon Williams, he talks about the confusion inherent in corporate public relations practice. "Not only is such confusion bound to bring waste and dissatisfaction; but also it is unnecessary. . . . The (public relations) practitioner . . . performs a straightforward, skilled and professional task, learned through long experience and clearly definable. He is not a wizard; his successful campaigns are not compounded out of 'blue smoke.' He is without crystal ball or clairvoyance." With cogent examples, Yutzy shows that effective public relations does not only come from millions spent but also from the wide variety of mechanisms used by the professional to tell the right story and the effort of the staff in "achieving an accepted service to these media outlets." Public relations should be managed as an activity that is an adjunct to strategy; in a basic form, it can be controlled and effective. If management makes too much of it, public relations can get out of control, and begin to dominate the company's activities.

Building on these thoughts, "You Have to Manage Public Relations," written this time with Caroline Bird, Yutzy does recommend centralizing PR within one department in the company to keep it independent and critical. But that centralization, and nearness to top management, should also make the function more controllable, and easily accessible. Top management should

217

make clear what the PR people can do, and give them more freedom, all the while monitoring their activities. Given guidelines, the PR department can be creative up to a point. Otherwise, it will tend to "play it safe."

Jumping ahead, Joseph Nolan's 1975 article, "Protect Your Public Image with Performance," points out that PR failures result from the lack of an overall management philosophy for the function. Public relations purpose is not "to conjure up a good story when performance fails," but rather to understand social and political trends and adjust to them so "there will, in fact, be a good story to tell, if and when it's necessary." Part of the PR function should be to create an early warning system that will give top management signals of impending new public ideas, and then advising the company on adjusting to them. The ultimate responsibility is up to top management but the public relations function can help management if given the right mandate.

Robert Mason explores the parameters of this mandate in "What's a PR Director for, Anyway?" Once again, he counsels managers to understand what they want the PR function to do—providing clear, but not too strict, boundaries and limits—before they will be able to manage it successfully. Most companies today need someone who has the experience to take part in policy making, since most business decisions have some public impact. The PR director must have corporate stature, however, to make his opinions count. Otherwise other executives will not heed his warnings.

While Kenneth Henry's "Perspective on Public Relations" discusses books written in the late 1960s on the topic, it has much to say to us today. It will get the reader started in thinking about how broad a function PR should be, and the role it should have within the company.

15

You Have
to *Manage*
Public Relations

CAROLINE BIRD and THOMAS D. YUTZY

It's not enough to recognize the value of PR services, or to hire a good PR staff, or to fit the PR function neatly into an organization chart—

☐ Is the public relations box on your organization chart really just a catchall for odd jobs?

☐ Is the public relations director in your firm the *last* to know company news? Does he have to "needle" department heads for information? Is he trusted to release news items when he thinks best?

☐ Is cooperation with the rest of the company made easy for the public relations department, or is it made awkward by oversupervision of overlapping areas of authority?

☐ What qualifications determine the choice of a public relations director?

If public relations has not quite lived up to its early promise, it is not because business leaders are insincere either in identifying their purposes with the public interest or in recognizing the need for specialized help in articulating company policy. On the contrary, public relations may have come too far too soon. Enlightened chief executives seem to subscribe to the most idealistic concepts of public relations and provide enthusiastically for it in their organization charts.

The failure of public relations which draws snide comment is, we believe, a simple failure of management to manage it. All too often, a company buys public relations without knowing what to do with it, where to put it, or what to put into it. Any corporate function needs clearly defined responsibilities and authority, a visible location in the organization, and clear-cut channels to other functions. No department head can define the role of his or her department without guidance—and if he or she tries to, as many public relations directors are forced to do, then this is a diversion from doing the very job he or she is trying to define!

In order to find out how public relations departments operate, the firm of Dudley-Anderson-Yutzy sent a questionnaire to the chief public relations officers of the country's 149 biggest manufacturing, finance, merchandising, transportation, and life insurance corporations. We wanted to find out the things a company president would like to know about *any* corporate function, so we asked:

- ☐ What do you do?
- ☐ For what are you responsible?
- ☐ What authority do you have to discharge these responsibilities?
- ☐ To whom do you report?
- ☐ How do you work with others in the company?
- ☐ What do you need that you do not have?

Of the 149 companies queried, 79 replied, providing a mass of detailed data about the workings of public relations in our biggest and best-managed enterprises.

The answers confirmed several of our own observations: that internal relationships are the principal concern of public relations directors, that their role is highly fluid, ill defined, and uncomfortable. There appears to be no rhyme or reason to the arrangements in some companies. Activities seem to have multiplied without reference to the essential purpose of public relations. No pattern applying to all companies emerges, even in the broad outline that a similar study of accounting or sales departments would provide.

Undefined Job

One of the hardest questions a public relations specialist has to answer is the frequent query, "But what do you *do* all day long?"

In order to collect concrete data, we offered 88 different tasks for check. Exhibit 1 gives a nose count of those most commonly performed, but it is not a job definition for any one department. Attempts to correlate duties with other data failed. For instance, the number of tasks checked bore no relation to the size of the public relations staff: a one-person department checked 36 of the 88 jobs, while the head of a 300-person department checked only 27. Many of the duties bore no visible relationship to anything that

Exhibit 1. Most Frequently Checked Duties of Public Relations Departments (number of mentions out of a maximum of 79)

Suggesting and arranging press conferences—73
Publicizing the annual report—70
Issuing financial publicity—68
Publicizing stockholders meetings—66
Publicizing speeches before investors' groups—63
Publicizing plant hospitality—62
Suggesting institutional advertising—60
Advising on product publicity—60
Writing the annual report—60
Publicizing awards—60
Publicizing sales speeches—59
Writing product publicity—58
Publicizing safety education—58
Arranging plant hospitality—56
Publicizing the recreation program—56
Approving press conferences—55
Publicizing exhibits at convention and other places—55
Advising on institutional advertising—53
Suggesting exhibits elsewhere than conventions—53
Initiating product publicity—52
Publicizing the medical program—51
Preparing employee periodicals—50

could be considered a public relations skill. Six directors, for instance, said they supervised employee recreation programs.

But the real shocker, from a management point of view, was the additional tasks our respondents wrote in. A partial list is eloquent testimony of the flexibility if not the courage of public relations staffs:

☐ Handling customers' complaints.
☐ Arranging office moves from city to city.
☐ Advising on pricing.
☐ Advising on product nomenclature.
☐ Checking advertising claims.
☐ Making market surveys.
☐ Handling credits and collections.

☐   Arranging skits for customers' meetings.
☐   Handling scholarships.
☐   Handling programs for visiting spouses.

While no one public relations director wrote in all these things, the variety of jobs regarded as appropriate for public relations people suggests a tendency to regard the department as a catchall for chores which fall within no other jurisdiction.

Further evidence that the public relations department takes for its province what no other department wants is provided by the findings on another question: What "public" do public relations directors take major responsibility for reaching? Here is a summary of the five main publics and the number of mentions each received (out of a maximum of 79):

Community	65
Stockholders	44
Government	28
Customers	27
Employees	22

Community relations fall to public relations by default, while customers and employees—a company's most important publics—are not regarded as major responsibilities by most of our respondents.

Messages to these two groups appear to be controlled by the sales and personnel departments, whose special interest may not always reflect the long-term objectives of the enterprise. Moreover, even when the sales and personnel departments do feel the need of public relations skills, they still tend to control the policy, using public relations only as a service organization. We found that 22 sales departments supervise public relations assignments executed for them, both in principle and at every step, while 36 personnel departments exercise this close supervision over projects.

Cost of Disorganization

What does so scattered a work load do to the public relations director? It forces him to jump from one minor emergency to another. As many of them privately complain, they are so busy putting out fires that they cannot set priorities on projects of real importance. The very variety of tasks involves public relations directors in constant shifts of role. Their relations with sales, advertising, accounting, industrial relations, personnel, and operating chiefs must be structured anew with every project. Sometimes they advise; at other times they execute upon the advice of others. Sometimes they are sounding boards; at other times they are initiators.

Unless top managements can plan the public relations job, they will have to choose public relations directors who have that rare talent of making their own jobs; for when the job is unstructured, critical responsibilities are lost in a welter of detail. This is one of the leading causes of public relations by default—of costly failures like the following:

☐   On the basis of legal and engineering advice, a company president acquired a new plant site in another community. He failed to ask his public relations director's advice on announcing the acquisition. When rumors started that the proposed plant would pollute the air, the public relations director reported them and urged a public meeting at which top representatives of the company would explain the facts to towns-people. His advice went unheeded—partly, it appears, because such action was not considered one of his main responsibilities.

Consequently, although the proposed plant would not have created any air pollution whatsoever, local feeling ran high unhampered by the facts. A hostile petition was circulated, and the company was forced to find a less desirable site elsewhere.

☐   Not so long ago a nonunionized manufacturer decided to initiate a wage increase. Public relations was not informed—perhaps because it had been commandeered to do a special job for the sales department, or some similar reason. Announcement lagged behind rumor of the action just long enough to allow an aggressive union to report it to the newspapers as a capitulation to union threats.

Although the union had never been able to get a foothold, the impression prevails with the community and the company's employees that the union forced the raise. The union now has a chance.

Need for Principles

There is, of course, no blueprint for the responsibilities of public relations departments in general. Every enterprise has its own style and its own public relations problems. But it is possible to frame two general principles of public relations responsibility against which any specific duty can be measured:

1   Public relations must be held accountable for counsel on the probable public reaction to any policy affecting the public interest and the effect of this reaction on the enterprise.
2   Public relations must be responsible for the timing and the execution of company statements affecting policy once they are approved for release.

By these yardsticks, many of the chores reported by public relations directors become frills or subordinate matters worth doing only if they do not interfere with the discharge of critical responsibilities.

Power to Act

What authority does public relations need to discharge these responsibilities? Since the unit of public relations work is information, the authority of the public relations department can be measured in its right to get company information and to release it.

Access to Information

Although 50 public relations directors said they were generally satisfied with their access to company information, most of them qualified their answers, and a few were bitter. The methods by which they said they acquired information are revealing, with such comments made as: "watch them," "police with discretion and understanding," "dig and hope for the best," "grapevine," "needling," "discovering items after they break in the papers!"

Free access to the president—claimed by all but four—does not seem to dispel the uneasy feeling that the public relations director may be the last to learn of an important company development. Nor do those who report directly to the president or board of directors feel any better informed than those who report at the vice-presidential or middle-management level.

Rather than a conspiracy to keep public relations in the dark, the difficulty seems to be that no one realizes that there is certain information that public relations directors must have. When they are not informed, there can be serious consequences. Here are some typical situations that could have been avoided:

> "Just got a tip your company is going to double the capacity of your plant," the newspaper reporter phoned.
>
> "Nothing to it," the company's public relations director answered flatly. He had not been told that his management had decided on the plant expansion two days before. As so often happens, the story had leaked.

Aside from putting the public relations director in a most embarrassing position with one of the people whose respect and confidence he always needs—and aside from the severe damage to his own morale—the result was to make the reporter and his paper distrust the company, which now can expect no favors or consideration when it may need them.

A company launched an improved product without informing the public relations department. Left in ignorance, the public relations director launched a publicity campaign to revive interest in the original product. When the new product was announced, it had to buck publicity on the older product.

Result: confusion, waste of money, embarrassment, and needless competition. And both products suffered.

Need for a System

What kind of internal communication system should be set up for the benefit of public relations?

The question is not an easy one to answer; it is hard enough to answer for sales and production, and their roles are better defined than that of public relations. At the very least, management should try to see the problem and accept responsibility for it (as it does for sales and production).

Ideally, the public relations director should have in advance any information that will be learned by the public, including messages in paid advertising as well as those which are bound to leak out as rumors. However, this is a tall order and, if construed literally, would swamp the public relations director's desk and phone. A great deal of experimentation is needed to work out the mechanics, but the task will be easier if management accepts the following principles:

1. The public relations director must be the judge of what information she needs. If she cannot be trusted with company secrets, she should be replaced by someone who can be trusted.

2. Management must support her right to be answered whenever and wherever she asks questions. She should not have to waste her time "stumbling" over information, cajoling it out of suspicious department heads, or winning it only after proving that she can help them in their work and in their personal ambitions to rise in the company.

Right to Release

Our survey suggests that public relations directors are not always sure whether they have the authority to release information or not. Not one claimed to participate in the public release of *all* kinds of information, and there was no agreement among directors on who should release any standard item of company news. In some companies, for instance, announcement of research grants is made by the department involved, but in others the news is released by the executive committee, the research division, a company foundation, the board of trustees, or the president.

In 33 companies, the public relations department has no part at all in releasing news of grants. As for the release of common news items about plant accidents, air or water pollution, contributions to charities, executive changes and obituaries, and company finances, public relations divides the responsibility about equally with other departments.

It is usually necessary, of course, for public relations to cooperate with other departments in releasing news. Which partner decides whether information should be released at all? Which decides how it will be released? When a public relations director cooperates with a plant manager in releasing news of an accident, for instance, does he (a) get the information from the manager and release it himself without clearing with anyone, (b) write a release and clear the facts with the plant manager, (c) write a release and clear every word with the plant manager, or (d) distribute a story written by the plant manager?

Explanatory comments disclosed two management attitudes toward release authority. In authoritarian organizations a typical comment was, "No one can sound off in public without checking with us." In "happy ship" organizations control was concealed or even abandoned, with such comments as "Anything—at their own risk," or "We do it together."

In the absence of clear mandates, public relations people tend to play it safe. In theory, they cannot clear every routine piece of news with higher authority or the department involved, but should clear all releases involving policy. But what is routine and what is policy? They have no way of knowing.

The result is not only that rumors go unchecked, as we have seen above, but that the public relations department becomes a closed door instead of a window to the public and creates ill feeling instead of goodwill. The public relations director who was genuinely ignorant of his management's decision to expand lost face with the reporter checking the rumor. Imagine how much more face he would have lost if, as is often the case, he had pretended ignorance because he was not sure whether he would be criticized for talking. While every reporter respects an honest refusal when there are reasons the information cannot be released, a nervous evasion simply encourages reporters to bypass public relations and management loses control.

Public relations departments cannot, at least with their present staffs, release all the information a great corporation must give to its many interested audiences. It is not even desirable, perhaps, that they be organized to control every statement. But a beginning can be made in defining the authority to release:

1.   There is some information which public relations should always have the right to release, such as any data which have been previously cleared or are already on the public record, and the facts of emergencies such as accidents or walkouts.

2.   On policy matters, public relations should advise on the public reaction to an announcement but should not claim sole authority to decide whether the announcement should be made. Legal, financial, and sales promotion chiefs have important views on the timing of new-product announcements, for instance. Public relations counsel must be based on public relations considerations alone; it must be kept within its own bounds. After the decision to release is made, however, public relations should have full control over how and where the information is distributed.

Fitting In

Public relations fares well on organization charts. The only company that does not have a place for it is the single respondent that has no chart. There are 66 departments enjoying annual budgets, 62 submitting periodic written reports to higher authority, and 72 with free access to the president of the company at any time.

The highest-ranking full-time public relations executive carries a middle-management title in 57 companies, but in 22 he or she is either a vice president or an assistant to the president or the board. As for lines of authority, 59 chief public relations executives report to top management, usually the president, and, rather surprisingly, 17 report directly to the board of directors or some member of it.

Too Many Cooks

There is some evidence, however, that the formal organization chart does not adequately represent the true state of affairs. Many public relations directors want better accountability, in one form or another. As many as 14 of them report to more than one person, and some report, vaguely, to "top management" and "chief executives."

Public relations directors have to work with every ranking executive, and unless their accountability is defined, they can get the feeling that they are at the beck and call of anyone in the company. In some cases, industrial relations, marketing, administration, economics, and advertising share a supervising vice president with the public relations department, suggesting the context in which top management perceives the public relations function. Where public relations reports to advertising, it is reporting to a middle manager removed from many policies of interest to the public.

Public relations activities of other departments irritate those who want control over product publicity, community relations, or some other area preempted by nonprofessionals. Double-harness with advertising irks still others who want to be "set up independently." As might be expected, better status in the company is high among the changes public relations directors want, but those who expressed the hope that they would be better off as vice presidents or reporting to the board chairman will be interested to learn that others who have achieved this rank do not find it a panacea.

There was a surprising absence of the bid for understanding on the part of top management, a plea which clogs the literature of public relations. Those reporting to top management or above, however, frequently mentioned that operating personnel and middle management were ignorant of public relations needs.

Divisionalization

Several public relations directors said they hoped to improve the organization of their departments, particularly in companies recently organized into semi-autonomous divisions. The 29 companies experimenting with some plan for local public relations people attached to units, however, do not seem to have a rational system. Some divisions of a company would have their own public relations representatives, other divisions none, and still others might retain outside counsel. Coordination of public statements by outlying branches is a vexing puzzle for the giant corporation. Three patterns emerge:

1. Each division may be wholly autonomous to the point where its officers or public relations directors do not even check with headquarters.

2. In the fully centralized company, the central public relations department may dispatch staffers to handle public relations for divisions with little or no responsibility to the operating division managers.

3. To allow for local differences, the divisional public relations offices may be operationally responsible to division managers and professionally responsible to the central public relations department.

Here relationships can vary widely, depending on the philosophy of decentralization the company itself is pursuing. The central public relations department may serve the divisions as coordinator, adviser, clearinghouse, or even as a source of extra staff. It may initiate companywide programs for execution by divisions, or it may confine itself to public statements on finance or central policy matters outside the bailiwick of any of the operating divisions.

The problem of divisionalization in public relations is an especially acute one in the larger corporation. It cannot be solved until it is clear how manufacturing, selling, accounting, and other functions are to be decentralized. The sooner this can be done, the better as far as public relations is concerned, for the hazards of uncertain division of authority and responsibility are very great. For instance:

☐ Three of the nine divisions of a large corporation manufacture products in the same general equipment field. One division does a fair job of publicizing its own products; the other two do not. Satisfied customers of one division who could be satisfied customers of other divisions remain for the most part unaware that this company could supply all their needs. Publicity in trade journals is not coordinated. The company and its stockholders are not enjoying the full benefits of its reputation and size. In short, public relations cannot do the job that it should be held accountable for doing.

☐ Dust is a problem in competing companies operating side by side in a western state. Both companies have the same dust-control system, and one is actually no dustier than the other. One of the companies, however, enjoys the goodwill of the community, including cooperation from the city council and a reputation as a good employer, while the other company is blamed for dust.

The difference is due entirely to the fact that the local public relations manager of the favored company has authority to act on the spot. He has been quick to answer every inquiry about dust control and has issued full information about everything his company has done to abate the dust nuisance. But the other plant manager can answer no inquiry without clearing with the company's headquarters in another city. Local newspapers and employees get the impression that the company is doing nothing because it has nothing to say.

Need for Guidelines

In organizing public relations in the large, multidivision corporation, management should keep in mind these principles:

1. The public relations policy setter must be close enough to top policy formation to give advice on public reaction to it and to coordinate publicity programs with it.

2. The public relations department should not be combined with other departments no matter how important their public relations problems are. New problems are always arising in all departments and will demand critical judgment. Public relations advisers must be encouraged to think of the company's total reputation rather than the short-term needs of any part of it.

3. The central public relations department should be informed of and have the right of review over public statements made by divisions. At the same time, local or divisional public relations officers should be given specific areas for which they will be held accountable *after* action.

Choice of a Director

It should be clear by now that public relations problems will not be solved simply by slapping the title "public relations" on somebody in the management family who is temporariily without portfolio or by hiring any reasonably good "public relations person." Management will have to exercise as much care in choosing a public relations director as it does in choosing a chief engineer, a head of research, or a sales manager. Incompetence in public relations directors is particularly embarrassing because their mistakes cannot be concealed from the public. When they blunder, the whole world knows about it. For instance:

> One vice president in charge of public relations is an affable person whom everyone likes, but his previous training has been in retail selling. Queried by financial reporters on a technical matter outside his field, he fumbled so badly that unfavorable publicity resulted in the financial press. The company's stock tumbled just at the moment it was negotiating for the acquisition of another concern on a stock exchange basis.

Unfortunately, the field is so new that top management is not sure what qualifications are needed for the work, and there are few yardsticks in past experience that can be applied to the men who are candidates for the position. The lack of yardsticks is compounded by another difficulty: public relations has as yet no proven training ground. Schools of public relations have not been operating long enough to produce a generation of graduates who have proved the value of the curriculum.

The best a company president can do at present is to measure the people available against the realistic demands of the job that needs to be filled and choose candidates with a strong desire to pioneer new fields. The

importance of the post itself and the need for structuring it demand exceptional talent of the type needed for top management itself. Here are a few
of the qualifications to look for in a public relations executive (although only
a paragon would have them all):

1 He must be able to structure his job and that of a large number of
helpers with no precedents to guide him. (The average staff of
public relations departments we surveyed was 27, the highest 300.)

2 He must be able to resist internal pressures from competing department heads who find public relations an ideal battleground for
policy clashes.

3 He must share the top-management viewpoint enough to understand the *why* as well as the *what* of the policies he must interpret.

4 He must get along easily with every department head in the company, not by back-slapping, drink-swapping cordiality, but through
insight into the needs of each.

5 He must have judgment, not only to choose among the tasks suggested to him but also to face phone inquiries from the press with
the poise of a Jim Hagerty.

6 He must be able to think on his feet and to handle himself well in
meetings and before large groups.

7 He must be able to express himself in good, clear English.

8 He must be the kind of man whom all top managers will trust with
confidential information.

9 He must be willing to perform anonymously. He must enjoy his
role as a transmitter rather than an initiator of concepts.

10 He must have a professional approach to his role and hold himself
as accountable to the public relations profession as a company
lawyer or an accountant holds himself responsible to his profession. When public relations is headed by a company officer who
has arisen from some other field, he should have a professional
public relations man as his righthand man.

Conclusion

Organizing public relations is a challenge to managerial competence which
requires all the skill in structuring and in identifying talent which top managers have successfully applied to other functions. So far, it has received
less attention than it deserves because the penalties of poor management in
this area so often turn up under other labels, such as absenteeism, low
employee morale, excessive tax assessments and taxation, punitive laws,
sales resistance, financing difficulties, and other problems apparently far
removed from the day-to-day work of public relations departments as now
constituted.

If the full price of public relations mismanagement could be segregated and identified on the books, top management would make sure it had the best public relations director it could find and then would give her the authority, organization, and freedom needed to hold her responsible for public understanding of the company.

16
New Perspective on Public Relations

THOMAS D. YUTZY and SIMON WILLIAMS

In every field, as knowledge has outstripped the capacity of individuals to comprehend it all, specialists have come forth and converged into professional groups to meet the challenge.

Existing interpretations of public relations to management are thrice damned: Once by the very name "public relations," which has encouraged sweeping, heady claims in staking out boundaries between it and other specialist functions. Twice by generality, which has made public relations doctrinaire and baffling to grasp. Thrice by oversimplification, which in pulling public relations "down to earth" has flattened it against the ground merely as the strategy and execution of "communicating information about the company."[1]

Damned is the word, because persuasiveness has exceeded understanding, and too often management accepts the need for public relations before adequately appreciating what public relations does that is different and worth the price. Too often "good public relations" is supported as a matter of policy while management proceeds to violate sound public relations practice at every turn.

More and more money is being spent or requested for public relations; the staff devoted to it, both executive and otherwise, is increasing steadily; and there is an ever-widening scope to its services—for example, in its use as an adjunct to sales promotion. Hence, the fact that confusion about its practice still persists is unhealthy. Not only is such confusion bound to bring waste and dissatisfaction, but also it is unnecessary.

These practitioners in reality perform a straightforward, skilled, and professional task, learned through long experience and clearly definable. They are not wizards; their successful campaigns are not compounded out of "blue smoke." They are without crystal balls or clairvoyance or special rights to management's ear. They exist only by virtue of a unique contribution to the variety of vital counsel available to management from specialists in advertising, marketing, law, finance, research, and other service functions—at least, this will be the basis for their long-range existence.

What they do and why they do it can be understood by management— and *must* be understood by management in any situation where it is considering the use of public relations advice. There are always three important decisions for management to make:

1 Is a given problem properly in the realm of public relations?
2 If so, how important is the problem relative to all others demanding attention?
3 Does the relative importance of the problem justify the cost in money and staff that must be expended in the effective use of the most appropriate techniques?

Here awareness of the specific, distinctive characteristics of public relations practice is needed by management. For these decisions must be made by the top executives concerned—preferably in conjunction with the public relations practitioner, but his words will not be given the proper weight or he will not even be listened to unless some recognition of his potential contribution exists first.

Essential Characteristics

Two characteristics of public relations programs make them different from other types of staff programs: (a) the use of a wide variety of methods to present a point of view; and (b) emphasis on servicing rather than buying the media of communication. An actual case may serve to identify these:

Management stated its problem to the public relations specialists this way: The cars we manufacture are known to be universally accepted as tops in engineering. Price is strictly competitive. Advertising is at a peak. Yet sales volume is unsatisfactory; traffic through the showrooms inadequate. Could public relations serve as an adjunct to sales?

Analysis in the field quickly revealed at least two interrelated factors in sales resistance: (1) The car did not appeal to women. An opinion and attitude check revealed that women were blocking sales, despite the car's mechanical appeal to men. (2) There was a serious dealer situation, and lowered morale was affecting performance.

A typical, basic device was employed to kick off a public relations program aimed at influencing both attitudes. The first nonstop, transcontinental automobile trip had been made in one of the early models of this company's line. Using this as a peg, a duplicate trip was set up, this time with two women drivers to symbolize improvements both in the automobiles and in travel conditions, and to create an activity which flattered women and which would get attention on the women's pages of newspapers and on women's radio and TV programs.

To add significance to the trip, it was tied to highway safety. A checklist of traffic violations was compiled with the aid of experts, and tabulations of the driving habits of men and women, state by state, were made.

Once the nonstop, one-way trip was completed, a slow return trip was begun. Wherever along the route dealers were located, a stop was made. Interviews and speeches were prearranged, with emphasis on women's programs. State and local highway safety officials cooperated completely, pleased by any effort to bring the story of safety to the public. The dealer in every community was host, his showroom usually the center of activity. Frequently, the dealer was interviewed along with the drivers.

After the return trip the company sponsored such events as safe-driving demonstrations and driver-reaction tests, each designed to develop maximum local news attention and traffic through the showroom, in order to capitalize on the momentum established by the cross-country event.

In no case during the public relations program was the brand of car emphasized. Advertising and salespeople still had to do the final job of selling cars. Public relations only made it easier to do so. Dealer attitudes and showroom traffic in communities touched by the program indicate that it has served its purpose well.

Note the two earmarks of public relations practice:

1.   *A wide variety of mechanisms was used to tell the story and capture attention.* All the known media of communication, oral, written, and visual, were utilized. Special events were created which provided material suitable to the needs of these media. The design of the program was such as to involve prestige, opinion leaders, so-called "third parties" telling and supporting the theme of the campaign. Such diversity of publicity is probably the most widely recognized characteristic of public relations.

2.   *No money was spent for the outright purchase of time and space with which to relay the company's message.* It is true that advertising space and methods are sometimes used (as witness the public interest advertisements in such magazines as *Harper's* and *The Atlantic Monthly,* or the practice during strikes and sometimes court cases of presenting one side of the issue in local newspaper advertisements); but it is more characteristic for the public relations specialists to proceed as they did in this case—capitalizing on an event, or creating an event to make capital of, and then

skillfully exploiting the action far and wide, relaying the public relations message from one medium to the next, with a minimum of cost.

In other words, what management pays for is *not* the accumulated cost of media time and personnel, but rather the effort of the public relations staff in achieving an accepted service to these media outlets. And, significantly, in order to be acceptable to the medium, the service must be valid, pertinent, and of sufficiently good quality to justify the space, time, or other forms of attention it seeks from the medium.

Note, also, that the need which public relations was called upon to meet—in this case, increased sales—apparently could not or was not being satisfied by the applied skills of other kinds of specialists. Analysis revealed that *part* of the problem of sales resistance lent itself to solution by public relations techniques. It is normal for a problem to be broken down in this way. The sensitivity of the public relations staff to cause and effect interacting among people of importance to the growth and prosperity of a business is part of what management should *expect* to buy when retaining counsel (whether staff or consultant).

Of course, not all human relations are properly the concern of public relations. The fact remains that every public relations program worth the name is concerned with some opinions and some attitudes. Therefore, when all that is known about a problem is that human relations are involved in a manner yet undefined, this is the time to seek public relations advice—the time to determine whether public relations techniques are applicable and, if so, how.

Fight for Publicity

There are more than 10,000 newspapers and 14,000 magazines published in the United States alone, each with a special audience and editorial viewpoint. There are roughly 100,000 school districts, almost 3,000 radio stations, and 423 TV stations. Places of worship, clubs, and conventions are legion. Name a religion, a profession, or a hobby, and you can find a channel of communication flowing freely between those sharing a common interest.

Now, public relations practice created none of these. Rather, their growth and proliferation into our society created public relations practice. The reason is simple. Every channel of communication must contain a flow of information, whether fact or fancy, whether oral, written, or visual. Those who guide and control this flow must either reach out for information and shape it to their needs or accept communications already satisfactorily shaped.

Here is where the skill of the professional public relations practitioner comes in. They have developed a sense of form and style as demanded by each outlet. They can recognize in a public relations message which elements appeal to some and not to others, or how to transform certain unappealing elements to an acceptable basis. Nevertheless the management–public relations counsel–editor (or producer) triangle is often a source of frustration to all concerned.

Results from News Stories

Newspaper publicity is an excellent case in point. Perhaps no other technique is so widely used and abused. Perhaps nowhere else in public relations practice does the unwise insistence of management force the practitioner into unhappy, wasteful practice, such as the accumulation of vast volumes of clippings or the constant mass mailing of releases known to contain nothing of real news value, known to irritate a busy editor and to go into the wastebasket, and known to plague the reputation of public relations among newspaper people—all this while more promising projects go begging for the lack of time and money.

In fact, newspaper publicity, in the minds of too many executives, *is* public relations, even though it can be demonstrated that sheer volume of clippings may accomplish no measurable effect and in some circumstances may actually generate negative reaction—while, by contrast, just one story properly placed *could* be the key to reaching a specific goal. Two simple cases will illustrate the need for more sophistication:

> *1. The first case involves an important ethical drug manufacturer in the highly competitive and swiftly changing field of antibiotics. Most of the products used to control or combat human disease are available only through prescription; hence the attitudes of doctors and druggists toward the company and its products are of vital importance. But it is also deemed important that the general public be informed of new developments by the company, in order to build confidence and also to answer the complaint that the new drugs are priced too high, with information on the vast costs of research and development necessary to produce drugs as well as the economies which the new drugs have effected in sickness costs.*
>
> *This creates a delicate situation because of the danger that an informed public, to the degree that it seeks to diagnose and prescribe for itself, will threaten the qualified authority of doctor and druggist. Is there a way out of the dilemma?*
>
> *Direct consumer advertising is of little use in the case of drugs available only through prescription. It is equally clear that a barrage of releases to newspapers, magazines, and radio is not the solution either; not only is the amount of coverage which will be given a mass release highly unpredictable, but there is grave doubt that it can do the job management wants done. Is not the information that interests the readers of one publication likely to bore readers of the other? Will information satisfying to the* Park Region Echo *reader in Alexandria, Minnesota, meet the needs of the* Philadelphia Bulletin *reader, or vice*

versa? What about the newspaper that has had a wide readership of medical columns by Dr. Brady, Dr. Alvarez, or others, as opposed to the paper that has not?

What is called for, rather, is a closely controlled flow of scientifically correct information skillfully directed at defined kinds of readers—a "rifle" approach rather than a "buckshot" attack.

2. This case is about certain conservative interests who are going into the mining business for the first time in a small but substantial manner. The company has exciting potentials. The owners naturally want to call the attention of investors to the new company in order to expand the stockholder list. Yet it is clear that since mining developments tend to be suspect, the release of information has to be carefully guided.

The problem raises several tricky questions as to how and where to tell the company's story first. It is obviously desirable to reach the widest possible audience of prospective investors. At the same time, management wants to maintain a sense of sobriety, financial substance, and sincerity of intent about information released.

These two objectives seem to be and are conflicting in the case of a mass release. *But not so if the company relies on a well-timed series of efforts to reach specific investor groups through selected media. Thus, in well-mapped-out campaign, one would expect to see media like* The Wall Street Journal, Business Week, *and special business newsletter services used at different points along the way and presenting quite different types of stories.*

Now, placing worthwhile news stories that people will read at the points of maximum return to the public relations objective is a tough, competitive fight. For example, a study in Wisconsin showed that on an average day, out of some 77 items and 13,352 words received from out-of-state sources via Associated Press wires, roughly 27% of the items and 24% of the words were actually relayed to Wisconsin dailies. Again, the Continuing Study of Newspaper Reading shows that the average person reads only one-fourth to one-fifth of the stories printed in the newspaper.[2]

As veterans in the battle for newspaper space know, newspaper content takes several ditinct forms—spot news, features, columns, editorials, fillers, and pictures. Ideally, a public relations program of more than local scope, in which newspaper publicity is deemed a useful tool, should seek to generate *all* the kinds of news in order to gain a repetitive impact, but at different times and in different papers, depending on the case.

To do this obviously calls for a variety of skills. A good reporter may never learn to write editorials; a good editorial writer may never learn to report. Few master all the subject matter covered by the many kinds of columns that might be reached. Similarly with pictures: few portrait photographers learn to take a good newspaper picture, capturing as it must all the action and human interest that make the story come to life.

Further, whether or not an editor uses material depends on many factors. Let us look at the four most important ones in terms of their bearing on public relations:

1. *Timing.* Much depends on whether news is light or heavy on a particular day. Also, some startling event may coincide with the release and bury the story. To illustrate, in a recent case the strategists of a trade association program very carefully planned how to present the association's stand relative to some pending federal legislation. But the day before the first newsbreak was to be made, one prominent association member released a letter to his congressman which received wide publicity, blew the lid off the project, and almost killed the newsworthiness and accuracy of all the work that had preceded.

Many executives fail to realize that news about an event that happens on Monday must be in the editor's hands on Monday or even sooner. If copies of an important speech are not available until the day of the event, a very poor reporting job can be guaranteed unless the speaker is more news by himself than most. For good coverage, particularly in the light of the next factor to be discussed, many days of preparation are required, and nothing is so frustrating as to have management sit tantalizingly on the news until the last minute and then frantically apply pressure for coverage.

2. *Local angle.* Does the company's story realistically take into account the readership of each paper to which it is submitted? One of the basic causes of wasted effort in so many mass-mailed news releases is that this matter of local angle is not stressed. Local color is particularly important in public relations stories because often they have no other news peg; they are not like stories of war or murder or baseball, which carry every time.

To obtain local flavor among the thousands of papers from coast to coast is a difficult, expensive job. Yet it is certainly just as expensive to grind out useless releases. Therefore, a vital preliminary decision for management to make in consultation with the public relations specialist is whether newspaper publicity is truly the most effective mechanism in light of all practical considerations.

Furthermore, if it is decided that widespread newspaper publicity is required, then care must be taken to examine the facilities of the staff, whether internal or retained counsel, and to consider whether the desired form of publicity can actually be attained. The experiences of the authors' own firm, for example, indicate that even to approach effective local distribution in the press requires a nationwide network of permanently affiliated field editors, each selected because of demonstrated ability and long residence in the area.

3. *News value.* What makes for news and what does not is sometimes a baffling question to management. Executives with a story to tell often cannot understand why editors are not imbued with the same sense of excitement and importance about the story that company people feel.

This is especially true if a competitive company or industry gets treasured space, let us say, in *The New York Times.*

Recently, such a situation rocked an entire public relations program of many years' standing. Two leading executives, each speaking for competitive industries, appeared before a national convention of scientists. The day after their talks, one received very generous treatment by *The New York Times,* the other practically no notice at all. The wrath of vengeance fell upon the public relations staff representing the overlooked industry. When it was discovered that its executive's speech had not been given to the public relations staff for preview, and that advance copies had not been made available, whereas the competitive speech clearly had been written with newspaper coverage in mind, the issue was dropped. But echoes of such misfortunes haunt a program for months and are, of course, quite unnecessary.

4. *Acceptance of the source.* Whether or not editors consider the information in a release reliable depends on a number of things, including: amount of personal contact over a period of time; previous satisfaction with company releases; amount of personal contact just prior to a story release (providing helpful background and otherwise establishing the validity of the story); quality of pictures, if used; general reputation of the source for reliability; and, of course, news value.

What all this means is that making effective use of newspaper publicity for public relations purposes calls for a skilled, professional job—far more than just a reporting job. Getting news coverage requires much more money and personnel than is generally realized by management. Moreover, what applies to newspapers applies with similar force to other media, such as movies, magazines, TV, and schools. The complex, highly organized skills in utilizing these media are part of what management should expect to buy and be willing to pay for when it seeks public relations advice and endorses a program.

Guiding the Client

Up to this point we have been discussing the function of the public relations specialist when he or she carries the burden of action. Actually, one of the most important services of the specialist is to guide clients to good public relations practice themselves. To illustrate:

The industry in question comprises a large number of units, operating under many different, independent owners, widely scattered geographically. It is an industry where labor costs are the single most important cost factor, and one whose technology is shared around the world. Consequently, it has always been threatened by imports from low-wage areas of the world and has required the protection of tariffs.

In light of the trends of recent years to lower United States tariffs as a means of stimulating free trade, it is vital to the industry for

Congress and the general public to understand fully just how sensitive the industry is to foreign competition and so avoid hastily conceived legislation. At the same time, industry leaders do not want to appear obstructionist or reactionary, since they sincerely believe world prosperity depends on free trade (obtainable by different methods than wholesale tariff reduction).

The industry has undertaken two types of action: (a) participation in congressional hearings, and (b) stimulation of informed action at the community level.

When resistance to low tariffs on the part of Congress was first evidenced, leaders of the industry were prone to disregard constantly the dictates of sound public relations practice. There was a tendency to believe that insistence could win over Congress; that the sheer logic and rightness of their position would make news and win support. Spokesmen would feel urged to express their views impulsively without waiting for the preparation of written statements; there was no advance copy from which accurate news releases could be prepared, and no time to assess the impact of what they said and how they said it on reporters, the public, or members of Congress.

In this situation, the function of public relations counsel for a long while was entirely that of mentor, helping the client to become aware of the concept of timing in news; the necessity for reasoned, commonly supported argument rather than insistence; the need for written copy to avoid the ambiguities of reporting verbal, impassioned statements. In this case, the problem was to get the actors to play a professional role.

Similarly, at the community level, the need was to develop locally held skills in working with press, radio, TV, and other media in the town. The action taken involved the development of community relations clinics; kits of sample speeches, news releases, radio and TV scripts; written and visual material for distribution from management telling why the industry felt its position in relation to tariffs was valid. But always the end point was to equip management to act skillfully when the public relations staff was not at hand, so no opportunity would be wasted.

Distinctive Problems

Having examined some of the characteristic things that public relations specialists do, let us turn now to the identifying marks of a public relations *problem.* Top management has to know which problems can be handled by operating executives and which require the services of specialists; and also, if specialists are to be called in, which ones—public relations or some other such as advertising or industrial relations.

Obstructive Viewpoints

Every public relations problem is entirely concerned with differences in beliefs, opinions, attitudes, and actions among people which in some way and to varying degrees interfere with the harmonious operation of an organization; for example, this group or that "won't buy," "won't work," "won't cooperate," "won't listen," "won't legislate 'properly,' " "won't understand 'fully,' " and so on.

Contrary to the recommendations of others that management should employ public relations specialists only "where the scale of informational and persuasive activities is large," we feel that public relations problems are frequently serious and demand the attention of specialists when the differences of viewpoint are held by a very limited group.[3] For example:

☐ The dealers in the automobile company case cited in the early pages of this article form a relatively small group, and the fact that they are widely distributed geographically does not indicate a wide-scale informational program.

☐ Again, in the tariff legislation case described in the preceding section, the members of the federal regulatory body are very limited in number and location, yet constitute a vital public for the industry concerned.

The area of public relations does not cover *all* possible differences in viewpoint and action which might threaten an operation, but only those which are in the realm of free choice. If the troublesome viewpoints can be made to yield to the traditional pressures of management regulation, to financial incentives, or to other direct operational forces, the problem is not one for staff experts but for operating executives. But if the desired changes in behavior cannot be ordered, if the people involved must be persuaded by means which they will voluntarily accept as in their best interest, then and only then does the problem continue to qualify as one for public relations. Suppose a company has a problem like this one:

An important product line consists of control and meter-type instruments for use in community water-distribution systems. Sales difficulties stem from two major sources. One is widespread community resistance to charges based on actual consumption rather than a flat service fee. The cost of water has never appeared as a direct charge, and its effect on tax rates has never been made clear. The other is the long-standing custom in many towns, now widely supported by law, of automatically accepting the low bid in purchasing supplies for municipally operated departments. Because of a long and treasured history of high quality, the company is constantly at a price disadvantage in such towns, although it can demonstrate long-term savings by virtue of maintenance costs, precision of operation, and other service features.

Now, obviously management has no means of coercing nor desire to coerce the water engineers or town officials. It must "sell" them. But sales representatives are not enough to do the job. They will be needed to make the sale, but first a lot of spadework must be done by others. There are basic attitudes about such matters as regulation, water conservation, and municipal economy to be changed. This means influencing a lot of people whom sales reps and company executives will never know, for the attitudes of the engineers and town leaders are intertwined with the feelings of other groups; and it means reaching these people with information that might seem to the uninitiated as having little to do with the immediate problem of adding customers— but it does pave the way for sales.

PR Versus Advertising

Not all problems in the realm of free choice are for public relations, either. Clearly, many such problems will be handled best by the advertising specialist. Choices between brands and between price brackets, overcoming traditional resistance to some product such as prunes or dried milk—these and similar matters are everyday grist for the advertising mill. What, then, is the difference between public relations and advertising in the specific cases where increasing sales is the dominant objective? This is an important question to answer for two reasons:

1 The first is the definite trend toward the use of public relations methods as an adjunct to sales promotion. Thus, among the cases described in this article (deliberately chosen for representativeness), sales clearly emerge in the majority of instances as the direct basis of management interest.

2 Related to this is something that gives rise to one of the bemusing, often bitter debates which has helped obfuscate the role of public relations in industry. Inevitably, in promoting sales, the advertising and public relations methods interact and intertwine all along the line, merging insensibly at frequent intervals in the long process between raw materials and customer, emerging more often as distinct but complementary actions.

It is vital to the effective use of both skills that management understand the role of each. The fact is, moreover, that a number of differences mark the contributions of the two functions—some superficial, others more fundamental:

1. *Different techniques used.* These differences are obvious. Advertising makes a frontal attack, the advertiser choosing his message, making the final decision as to how and when to deliver it, purchasing space or air-

time, and appealing directly to the consumer. Public relations, by contrast, more often relays its message indirectly. That is, a basic story is put into the hands of "third parties"—editors, speakers, program producers, teachers, and the like—who, while accepting the material for use, still retain the position of censor or selector for the medium being used.

Advertising and public relations both use oral, written, and pictorial methods. However, as already noted, public relations employs many more devices—speeches, letters, personal contacts, events which generate news, school aids, and so on. On a large scale, advertising costs more than public relations; certainly advertising is better understood and more widely used.

Also, advertisers have methods for measuring results, which, though far from exact, are accepted by experts and management as useful guides. These methods are not directly applicable to the evaluation of public relations, where the time element is on a different scale (much longer) and where the measurement of opinion and attitude change is much more subtle (and expensive) than the measurement of movements in the marketplace. Furthermore, as advertising and public relations are more and more used together to promote sales, it is increasingly difficult to isolate the impact of each.

Note that, contrary to what some have implied, public relations impact *can* be measured. The hindrance is simply the economic one of expense, which makes it unfeasible to budget such evaluations in the average public relations program. The public relations profession is striving for practical, universally applicable methods of evaluation, but it must be frankly admitted that for the time being the practitioner and management are obliged to put their faith in personal observation and the empirical evidence of the many public relations programs which have been followed by good results.

2. *Different motivations aimed at.* There are also more basic reasons why advertising and public relations are neither interchangeable nor competitive in function, but complementary. In years past, when both advertising (the older of the two arts) and public relations were evolving from the tempest of industrial revolution and the building of an economic empire, the question of overlapping function never occurred; the publicity functions that gradually were assumed by public relations just were not related consciously to sales. As a matter of fact, until recently the predominant task of public relations has been to sell the virtues of the business enterprise itself not its products.

It is only with the emergence of the social sciences in the past decade, revealing an almost frightening spectrum of variables affecting human behavior and, more specifically, consumer motivation, that the objectives of both advertising and public relations have been associated with sales.

The essential difference is that public relations and advertising deal with different ends of the spectrum of consumer motivation. Advertising meets the needs of customers to know that a product exists, to be comfortably familiar with its brand name, to know about cost and availability and what the product does that is different and worth the cost, to know the form the product takes, and to be able to envision it in business or at home. In a sense, these and similar needs are satisfied with direct statements of fact, made appealing and quickly understandable by design, color, and word form.

At the other end of the spectrum are new concepts of consumer behavior which have become more the province of public relations than of advertising. Here we find defined social pressures toward conformity; the stubborn persistence of cultural mores brought to our society by a multitude of nationalities; noneconomic needs for status, personal identification, and acceptance. In the last analysis, these are the beliefs and attitudes which together form the climate of opinion in which an advertising campaign thrives or withers; but advertising itself is not effective in coping with them.

In fact, one of the major identifying characteristics of a public relations problem, which is revealed most clearly when barriers to increased sales become the primary concern of management, is that the problem embraces deeply held opinions which block acceptance of the direct message of advertising. These opionions may result from ignorance, loss of confidence, fear, or tradition; to be modified they may require the persistent, diversified attack of public relations concurrently with other methods of sales appeal. To illustrate:

☐ A leading manufacturer of appliances has an exciting new product to sell. But release of the product is being held up because its use is deeply involved in a concept of personal hygiene entirely novel to United States culture. The company must first find ways to introduce the gadget in a manner acceptable to good taste and yet forthright enough to command attention, understanding, and acceptance. This is a problem for public relations.

☐ A real estate development is faced with a stereotypic image of the colony. Because of its name and history and location, too many of the kind of people being sought as purchasers feel that the area is too rich, too snobbish, and too isolated socially. At the same time the leaders of the development want to maintain certain restrictions and social conditions in order to preserve their dream of community.

How to eliminate the stereotype and yet maintain the concept of privilege in being a member of the settlement is the problem which public relations is working to solve.

Attainable Objectives

According to Mr. Pimlott, "it seems fair to say that intelligent public relations 'pays off' to the extent that its objective is specific and noncontroversial and does not entail changing people's deep-seated habits of mind."[4] With specificity of objective we hold no argument; but if the rest of that recom-

mendation were to be accepted, we hold that there would be little of significance for public relations to accomplish. For example, should or should
not the following problem have been attacked with public relations methods?

*This industry has developed large potential markets for a variety
of new products among food processors, demonstratively safe for human consumption and offering decided advantages in materials handling.*

*But sales resistance of several kinds has been met. The food
industry is very sensitive to tradition, both in the art of food processing
and the mores of consumers. Rooted deeply in the craft and habit of
yesterday, opinions of "what is good" and "what will work" easily
come in conflict with advances in technology, slowing down the acceptance of new products, often in an irritating, exasperating manner.*

*In addition, use of the new products has been handicapped by
the strict regulation of food content and food labeling. Because of the
newness of use of the products in question, even though admittedly
harmless, regulatory agencies have insisted on special label identification until such time as it can be demonstrated that public knowledge
and acceptance of the new products is widespread.*

*The problem is: how to generate widespread, articulate aware-
ness among the general public; how to create understanding among
the processors that public acceptance does, in fact, exist; how to convince government regulatory agencies that discriminatory labels should
be eliminated.*

*Several years ago, this industry decided that public relations tech-
niques, patiently, and systematically applied, could help. In schools,
among homemakers, with home economists, science writers, doctors,
and others who may influence food habits, the subject of the interaction
of food content on basic food requirements, digestibility, preservation,
and packaging is emphasized. Wherever possible, the particular ad-
ditives of the industry sponsor are used to illustrate the nature and
value of changes in food technology. Note that throughout the program, it remains the job of each company in the industry to capitalize
on increased knowledge and acceptance by vigorous selling of its own
brand.*

*The story is told by developing teaching aids, written and visual;
by servicing the needs of radio and TV programers with scripts, props,
prominent personalities; by promoting industry tours, among other
standard devices. Similarly, a more technical description is prepared
for the trade press serving industrial customers. Special operational
guides are designed for specific industries, illustrating cost and quality
benefits and how to attain them. Regional and industrywide seminars
are sponsored, at which time scientists of the sponsor industry contribute and so enhance institutional prestige and confidence among
customers.*

The industry itself sponsors a fundamental research program which has become internationally recognized, carrying forward its investigations at universities and other reputable laboratories. The scope of the program is kept constantly before regulatory agencies by means of personal contact, reprints of all technical publications, and special meetings called to analyze and correct differences of understanding.

Surely we know and accept with humility the fact that deeply held viewpoints, particularly among adults, are changed with great difficulty. Beliefs and even opinions are among the toughest of human fabrications. Yet we know changes do occur. If we bend and flex and twist systematically and repetitively, revisions in viewpoint can be anticipated. If we pinpoint our attack catering to the multitude of relatively small special-interest groups, entering wedges can be driven into preconceived notions.

True, it may take lots of time and money. Equally true, not every effort will be successful—and some will be judged fruitless in advance. But management is justified in taking a far more ambitious view of public relations than that proposed by Mr. Pimlott. The elements of controversy and deep-seated habits of mind are present in almost every major marketing problem faced by management. To block off consideration of a public relations program because of their presence is to defeat the main purpose of having public relations advice.

Conclusion

There is a seemingly endless variety of problems posed by the complexities of American business. Taken together with an apparently endless variety of publicity devices created for solving them, these problems tend to make public relations look like a pretty tricky business. In practice, however, public relations jobs actually fall into a limited number of categories, and fundamental methods of solution (in contrast to media) are equally few.

The fact that there are subtle variations in problem and procedure—that in one case we may be talking to farmers and in the next to city dwellers, or once to labor and then to stockholders, or first to all women and next to housewives—should not confuse the basic simplicity of public relations analysis. This is not to say that the solution of problems is simple. Rather, it is to say that defining a problem and choosing methods of attack are procedures that management can and should understand.

But are the special knowledge and skills attributed in this article to the specialist too vast to harness? Are we public relations practitioners guilty of arrogance in staking out professional competence?

To the skeptics, our answer is that the unique experience of the specialist is no more vast, probably far less so, than the precedence of law on which legal counsel rests, or the facts of the natural sciences whose mastery has become vital to modern industry. Experience in dealing with the accumulations of relevant information becomes the hallmark of usefulness in every field. In each, as knowledge has outstripped the capacity of individuals to comprehend it all, specialists have emerged and converged into professional groups to meet new challenges. So it is with public relations practice as it has evolved from the nameless, formless activity of a decade ago to the professional operation it is today.

Such is the picture management should have before it when it seeks public relations advice. If to some we seem naive and idealistic in defining public relations as we have, we can only say that elimination of the quacks, of the less responsible and less capable, depends in no small way on what management demands. If management does not see what public relations is driving at and how, or if management supports a lesser effort, then the cynics will always have a reference. Without the ideal as a sharpening stone, a useful and important tool for management will be blunted and destroyed.

Notes

1. J. A. R. Pimlott, "Public Relations Down to Earth," *HBR*, September–October 1953, p. 50.

2. S. M. Cutlip, "The Flow of News," *Public Relations Journal*, October 1954, p. 6.

3. See J. A. R. Pimlott, op. cit., p. 52.

4. Ibid., p. 58.

17

Protect Your Public Image with Performance

JOSEPH NOLAN

If the last five years or so have taught U.S. business anything it should be in the area of public relations. But when the public, advocacy groups, and political reformers start clamoring for business to change some of its practices, it appears, sadly, many companies have yet to learn that something might really need changing—and that the changes required need to be substantive, not merely cosmetic or the old ways, better communicated. The author of this article discusses three reasons businesses continue to fail in this area. One, they fail to learn from others' mistakes; two, they ignore signs of impending changes in public opinion; and three, they neglect to match their performance with public expectations. He concludes with some suggestions for avoiding these mistakes.

In many areas, U.S. business has proved itself a remarkably fast learner. When one company markets a new aerosol shaving cream that captures the consumers' fancy, competitors rush to catch up. When another strikes it rich among grocery shoppers with a novel frozen-food package, rivals move quickly to follow suit. And when a company misfires with a new product, others promptly learn from the mistake.

One of the few areas where benefiting from the mistakes of others seems to be neglected, however, is in public relations. Here, industries and companies view one another's problems with the same lofty disdain that Sherlock Holmes reserved for the dimwitted Inspector Lestrade.

So while constantly lamenting the lowly standing of the "business image," business executives themselves are so preoccupied with the communication and cosmetic dimensions of their problems that they tend to overlook everything else. M. A. Wright, chairman of Exxon, USA, echoed the conventional wisdom of a generation of his corporate colleagues when he declared that "business has failed to do an effective job in communicating its point of view to the general public."[1]

It is hard to argue with the proposition that there is room for improvement in business communications. But nine times out of ten, the trouble lies not so much with the communications as with two other aspects of the broad management function of public relations: perception and performance. The essence of improving the business image rests not in trying to conjure up a good story when performance fails, but in sharpening corporate perceptions of emerging social and political trends and in adjusting performance so there will, in fact, be a good story to tell.

In short, doing a plastic-surgery job on the business image is no substitute for reforming some substantive business practices.

Aside from a lack of understanding that real and not cosmetic changes need to be made, there are three reasons companies seem to needlessly repeat blunders that can have drastic consequences for their images: (1) they don't learn from others' mistakes, (2) they don't read early warning signs of trouble, and (3) they don't take steps quickly enough to bring their performance into line with reasonable public expectations.

In this article I want to discuss these three mistakes companies commonly make, and suggest some ways organizations can learn to take action before public relations disaster srikes.

Learning from Others' Mistakes

Before their own public relations bell tolls, industries and companies go blithely on their business-as-usual way, naively assuming that disaster can't strike them as it has others. For example:

☐ A few years ago they saw the pharmaceutical companies hauled up on the congressional carpet for allegedly overcharging customers on miracle drugs.

☐ They watched the steel companies bombarded with scornful broadsides for ill-timed price increases.

☐ They witnessed General Motors being forced to acknowledge, before the world, that it had assigned gumshoes to trail Ralph Nader in hopes of finding evidence of misbehavior.

☐ Now, as the public grows increasingly concerned about the galloping rate of inflation with its high interest rates and soaring prices for energy and food, businesspeople can see banks, oil companies, utilities, and grocery chains taking their lumps in the public opinion polls.

They *see* all these things, but they *learn* very little from them. If business leaders had absorbed the lessons of the past, they might well have struck a better balance between the economics and safety requirements of the consumer protection movement. For example, auto manufacturers might not be saddled now with many of the inconveniences, such as reinforced auto bumpers and extensive engine modifications, that make for lively luncheon conversation in executive dining rooms.

Instead, the individual businessperson in a currently trouble-free industry has a tendency to sit back complacently, like the pharisee in the Bible, thanking God that he is not like the rest of them, who are sinners, adulterers, and scoundrels in general.

Consequently, when his turn comes—as can readily happen in our "whistle-blowing" society—he is unprepared for the ordeal and usually fares even worse than those who preceded him. As Charles Dickens demonstrated in *Pickwick Papers,* when the Reverend Mr. Stiggins appeared at the Temperance Society meeting far gone in rum-and-water, nothing gladdens the public heart so much as a fall from grace by the excessively righteous.

A classic case of corporate ignorance of whistle blowing—one which should be required reading for every businessperson in America—is Eastman Kodak's controversy with a minority group over discrimination in hiring in its hometown of Rochester, New York. This conflict, coming as it did in 1966 and 1967 when public sympathy for the civil rights movement was cresting, attracted nationwide attention in the press and on television.

The highlight of the case was Kodak management's dramatic repudiation of an agreement that a lower-level Kodak officer had negotiated, in good faith, with a community group. As longtime PR practitioner, author, and teacher Edward L. Bernays described it, this was "a colossal public relations blunder."

When Kodak finally made its inevitable capitulation to the community group's demands, which were framed by "professional radical" Saul Alinsky, the lessons in public relations were clear for all to read:

☐ Regardless of how good its past record of socially responsible behavior is, a very visible company is also very vulnerable.

☐ A single blunder in performance—in this case, the repudiation of the accord—can undo a lot of good works and good communications.

☐ The prevailing climate of opinion can be decisively important to the outcome of any confrontation.

☐ A David-and-Goliath contest is a "natural" for the press and television and, hence, likely to generate unfavorable publicity for a company for the duration of the struggle.

☐ Arguments emotionally expressed by underdogs will override the stodgily factual ones that many companies insist on using.

The Kodak case makes these truths obvious. Yet in the ensuing years, companies have ignored them and consequently have run into PR disasters similar to Kodak's:

☐   Because it failed to recognize that its great visibility made it extremely vulnerable to the emotional arguments of its critics, a major utility seriously tarnished its reputation in a protracted conflict with a community group.

☐   Because it took an unyielding position against church activists on doing business in South Africa, a large financial enterprise encountered formidable public relations problems.

☐   Because it foolishly resisted compromise with local environmentalists when prevailing public opinion clearly favored accommodation, a diversified manufacturing company came to grief.

It would be hard to imagine a more flagrant example of a company's ignoring public opinion than the tender offer of Mobil Oil Corporation to Marcor, Inc., parent company of the Montgomery Ward chain.

As the price of gasoline and the profits of petroleum companies rose sharply, so did motorists' tempers. To reverse the tide of criticism that was rising against them, Mobil and other companies tried to convince the public through a barrage of institutional advertisements that the industry desperately needed those higher prices and higher profits to invest in new exploration, new refineries, new pipelines, and new supertankers. Never in any of the defenses of higher prices, however, did Mobil talk of its need for huge sums so it could go out during a national emergency and buy department stores.

As an exercise in supreme indifference to public opinion, this was in the fine tradition of Nero with his fiddle, Chamberlain with his umbrella, and Marie Antoinette with her cake.

In heartening contrast, Union Carbide Corporation did learn from its own mistakes and those of others and responded to an environmental issue with performance instead of puffery. After an initial period of fretful foot-dragging, Carbide determined to do something about its ferroalloy plant in Alloy, West Virginia—a plant that environmentalists had scornfully branded "the world's smokiest factory." By installing the best available pollution-control equipment—at a cost of almost $35 million—the company has succeeded in cutting particulate emissions by an astonishing 97% over the past four years. Carbide's widely acclaimed environmental success story is a symbol of what can happen once corporate management recognizes that good public relations involves more than a facade.

Heeding "Early Warning" Signs

It is hard to understand how companies can ignore prevailing public opinion and other indicators of change when dealing with issues that cast giant shadows before them. Still, the recent past is littered with examples of business's inability to perceive social and political trends before they become issues of great public concern.

This breakdown in the corporate early warning system is all the more inexcusable when even a cursory examination of public issues suggests that over an extended period there are certain readily identifiable phases in their growth:

1.   First, there is the dormant phase when the issue is recognized by relatively few. If caught here, it can frequently be handled through the private actions of individual businesses. A striking example is the large corporations' response to demands that they place more blacks and women in high-level jobs.

As soon as this issue of representation began to surface, several corporations actively sought out talented blacks, women, and consumer representatives for positions on their boards of directors. New faces began turning up in boardrooms: Patricia Harris, Catherine Cleary, Reverend Leon Sullivan, Mary Gardiner Jones, Cecily Selby, William Coleman, and others. Simultaneously, some companies made similar efforts to broaden opportunities for blacks and women in the ranks of senior management, although progress in this area has been somewhat slower.

2.   The next phase is one that might be described as the opinion development phase. By this time the issue has been subjected to scrutiny in the newspapers and on television, and has begun stimulating open debate. At this stage voluntary cooperative action can often prove helpful.

The National Alliance of Businessmen, which spearheaded the campaign for the hiring and training of minorities, offers an apt illustration. The alliance succeeded in convincing the business community of the advantages to be gained by changing their employment policies and accepting men and women once regarded as "unemployable."

3.   Finally, the institutional action phase occurs when Congress, the state legislatures, and the courts crowd into the picture. By this time it is usually too late for the private sector to exert much influence. Yet, amazingly, this is the stage at which most businesses wake up to the fact that something is going on and try clumsily to get into the act.

Only when the auto safety proposals had escalated to the level of congressional debate did the industry start talking seriously about self-regulation. What it was doing, though, was proposing a phase-one solution for a problem that had already advanced to phase three. At that stage, the initiative had clearly been preempted by government.

Industries' tardy recognition of other public issues has followed this same pattern. Concern for the environment had existed in the dormant phase for 25 years or more, but the environmentalists were brusquely dismissed as "fanatics" and "do-gooders." Then a dedicated public servant named Rachel Carson wrote a book about what pesticides were doing to the environment. Almost overnight, *Silent Spring* became a best seller, and public consciousness became sharply focused on the deterioration of our air and water. The issue moved rapidly through the opinion development phase, and before long Congress and the state legislatures were grinding out laws aimed at combating pollution.

Consumerism traveled a similar route. As far back as 1887, with the passage of the Interstate Commerce Act, the federal government had begun taking steps against particular abuses. But for 75 years or more isolated grievances had no common outlet, until they found a charismatic champion in Ralph Nader. Again it was a book, *Unsafe at Any Speed*, that provided the main impetus for nudging consumerism into the opinion development phase, and persuading consumers that somebody was listening. As with the environmental concerns, the passage from the second to the third phase was uncommonly swift.

On both matters, trade associations and individual companies badly miscalculated public reaction. Many organizations thought the environmentalists were simply a flash in the pan. In a year or so nobody would hear any more about them. Ralph Nader? Just a publicity-seeking guru who would be forgotten in a few months. Having thus underestimated the gravity of others' concerns over these problems, the affected industries were scarcely in a position to deal decisively with them.

Business has been largely oblivious as well to the changes that have taken place over the past few years in public expectations of corporate conduct. Often it cannot understand and is not prepared for public outcry over its actions.

At a time when the newspapers were filled with indignant editorials and letters to the editor deploring ITT's dealings with the White House, Department of Justice, CIA, and other government agencies, ITT Chairman Harold S. Geneen told the Senate Judiciary Committee:

> As a businessman, fundamental in my mind is the question of "What does a diversified company such as ITT do that is good for the economy and/or bad for the economy?" On this basis, knowing the degree of effort that our company has consistently in the last 12 years expended as well as the personal effort of our management and myself to strengthen the company within the domestic economy. . . . I am surprised to find a company such as ours—and there are others—without much chance of stating its case, put in the category of a nonconstructive and fearsome force within our society.

Another harassed chief executive complained:

> I don't understand it. I'm doing the very same things now that I did in the early 1960s. Yet, then, I was applauded as an enlightened and pro-

gressive business statesman; now I'm vilified as a stubborn defender of
the status quo.

This executive and others like him could learn a lesson from the words
of the bard of Tin Pan Alley, Eddie Green: "Then was then, and now is
now!"

Ironically, public relations professionals are the first to acknowledge
the primacy of perception and performance over communications in trying
to enhance the corporate image, but some are regrettably hesitant about
putting it quite so baldly to the chairman or president. When asked why there
is this curious reluctance to speak up, the senior PR officer for one of the
Midwest's largest manufacturers explained:

> As long as the business image is perceived as a communications problem,
> top management can slough it off by saying it's something for the PR
> boys to worry about. But once you suggest that it is tied in with the
> company's overall performance, then you're talking about senior man-
> agement's direct responsibility, and that's risky business. It's better to
> take a little heat, from time to time, in the PR Department and let it go
> at that.

The trouble with "letting it go at that" is that matters rarely get any
better, while the challenges keep mounting. Unless steps are taken consistently to bring performance more closely into line with legitimate public
expectations, issues and problems that now appear just on the horizon will
have a profound effect on business and industry in the years ahead.

Matching Performance with Expectations

It is not surprising that industries and companies fail to act quickly enough
to improve their performance, because they seldom learn from the mistakes
of others and they frequently overlook early warning signs.

Obviously, no business can satisfy all expectations all the time. This
is particularly true when the threshold of acceptable performance is steadily
rising. Yet a business should be able to keep its performance generally within
the boundaries of acceptability and avoid actions that would predictably
outrage large segments of the public.

Despite scores of danger flags, the automobile industry did not alter
its performance with respect to safety until the federal government intervened on a massive scale. The packaged goods industry dragged its feet for
years on patently needed reforms and finally had truth-in-packaging legislation forced on it. And in the face of compelling evidence to the contrary,
the banks insisted that they were telling the small customers all they needed
to know about finance, thus inviting truth-in-lending legislation.

To avoid enforced regulations, business will have to start making more
voluntary changes before issues become inflammatory. And in the future

there are likely to be a variety of public expectations that companies and industries will have to accommodate.

One of the most obvious issues that will face business over the next decade will be how to deal with what has been termed "the new labor force." To satisfy the increasingly demanding work force, business will have to provide jobs that offer self-fulfillment and participation in the advances of the enterprise. This means not only opening up entry-level positions for minorities and women, but also establishing comprehensive training and equitable promotion opportunities all along the line. To forestall costly federal intervention, grandiose 10-year plans for upward mobility need to be augmented by immediate and specific steps.

Senior management has a penchant for saying to its staff officers: "Show me the impact on the bottom line." On the labor force issue, there is a persuasive response. Failure to comply satisfactorily with federal equal opportunity standards has already cost the steel industry $30 million and AT&T $50 million in raises, back pay, and promotion adjustments, and the end is nowhere in sight.

Another issue that will loom even larger is consumerism and the business community's response to it. The more knowledgeable and sophisticated consumers in tomorrow's marketplace will expect products to perform efficiently, to provide satisfaction, and to be completely safe. They will become increasingly impatient with those manufacturers and retailers who leave them with problems once the merchandise is in the home.[2]

For a variety of reasons, such as haste, carelessness, or dreams of ownership outweighing judgment, many consumers do not read the fine print on the products they buy. Under the mandate of consumerism—"Let the seller beware!"—it is the business's job to read that fine print for them, or suffer the consequences.

One of these consequences will likely be that the frustrated consumer will address more and more of his or her inquiries to government, where even top-ranking officials lend a solicitous and sympathetic ear. That could very well result in stricter regulation and more consumer/public interest legislation.

For example, banks and other savings institutions will, in all probability, be forced to disclose more fully the terms under which interest will be paid on savings, so the consumer can make intelligent comparisons. The terminology used in referring to interest will be standardized so there will not be, as there are today, dozens of different ways to compound interest on a savings account.

In retrospect, the business lobbyists' widely heralded 1974 "victory" over the bill to create a Consumer Protection Agency is likely to prove costly indeed. For one thing, in the new Congress the bill's proponents are likely to make even greater efforts to enact legislation that will be much tougher from business's viewpoint. For another, the business lobby's success underscores anew the dismal fact that business has not originated a single piece of constructive consumer legislation and that the consumer laws now on the books were put there over sustained business opposition.

Recalling his half-century of public relations practice, John W. Hill, founder of the nation's largest PR firm, Hill and Knowlton, pointed up a lesson for business leaders to ponder: "Whenever business adopted an adversary posture toward government and failed to make effective efforts to help shape legislation constructively, it usually lost not only the legislative battle but the esteem of the people as well."[3]

Still another issue that will become increasingly prominent in the future is advertising. A recent Roper Poll showed that the man-in-the-street holds business strictly accountable for the honesty and accuracy of its advertising claims. He deeply resents any shading of the truth in the claims that ads make and will retaliate against those companies that offend.

To consumers, advertising reflects industry's intentions, will, strengths, and weaknesses. More than merely reflecting them, though, it projects them on a giant screen, magnifying the differences between the casual ethics of everyday life and the much stricter ethics to which we all in our best moments aspire.

Any ad executive worth a double martini used to argue glibly that it was unrealistic to assume that advertising had any responsibility for maintaining ethical and cultural standards. He used to assert that, by its very nature, advertising dealt in half-truths and that that practice was perfectly acceptable in our society.

This is not so any longer. There have been so many examples of deception by manipulation that honest advertising and informative labeling have become central to the consumer movement. Eventually, tough truth-in-advertising legislation will very likely require all advertisers to furnish consumers with specific documentation of their claims to safety, performance, and efficiency. And just as a healthy respect for truth is indispensable to the functioning of our democratic society, so is a healthy respect for the public's opinion indispensable to businesses serving their economy. It pays to be prepared.

Taking Protective Steps

If this scenario of future issues has any validity at all, it should raise one major question in the business executive's mind: Why wait for PR disaster to strike? Several courses suggest themselves as ways of avoiding trouble:

☐ Study the mistakes of others in public relations as intently as in other areas of business and draw lessons from them. As Chief Justice Holmes put it, "The first step toward improvement is to look the facts in the face."

☐ Learn to read early warning signs more accurately and to interpret them in terms of individual businesses. Social scientists are furnishing increasingly sophisticated tools to aid in this effort, and business should use these to their fullest.

☐   Reassess policies and performance constantly in light of new social and political trends. Good public relations must be based on solid performance, not on flimsy facade. Some desirable changes in performance may seem costly in the short run, but these costs should be weighed against the costs of an all-out fight with consumer groups or government agencies on a particular issue, and against the far greater costs of radically altering a business system, which will likely be required if present business policies are not modified.

Over the years, business has shown extraordinary resilience in adapting its policies and performance to emerging trends. Despite what critics say, it is hard to conceive that it will not be flexible enough to accommodate present and future shifts in style and mood.

Inevitably, this adaptation will involve the development of new concepts of the corporation's role in society. In this role it will be more sensitive to the needs and aspirations of people, more keenly attuned to human as distinct from material values, and more alert to demands for an improved balance between man and nature.

Businessmen should never underestimate one fact that Ralph Nader and his associates stress endlessly: that nobody has a larger stake in our economic system—or a larger say in our society—than U.S. business. Whether that system and that society continue to work to the satisfaction of business will depend, ultimately, on how successfully individual businesses demonstrate that *they* can work for the good of everybody.

Notes

1. Address given at the 26th Annual Business Conference, Rutgers University, New Brunswick, New Jersey, May 31, 1974.

2. See also Lawrence A. Bennigson and Arnold I. Bennigson, "Product Liability: Manufacturers Beware!" *HBR*, May–June 1974, p. 122.

3. Address given at the 16th Annual Institute of the Public Relations Society of America, University of Maryland, College Park, Maryland, July 10, 1974.

18

What's a PR Director for, Anyway?

ROBERT S. MASON

Don't hire that new public relations director until you've determined what you have for him to do, how he will work with other top executives, what your PR goals are, and what PR can add to your organization. Such a presearch will show whether you need (or want) someone who can take part in policy-making or simply a PR technician—at half the price. The former is more likely to be the case, the author suggests, since nearly every major policy decision has its public relations implications. What is more, the independent orientation that is typical of most PR directors adds a significant dimension to the decision-making process.

Executive recruiting companies are reporting a dramatic increase in the number of searches for public relations executives. Apparently, consumerism, environmentalism, and many other popular and special interest movements that are echoed daily in the media are accelerating management's search for public defenders, communicators, and spokespeople—that is, for PR men and women.

However, the typical job description management is handing search companies is not very different from what it was 10 or even 20 years ago. In other words, management is responding to growing public pressures by seeking more PR help, but it is giving the critical presearch process little attention. Considering management's past disappointment with public relations (which paradoxically is another factor in the upsurge of PR recruiting), using the same old approaches to staffing seems likely to lead only to the same old frustrations with PR.

In a few leading companies, however, management is doing its homework *before* bringing in the search company and *before* hiring a new public relations director. Executives are asking themselves these hard questions:

☐ What responsibilities can we delegate to the new public relations manager, and how should these responsibilities mesh with the other staff functions?

☐ What specifically do we expect the new PR director to accomplish?

☐ How will we integrate this new person into our organization?

☐ How will we evaluate his or her performance?

It is too early to tell whether the companies that are using this rigorous presearch discipline are achieving "better public relations," but they are certainly getting a better grip on this elusive function.

My purpose is to suggest applications of this approach that will be useful to other managements with PR staff problems and related issues. I will explore each of the four key questions mentioned earlier, not to provide a formula that will serve all companies, but to bring out the critical choices for management that each question raises. The alternative to facing and making these choices is mere repetition of unsatisfactory experience with PR people, leading perhaps to Robert Townsend's well-known solution of simply abolishing the function.[1] The first step is to determine what you need.

Spectrum of Responsibilities: Technician to Strategist

The public relations director's responsibilities are just what top management decides to delegate, no more and no less. The spectrum of possibilities is much broader than is generally conceded, ranging from policy to technique.

The technique end of the spectrum is easily dealt with. Obviously, the person should be able to do (or get done) with a degree of excellence the usual chores: quarterly and annual reports to stockholders; development, writing, and placement of articles and speeches; publicity, including press releases; organization and implementation of special events (exhibitions, conferences, receptions, tours); and so on.

These activities constitute the canon of PR expertise and have in the past few decades become highly refined. Management may reasonably establish mastery of these skills as a sine qua non of candidates for the top PR job.

It is, however, at the other end of the scale—the policy end—that problems begin to arise. The techniques of PR, like those of any other staff function, are the raw materials that top management molds to its purpose. But it is for management to decide whether, and to what extent, it will consult with PR on matters of policy. Looked at another way, the question is: To what extent will the PR director be "let in on" corporate strategy?

The kicker in this question is the near impossibility of separating PR policy from overall corporate strategy. The fact is that every major decision has public relations implications. The bigger the decision, the larger the company, and the greater the number of people that are affected, the more significant the PR component becomes. More often than not, however, the chief executive officer would no more consult with PR about a major policy matter than ask his barber for stock market investment advice. And yet major public relations problems continually arise from policy decisions in which PR has had no part:

☐ A new pricing policy arouses a storm of protest among consumers.

☐ A financial reporting decision creates panic or euphoria in the investment community, causing stock market prices to seesaw.

☐ A design or packaging decision creates suspicion or hostility, ending in government regulation.

☐ Communal wrath against the company is stirred by decisions involving location or relocation, waste disposal, and so on.

☐ Hiring or firing policies bring charges of discrimination by one faction of labor or another.

☐ Decisions to deal with certain governments, domestic or foreign, precipitate protest marches.

The newspaper clipping files of most *Fortune* "500" companies provide ample documentation of these generalized examples—and many more. Whether the management decisions that reaped these bitter public relations harvests were "good" or "bad" is not the issue here. The point is that whether or not management includes consulting on policy issues among the responsibilities of the public relations director, policy decisions still carry PR implications.

Management may think, perhaps rightly, that public relations people don't know anything about pricing, finance, product design, waste disposal systems, or personnel, and may decide that it is therefore pointless to include them in policy-making deliberations. But by making this decision, management has simultaneously and implicitly assumed the public relations burden itself. The public relations director may not be sitting at the conference table, but like the ghost of Banquo, the "publics" are.

Presearch a Prerequisite

Management should decide at the presearch stage of recruiting a public relations executive what degree of policy-making participation PR will have since this decision will greatly influence the kind of person management will be searching for. If top management decides to assume exclusive responsibility for the PR implications of major policy decisions in all areas and to delegate to PR responsibility for only the implementation of policy, the staffing problem is a relatively simple one. Indeed, many managements state very clearly what they want a PR director to do. For example, the CEO of a large consumer products company said:

> I just want a guy with a good news sense who can travel around our divisions, spot stories, and get them written up in the business papers and some popular magazines. . . . The annual report? Well, that's our financial VP's baby. The PR man can doll it up, but it's the financial man who's in charge.

The head of a major financial organization stated:

> I must make a hundred speeches a year. I need a PR man who can help me write them or get them written for me. Whatever else he does is incidental. He can always find good people to help him with the other things. When I started this job I struggled with a speech for days, writing it myself, and it was a bomb. I never want to be in that position again. For me, a good PR director is one who can consistently give me excellent, polished speeches that say what I want to say the way I feel comfortable saying it.

Job Descriptions Should Mean What They Say. When the PR director's role is clearly limited, the job description writes itself, and the position is relatively easy to fill. However, the broader the definition of PR's role and the closer PR gets to policy-making, the more difficult the recruiting problem becomes. It's the difference between hiring a technician to management and hiring a member of management. If the PR director is to be an important part of management, she must have ideas of her own, and other executives must be prepared to listen to them.

In a determined effort to upgrade its public relations, one of the largest life insurance companies went outside the PR field and recruited a professional sociologist with a Ph.D. to direct its PR. In this instance management clearly wanted an authoritative voice presenting—if not necessarily *representing*—public opinion in the organization's highest councils. Evidently, management meant what it said, for the sociologist has had an impact on decision making, and subsequent public relations policies bear the imprint.

On the other hand, a major investment banking firm carefully recruited a top-level PR director at a substantial salary plus considerable relocation costs. Within months it became clear that the communications gap between the new PR man and top management was as wide as the Grand Canyon.

The PR man had understood that he was being brought in at a policy level. The chief executive officer, however, was not accustomed even to discussing the public relations implications of his decisions and resented the PR man's efforts to do so. On every issue from financial reporting to fair employment to internal communications, the CEO knew exactly what he wanted and felt it was the PR man's job merely to implement these decisions. When the decisions proved unpopular or ineffective, internally or externally, the PR man's job was to make them look good. The PR director finally left and was replaced by a man who simply did as he was told—at less than half the salary.

Thus failure to distinguish between the need for an executive or a technician and to make an appropriate choice attracts the wrong candidates, lays the groundwork for early disillusionment on both sides, and contributes to the quick turnover that characterizes many top PR jobs.

Fitting PR In

How well the PR director fits into the organization depends on how well his relationship to the rest of management has been defined. The company cited earlier whose annual report was the responsibility primarily of the financial VP lost its public relations VP around annual report time. The two officers clashed, but it was the PR man who was obliged to leave.

The outcome of this situation suggests that the PR function was of less importance to management than other staff functions and therefore was subordinate to them. PR was, in effect, supporting the rest of the staff rather than functioning in its own right. The PR director's role was, as the CEO indicated, a modest one—to "doll things up" for the other officers. Presumably, management could have headed off organizational grief if it had precisely defined the limited nature of the PR position at the presearch stage.

When management limits PR, however, it must realize that it will be recruiting a technician and not an executive. Of course, the PR person in these circumstances must still exercise certain executive responsibilities—for example, setting priorities in handling other staff officers' requests.

The PR director of one of the largest professional service organizations was placed in precisely such a priority-setting situation. He was asked primarily to assist the various divisions of this loosely organized company with printed materials and conferences. Since it was a principle of top management not to interfere in operational matters, the PR man was obliged to choose among the demands made on him (from both staff *and* line officers) and thus to set PR policy by default. Inevitably, he aroused considerable resentment among those divisions he served less than others. Moreover, the key "publics" of the company remain, to this day, undefined, unidentified, and largely ignored. The company is being reorganized.

Thus defining the relationship of the PR director to the rest of the members of the management team is as important to successful PR staffing as determining the range of his responsibilities. In fact, the two considerations overlap.

For example, the PR director may not know much about marketing as such, but his sensitivity to the media and how they are likely to respond to, say, a new product could be a valuable asset in planning marketing policy. The degree to which PR will be expected or allowed to make this kind of contribution should be determined during the preselection process. If the company wants a PR director primarily with technical expertise rather than ability as a policy planner, and if PR's relationship to the marketing director is to be unquestionably subordinate, the job description should reflect these facts. The description, in turn, will influence the kind of person sought and ultimately selected. It is obviously wasteful to kill flies with cannons.

The sooner management makes these decisions, the more efficient the search process will be, and the greater the new PR director's chances to succeed.

PR at Work

Having determined the nature of the PR director's responsibilities and his relationship to the organization, management must then decide what specific goals it expects him to achieve.

Setting Goals for PR

As in other functions, specific goals make the task easier—in the PR director's case, the task of improving the public relations of the organization. Most sophisticated managements have learned that hiring a person "to improve the company's image" is the same as giving someone a clock without hands.

In the absence of specifically designated goals, PR directors—like others—will make their own. Floundering for management approval (and reward) they may try to make a star of the chief executive officer, arranging for personal profiles in large circulation publications. Or they may try to win prizes for the company's annual report or awards for plant tours and community programs.

In and of themselves there is nothing wrong with any of these efforts or activities, except that they may be quite irrelevant, indeed antithetical to the company's interests. The profile may come at a time when it is important for the organization to play down its reputation as a one-man show. The annual report prize may be an absurdity if earnings are plummeting and market share is diminishing.

In other words, PR "breakthroughs" have less meaning the further removed they are from the company's strategy and situation. Conversely, by tying PR goals to corporate strategy, management is in a much better position to offer the new PR director a realistic mandate, and the nature of these goals will help clarify the qualifications the person should possess.

Consider a company with excellent performance and prospects and a determination to accelerate growth by increasing its use of debt financing. Management has traditionally favored a "low profile," typified by its modest annual report. Now, however, in active pursuit of growth through increased debt strategy, management would like to present the company in "glowing technicolor." In such a situation, the PR director who has won awards for annual reports may be eagerly sought.

Except in times of crisis, public relations goals are very difficult, though not impossible, to specify. Crises, of course, dictate their own terms. Discovery of botulism in a food-canning company's product could (and in at least one recent instance did) put a company out of business. A serious charge of fraud against management, the breakdown of a delivery system, or poor customer service are other examples of problems that seriously damage a company's reputation. A prompt and thorough campaign of public information, supported and integrated at the highest levels of management and staffed by the best available PR talent, both external and internal, becomes critically important during such events.

When the heat on management is not so intense, however, goals are harder to identify and define; but it is still easier to formulate them before a new person is hired rather than after.

It is critical for management to distinguish between what PR routinely does and the particular problems and opportunities of the individual company. The PR needs of a consumer products company are radically different from those of a professional service organization, and even within industrial categories each company is unique. The more clearly management defines this uniqueness, the easier it is to identify the PR personality management should engage to cope with it.

Outsider in the Executive Suite

As many top managers have found, PR people are "different" and as a result harder to integrate into the management team. Understanding and anticipating the difference at the presearch stage spares much unnecessary conflict and waste.

The contrast between PR people and those who customarily fill other staff functions need not be labored. The financial officer typically is a product of an educational and training path that may include a graduate school of business, experience on Wall Street or the equivalent, and perhaps a stint with a management consulting firm or with another corporation as a sub-officer in the financial department. Similar career paths may be traced for other key staff officers in marketing, production, distribution, personnel and industrial relations, legal and economic counsel, and so on.

Oddballs and Ombudsmen

Most of our large corporations draw their chief executive officers from the ranks of the key staff officers. Public relations officers, in contrast, are oddballs. Their training is usually in the liberal arts or in the "soft" sciences, like sociology. Many PR people have come out of journalism, some have been teachers (usually of nonbusiness subjects), some have come out of government; only rarely do they come up through the ranks of business, demonstrate a public relations "flair," and thus acquire the PR personality.

The contrast in orientation between those in PR and their fellow corporate officers is both a liability and an asset from management's point of view. It is a liability to the extent to which PR people speak a different language and march to a different drummer. They may understand the business ethos and management skills, but this knowledge is central neither to their interests nor to their orientation. Indeed—and this is the main paradox—their usefulness to the corporation hinges on their ability to retain a degree of detachment from the motives that drive other members of management.

To be ombudsman, advocate, and communicator, PR people must at least be receptive to the forces that lie outside but impinge on the corporation:

☐ The PR director may be as enthusiastic about the company's new product as those in marketing, but he also knows that newspaper and magazine editors will not print a press release that reads as if it were a sales promotion piece.

☐ The PR director may sympathize with the CEO's motives in putting the company's bad news in small type between illustrations of its glowing prospects in the stockholder report, but she is also aware that publications like *Barron's* are more than likely to blow up the evasion in very large type.

☐ The PR director may spend nights studying the intricacies of the company's new billing system and may think it very ingenious, but he also knows that the system will have to be explained to customers who won't stay up nights to understand it and who may be very irritated by it.

The list may be elaborated but the point need not be: the PR director must view corporate policies with multiple vision to an extent that is not done by any other staff officer. For those in PR, loyalty to the company is never an excuse for failure to observe it from every point of view, including the most hostile, actual or potential.

Thus, both by orientation and function, the PR director tends to be an outsider in the executive suite, integrated with management but not stifled by it. It takes subtlety and skill on the part of top management to preserve and use this independence in the long-term corporate interest. Some companies have used the presearch stage to lay the groundwork for the new PR director.

For example, one CEO formed a PR search committee of key corporate officers. Charged with writing a detailed job description, the committee members quickly perceived sharp divergences among themselves of what constituted PR, what the company's stance should be on specific issues, how the PR director should function, and what his relationship to themselves should be. Some issues were resolved, some not. But there was a clearer understanding within management of the role of PR when the new PR person arrived on the scene and thus a better chance for collaboration and integration than would have been likely without the stage setting.

Evaluating PR

A discussion of the problem of evaluating the contribution of public relations might well start by considering these two contrasting cases:

In the early part of this century a young door-to-door peddler of stockings and undergarments, who worked a few towns in upstate New York, tried an experiment. He got up very early one morning and drove to a town he'd never worked before. He was a good salesman and managed to sell several dozen pairs of ladies' cotton stockings that day. The next morning he started out even earlier, drove to the same town, went back to each of the women he'd sold stockings to the day before and said, "I'm very sorry, madam, I overcharged you one cent a pair on the stockings I sold you yesterday. I discovered the mistake when I got home last night. I just want to return the difference."

Within a couple of weeks his business in that town multiplied several times. It was a carefully controlled experiment. He didn't try that ploy in any other town he worked. He sold the same merchandise at the same prices in the other towns. The experiment was successful, and he came to be known as "Honest Phil." He moved his family to the town of his experiment, opened a retail dry goods store, and prospered. The total cost of his successful public relations program—if it can be called such—was about 35 cents.

At about the same time, John D. Rockefeller, supposedly on the advice of PR counselors, began to give away dimes to "improve his image."

The contrast between the examples illustrates the importance of setting objectives: the more specific the goal, the easier it is to establish a cost/benefit relationship.

For instance, the cost of the stockings salesman's PR effort can easily be measured in terms of the amount of his increased sales. But it is much harder to determine how much it cost John D. Rockefeller to improve his image—if it can be assumed that it was affected at all. Therefore, the more specific management is in its expectations of PR, the easier it will be to evaluate its performance.

The suggestion is not that goals be firmly set at the presearch stage, but that management anticipate performance evaluation factors at this point. Management should not inhibit the contribution of the new PR director by presenting him with a set of programs cast in concrete but rather should lay the groundwork for a rigorous cost/benefit approach to PR.

Meaningful evaluation of PR's performance can only occur in an environment where PR itself is managed consciously as a rational function.

Notes

1. *Up the Organization* (New York, Alfred A. Knopf, 1970).

19

Perspective on Public Relations

KENNETH HENRY

A proliferating literature in the past few years examines how—and how well—management is using public relations to maintain and improve the corporation's reputation. Here Mr. Henry looks over this literature and singles out several books that executives should find especially interesting, readable, and helpful.

Three ideas emerge strongly from the more thoughtful books on public relations published since 1963:

1. It is argued that U.S. business has become urgently aware of its social responsibilities, and that it sees PR as playing a key role in deciding and executing those actions of the corporation most appropriate to the "public interest."
2. It is claimed that the corporate PR manager of the future must be a trained behavioral scientist.
3. It is predicted that effective PR programs will be increasingly based on and judged by responsible, continuous research on the attitudes of the many publics that ultimately grant the corporation its permit of social survival.

These major themes are forcefully presented in the two books published since 1963 that I consider the most helpful to management. One is *Corporate Public Relations*,[1] by Paul Burton, a journalism graduate and former wire service writer who has practiced his craft in two large industrial corporations and in a major PR counseling firm. His book is sensible, clear, concise, and complete. He discusses just about all the issues and arguments concerning corporate PR that top management would want or need to know in order to appraise or set up an inside department, or to hire outside counsel.

Burton offers no original thought or research (beyond using illustrative cases from his own practice), but he does synthesize everything of major current relevance in the growing PR literature. His approach is practical without being "cookbooky"—though he does occasionally give examples and advice on such routine requisites as writing press releases and cropping photos. But since such recipes constitute nearly all of the many so-called handbooks, a PR book that uses well under 10% of the text for how-to-do-it instruction is welcome indeed. Most top managers would find the majority of the book's compact 225 pages well worth the reading time.

For the larger issues surrounding corporate PR, thoughtful managers will probably also find stimulating *The Corporation and Its Publics: Essays on the Corporate Image,*[2] edited by John W. Riley, Jr. and his assistant, Marguerite F. Levy. This book, consisting of a series of nine scholarly but readable and provocative papers first presented in a symposium of the Foundation for Research on Human Behavior, examines PR from the social science point of view. This is not surprising; Dr. Riley is vice president and director of social research at The Equitable Life Assurance Society of the United States, which is sponsoring this project.

The entries are by an economics professor, two sociology professors, a college dean, two research organization executives, a corporation research psychologist, and Dr. Riley and his assistant. Dr. Riley himself is a sociologist and former chairman of the sociology department of Rutgers—The State University. Like Burton's book, Riley's is comfortably short—189 pages.

If management had time to examine only two books on PR, these two would probably be the most rewarding of any I know. I shall examine them in some detail, then mention a few other volumes that contribute to thinking on this subject.

Comprehensive Handbook

What *is* PR? The answers on record to this question could fill this magazine, and then some. But Paul Burton's answer will do as well as any: "Corporate public relations is a function of management which helps a company establish and maintain a good name for itself and its products or services through professional communications techniques." It is self-evident, Burton adds, that a company must deserve a good name in order to maintain it. Therefore PR people must know at all times the mainstream of public thought and help management predict how the public will react to any major decisions.

Social History.   The book begins with a brief social history of PR, reviewing the contributions of Pendleton Dudley and Ivy Lee, who opened counseling firms in the first decade of this century, as well as others such as Edward L. Bernays, who set up a practice in 1919, and Paul Garrett, the man "generally credited with establishing public relations as a management function within a large corporation." (Garrett became PR director and a one-man department for General Motors in 1931. He saw PR as a philosophy of management that "deliberately and with enlightened selfishness" made every business operating decision in terms of the customer's broad interest.)

Is PR a profession, like law or medicine? In asking this question, Burton addresses himself to the intramural debate that is current among PR practitioners. Actually, he answers, the question does not matter a whit to the PR man's boss. PR evolved to fill a need. The PR man does a job. And if the job fails, it is probably a PR man who promised management something that PR could do, or who failed to sell management on the merits of what the job could do.

Next, Burton asks a question that surely many managements have pondered: What makes a good corporate PR practitioner? Several things, he says in answering his own question. Foremost are "personality and compatibility within the corporation." Also, the PR person must be a competent writer, or be able to spot others who can write. Burton checked a leading PR personnel placement agency in New York; the records showed that 94% of the placed applicants had demonstrated writing ability and 77% of them had worked for wire services, trade magazines, or newspapers.

But a former newspaperman may fall flat on his typeface when he becomes a PR executive for a corporation. His job is no longer objective news reporting, letting the chips fall where they may. Now he gives advice about how the public will react to the news the corporation makes. He will also probably be amazed to find that external publicity, including press releases, accounts for as little as 10% of his time and thought. The balance of the work may be entirely new to him. Also he sometimes fails to grasp corporate protocol. Thus, some of the best news reporters have failed at PR, while some mediocre news reporters have "readily adapted to corporate life, discovered how to operate creatively, and carved a nice niche for themselves."

At present, on-the-job training in corporate PR departments is rare, Burton notes, probably because the field is new and still growing fast. As growth levels off and the field stabilizes, perhaps on-the-job training will become more prevalent. But if management wants good PR performance, one thing is essential: a new employee should be given time to learn the history of the company, its problems, its products, its competitors, and, most important of all, its objectives and policies. She should visit plants, and talk with top management and many department heads and employees before being permitted to communicate with the public on behalf of the company.

PR and Top Management.   This raises Burton's next point, the relation of PR to top management. The ultimate responsibility for PR, he insists—and almost all PR managers would agree with him—falls on the company's chief executive officer. Company PR can fail when a chief executive rejects the obligation and turns it over to an unqualified person. A PR program can also fail when management hires qualified personnel but hems them in because of a "basic anticommunications attitude." The PR director, like members of the financial and legal staffs, must have free access to, and the full support of, the top corporate executive. This ideally should be a reciprocal relationship, judiciously exercised, Burton believes; and there should be mutual confidence and consultation on policy decisions that may affect the company's relations with its publics.

It is therefore important, he argues, that the status of PR directors be at least equal to that of the people with whom they will be dealing most of the time.

The author fleshes out these skeletal points with a discussion of such factors as personality (is the boss press-shy or a publicity hog?), company size, the magnitude of the PR program, industry trends, and government and legal situations. He conveniently summarizes cogent cases from the public domain of top managers as industry spokesmen—e.g., Romney's famous speech on "The Dinosaur in the Driveway," and Connor's rebuttal, in behalf of Merck & Co., to the governmental attack on the pharmaceutical industry.

Finally, Burton spells out just how and what (with abundant specific examples) PR should regularly report to top management, ranging from immediate reporting of any major news or publicity that affects the company to "a bird's eye view of accomplishments at least once year."

Research—A Must. A chapter on PR research and programming in Burton's book opens with a recommendation to use the widely accepted principles of conducting preliminary research, isolating problems, setting policy, doing more systematic or deeper research, determining objectives, developing a plan of action, and carrying it out. In discussing each of these phases, Burton argues for a detailed "company profile," including a dozen categories of descriptive information and a set of solid questions that will almost automatically isolate the problems which require PR attention. This analysis calls above all for "realism." The author defines realism as "a thorough understanding of what PR can do and cannot do, what its potentialities and limitations are." He warns against the two extremes of the noncreative: "can't do" PR managers and the sharp practitioners who believe they can fool some of the people some of the time.

Research can throw light on corporate objectives, Burton explains. These should be as specific as possible. Two good starting questions are: "What is my company? What does it want to be?" Answers to these questions will guide the final program of action selected, and suggest the themes that "will make it palatable to the group or groups which the company is trying to reach." If publicity is part of the program, themes must also meet editorial needs. Burton demonstrates the value of his point by citing the case of a small, precision-bearings company which established an awards program to recognize scientists, inventors, or companies that made the greatest contribution to the field of miniaturization. Through this PR program, the company became "the best single source of information on the subject." And in time no writer on the subject could bypass this source.

12-Point Appraisal.   Other chapters in this book deal with PR departmental organization, the benefits and problems involved in selecting and using outside counsel, and that perennial PR headache—measuring results and effectiveness. Until the day comes when "a simple, effective and airtight system of measurement is developed," Burton proposes 12 methods as the best means available. To convey the gist of them, let me rephrase these recommendations into a set of questions:

1   Does product publicity produce a satisfactory number of promising inquiries?
2   If opinion research can be budgeted, what do people think of a company or some aspect of it before and after a PR program has been launched?
3   Is the company's stock price at an equitable level?
4   If a company suffers negative publicity, how does it preserve its original reputation? (Burton cites the cases of two companies convicted of price-fixing. One's reputation withstood the clamor because of an immediate and effective PR program; its stock returned to a normal market price within a few weeks. The stock of the second company had not recovered after several years.)
5   Does the company consistently receive favorable publicity? (Is it, for example, usually mentioned in roundup stories on the industry? If not, Burton suggests, the company's press relations may be inadequate or poor.)
6   Does the company's reputation help it to recruit easily the best people available?
7   Are labor difficulties fewer for the company with a good PR program than they are for the one without such a program?
8   Does the company experience a greater-than-average turnover because of management's failure to communicate effectively with its employees?
9   Does the company receive frequent inquiries? (Burton says that there seems to be a relationship between the number and type of inquiries a company receives and the success of its PR program.)
10   How often are the company's executives asked to speak?
11   If the company is scientific in nature, how many requests do technical media make for bylined articles from its research and development people?
12   Granted some awards may be regarded with skepticism, how often do the company and its personnel receive award recognition for genuine accomplishment?

Burton does not pretend that the 12-measurement methods he outlines will cover every company or situation that calls for evaluating PR effectiveness. However, PR people are accountable to management. They "should never stop trying to evaluate their own work. They should always attempt to measure it and then interpret these measurements for non-PR people." There are also some intangible, and unrecorded, factors in successful corporate PR, such as keeping unfair and inaccurate news stories from appearing in print. For this reason, among others, Burton argues against efforts to measure PR in just dollars and cents.

The negative publicity situation, he says in a later chapter, is almost inevitable for all but very young or very small companies. He discusses the PR techniques appropriate for handling, and often alleviating, three typical negative situations: a disaster, a strike, and an antitrust investigation. Management will find this discussion informative, helpful, and vividly documented with actual cases. To mention just a few of the specific suggestions Burton offers:

☐ "Truth" is the guideline to handling the negative situation as well as to obtaining favorable publicity.

☐ "A disaster is always headline news, and the sooner the news media get all the facts, the sooner the story disappears from the headlines."

☐ As for attempts to obtain favorable publicity, PR men should never lie to the media. "Situations arise in which a lie may seem to be the easiest way out, but when the truth becomes apparent—as it inevitably will in time—the lie will be much more damaging."

The same truism applies to the timely disclosure of bad financial news, Burton argues. He calls this function one of the most important and difficult of corporate PR. His excellent 30-page chapter on "Financial Communications" spells out the SEC and Stock Exchange requirements that prescribe and circumscribe financial PR. PR people must have some knowledge of these regulations. The author discusses timely disclosure—a far from unambiguous requirement that plagues current PR judgment—in terms of major corporate matters and rumors. He also presents the most effective PR techniques for handling the annual report and dealing with security analysts and shareholders, two of the corporation's admittedly crucial "publics."

The book closes with a two-page chapter called "The Future." Here Burton predicts the disappearance of "flim-flam artists" and the rise of responsible PR, based on solid communications efforts. "Public relations as a sales tool is successful—it works." But good PR needs better research. Research methods are still in a primitive stage. They can indicate what people think, but not why. PR men need to have both kinds of knowledge to do what Burton regards as their primary job: "to break down the barriers which prevent men from viewing the truth as it actually exists."

Searching Symposium

John Riley's symposium on *The Corporation and Its Publics* is more abstract than Burton's book, but probes deeply into some fundamental issues of corporate behavior and the corporation's relationship with the larger society that ultimately sanctions its continuance.

Image and Reality. Riley says that the contributors' chapters "do not constitute a how-to-do-it manual for managers who want to know how to go about finding and developing a corporate image. Rather they explore the contents of the concept and then try to see it within a broader frame of reference." Nor was any preliminary definition of "corporate image" offered to the contributors. Each defined the term, if at all, as he chose. In the concluding chapter, Riley and Levy note that the words "corporate *reputation*" mean essentially the same as "corporate *image*."

How do the contributors to this symposium face the issues that they see regarding corporate reputations? And what are the issues that they select as crucial? Gerhart D. Wiebe, Dean of Boston University's School of Public Relations and Communications, notes that thought, planning, and discussion of the corporate image all too often stop at appearance and seldom probe the substance. He sees the real issue as the social dynamics that relate corporations to the larger society. Wiebe insists that the time has come to reexamine the nature of the underlying company-public relationships.

The small business of an earlier day was usually dominated by a single personality, well known in the small community as Mr. Big, who was in continuous and effective communication with the public. Mr. Big *was* the corporate image. Today's notion of corporate image, however, is a "by-product of the increasing size of business institutions." Plants are dispersed, products or services are distributed nationwide, and employees number in the thousands. Many corporations have replaced the single dominant executive with team management. Thus present-day corporation management is hard put to sustain a unified corporate personality.

Another problem of the corporate image, according to Wiebe, is that "so few corporations have decided what they *claim* to be, or what they *aspire* to be." Thus the first question becomes: Is there an integrated corporate personality—a body of policy or articulated self-perception—to which people can relate? Granted such a self-concept, image research can then reveal the accuracy or distortion with which the public perceives what the company believes it projects.

Corporations can remain going concerns only in a vigorous and economically sound society. Popular culture tends to portray the little businessperson as a good guy, the big businessperson as a bad guy. In good times, this belief recedes. But bad times could revive it, so that business must keep the public esteem it has earned since the depression. A vigorous and growing society is the best overall insurance for corporate images. "The price tag is forthright involvement in the nurturing of the society,'' Wiebe states. So one must also ask: Does the company promote the kind of society that will continue to grow and prosper?

The corporation, Wiebe believes, must conduct research to find out whether people receive and believe the messages released by the company. But one hard fact is ''that corporations as such are not very interesting to most people.'' PR messages that tell only the corporation's achievements and plans have a narrow and specialized appeal. No wonder that people, if asked, say they think highly of a corporation, but ''don't as much as write a postcard if the government threatens to break up its corporate structure. . . . The corporation's messages about itself have only minor saliency in the individual's perception of his relevant world.''

Wiebe summarizes his points by urging that companies ask themselves these questions about their public relationships.

1 Does the company have an integrated, recognizable self-concept?
2 Does it appropriately nurture the larger society that sustains it?
3 Does the company tell its publics what it is doing to solve problems that these publics perceive as their own problems?

What Do the Publics Think?   Another contributor to *The Corporation and Its Publics* is Robert O. Carlson, PR counsel for the overseas affiliates of Standard Oil of New Jersey. Carlson reviews research done during the past two decades to examine what people think of corporations. He finds no sizable body of hostile feeling in the United States today, but says that this appraisal rests on fragile evidence.

The information that the average American has on some large companies is nil and on others, dead wrong. Like Wiebe, Carlson sees the lack of public antagonism toward companies as no ground for complacency. ''Today's corporate executive worries not so much about overt antagonism from his publics as he does about their indifference and apathy.''

Carlson asks a penetrating question: If surveys show that a majority of citizens express apathy and disinterest toward large corporations, does it make sense for companies to strive for higher visibility? What benefits can be expected from increased public awareness of a corporation's personality? Survey after survey shows that people have no impression of the companies that contribute most to the economic life of the United States. It cannot therefore be assumed that every company has or should have a corporate image. We need, says Carlson, to have a much clearer rationale for showing how the corporate image influences behavior toward the corporation.

Survey findings show that people who like a company's products tend to like the company that makes them. But the surveys do not show which attitude comes first—liking the product or the company. The same surveys show that people can like the company without buying its products, or dislike the company and continue to buy what it makes.

The notion that a favorable corporate image is desirable assumes that favorable attitudes toward a company are translated into desired actions. This proposition is "audaciously exciting," Carlson says, and explains the "present rash of interest in the corporate image." It "looks like an easy answer to harassed management's dream of being loved by more and more people with each passing year."

But responsible studies repeatedly show that effective public information programs do not necessarily change attitudes in a desired direction. Little research has been done to get at what company knowledge or ignorance means to the respondent.

Does the corporation in time become the prisoner of its image? Carlson calls this an intriguing question. An obvious example is the corporate name that has become obsolete or misleading (e.g., Minnesota Mining and Manufacturing Company, Great Atlantic & Pacific Tea Company, Inc.). Even more fascinating, Carlson suggests, is the possibility of the self-fulfilling corporate image. For instance, what of a corporation that strikes a pose, and then must behave accordingly because it finds the public forces it to? The corporate image is far from static. We need research which specifies the internal dynamics that cause corporate images to change.

Carlson concurs with Peter Drucker in calling the corporation primarily a political being. This suggests that programs designed to create favorable corporate images should concentrate greater attention on specific target groups which exercise power in the political sphere. Nor is it possible to reverse curiosity about the corporation, once aroused. "The company which proclaims that it wants the public to know it better must be ready to answer some very searching questions on occasion."

In a downbeat concluding sentence, Carlson states, "We are tempted to wonder whether . . . large companies may not be so remote from the lives of ordinary individuals that they are no longer targets for strong, personal feelings of any sort." This may be an unduly pessimistic view. But it raises assumptions and questions that most writers on PR and most practitioners ignore. This is the real value of the Riley symposium: it raises tough questions that deserve management consideration.

Clusters and Segments.   Reuben Cohen, vice president of Opinion Research Corporation, and Herbert H. Hyman, professor of sociology at Columbia University, contribute informative articles to the symposium on how social science measures attitudes toward corporations. They examine the available useful techniques as well as some unsolved problems of present methodology. Cohen demonstrates the generally satisfactory results so far obtained by "cluster analysis"—a procedure that groups related factors which can be simply scored for statistical analysis (e.g., "corporate leadership" includes notions of a company as progressive, outstanding in new product development, well managed, and so on, to yield a cluster of seven related components).

Hyman argues against the value of research which is undifferentiated by "strategic publics." The blended, mass image may obscure "critical images held in small pockets of society." The blandness of the current public image of the corporation, he suggests, may in part be an artifact of the research to date. Thus, research must focus on segments of publics, such as ethnic groups. Research might also seek to distinguish whether people think well or ill of the corporation because of "the personnel involved or the corporate body itself."

How do Americans view corporation executives, and does this influence how they react to the corporation? Hyman suggests studying the corporation, as it has been portrayed in the mass media, by the method that has come to be known as content analysis. What are the particular actions or parts, he asks, in the complex and historic structure of the corporation that produce the end-product image?

Other contributors to the Riley book discuss the effect of automation and such demographic changes as population growth on corporate images, and the difficulty of developing corporate images overseas (in the face of such problems as illiteracy, negative attitudes toward private enterprise, the shift of ruling political elites, and the resentment of the underprivileged toward corporations symbolizing U.S. wealth.)

In another chapter, Kenneth E. Boulding, professor of economics at the University of Michigan, argues that the distinction between profit and nonprofit organizations is breaking down. His key point is that the outside social environment is continually pressing the economic decision maker. The role of PR, he says, testifies to the importance of the nonmarket environment. The purpose of PR, as Boulding sees it, is to sell the organization, not the product.

In a concluding chapter, Riley and Levy summarize the corporate image debate as taking "shape around the problem of legitimation of power. . . ." General agreement exists that the modern American corporation is the major nongovernmental institution in the society. It is therefore often described as a quasi-public institution, and the United States as a corporate society. The legitimacy of corporate power has been satisfactorily based on the old doctrine of natural rights. An alternative argument, the writers note, is that the corporation contributes to the general welfare by providing employment and other community services. But no clear agreement has been reached on just what are the corporation's commensurate obligations to society, or whether social responsibility should be institutionalized in the private corporation or in public government.

It seems reasonable, Riley and Levy conclude, "to interpret the concern of many corporate leaders with their public images as an expression of their need for a clearer understanding of their responsibilities to the public and, in turn, of the public's expectations of them."

The "Public Interest"

The foregoing conclusion suggests a deeper underlying problem: What is the public interest? John W. Hill, founder in 1927 of the PR counseling firm of Hill and Knowlton, has tried to answer this question in his business auto-biography, *The Making of a Public Relations Man,*[3] which, in a sense, has some of the characteristics of a long love letter to the steel, natural gas, aerospace, and other industries he has served as counsel.

Hill states as an article of his personal faith that PR is the ultimate ruling force in the free world. But PR has no power to create any lasting value where none exists. Therefore corporate management, to earn public confidence, must make decisions in terms of what it genuinely believes to be the public interest. Granted that the corporation's primary responsibility is to make sufficient profits to survive, it may be viewed by the community "as a bearer of social responsibilities that are inseparable from its economic function." The corporation must develop its own definition of national purpose and also a publicly defensible concept of its own contribution to that purpose. According to Hill, sound business policy must pass two tests: profit production and public approval.

Hill devotes his two key concluding chapters to defining the public interest that the corporation must serve to ensure its own survival. He assembles philosophy on the subject from many armchairs—answers to queries he made of 50 leaders in education, government, theology, and labor. Predictably, no pat, single definition evolved. The varied answers, he reports, suggest that the public interest must be specified in given instances for given audiences. Public and private interest are not necessarily opposites. Long-range considerations appear important. In the words of one of Hill's respondents: "The public interest requires doing today the things that men of intelligence and good will would wish, five or ten years hence, had been done."

Hill quotes other respondents extensively, by name, in a discussion worth the careful attention of everyone who has ever uttered the phrase "public interest" as a decision criterion. He urges every management group that invokes the public interest in support of any action to:

1   Study the issue and explain why the position or proposal is in the public interest.
2   Never use the term loosely or too briefly on the assumption that it will be automatically accepted.
3   Consider the long-term effects of the position taken.

4 Recognize that the better informed people are, the more capable they are of judging where the public interest lies.

The Coming "Publicombine".   At one point in his autobiography, Hill incidentally observes that the future PR counseling organization will be expected to offer a broad spectrum of services. This is the basic premise of another book, *The Relations Explosion,*[4] by William L. Safire.

The maverick manager, Safire argues, will force a new breed of executive to enter the field of business communications within the next 10 years. This new executive will be a maverick too, and he will be a generalist. He will be knowledgeable about advertising, PR, product publicity, labor relations, community relations, and stockholder information services, but the specialists working under him will know more than he about any of these present specialities. He will be the corporation's "communications generalist." He will be goal-oriented, and his goal will be to pull together all of the activities dealing with the company's relations (public, industrial, employee, and so forth) so that they serve "a single, clear-cut goal of management." He will need to know what varied communications techniques can do, then use these to manage "persuasive missions." The fused communications specialties, directed toward a common goal, will produce synergism; the sum will be greater than the total of the parts. A new communications combination will come into being. Safire calls it a "publicombine," defined in his glossary as " an amalgam of relations services that can act in a unified manner to define and accomplish corporate missions."

Corporations in the past have moved from the influence of bullheaded robber barons to do-gooders trying to be all things to all people. But corporations are learning, Safire believes, that to stay on their toes they may have to step on other people's. Many executives wonder whether there may be a happy medium between damning and pandering to the company's publics. Communications men of the future will drop their messianic pose and adopt a more sophisticated attitude, considering both profits *and* ethics. The company will then aggressively obtain information about the needs and rights of its publics, "evaluate the information in the light of its own needs and rights to determine company conduct, and then—with the conduct decided on and the outgoing communications mission clearly drawn—use every organ of its corporate body to sell, argue, plead, persuade, affect, and convince."

Safire discusses a number of the individual communications areas and techniques that he sees as fusing in a future service publicombine; he also looks at relevant social science theory and research. He shows that he has done his homework well in the social sciences; he cites studies and theories of Katz and Lazarsfeld, Bohlen and Beal, Leon Festinger, and others. He also devotes a well-documented section to Abraham Lincoln's impressive PR skills and techniques, and seasons the pot further with name-dropping that includes Napoleon, Judge Learned Hand, humorist Finley Peter Dunne, novelist Herman Melville, and pollster Elmo Roper. The result is a jazzy, provocative, neologistic—but cogent and solid—book on business communications. His aim, he admits, is "to alert, annoy, and goad." Some readers may dislike the spangles and slang. But the substance behind the gaudy style is firm.

Other Points, Other Views

A number of other books deserve at least brief mention.

Use of Social Sciences.   Dr. Edward J. Robinson, in *Communications and Public Relations,*[5] pushes even further Safire's implied pleas that PR practitioners make far more use of the social and behavioral sciences. Robinson's 600-page textbook, responsibly reviews, translates, and evaluates social science theory and research directly relevant to PR applications, and repeatedly PR men are urged to use more research to provide feedback for evaluating the effectiveness of PR programs. I only wish that in these chapters the author had acknowledged the fact that his views are not without precedent; the importance of applied social science to PR has been stressed for years by Edward L. Bernays,[6] Rex F. Harlow,[7] and Verne Burnett,[8] among others.

Case Histories.   Another textbook is John E. Marston's *The Nature of Public Relations,*[9] currently recommended to members of the Public Relations Society of America who apply for accreditation. Its chief virtues are complete coverage and more case histories than any other book reviewed here. Its drawbacks, at least for the general reader, are probably the prodigality of cases which are too often trivial and a style as pedestrian as Robinson's.

Role of Chief Executive.   Many managers will be interested in a brief study (36 pages) by Robert W. Miller, *Corporate Policies and Public Attitudes,*[10] which "stresses the views of the chief executive and his role in public relations and policy formulation." Miller was led to make the study because of the dearth of information about how the chief executive officers of large corporations go about attacking the PR job. He reports highlights from the findings of a questionnaire survey of 250 chairmen or presidents of the largest corporations in the United States. He also conducted personal interviews, from which he quotes liberally, with the presidents or chairmen of 24 major corporations.

Miller opens the report with a summary of the research. Here, in brief, are the 10 main findings:

1   PR has achieved a secure place in the corporate structure, with large expenditures for PR programs and activities which are now recognized as essential.

2 The PR director in an increasing number of companies (31% in Miller's study) plays a part in principal policy discussions and formulation.

3 In the majority of companies, the chief executive recognizes and accepts his ultimate personal responsibility for PR.

4 The growing local, state, and federal regulation, restraint, and control of business have multiplied the need for companies to engage not merely in public, but also in government, relations.

5 Top management is frequently critical of its own PR people, largely on the grounds that they understand inadequately the overall economic picture and the total corporate situation.

6 Most executives consider public attitudes a vital factor in determining corporate policies, but few feel certain of what the public actually thinks about their company or of how public attitudes might be measured and defined. (Riley's previously discussed book should be helpful to managers in this respect.)

7 More than half of the respondents claim to be personally much concerned with public attitudes and with the effect of public thinking on long-range company sales and profits.

8 About one fourth of the responding executives expect to make increasing use of outside counsel in the next five years, especially for business-government relations; further, they expect outside counsel to work directly with the chief executive officer rather than with the PR department.

9 Nearly all respondents expect PR to become more important and effective in their corporations in the next five years.

10 The executives view public attitudes as a persisting, long-range problem—one to be "continually faced up to, solved and solved again."

Miller documents these conclusions with a number of tabulations from his survey and a highly readable sampling of quotes from the men he interviewed. John Hill's discussion of the public interest is underscored in the words of one chief executive who told Miller: "Even if you have some weight to throw around, I think you should not throw it around unless you are certain that your cause is a good one, and a just one—and in the public interest."

Some 51% of the companies report conducting public opinion or attitude polls, and in 46% of these companies the chief executives were involved in survey evaluation. However, there is uncertainty that the currently used methods dependably measure public opinion. Some executives point out that they *expect* their PR experts to be proficient in finding out how the public feels about the company—but confidence is lacking that such proficiency exists in fact. Management further specifically criticizes PR people "for not having a solid background in economics, finance, management, organizational philosophy, and the behavioral sciences."

This leads Miller into a report of the educational and business training of top PR executives in the companies studied, and a suggested PR curriculum for graduate business administration schools. He strongly recommends study of communications theory, the behavioral sciences, business-government relations, and a seminar in PR cases. This may suggest to management some qualifications which it should consider when hiring new PR personnel for the future.

Apparently, Miller's executives are fully aware that the private corporation exists by, and must maintain, the consent of the public and the government. He concludes with this sentence:

> The chief executive officer of America's largest business corporation seems to feel that, unless the public as a whole accepts the philosophy of private enterprise—and believes in big business and in the rightness of big business—then, so far as his particular corporation is concerned, all short-range interests become merely academic.

Miller is now updating this study for a full-length treatment of corporate public affairs, to be published by the American Management Association.

Business and the Government.   In a newly published book, *Corporate Management in a World of Politics,*[11] Harold Brayman, director of public relations for DuPont for 20 years until his retirement in 1965, underscores the main theme of the recent literature—corporate behavior in the "public interest." His key premise is that public opinion must be won by both the government and business if they are to operate their programs effectively. Thus, business and the government must act as partners in public service and, when they differ on what the public interest is, seek the support of public opinion, which is the final arbiter. Brayman illustrates his argument with some dramatic DuPont PR victories.

Although the book has some of the built-in obsolescence of ephemeral journalism (topical references to people and events as late as early 1967), it is timely now. More important, it speaks in corporate management language about practical strategies in dealing with the government in jurisdictional disputes about who serves the public interest—and how. Some readers may find Brayman too exhortative at times, but few will fail to find some practical suggestions to apply to their government-relations programs.

PR Counseling.   For company managements interested in how the relatively large PR counseling firms operate, *Inside Public Relations,*[12] a staff-written Prentice-Hall "Executive Report," gives portraits of eight of the big firms, plus illustrative, capsule case histories. The 56-page brochure is practical, factual, and journalistically breezy—without becoming windy. It pulls no punches, reporting some of the seamier shenanigans of public record that other books usually cite vaguely. This book predicts, as Safire does, that PR in the future may be practiced by giant, integrated organizations performing a variety of communications services.

Collected Articles.   A sampling of articles by PR practitioners and social scientists is provided by *Perspectives in Public Relations,*[13] edited by Raymond Simon.

The problem of all such books, of course, is what they include. Who has read what before? And what is their scope? Specialists may be frustrated because they have read most of the entries, and decry the failure to include relevant but unfamiliar articles from other disciplines. Generalists may misjudge the subject because of the specific sample of articles the editors have chosen. Simon's book gives space to the writings of people who practice PR, including a number of speeches which would otherwise be inaccessible to the average reader. Simon also draws on PR journals for much of his material.

Around the World.   Another new book, *International Political Communication,*[14] is important for any company currently concerned with the media problems involved in international PR. Although the author, W. Phillips Davison, has focused on political communication, nearly all of his comments in this carefully researched and documented work suggest business applications.

Message or Massage.   And perhaps one should now take account of Marshall McLuhan's *Understanding Media: The Extensions of Man.*[15] The author, who in November 1966 joined a Toronto PR firm, alternately describes the medium as the message or the massage. McLuhan is more quotable than readable, and may have produced nothing more than an extended metaphor of perception. But he can stimulate thinking about communications from unlikely and provocative angles in his Alice-in-Wonderland logic of private free association.

In Political Campaigns.   For readers interested in PR as a tool in political campaigns, Stanley Kelley, Jr.'s *Professional Public Relations and Political Power*[16] has become newly available in paperback. It presents three case studies:

1   California's Campaigns, Inc.—how the Whitaker and Baxter firm has helped put men in office on the West Coast.
2   The American Medical Association's campaign against national health insurance.
3   The 1950 Maryland senatorial campaign of unknown John Marshall Butler against four-term Senator Millard E. Tydings.

These are fascinating accounts, with cogent relevancy and analogies for such gubernatorial campaigns as those in California and New York, where PR became highly visible, if not a primary issue.

Mirror Images. If three books signify a trend, we are in for a spate of autobiographies by PR practitioners, which John W. Hill launched in 1963 with the book cited earlier.

The publication of Edward L. Bernays' autobiography in 1965,[17] and last year Herbert Cerwin's *In Search of Something: The Memoirs of a Public Relations Man.*[18] Bernays offers, in addition to his operating principles and some inside stories of PR campaigns, a fascinating social history of U.S. business (including show business) events and personalities. Cerwin is a raconteur, and has provided more entertainment—though very good entertainment indeed, including a wild PR involvement with Salvador Dali—than insight into PR practice.

An excellent biography on pioneer PR practitioner Ivy Lee is Ray Eldon Hiebert's *Courtier to the Crowd: The Story of Ivy Lee and the Development of Public Relations.*[19] Bernays believed in engineering consent; Lee, in seeking consensus. Bernays claimed to crystallize opinion; Lee courted the opinion he believed the crowd held. Both Bernays and Lee served some of the most famous personalities among U.S. business managers in this century. The Bernays and Hiebert books are worthwhile social histories in their own right.

Increasing Role

This sampling of books since 1963 about PR suggests that the subject is growing in importance in the marketplace and on the campus. The writers foresee impending changes in the practice of PR. They see PR as playing an increasing role in shaping and documenting the corporation's social conscience. They see PR as applying the behavioral sciences more. And they see research as charting the course for PR programs and measuring their effects.

Notes

1. New York, Reinhold Publishing Corp., 1966.

2. New York, John Wiley & Sons, Inc., 1963.

3. New York, David McKay Company, Inc., 1963.

4. New York, The Macmillan Company, 1963.

5. Columbus, Ohio, Charles E. Merrill Books, Inc., 1966.

6. *Public Relations* (Norman, Oklahoma, University of Oklahoma Press, 1952).

7. *Social Science in Public Relations: A Survey and an Analysis of Social Science Literature Bearing Upon the Practice of Public Relations.* (New York, Harper & Brothers, 1951).

8. *Public Relations Handbook* (Englewood Cliffs, New Jersey, Prentice-Hall, Inc., 1950).

9. New York, McGraw-Hill Book Company, Inc., 1963.

10. Washington, D.C., The American University, 1965.

11. New York, McGraw-Hill Book Company, Inc., 1967.

12. Englewood Cliffs New Jersey, Prentice-Hall, Inc., 1963.

13. Norman, Oklahoma, University of Oklahoma Press, 1966.

14. New York, Frederick A. Praeger Publishers, 1965.

15. New York, McGraw-Hill Book Company, Inc., paperback edition, 1965.

16. Baltimore, The Johns Hopkins Press, paperback edition, 1966 (first published in 1956).

17. *Biography of an Idea: Memoirs of Public Relations Counsel Edward L. Bernays* (New York, Simon and Schuster, Inc., 1965).

18. Los Angeles, Sherbourne Press, 1966.

19. Ames, Iowa, Iowa State University Press, 1966.

PART FOUR

TAKING ON THE MEDIA

AN OVERVIEW

Business has a love-hate relationship with the media. Companies love publicity, but hate the price that must be paid to obtain it. The most sophisticated organizations, however, have learned the importance of candor, especially with regard to delicate situations. After all, the media wields a great deal of public power; that fact must be accepted and worked with. The articles in this section offer advice on how a company can best live with the institutions of information.

Chester Burger's article, "How to Meet the Press," is a very pragmatic attempt to counsel businesspeople on talking with journalists. It doesn't pretend to offer magic solutions, but gives concrete guidelines based on the author's experience with public relations and television news. While the advice looks "obvious," if more executives took it to heart there would be less animosity between the press and business.

Louis Banks follows with his own advice for "Taking on the Hostile Media." Banks goes to the heart of the problem by suggesting that business has never truly placed its case before the public, and endorses the use of issue advertisement as a way for companies to put their best foot forward. He also suggests that firms learn to provide technical information about their individual experiences to journalists as a way to deepen analysis.

"Bad Day at Bunker Point," by Edmond Marcus and Richard L. Heaton, takes the reader inside seminars put on by Gulf Oil Corporation to teach executives both the kind of reaction they can expect from the media to a particular event, and how they should respond. While it may seem artificial, the authors admit that the method "is a shock to most of those (executives) who attend. (But it works.) Seminar-trained Gulf managers have successfully applied the principles in (several instances. . .)."

Commenting on the recent trend in corporate issue advertising, David Kelley's "Critical Issues for Issue Ads" endorses the technique's principle, but analyzes why business has failed to stem the tide of public criticism in practice. The problem, he suggests, is that companies have used the language and beliefs of their critics to justify their actions. In doing so, they have been unable to change anyone's mind. Kelley counsels companies to fight the ideological assumptions behind their critics, and extol the virtues of the capitalist system, rather than trying to print out myriad corporate *mea culpas*, which fall on deaf ears.

Solomon Dutka's short piece, "Business Calls Opinion Surveys to Testify for the Defense," explains how sophisticated organizations have used the discipline of survey research and statistical sampling to buttress their opinions, and put their messages before the public. While companies have used the technique mainly to solve legal problems, their use in dealing with other public matters is straightforward.

Finally, another *HBR* case, "The Case of the Suspicious Scientist," examines a particularly touchy environmental incident handled poorly by the company involved. Three commentators offer advice on how companies can better handle public relations.

20
How to Meet the Press

CHESTER BURGER

One of the continuing problems facing a top executive or spokesperson of any organization in times of stress or major change is how to tell his company's story to a press, radio, or television reporter. The dilemma is that the official is fearful of putting his foot in his mouth by saying the wrong things. He knows he is at a disadvantage in talking with a reporter who is skilled at asking provocatiive questions in order to get provocative, interesting, and controversial answers. But the advantage need not be so one-sided. As this author discusses, there are certain guidelines that any executive can learn and remember which will enable him to meet the press with no postmortems necessary.

Why cannot business find a way to tell its story through the news media? Is the press really dominated by hostile, antiestablishment reporters? Are leftist editors biting the business hand that feeds them?

Many corporate spokespeople are convinced that today's news media, or at least their young reporters, are imbued with a fundamental bias against business.

Journalist Edith Efron believes, for example, that American news reporters are hostile to business, to capitalism itself. Referring specifically to television, she writes: "The antagonism to capitalism on the nation's airwaves, the deeply entrenched prejudice in favor of state control over the productive machinery of the nation, is not a subjective assessment. It is a hard cultural fact."

That, however, is an assessment with which one can reasonably disagree. As NBC commentator David Brinkley reminds us, "When a reporter asks questions, he is not working for the person being questioned, whether businessman, politician, or bureaucrat, but he is working for the readers and listeners."

If indeed the working press, reporters, and correspondents bear an antibusiness animosity, opinion polls tell us that such attitudes are quite representative of public opinion generally in the United States today. Rather than dismissing newspeople and news media as hostile, these may be the very ones to whom business ought to increase its communication because they typify the attitudes of millions of Americans.

Further, while the corporate president often finds his life and circle of personal contacts circumscribed within the territory of his management team, his luncheon club, and his country club, the working reporter's duties bring her into daily contact with broad strata of the population, ranging from politicians to factory workers and activist leaders. She cannot be dismissed lightly. Nor should she be written off.

So it would seem essential for corporate presidents and spokespeople to learn how to tell their stories effectively to the press, radio, and television reporters. But there is more to it than that. Unless one knows how to tell what commentator Eric Sevareid calls "the simple truth," one may fail to communicate. Although businesspeople are as intelligent as members of the working press, they are unskilled in the art of effective communication.

As Bos Johnson, president of the Radio-Television News Directors Association, says, "Businessmen are often so frightened or wary of the reporters that they come across looking suspicious. And there's no reason to be. They should put their best foot forward, speak out candidly, assuming they have nothing to hide."

Corporate presidents are not chosen for their outstanding abilities to articulate corporate problems. They are selected by their boards of directors because of their management know-how, or their financial expertise, or their legal proficiency, or whatever particular combination of these talents may be required by the immediate problems facing their companies. In utilizing their own skills, they are usually very good indeed.

But the skills of management are not the same as those required to deal with the news media. Reporters, whether they are employed by television (where most people get their news these days), newspapers, magazines, or radio are trained in the skills of interviewing. They excel in their ability to talk with someone and unearth a newsworthy story, one that will stimulate their viewers or readers. That is why they were selected; that is their surpassing talent; and that is precisely what unnerves corporate managers who choose to face their questions.

The elaborate files of newspapers and the film and tape libraries of television stations are replete with examples of boners, indiscretions, and insensitive statements voiced by corporate spokespeople. My own experience, first as a television network news executive and later as a management consultant, convinces me that there is no more mysterious reason for management's failure to communicate effectively with the news media than that it simply does not know how.

Business executives, rarely fearful of meeting their stockholders or their bankers, tremble before news reporters for fear they will accidentally or deliberately misquote them or pull their words out of context.

This can indeed happen, and it occasionally does. But every reporter knows that if he sins or errs more than once or twice, his job will be endangered. Newspapers do not like to print corrections of their errors—only a few do—but editors like even less to see errors break into print or be broadcast on radio or television.

The problem usually is not with the reporters. They try to get things straight. More and more these days, in fact, they are showing up for interviews armed with cassette tape recorders. This is an encouraging trend for the business executive because it ensures more accurate quotation. It also frees the news reporter from the note-taking burden so that she can concentrate on the subject under discussion.

But a recorded interview is hell for the executive who says the wrong things. If he puts his foot in his mouth, his words will be quotable and, most likely, quoted. No longer will he be able to blame the reporter for misquotation.

Business managers know from experience that news reporters will not hesitate to cover (i.e., write or film) a story that may be damaging to their company. From this perception, it is easy to conclude that the reporters are basically hostile to business. However, management often fails to understand that the reporter's first responsibility is to produce a newsworthy story that will interest the audience. The reporter frankly does not care whether that "public interest story" will help or hinder the company. The reporter will select, from his bag of techniques, whatever method he believes will produce an interesting and informative story.

So the lesson is clear: if the corporate executive has something to say, she must present it to the reporter in an interesting way. A skilled reporter, hot on the trail of a noteworthy story, uses standard techniques to get it. Business executives ought to know what these techniques are, and to decide that it is worth the effort to learn to cope with them. Kerryn King, Texaco's senior vice president in charge of public affairs, put it sharply and well when he told a public relations conference:

> Industry, and especially the petroleum industry, has an urgent need to dispel its reputation for secrecy and its reputation for indifference to public opinion that this supposed secrecy implies. I believe that when you once lay the full facts before a journalist, he is less likely to be taken in by critics who know less about your business than he does.

> The more information you can get out, the more light you can shed, especially on misunderstood economic matters, the better your standing with the public, in my opinion.

> A principal reason that people become frightened during a crisis is misinformation or noninformation. That is what moves them to action, whether that action be violence or demands for nationalization.

The Rules of the "Game"

Rather than abandon the field to misinformation, it is better to learn the rules of critics, journalistic or otherwise. These guidelines are simple, and they can be learned. Hundreds, and probably several thousand corporate managers, have learned them. They have discovered that when you know the rules of the reporter's "game," you can communicate your story effectively and truthfully, with no postmortems necessary.

For the businessperson to be successful in speaking with press or public, there are two general criteria and 10 specific guidelines to learn and remember. I shall present these respectively in the balance of this article.

General Criteria

First, it is necessary to have a sound attitude. That attitude is not one of either arrogance or false humility. Rather, it is an attitude in which the business executives respect their own competence and greater knowledge of their own subject, but realistically recognize that the reporter or critic is skilled in the art of asking provocative questions, hopefully to elicit provocative, interesting, and perhaps controversial answers.

Second, it is always wise to prepare carefully for a press interview. Never should an executive walk into a meeting with the press, planning to "play it by ear" (i.e., to improvise). Preparation is essential. The best preparation consists of anticipating the most likely questions, attempting to research the facts, and structuring effective answers to be held ready for use. Probably it is unwise to carry such notes into the interview. It would be better instead to have the answers well in mind, although not literally memorized.

Specific Guidelines

Let us now turn to the 10 specific rules of effective communication found most useful by corporate executives.

1. *Talk from the viewpoint of the public's interest, not the company's.* This important rule presents difficulties for most corporate presidents and senior executives. Their difficulty is understandable. When you have spent years struggling to manage the company, it is difficult to step back and look at your problem and your own company from a different perspective.

For example, often during negotiations for a new union contract, corporate spokespeople will tell the press, in effect, "We can't afford the increase the union is asking." That may be true, but why should the public be concerned with the company's financial problems? Employees often respond with hostility and resentment. It is much better to say, "We'd like to give our employees the increase they seek. But if our costs go up too much, our customers won't buy. That will hurt us, and in the end, it will endanger our employees' jobs."

Or an electric utility challenged, say, on its policy of requiring deposits from new customers, may respond, since it is a truthful answer, "We don't like to ask for deposits because they annoy our customers; they're a nuisance to us. Also, we have to pay interest on the money.

"But we don't think it fair that you should have to pay part of someone else's electric bill when he fails to pay. And that's just what happens: the cost of his service is passed along to all other users. If a new customer pays his bills promptly for six months, we refund his deposit, and we're glad to do it."

Sometimes, in their efforts to present their story from the public viewpoint, companies seem to assume the pose of philanthropic institutions. They claim to be acting in and serving the public interest in whatever course of action they are following. And indeed this may be true.

But to a skeptical public, such talk falls on unhearing ears. The public knows, or believes, that a company primarily acts in its own self-interest. When this self-interest is not frankly admitted, credibility is endangered.

So it is desirable always to indicate your company's position in a given course of action. The soft-drink bottler who launches a campaign for collecting and recycling its containers can frankly admit that it does not want to irritate the public by having its product's packaging strewn across the landscape. Because this is the truth, the public will find the entire story of the company's environmental efforts more credible.

Every industry has its own language, its own terminology. When corporate spokespeople use company lingo, they know exactly what they mean. But the public generally does not. So speak in terms the ordinary citizen can understand.

Instead of saying, "Our management is considering whether to issue equity or debt," it might be better to say, "We are considering whether to sell more stock in our company, or to try to borrow money by issuing bonds."

2. *Speak in personal terms whenever possible.* Any corporation, even one of modest size, involves many people in decision making and other activities. So corporate executives early in their careers learn never to say "I," but rather "we" or "the company."

When dozens or a hundred people have worked on developing a new product or adopting a new policy, it becomes difficult, if not impossible, for anyone connected with the project to say "I." Yet the words "the company" or "we" only reinforce the public image of corporations as impersonal monoliths in which no one retains his individuality or has any individual responsibility.

To avoid reinforcing this impression, if an executive has participated in a project she is proud of, she should be encouraged to speak in the first person and to reflect that pride. For example, "I was one of the team that worked on this product. My job involved the product design." Of course, it is wrong to claim personal credit where it has not been earned. But the top executive who can speak in terms of personal experience will always make a favorable impression.

Executives sometimes even hesitate to use the term "we" because they are reluctant to speak officially on behalf of the company. Unless they have been properly authorized by management, their reluctance is justified. But when middle-level or even lower-level managers have been carefully briefed and know the answers to the questions under discussion, they often make quite effective company spokespeople.

One telephone company, for example, invited its chief operators to speak to the press on its behalf in small communities where their position had considerable esteem. In this case, if a chief operator discussed local matters within her range of responsibility, such as changes in local telephone rates, she would provide considerable credibility. The press and public would rightfully assume she knew from personal involvement what she was talking about. But if she were to discuss overall corporate financing, obviously her credibility would vanish.

3. *If you do not want some statement quoted, do not make it.* Corporate spokespeople should avoid "off-the-record" statements. There is no such thing as "off-the-record." If a company president tells something to a reporter off-the-record, it may not be used with his name attached. But it may well turn up in the same published article, minus his name, and with a qualifying phrase added, "Meanwhile, it has been learned from other sources that. . . ." The damage is done.

Therefore, experienced company officers quickly learn that if they do not want something published or used, they should not divulge it to the reporter on any basis. And although naive company officials sometimes assume that an invisible line divides informal conversation from the beginning of the formal interview, no such dividing line exists in the reporter's mind. What is said may be used, either directly or as a basis for further probing elsewhere. The same off-the-record rule applies to telephone conversations with the media: whether or not you hear a beep, your words may be recorded. A recording makes it impossible for you to deny later what the reporter has taped in your own voice.

4. *State the most important fact at the beginning.* Years of training and experience, often without conscious thought, have accustomed the typical corporate executive to respond to questions in a particular way. If the executive is asked, "What should we do about our new product?" he will frequently respond along these lines, "We are facing shortages of plastics. And their cost is rising so fast I don't think we can price the product at an attractive level. Moreover, we have a labor shortage in the plant. So I recommend we don't take any action now to develop the product."

The executive's format lists the facts that lead to his final conclusion and recommendation. But such organization of his material will fail when it is used in talking with the news media. There are both psychological and technical reasons why.

Psychologically, we tend to remember most clearly the first thing that is said, not the last. So when you speak to a reporter, you should turn your statement around to begin with the conclusion, "We don't plan to develop the product. We are facing materials shortages. Our costs are going up, and we also have a shortage of skilled labor." In such a reverse format, the most important statement is likely to be best remembered: "We don't plan to develop the new product."

Technical consideration in printing and production are also an important reason for giving your conclusion first. The newspaper reporter who writes the story seldom knows in advance how much space will be available for its publication. So she has been trained to put the most important fact at the beginning, using subsequent paragraphs to report items of declining importance. If the most important fact is buried at the bottom of the story, it may simply be chopped off in the composing room to fit the available space.

On television, time pressures and broadcast deadlines often make it impossible to screen all filmed material for selection of the best footage; frequently, program producers or news editors are compelled to select segments from the beginning of a film. So, I repeat, the most important fact should be stated first. Afterward, it can be explained at whatever length is necessary; but even if the full explanation is cut, the initial statement will survive.

5. *Do not argue with the reporter or lose your cool.* Understand that the news reporter seeks an interesting story and will use whatever techniques are necessary to obtain it. An executive cannot win an argument with the reporter in whose power the published story lies. Since the executive has initially allowed herself to be interviewed, she should use the interview as an opportunity to answer questions in a way that will present her story fairly and adequately.

If a reporter interrupts the executive, it is not rudeness; it is a deliberate technique that means he is not satisfied with the corporate response he is hearing. The solution is for the executive to respond more directly and more clearly.

An executive should never ask questions of the reporter out of anger and frustration. I remember the following example:

Reporter: *How many black executives do you have in your company?*

Executive: *[Irritated] Damn it, how many black editors do you have on your paper?*

Reporter: *I'm here to ask you the questions.*

An executive may occasionally win the battle with that sort of tactic, but will always lose the war. The reporter, not the executive, will write the story. The published interview will reflect the reporter's own hostility.

6. *If a question contains offensive language or simply words you do not like, do not repeat them, even to deny them.* Reporters often use the gambit of putting words into the subject's mouth. It is easy. Politicians do it, too. The technique works like this: the reporter includes colorful, provocative language in the question. For example, "Mr. Jones, wouldn't you describe your oil company's profits this year as a bonanza?" If Mr. Jones bites, he will answer, "No, our profits are not a bonanza."

When Senator Abraham Ribicoff asked a similar question during the 1974 Senate Committee hearings, President Harry Bridges of Shell Oil Company (USA) was trapped. That is exactly how he did answer. And his answer was headlined "Oil Profits No Bonanza, Executive Says." Even though Bridges denied the charge, in the public's mind he associated the world "oil profits" with "bonanza." He might have answered the question this way: "Senator, our profits aren't high enough. To build more refineries and increase the oil supply, we're going to need to earn much more money."

Most executives have never noticed, but the reporter knows well that the questions will not be quoted in his article; only the interviewee's answers will be. It is not important, therefore, whether a reporter asks a question loaded with hostile and inaccurate language; the important thing is how the question is answered. As long as an executive does not repeat the offensive language, even to deny it, it will not appear in the published report.

On some occasions, overzealous reporters have even been known, with dubious ethics, to ask an executive to comment on a so-called "fact," which may be an outright untruth. The quoted "fact" has the ring of plausibility.

For example, one reporter asked a plant manager, "*Ecology Magazine* says your plant is one of the worst polluters in this state. Would you care to comment on that?"

The manager immediately became defensive and insisted to the reporter that his plant did not really pollute too badly, considering all the other sources of pollution in the local river. The manager did not know that no magazine called *Ecology* exists. The false quotation had been manufactured by the reporter. But it served its purpose. It put the manager on the defensive and induced him to talk. The reporter's false "quotation" was never published.

If you are asked a question based on a "fact" about which you are uncertain, be wary of a trap. The so-called "fact" may indeed be a fact, but if you are not sure, it is better to dissociate yourself from it. You might say, "I'm not familiar with that quotation," and then proceed to answer the question in your own positive way.

7. *If the reporter asks a direct quesion, he is entitled to an equally direct answer.* Sometimes, executives who have been interviewed complain afterward that they answered all the questions the reporter asked, but that they never got a chance to make their points in a positive way. They fail to make the points they wanted to make, and then they blame the reporter. Usually, it is their own fault. They have been playing what is called the "ping-pong game." The reporter asks a question; they answer it. Another

question is asked; they answer it. Back and forth the ball bounces, but the executive does not know how to squeeze in what he regards as *his* important points.

This common error in dealing with the press is one the executive is particularly prone to make. Management training accustoms executives to answer questions directly, without undue amplification. Such conduct is appropriate when talking with the boss, but it is inappropriate when talking with a reporter. Here amplification is often in order.

Corporate officers incorrectly assume that they somehow protect themselves by giving simple yes or no answers to questions. Their theory is that the less said, the better. The yes or no answer is not, however, interesting to a reporter. Usually, the reporter will react by provoking the executive in the hope of obtaining a more informative and colorfully expressed response.

This rule is not intended to suggest that an executive answer with either evasion or wordiness. But interviewees should not stop with a one-word response. Instead, they should amplify the point until they have said what they want to say.

For example, suppose a reporter asks, "Aren't you still polluting the air and river?" The answer should be positive and broad, rather than simply "No." A factory manager might respond, "Protecting the environment in Jonesville concerns us greatly. We've eliminated the major sources of pollution. The smoke from our factories is gone; we spent $3 million to purify the exhaust fumes from our furnaces. We've added filters to remove waste from water that flows back into the river. But we still haven't solved the problem of cooling our waste water, and we are working hard on that."

8. *If an executive does not know the answer to a question, he should simply say, "I don't know, but I'll find out for you."* This response does not make the executive look ignorant. Nor is this lack of knowledge newsworthy. Even in an interview filmed for television, such an answer would find itself "on the cutting room floor."

However, if the executive replies simply, "I don't know," it might appear to the reporter or viewer that he is being evasive. So executives are advised never to answer "I don't know" alone, but always to qualify the answer with a phrase like, "I'll put you in touch with someone else who can answer that for you," or similar words. Of course, the executive then assumes the responsibility of following through to ensure that the requested information is provided promptly.

Occasionally, a reporter will ask a question which the executive does not wish to answer. There may be a legal reason, say, because the company is in registration in connection with a new securities issue. Or the requested information may be a proprietary company secret. In such circumstances, the recommended course is to respond directly, without evasion or excuses, "I'm sorry. I can't give you that information."

However, if the question seems appropriate, and it usually is, it is desirable to explain to the reporter why the question cannot be answered.

Executives are cautioned never to "play dumb," deny knowledge, or give anything other than a forthright refusal.

9. *Tell the truth, even if it hurts.* In this era of skepticism, hostility, and challenge, the fact remains that the most difficult task of all sometimes is simply telling the truth. This rule can be embarrassing for the executive and the company.

Neither individuals nor corporations (groups of individuals) like to be embarrassed. So to avoid embarrassment, they sometimes tell the press and public half-truths (which are half-lies).

Understandably, nobody likes to admit that business is bad, that employees must be laid off, that a new product introduction has been unsuccessful, that the company has "goofed" in one way or another. Yet telling the truth remains the best answer.

How much truth should a company tell? My experience answers, "As much as the reporter wants to know." When an executive change is announced, probably 99 out of 100 reporters will be satisfied with that bare fact, and ask nothing more. But once in a while a keen reporter may respond, "Mr. Jones, I've heard that you held Mr. Smith responsible for the severe drop in earnings your company had last year. Is that true?"

First of all, if the allegation were true, I would not deny it; denial would only lead to a loss of credibility later when the reporter confirmed it from another source. But neither would I invite a libel suit from Mr. Smith by blaming him for the company's problems. So the question might be answered, factually but tactfully, "When economic conditions are difficult, companies frequently make management changes and that's what we've done."

Executives, already fearful of the power of the press, find themselves terrified at the thought of having to report bad tidings. Countless examples can be found in the business press of attempts to conceal, or to grudgingly admit only portions of the truth, when it is unfavorable to the company.

My experience, however, convinces me that while the press and public do not like to hear bad news and will judge the company or its management adversely because of it, fair-minded people will understand that the difficulties of management make unavoidable a certain number of errors in judgment. Thoughtful people understand that no one is perfect; that each of us makes errors despite his or her best judgments and best efforts.

What the public will not understand or tolerate, however, is dishonesty. Concealment and lying will be neither forgotten nor forgiven by the press and public alike. Evidence exists to confirm this. An example can be found in the aviation industry.

In earlier years, whenever a commercial airliner crashed, certain airlines had standing policies to rush work crews to the site and to paint out the company name and emblems on the wrecked aircraft before photographs were permitted.

Today, that policy has changed. Most carriers currently cooperate fully with the media, furnish all available information, and provide all assistance needed for news coverage. The theory, and I believe it is the correct one, is that the crash will be reported anyway; the name of the airline will be headlined anyway; so it is better to cooperate with the press and get the story covered and forgotten as quickly as possible.

10. *Do not exaggerate the facts.* The American Bakers Association may have done just that. The president of the Public Relations Society of America, James F. Fox of New York, commented in a 1974 speech:

> Last winter, we heard a great deal about an imminent wheat shortage and bread at a dollar a loaf this spring. Well, spring has about two weeks to go; the cost of wheat is down a little, and bread is nowhere near one dollar a loaf. What was that all about? Under Secretary of Agriculture J. Phil Campbell suggested that the bakers' move to reinstitute stockpiling was motivated by their desire to have government maintain wheat reserves to carry inventory for the industry and lower its costs.
>
> I don't know whether that's the whole story or even a part of it. It isn't necessary that we settle the facts here; whether, as Campbell implies, the industry's self-interest overcame its discretion, or it was depending in good faith on bad information or inadequate projections.
>
> What does concern us is that the American Bakers Association looks a little foolish now. It's going to be that much harder for them to make themselves heard and believed next time, when they might just be right."

Telling the business story to an apathetic or hostile nation is not easy, but it is worth doing, and it can be done successfully. As one senior executive in an engineering company told me:

> I've been interviewed frequently over the past 20 years, and every time afterward, I felt sorry for myself. But now, I realize that I just didn't know the rules of the reporter's game. Since I started playing the game too, I've had a much better press. In one case, I even got a sympathetic newspaper editorial in one of our plant communities, where we always used to get clobbered. It's convinced me to look on a press interview as an opportunity, rather than as a cause for fear.

21
Taking on the Hostile Media

LOUIS BANKS

We all tend to generalize, and so does the media. So when corporations take unwarranted criticism lying down, and corporate officers do not speak out for fear of retaliation, the media antagonism toward business flourishes. One likely result of this hostility is that the political force in our country, the public, might move toward greater control of business. This control would hamper business's freedom in making decisions, and thereby effectively curtail one of the strongest voluntary institutions in our free enterprise system. Having learned from personal experience the degree of anger many businesspeople feel toward the media, the author of this article argues that to forestall the curtailment of business's freedom, its leaders need to enter the marketplace of ideas and debate their side of public interest issues in a rational, informed way.

My first bruising encounter with the visceral hatred and contempt that most businesspeople have for the media took place in the largest classroom of the Harvard Business School. I was fresh from the world of magazine journalism, a visiting professor ready to cast my first pearls before the senior corporate executives of the Advanced Management Program, in a two-session elective called "Business and the Media." We were assigned the largest classroom in Aldrich Hall because of the record sign-up for the class.

With considerable pride and anticipation I had written and assigned a case incorporating a vivid example of bumbling corporate relations with the media that had resulted in permanent wounds to the company and the executive involved. I had also prepared lecture notes on a "how to cope with the press" theme.

Alas, the case and the notes got little use that day, for five minutes into the first class the storm broke. Those executives had been waiting for a long time, it seemed, to tell someone from "the press" what they thought about media coverage of business, and so they did. Unfair, distorted, ignorant, slanted, conspiratorial—fill in the blanks and the reader will be close.

As for the maladroit executive in the case I'd written, he was something of a hero to this group, which viewed him as never having had a chance in any contest with the predatory media monsters. Their message delivered, they departed at the end of class. On the second day—when I finally had pulled myself together to respond—only about half of them came back.

As is not unusual for teachers, I got started down a learning path of my own that day. I soon discovered, first, that even the best-connected business journalists do not know the depth of emotion about the media's coverage of business harbored in the breasts of most corporate executives. And one of the reasons journalists don't know is that few business executives (and I have found this goes for public officials too) are brave enough to speak out openly for fear of retaliation. Second, the problem in today's business-media relationships is as crucial and fundamental as any on the current socioeconomic scene, for both institutions are vital to the voluntary or nongovernment functioning of our society. Third, despite the shortcomings of the press itself, there had better be a business response more thoughtful and intelligent than raw emotion, or everybody is going to be in trouble.

In this article I attempt to view contemporary antagonism between business and the media from a corporate point of view. While the conclusions are my own—combining, I hope, the best elements of a journalistic, business, and academic background—they involve a synthesis of discussion and debate among serious practicing journalists and television newscasters, business public relations leaders, corporate executives, and graduate students who have since taken part in more successful, more thoughtful Business and the Media seminars at the Harvard Business School and the Sloan School of Management. Needless to say, I am most grateful to that first group, however, for engulfing me in this particular problem.

In the Media Marketplace

Some years ago, the senior managers of the Mobil Oil Corporation took a long look at the future and decided the central question before them was whether they would be allowed to do business within a decade or two. They could see their way through problems of technology, finance, marketing, and even crude oil supply (always touchy for Mobil).

But they saw no easy answer to the converging social and political pressures, influenced by an increasingly powerful media with an antibusiness mind-set, which seemed likely to constrict industry in general and the oil industry in particular. Being a notoriously scrappy and uninhibited group of managers, the Mobil executives decided to compete in this area too. In the words of Herbert Schmertz, the vice president for public affairs who directed the susequent campaign, Mobil elected to "put itself into the marketplace of ideas."

The result was a many-pronged campaign of issues that has become something of a corporate classic. In the past decade, Mobil management has said what it thought and felt about public policy on oil companies, energy, profits, government regulation in general, and other people's business. These messages were conveyed consistently and periodically in short, well-crafted editorial advertisements that came to run in most of the key metropolitan newspapers as close to the editorial pages as possible. When Mobil management believed media reports to be wrong, it bought space to name names and answer back with factual tartness. Mobil's chairman and chief executive officer, Rawleigh Warner, Jr., Schmertz, and others in the company met with editorial boards of principal newspapers and magazines to debate the issues affecting the company and the industry.

Subtle shifts in editorial points of view are all but impossible to measure, if only because they usually are shrouded in claims of consistency, but I myself believe that the tone of many columnists and editorialists changed under the factual barrage. In discussions of energy matters, the bellwether *New York Times,* for one, revealed its awareness of the terse, newsy arguments in the small Mobil advertisements tucked into the corner of its op-ed page.

Schmertz and others noted with interest that President Carter's bruising attack on the major oil companies, made during the heat of congressional debate over his energy program, won remarkably few editorial plaudits. In fact many papers and network shows checked with oil company sources and gave equal play to industry responses. "This awareness that there might be another side never would have happened three years ago," Schmertz says, and most industry spokespeople agree with him.

Mobil's tactics may not be everybody's model of a corporate public affairs approach to public issues, and indeed Schmertz says "such programs should be a reflection of a company's personality." It is, however, one of the more dramatic examples of a new kind of corporate approach to the media, and thus to political attitudes, that adds a long-missing dimension to conventional concepts of public relations. The Mobil model begins with the acceptance of the fact that an increasing number of the major forces affecting corporate business are social and political—felt most dramatically, of course, by the oil industry, but in reality by the smallest paper mill in Maine as well.

The news industry—television, radio, magazine, newspaper—stands as the principal arbiter of social attitudes toward business (and all institutions). Broadly speaking, mass media news selection and interpretation feeds the public's suspicions about corporate practice (with a certain amount of help from business malefactors), and interprets corporate affairs with a negative bias. This situation has prompted the choruses of antimedia hates that dominate many business panel sessions and conversations.

But an increasing number of managers have graduated beyond this exercise in high blood pressure to compete in the "marketplace of ideas" themselves. Here the medium of competition is the carefully drawn, factual,

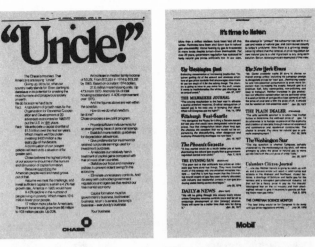

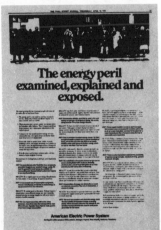

Illustrations for Media Ads

systematic argument on behalf of a corporate or industry policy—delivered by trained executives who know how to engage intellectually in debates that previously have been lost simply by default.

It is my thesis here that not only is an "issues" campaign the soundest long-range strategy for business-media relationships, but also that the effort involved is intricately connected with the future of the freedom of large corporations to operate as centers of independent managerial decision making. Whether U.S. business likes it or not, it lives and works in a capitalist democracy, and the virtue of the *capitalist* factor must continually be redefined and argued in current social context if the public *political* factor is to overcome its populist suspicions of corporate power and scope.

What Mobil and others are proving is that it is possible for individual corporations or industries to take part in the argument about specific issues *on behalf of the public interest,* and thus gain both media attention (if not affection) and a chance for the public to make up its mind from a broader set of arguments. In sum total, this may be the only feasible answer to "the media problem" for corporate business.

An Intellectual Effort

For the individual corporation to carry corporate affairs into the marketplace of ideas is as basic a decision as, say, that to diversify lines of products. Those who have moved in this direction discover that it involves a rethinking of management structure, and, frequently, a change of emphasis in the factors usually weighed in formulating major policies. Even more basic, if a corporation is to defend and advance its goals in public argument, it must force itself to define and refine the essentials of its operations, as well as their roles in the general scheme of things.

Thus for Mobil to take a lead in advocating a specific U.S. energy policy required it to make an intellectual effort far more extensive and subtle than a reflex action against any threat to earnings. The important consideration for the marketplace, however, was not only the policy itself (which in some aspects broke step with the rest of the oil industry), but also Mobil's ability to defend it as being in the public interest.

As surveys have shown, most chief executives of *Fortune's* "500" corporations find themselves spending ever-increasing amounts of time dealing with public affairs.[1] In the largest corporations it is not unusual for the chief executive officer or the chief operating officer to fill more than 50% of their respective calendars with appointments and engagements that relate to public issues affecting the corporation—ranging from the economic soundness of the surrounding metropolis to proposed changes in federal tax laws.

Yet relatively few chief executive officers have sponsored the drastic managerial changes that would institutionalize such new emphases. In piecemeal fashion they have, perhaps, beefed up the company offices in Washington or in state capitals, expanded the press relations department, allocated the time of top executives for public appearances, and so on.

But a managerial structure that puts the corporation into the idea marketplace has to be built on a redesign of those various functions into an office of external affairs or public affairs. (I am trying not to use the hackneyed term "public relations" because in practice this has come to mean a one-way propaganda apparatus.)

In theory this division should be a staff operation, encompassing such functions as media relations, government relations, contacts with relevant pressure groups, attitude surveys, and corporate advertising. In the late 1960s the Quaker Oats Company organized itself this way, naming Robert N. Thurston as senior vice president for corporate affairs. Thurston not only reports to Robert D. Stuart, Jr., the chief executive officer, but also, since 1971, sits on the board of directors and has the backing, or monitoring, of a board committee on public responsibility.

At Mobil, Schmertz, too, is a corporate director, and not only works closely with all ranking company officers but also has the direct support of Herman J. Schmidt, vice chairman, who is solely concerned with public affairs. Edward M. Block, vice president of public relations and employee information at AT&T, sits in on top management policy meetings. Additionally, Alvin von Auw, vice president of AT&T and assistant to Chairman John deButts, is a career public relations man.

Many vice presidents of public affairs are former journalists or public relations specialists. Thurston is a liberal arts graduate who came up through the public relations operation. Schmertz, however, is a lawyer by training, has a labor relations background, and for a while ran Mobil's tanker fleet, but admits he is by instinct a political animal—hence his sensitivity to public issues and willingness to use novel techniques in trying to effect them.

Schmertz's opposite number at Exxon, Stephen Stamas, is, at 44, the youngest of the company's 13 vice presidents, a Rhodes Scholar, and a Ph.D. in economics. Stamas managed Exxon's international petroleum division, and served in the U. S. Department of Commerce for six months before taking over the Exxon public affairs department; because of this varied background, his views are valued both within and outside the corporation.

In my Business and the Media classes with middle management executives, I find the growing conviction that prospective top officers should be rotated through the external relations vice presidency. Just as some periods in history demand legal genius in the corporation, and others financial top guidance, they reason that top management in the next decades will increasingly be involved in the public affairs area.

Regardless of his or her background, the vice president for external affairs should bring to the policy discussion a well-informed sense of prevailing social and political values. "Give me a man or woman who knows society," says Osgood Nichols, a New York consultant who has counseled a number of major corporations in redesign of the public affairs function. Most large corporate public affairs departments conduct attitude surveys, measuring the views of both influentials and the general public.

Quaker Oats, among others, has a small staff that is on a first-name basis with leaders of most of the pressure groups interested in its affairs, and has learned to separate real, legitimate causes from those of the professional troublemakers. In 1971, Thurston's department anticipated pressure group reaction to violence on TV and, with top management encouragement and support, set down guidelines prohibiting corporate sponsorship of programs portraying violence or antisocial behavior. Similarly, with Stuart's encouragement, the Quaker Oats corporate affairs department monitored the company's plans for plant expansion into smaller communities to ensure, in advance, that minority employees would find a hospitable climate in the new surroundings.

AT&T's public relations department has its own policy and planning staff, a kind of think tank that tries to spot problems—both within the company and outside—before they become public issues. Vice President Block discreetly describes the AT&T public realtions function as "nudging the behavior of the corporation into line with the expectations of the public." Such nudging has, for example, restrained the AT&T companies from increasing the rates at public coin phone boxes as much as simple tariff calculations might dictate.

Mobil, champion of profit incentives and increased production as a solution to the energy problem, considered carefully what effect its purchase of Marcor (Montgomery Ward—Container Corporation) would have on its public position. External affairs considerations contributed to a decision to finance the $800 million acquisition by borrowing against Marcor, with repayments to be made out of Marcor earnings. Thus Schmertz's staff could argue, with only a touch of sophistry, that not a penny of Mobil's energy resources was deflected to the diversification program.

Purpose of Doing Business

Of themselves, such external affairs considerations would not seem very novel to Edward Bernays, the late Earl Newsom, or to any other respected public relations counselor. What I am stressing here is that these issues should now be a part of a corporation's *total* approach so that it is prepared to meet the media—and the public—one-on-one to argue for the corporation's "right to be right" on controversial public issues. To establish this right, the corporation must understand a good bit more about itself and its function in the contemporary socioeconomic context than most corporations do.

"The power, respect, and freedom to act of an institution," Osgood Nichols told me, "are based on whether or not it is working, and is perceived to be working, in the interest of the citizenry." (Some public relations practitioners, edging in this direction, have chosen to stake out an area of expertise called "public issue management." The manipulative connotations of such a term are hardly likely to relieve the fears of the media or other corporate critics.)

Part of the function of the vice president for external affairs should be to probe deeply, perhaps on an annual basis, into the purpose of the business and prepare a report that puts the corporate function into social perspective. Of course, putting the corporate function in any social context raises the hackles of the Milton Friedman purists, who hold that the *only* legitimate social function of a corporation is to meet a demand and make a profit.

The most trenchant scholarly rebuttal to Friedman is "the social environmental model" of a corporation designed by Neil H. Jacoby, a member of President Eisenhower's Council of Economic Advisers and former dean of the Graduate School of Management at the University of California, Los Angeles. The central feature of this model, Jacoby holds, "is the explicit recognition that corporate behavior responds to political as well as to market forces."

He continues: "Whereas both classical and managerial theory ignored the impact of political forces, the social environment theory analyzes corporate behavior as a response to both market and nonmarket forces because both affect the firm's costs, revenues, and profits."[2]

No industry was more secretive or distant than the petroleum industry before it began to feel the relentless pressure of social and political forces. In its view it was doing its job—producing petroleum products, making money—and owed the world very little else in terms of explanation. But today Exxon, Atlantic Richfield, and Mobil, among others, have consulted with, or hired, some of the best intellects available to help them figure out the direction of, and reasons for, the powerful external pressures affecting them. All these companies have adopted a form of periodic self-analysis in public interest terms to help provide a consistent basis for their public argument.

AT&T inherited a sense of service from its founders and, in a regulated industry, has long known that it must make satisfied customers its most powerful allies, and its legions of small shareholders the second echelon. But under assault from new kinds of competitive pressures induced by proliferating technologies and new theories in utility regulation and rate making, deButts's and Block's staff have been forced to do a lot of redefining. The result is a campaign to involve customers, shareholders, and Congress in the battle to preserve the present structure of the communications industry.

DeButts and his colleagues are so confident of their arguments that they systematically try to provoke debate on the issues. This is not to say that they will be completely successful in heading off the competition, or even that they should be, but that they are ready to do battle from a sound intellectual base that relates their own self-interest, and their customers', to the public problem. This activity in turn broadens the debate. Thus far AT&T

Illustrations for Media Ads

has won remarkable support in the editorial pages of major national publications.

One sees evidence of a "purpose audit" in an increasing number of issue-oriented articles by business executives, and in such advocacy advertising campaigns as those of American Electric Power, U.S. Steel, and Union Carbide. These campaigns and articles are not to be confused with broadsides defending free enterprise as a religious creed and damning any interference with profits as heresy. It is my observation, backed by the opinions of some of the nation's leading corporate public affairs executives, that broadside attacks have very little positive effect on the unconverted—especially the media.

Power of One-on-One

The move to bring corporate policies and actions into the marketplace of ideas has come at a strategic time. In my view not only are we seeing a general weakening of ideologies—as Daniel Bell observed some 15 years ago—but we also are seeing a resurgence of pragmatism as the principal philosophy underlying both political and corporate decisions.[3]

This is a complex point, and I will not attempt to argue it here, but the public's shift toward pragmatism is revealed in a new respect for "what works." There is, as we have seen, a longstanding bias against corporate business in the general media—among general assignment reporters and editors of television, radio, daily newspapers, and many general magazines. The reasons are complicated and range from simple ignorance of corporate practice to a mindless pursuit of the kinetic or sensational. (One corporate public affairs vice president says: "If it doesn't light up or blow up, television can't handle it.")

More important, there will always be a tension between corporate managers and even the enlightened business press because the former are engaged in making individual decisions against an earnings discipline, and the latter, as knights and ladies of the First Amendment, are engaged in interpreting the results of those decisions as part of the whole social and economic fabric.

For example, several years ago one of Detroit's major corporations quietly underwent a major retrenchment; curtailing, cutting back, and closing marginal operations, it tried desperately to reestablish an acceptable level of profitability. A Detroit correspondent of a national business publication caught wind of what was going on, carefully researched and documented the cutbacks, and published the story. The news knocked the stock price down, and to this day his friends in the corporation cannot fathom his motives for "doing this to us." But, of course, the news of retrenchment was important to the financial markets and to thousands of readers who rely on the press to report just such informed detail on the general economic scene.

For all of that, *this* seems to be a time when journalists, too, are beginning to abandon dogmas and ask new questions. Attitude surveys show that faith in government solutions is fading fast in all sectors, and one has only to carry on classroom discussions with succeeding generations of graduate students to be assured that this trend can be projected well into the future. Daniel Yankelovich's research has long shown a generalized favorable disposition toward the free enterprise system (sometimes ranging up to 93% of his samples), along with mistrust of corporate managers.[4]

But today the thoughtful elements of the media are willing to listen to corporate arguments on specific issues—if they are rational, and shown to be in the public interest. It would be difficult for any broad-minded editorial writer not to be grateful for industry's contribution to the energy crisis debate—no matter how much he or she might suspect corporate motives or be swayed by presidential rhetoric. Likewise it is hard to imagine that the legions of honest corporate executives, long vexed by the under-the-table dealings of unscrupulous competitors, would not be pleased with the strong ethical component of intelligent business investigative reporting.

This ameliorative mood was strongly suggested in a pioneering pilot study conducted by four graduate students of the Sloan School.[5] The study questioned both business executives (then enrolled in executive programs at the Sloan School) and general assignment reporters and editors (at *The Boston Globe*) on 37 points relating to business-media assumptions and relationships.

Both groups agreed that the role of the media is critical in shaping public attitudes about business. Both agreed that business is fundamental to the operation of the American system. Both doubted that the media provided balanced coverage of business; yet both strongly endorsed the guarantees of press freedom encompassed in the First Amendment, perhaps because both agreed that government wields too much power. In fact, the only point of sharp conflict came in the questions that dealt with the *power* of business in American life. The corporate executives believe that business has very little power, and the journalists believe strongly that business has too much.

These findings—at the moment still tentative pending a wider survey—suggest a lot about corporate responses to media pressure. First, once executives work off their emotional hates and fears of the media, such as those reported at the beginning of this article, they can come to see a broad area of neutral ground where they and the media may even have common cause. Second, one can extrapolate that the traditional corporate public relations approaches have a better chance of succeeding if a corporation can explain itself in public as well as private terms.[6] Third, and perhaps most important, when the media views business in the aggregate, its fear of corporate power is understandable.

It is because of this fear that I think the corporation's plunge into the marketplace of ideas is so important. The media view, as well as the public's, of a single corporation or industry arguing an issue is quite different from their view of business in the aggregate fighting social values (as so often seems to be the case).

In a one-on-one relationship with the media, a corporation or an industry can offer its technical know-how, its experience or point of view on a particular issue in the public interest. The net effect is to broaden the debate, educate whatever segments of the public are important to the corporation or industry, and *perhaps allow them to learn something from the rebuttals*. If there is a touch of humility in the process, the corporation will appear honestly to be searching for the kinds of answers that we all desperately need. ("We're doing the best we know how, and we'd like to know how it can be done better.")

It is the accumulated effect of this issue-by-issue process that I believe holds the best possibility of changing the public view of corporate practice, and thus protecting the corporate freedom of decision which, in itself, is such an essential and underrated component of a functioning capitalist democracy.

Notes

1. The Conference Board, *Managing Corporate External Relations* (New York, the Board, 1976).

2. Neil H. Jacoby, *Corporate Power and Social Responsibility* (New York, Macmillan, 1973), p. 195.

3. Daniel Bell, *The End of Ideology* (New York, New York Free Press, 1962).

4. Daniel Yankelovich, *Dissent*, Fall 1974.

5. Pamela Chin, Andrew Moehlenbrock, Assen Nicolov, Anne Wood, "Business and the Media: An Assessment of Attitudes," May 1977.

6. See, for example, Chester Burger, "How to Meet the Press," *HBR*, July–August 1975, p. 62.

22

"Bad Day at Bunker Point"

EDMOND MARCUS and RICHARD L. HEATON

"Good morning," says the moderator, "and welcome to Bunker Point. Consider yourselves to be embarking on a survival mission here today. Your objective: help save the company's business."

Ship's officers, terminal and refinery managers, and others have heard introductory words like these in a series of seminars in Philadelphia, Toronto, Bantry (Ireland), San Juan, Houston, and London. Gulf Oil Corporation has sent many hundreds of line managers responsible for oil storage and transportation back to a different kind of school. At Gulf's school they are directed to consider a case based on these conditions:

☐ Restrictions on the oil industry's way of doing business, imposed as a result of oil spills, are increasing rapidly and becoming more stringent.

☐ The costs of spill cleanups have reached astronomical levels, threatening to bankrupt even large companies involved in major spills.

☐ No operational guarantees against massive spills exist, especially under adverse weather conditions, while the public outrage over these incidents is growing.

"Bad Day at Bunker Point," as the seminar is called, employs sophisticated training techniques to demonstrate the public anger, repeatedly, through an exhausting, tension-filled nine-hour day. Intense audience participation, role playing, audiovisual dramatizations, confrontations, and furious debate force the managers to live through a "real" oil spill. They go away convinced that they never want to experience the actuality, but they are better prepared should it occur.

"The main cause of oil spills—by far—is human error," the host tells the audience. "Bunker Point" is an awareness seminar, designed to demonstrate memorably the serious consequences of human error.

The job of the line managers these days is more difficult than ever. They find themselves increasingly besieged by social activists and special interest groups, isolated by the concurrent trend toward corporate decentralization, and suffering from the general decline of business esteem in the eyes of the American public.

Corporate executives too have had their trials. But they rarely face their adversaries except in tightly controlled situations, such as annual meetings, where they benefit from plenty of preparation and expert assistance. It's the line manager who—without preparation and without help—has to face the pickets, the cameras, and the politicians, often at the same time.

In the angry and violent social atmosphere of the late 1960s and early 1970s, Gulf experienced a series of local crises in which some operating managers performed very well. But others, faced with bomb threats, mass picketing, and similar unsettling confrontations, locked the gates, turned out the lights and hid; overreacted to the press, the public, or local government to the point of neglecting the crisis; refused to say anything at all, or said the wrong things; or succumbed to various forms of physical collapse.

These people often handled the physical or operational aspects of an emergency very well—for that, they were trained—but they failed to realize that its social, political, and economic implications were just as important. They did not understand that Gulf's ability to live and work in the community depends on community goodwill, or at least tolerance.

Crisis Piled on Crisis

As early as 1970, Gulf conducted a program to prepare line managers to deal with the threatening business climate. "Bunker Point" came into being in 1975 as a result of several tanker accidents that caused substantial oil spills and raised a public outcry in many parts of the world.

At the beginning of each seminar, managers are told to consider themselves, for the day, managers of Gulf's fictional Bunker Point terminal, a large oil storage and shipment facility located in a remote, idyllic, coastal community where tourism and fishing are the economic mainstays.

Throughout, managers are picked from the audience to play the role in ever more critical situations. On a telephone in the front of the room, they must answer calls from irate environmentalists and furious resort owners. They must, singly and in teams, decide how to react to critical newspaper editorials and hostile radio broadcasts.

They must submit to spill-scene interviews by reporters and appear on local TV talk shows to discuss the subject of oil spills and their consequences.

The interviews are recorded on videotape and played back for criticism.

Use of film, slides, television, and other audiovisual devices helps dramatize the situation.

A panel—consisting of experts in marine operations, terminal management, insurance, and legal and public affairs—criticizes the performance of each manager and needles the audience to provide better solutions. Even when they receive a satisfactory answer, the moderators, emphasizing that there is no single answer to every situation, probe for other opinions. Arguments between audience and experts become animated as the day progresses and the problems become more pressing.

In the afternoon, the managers must deal with the ramifications of such a crisis. Slides, film, and simulated radio and TV broadcasts report the grounding of a giant tanker just outside the Bunker Point harbor. The ship is spilling oil, attempts to refloat her have failed, she is in danger of breaking up, and the weather is worsening.

Tourist interests, fishermen, environmentalists, and local politicians running for reelection feel threatened by Gulf's disaster. They make their feelings known to the Gulf manager in pungent—even violent—language.

Members of the audience are called up to deal with each of these confrontations in turn, while they are being pressed simultaneously to handle the matters of the ship and the spill. They are given information the way it is received in a real emergency, which is piecemeal, incomplete, and often erroneous.

In the midst of this turmoil, the participants learn that a government official has flown to Bunker Point from the national capital and has demanded an immediate meeting with the terminal manager. He is accompanied by an unfriendly local politician and an environmentalist. Together they will prepare a report for the president.

"Do you meet with them?" demands the moderator of the audience. "Can you leave your post in this crisis? What are you prepared to discuss?"

Three managers are picked to attend the meeting, which quickly turns into a shouting match. The environmentalist chides Gulf bitterly, the politician makes extreme demands, and the federal official presses the managers for agreements on compensation and for assurance that such an incident will never recur.

Though patterned after real incidents that have happened to Gulf managers, "Bunker Point" is a shock to most of those who attend. And that is one of the purposes of the program. (Another is to indoctrinate managers in the company's pollution control program.)

Seminar-trained Gulf managers have successfully applied the principles of crisis management. Examples are in—

☐ Averting a near panic when distorted news reports of a plant fire alarmed nearby residents.

☐ Preventing the shutdown of a coal mine when reports about a minor accident gave rise to a false rumor that the mine was unsafe.

☐ Refuting inaccurate and irresponsible allegations in the press about company operations and policies.

Whether the managers are in the oil industry, in a manufacturing industry, or in a service business, the lessons to learn are the same. In a crisis they must be alert to the possibility of violent confrontation from a segment of the community; they must plan carefully for emergencies and rehearse those plans regularly; and they must remember the importance of dealing swiftly and frankly with the press, the public, and community groups.

23
Critical Issues for Issue Ads

DAVID KELLEY

U.S. companies get high marks for being concerned enough about public opinion to wage campaigns of advocacy, or issue, advertising in many newspapers. Often placed on the editorial page, these boxes are becoming well known as a sounding board in which business can show a "human side" by discussing everything from the excess oil profits tax to "Masterpiece Theatre." The ads may infuriate some and tickle others, but at least, say their advocates, companies have come out of the closet and aren't afraid to "take their case before the American people."

Despite their flashy campaigns, their big budgets, and a lot of intercompany backslapping, some companies are not pleased with the results. They complain that the message is still not getting across, that whatever their good intentions, they fail in the end.

It's not that companies aren't discussing the right issues, because they are. It's not that they don't speak in language that can be understood, because they do. No, according to David Kelley, companies do not make much headway with these campaigns because they use terms and a frame of reference that are fundamentally antibusiness. Companies are starting out from a position of inherent weakness instead of strength. Unless they change the way they state their case, it doesn't matter what they are trying to say. Here, Kelley explains just what companies are doing wrong and what they can do about it.

Concerned about what they see as a bias against business in the media, U.S. companies are increasingly taking their message on basic issues directly to the consumer. Company spokespeople use sophisticated techniques to package and target the message in issue advertising. But, as is the case with much advertising, they often pay too much attention to the form and too little to the content of the message.

Consider an ad by Amway Corporation—the one discussing the impact of government regulation on all of us and picturing the federal government

314

The Federal Nanny.

Domestic help we can't afford.

We used to worry about Big Brother. Now, there's a real threat—the Federal Nanny.

She's everywhere—regulating everything from ladders to land use. She inspects small business for the tiniest violations; she sets prices for energy production; she decides which expensive "refinements" will adorn the family car.

Over-regulation increases your cost of living. In 1979 it will cost each U.S. family about $2,000—a good start toward buying a new car! You see, it takes almost $5 billion to keep the regulators working in Washington. And business must spend $100 billion to comply with the regulations. Here's the catch...because those billions produce no more goods for sale, the costs are added to every product you buy.

Some people feel more secure with this kind of government "protection", and, of course, some government regulation is necessary. But it's gone too far. Nowadays, the Federal Nanny wants to run the whole house! Trouble is, we can't afford it.

In the last several years, the ideas of government regulators have added more than $600 to the price of a new car. Was it worth it?

We can all realize *substantial* savings if we all depend less on that expensive Nanny from Washington. Amway Corporation, Ada, MI., 49355.

Amway®

One of a series of messages to stimulate public dialogue about significant national issues.

Amway Corp. Ad

as the nanny shown in the Exhibit. It has a provocative subject. It reads well. It's visually forceful, if a little unsubtle. But is it effective? And worth the price of the space it will take? To find out, let's look closely at the text.

"We used to worry about Big Brother. Now, there's a real threat—the Federal Nanny. She's everywhere." This opener is right on target, we might say. Government regulation of business *is* an issue of freedom.

Amway's use of the Big Brother image is a good idea, for it points up the danger that extreme regulation poses. But regulators don't wear jackboots; they wear good, sensible shoes. And most Americans have no experience of the midnight knock on the door; their pride and independence make ridicule more effective than any appeal to fear. So Amway brings the subject to the more appropriate image of a nanny.

"Over-regulation increases your cost of living." This paragraph shifts our attention from our pride to our pocketbooks. It's a little jarring, but the ad succeeds here by asking us to think about the issue in personal terms: $2,000 per family is a lot of money. We'd like to decide for ourselves how to spend it, and we can appreciate businesspeople not liking being told how to do their jobs. This perspective puts the company and the reader on the same footing and the burden on the regulators to justify their intrusions into the lives of ordinary citizens. The argument of this paragraph is effective.

But notice what happens in the next: the ad asks us to shift from our own perspective to that of a legislator. "Some people feel more secure with this kind of government 'protection,' and, of course some government regulation is necessary. But it's gone too far." Well, we might say, I don't need a nanny, but others might. Maybe some regulation *is* necessary. If even companies say that some government regulation is necessary, it must be true. Maybe Nader's right. How much regulation do we need? Amway says it's gone too far because it comes to $105 billion. That's a lot of money— but the government spends a lot more on military defense, and no one calls it a nanny on that account. Maybe $105 billion is reasonable, but how do I know whether it is?

An important—if subtle—shift in perspective has occurred, one that alters the way "regulation" looks to the reader. At first, the simple image of a nanny, when amplified by a discussion of the impact of regulation on the individual's standard of living, easily conveys the problem with regulation: it takes away the freedom of responsible adults.

But then, the change of perspective destroys the impact of the advertising and shows just how companies can undermine their own messages. Once the ad allows that some regulation is necessary, it gives credence to the claims of business's critics. It also turns the issue into a matter of degree: how much regulation? The ad cannot possibly offer the lengthy analysis necessary to justify its position on this issue, so the position comes across as arbitrary, leaving the reader unmoved at best and probably suspicious: what has happened here, and why?

If we can judge by numerous corporate advocacy campaigns, speeches by top executives, and discussions in business publications, the defenders of business feel constrained to operate within a framework for discussion that is skewed against the free market system and corporate enterprise. Simply put, the critics of corporations have been allowed to set the terms of the debate in which everything concerning business is argued.

Accepting this framework is a fundamental mistake. Philosophy has long taught that assumptions granted at the outset of any argument help determine the success or failure of a particular point of view. These assumptions set the framework for argument and determine how the issue is stated, who has the burden of proof, what facts are relevant and how they are evaluated, which arguments seem convincing and which miss the point, what questions critics will ask and what they will accept as valid answers.

Unless business challenges the fundamental assumptions that define the framework in which we currently debate social and economic issues, it can expect nothing more than occasional local victories in the marketplace of ideas—bull rallies in a primarily bear market. I think this challenge should begin with a look at the three most important assumptions made:

1   The public interest is the ultimate standard by which we are to judge everything, including business.
2   Since it is founded on the pursuit of material wealth, business has a lower moral value than other activities.
3   Since it is subject to political controls, a company is a political as well as an economic entity.

Understanding these assumptions will help solve the difficulty business has had in making an effective case. Let's look at each in turn to find where they come from, how they structure the logic of debate, and how companies can avoid them.

Individual Rights and the Public Interest

The argument most commonly offered in defense of business is that it serves the public interest, primarily by creating jobs and goods that consumers want. The moral assumption is that the public interest is the ultimate standard by which we are to judge social issues.

A Citibank ad proclaims that "the American economic system is based on the premise that the public benefits from free competition and suffers from its absence." United Technology says that "we need unity of purpose and a sense of pulling together toward goals serving the broad public interest." DuPont's former chairman Irving Shapiro is encouraged to see a growing public awareness that "business is not the enemy of society but is simply its instrument."[1] *Fortune* editor Paul Weaver argues that "business needs to develop the ability to take positions that embody a clear notion of the public interest."[2]

The problem with such arguments is not that they are false. By any reasonable standard, a free market economy does serve the public interest. The problem lies with the implication. The argument boils down to the old advice not to kill the goose that lays the golden eggs. That's good advice—unless you happen to be the goose, in which case you might want a stronger foundation for your right to exist than the expediency of your masters. In other words, the appeal to the public interest implies that businesspeople are second-class citizens who must justify their existence and that they can do that only by serving others.

The basis for the argument comes from social critics of the nineteenth century who embraced a collectivist view of society, in which the public interest stands above private interests. In German philosophy and later in the American Progressive and Pragmatist movements, private interest even became a term of opprobrium. Utilitarians like John Stuart Mill talked of the duty to pursue the greatest happiness of the greatest number. They did not tie the public interest to the preservation of individual rights; on the contrary, they considered individual freedom a privilege that society grants and intends for service to the public good. This is the antithesis of the individualist philosophy espoused by thinkers like John Locke and Thomas Jefferson. In that philosophy, individual rights are primary; the public interest is simply the common interest we all have in preserving the framework of rights.

Statements linking business with the public interest without mentioning rights clearly invoke this collectivist framework and will naturally work against any argument for economic freedom that is made within it.

The history of social thought is littered with examples of how this works. Consider Andrew Carnegie's essay of 1889, "The Gospel of Wealth." In response to populist hostility toward the large corporation, Carnegie and other industrialists cast themselves in the role of the stewards of society's capital. Carnegie said that the moral imperative for those who acquire great wealth is to administer it "for the highest good of the people," to distribute the surplus in accordance with the general welfare. The moral justification for allowing wealth to accumulate in private hands in the first place, he claimed, is that in a free market, only those who can use wealth productively are able to acquire it. The market selects the best stewards. According to Carnegie, then, wealth belongs by right to society and must be used for its benefit.

Critics of capitalism, from social scientists like Lester Ward to Progressive philosophers like Herbert Croly, took the ball from there. They argued that if the wealth is society's, then its stewards must be accountable to the public. This argument became a key intellectual basis for the first wave of political controls over business—central banking, antitrust laws, and the early regulatory agencies.

Today companies occasionally use Carnegie's argument (although they don't call it the "gospel of wealth"), and it still plays into the hands of those who clamor for corporate accountability. But let's look at two other, more recent issues in which the same logic is at work—cost-benefit analysis and profits.

Cost-Benefit Analysis

Companies have won some of their battles against regulatory agencies largely because of the cost-benefit studies that economists have made of various regulations over the past 20 years. Murray Weidenbaum's estimate of $100 billion as the indirect cost of regulation has, through endless repetition, become a fixture in public debate. Even the Environmental Protection Agency, the group least affected by the pressure for deregulation, cannot assign infinite value to goods like clean air or impose limitless costs on industry.

Companies may win this battle but lose the war. A case for business freedom cannot rest on cost-benefit analysis alone, or the gold mine becomes a land mine. Cost-benefit analysis is inherently collectivist because it measures the public good and defines it as the sum of all benefits and costs to everyone affected by a certain action. Any argument based on it is simply a more precise version of the appeal to the public interest.

Critics of the market are happy to have this collectivist standard accepted as the criterion for forming social policy. At some point, they find it quite easy to reject the economist's definition of the public good. After all, cost-benefit analysis relies on market prices to quantify costs and benefits. What it measures is therefore the sum of values that individuals place on goods. Unless we accept the individual's right to choose values and to pursue them, we cannot accept cost-benefit measures. Advocates of regulation already attack them on precisely this ground.

How do we establish a right? Not by cost-benefit arguments. We never subject the rights to freedom of speech and press, for example, to this sort of test. If we did, we would have lost them long ago. We accept the right to intellectual freedom because our nature as autonomous intellectual beings requires it. Rights to property and contract have the same kind of basis: by our nature, we need autonomy in economic as well as intellectual matters.

A Citibank ad put it well: we are "intelligent beings whose nature requires us to be free agents." Once companies campaign to have these rights accepted, they can use cost-benefit analysis in particular areas of the economy to determine whether the market effectively integrates the activities of individuals exercising their rights. But companies cannot reverse that logical order.

Profits Immoral?

Moral attitudes toward business crystallize around the subject of profit, and profit takes on a distinct moral color in each framework.

In fact, business provides an array of benefits—to consumers, a range of products they could not otherwise enjoy, at prices they are willing to pay; to workers, a way of supporting themselves productively, at wages that make it worth their while; to investors, a return on the capital they put up at risk. From an individualist standpoint, each of these benefits has the same moral status: each benefit is good for the party who receives it, and that people can cooperate to their mutual benefit is good for everyone. To put it another way, it is no more to be expected—it would no more be right—for investors to undertake risk without return than it would be for workers to work without pay or for consumers to pay for things they did not want.

Collectivism, however, takes for granted the benefits to both workers and consumers. They are the public, and business merely does its duty to serve the public when it renders services to them. Collectivists see profits as a loss to society: without them, goods would be cheaper and wages higher than they are. That is precisely what the socialists have hoped to achieve by abolishing profit. But it doesn't work that way economically. Companies know that without profits, no one puts up the capital to make the other benefits possible. If they don't challenge this collectivist moral assumption, the fundamental economic fact appears as a necessary evil, a concession to the greed of businesspeople.

Accepting the collectivist assumption by stressing the social benefits of the profit motive or pointing out how low profits are—the two points about profit that issue ads make most often—simply backfires. In effect, the message of companies to the public is: "We wouldn't serve you at all without taking something for ourselves from the public till, and besides we don't take much." That message only encourages opposition to profit, even among those who understand its economic role. When the windfall profits tax was proposed, for example, no one pretended that it made any economic sense; with the doubtful exception of President Carter, no one really believed that the proceeds would trickle down to consumers. But the tax was absolutely unavoidable in the face of the moral hysteria over oil company profits. Despite heroic efforts to enlighten the public about the economic necessity of their profits, the oil companies did nothing to dispel the public's hostility.

Companies fear they will antagonize the public by vigorously defending corporate self-interest, but challenging the public interest ideology need not backfire. The secret lies in the way companies put their message across.

Everyone knows that the profit motive is not altruistic, and a clear acknowledgment of that fact would at least demonstrate corporate credibility. More important, Americans are not collectivists at heart, and it is possible to tap into their sense of individualism and independence with a message that reads, in effect: "You wouldn't put in a full day's work unless your contribution was recognized with a full day's pay. We won't either. Last year we made X in profit, and we're proud of every cent. Here's what we did to earn it."

The Moral Nature of Enterprise

If business wants to make an effective case for itself, it must also challenge the second assumption, that business is materialistic. The assumption takes many different forms. The root idea is that material wealth has a lower value than art, knowledge, or spiritual fulfillment. This evaluation spreads to activities of production and trade and makes them seem routine, mechanical, mundane, and uninspiring.

Although a moment's thought makes it obvious that business success depends as much on intelligence as does anything else, the public does not consider business an intellectual activity. Nor does it see business offering much room for individuality: in the popular image, executives are faceless and interchangeable. Even sympathizers think that business encourages the "bourgeois" virtues of rationality, industriousness, and financial rectitude and discourages the more "heroic" virtues of imagination, vision, passionate commitment, integrity in the face of pressure, and courage in the face of risk.

These attitudes have had a varied life in our culture. The animus toward material values is a heritage of religious traditions that emphasize the otherworldly: even the Puritan fathers of "the work ethic" prided themselves on "loving the world with weaned affections." The secular philosophers of the Enlightenment looked with favor on the motive of economic self-interest, but they did so because they considered it dispassionate and thus safer than the motive of personal glory, which inflames politics. That was the thrust of Samuel Johnson's remark that "there are few ways in which a man can be more innocently employed than in getting money"; commerce isn't noble, in other words, but at least it does no harm. Romantic thinkers rebelled against what they saw as the unheroic character of bourgeois virtues. Their attitude reappeared in the 1950s image of the organization man and the 1960s talk about alienation.

Businesspeople allow these attitudes to flourish more by silence than by active assent. Perhaps this silence comes from modesty, perhaps from a pragmatic belief that nothing so intangible can make any practical impact. If that is what businesspeople believe, however, they are making a mistake. We have only to look as far as the issue of regulation to see the results of these attitudes.

Here again, we can learn something by comparing economic with intellectual freedom. Journalists defend the freedom of the press in part by arguing that competition among ideas helps ensure that truth prevails over error—just as business argues that competition in the marketplace tends to ensure that good products and honest practices predominate. The arguments are exactly parallel.

Yet freedom of speech is more secure in this country than economic freedom. One reason is that, when threatened, journalists do not rely solely on the argument that competition promotes quality but rather cast the issue as an assault on the mind, an attempt to suppress their integrity as individuals. They invoke the tradition of heroic thinkers standing alone against orthodoxy and popular prejudice. Freedom itself becomes the central issue, and it moves us because a long line of victims, from Socrates to Solzhenitsyn, have shown what human qualities the loss of liberty would destroy.

Business freedom, in contrast, remains largely an abstraction. The popular mind has no sense of what human qualities this principle protects.

Business has never pointed out that what the government regulates is people and that regulation is a way of censoring their ideas, their values, and their imaginations. As a result, regulation is seen as only one of the devices governing that vast, mechanical, impersonal machine we call the economy; arguments that the device does not work well do not inspire outrage even when they convince. The Amway ad begins to make this point with its image of the federal nanny but quickly drops the point and returns to the usual cost-benefit approach to regulation.

So those attitudes are potent. Business could take various concrete measures to counter them. The first is to respond effectively to hostile portrayals of business in the media. A recent study done by the Media Institute found that in two out of three cases television presents business-people as foolish or evil; nearly half the business activities shown are illicit. Business's response to the study never quite hit the mark. A United Technology ad, for example, wound up its discussion of the study with two ironies—that TV is itself a business and that business advertising supports it. In logic, that sort of reply is known as a *tu quoque* ("you're another!"), and it is a fallacy: you can't refute one insult with another.

United Technology probably avoided a more direct rebuttal for fear the public would say it was blowing its own horn. That fear is unnecessary. There is a perfectly simple, dignified, effective response to make in this context: TV writers and producers would never allow themselves to treat blacks, or women, or schoolteachers, or any other group with such blind hostility. Should they be any less ashamed of their prejudice toward people in business?

A second measure for companies to take is to launch programs in economic education. The programs that now exist tend to focus on how the economy works as a whole. This effort is all to the good, for the public has become familiar with the standard economic concepts of the market. What is missing is an idea of what goes on *inside* the corporations that compete in the market. Without this, it is natural for people to think of business, especially big business, as a kind of impersonal machine. They need to see real people at work on real problems within companies. Public television's series "Enterprise" has had several episodes that illustrate the sort of thing I mean: without sentimentalizing their subject, the producers make business engrossing and dramatic.

The most important measure, however, is to speak out about government interference in business life in a very personal way. When Sohio announced that it was abandoning its California-Texas pipeline for Alaskan crude in 1979 because of regulatory delay and the threat of further litigation, the public was surprised—surprised by the unmistakable note of weary frustration in the company's statement; surprised by the unprecedented revelation that business is not a workhorse that will plod along no matter what burdens the public authorities place on it.

This kind of revelation ought to occur more often. Regulations have driven companies out of business and subjected whole industries to a kind of prior restraint, an assumption of guilt until innocence is proven. Where is the outrage at such injustice? In private conversation, businesspeople speak with bitterness of talented people giving up in frustration and of innovations drowning in a sea of paperwork; but official statements are normally couched in colorless terms of costs and benefits, drained of all moral force. Business can no longer afford this sort of gray silence about its own victimization.

Corporations as Political Entities

The third assumption skewing the case for business concerns the corporation as a social institution. Writers on the left have labored hard to erase the distinction between economic and political power by portraying large corporations, which undeniably possess great economic power, as political entities that should be subject to popular control. John Kenneth Galbraith has argued that while small companies are competitive and genuinely private, large corporations possess something like political power in their ability to "administer" prices, mold public opinion, and influence the government. The New Left, fundamentally opposed to capitalism and the profit motive, has nevertheless waxed eloquent about the virtues of small entrepreneurial enterprise in order to rail against the power of big business.

The reason the Left wants to blur the line between business and politics is obvious. If we can apply to business the conceptual framework in which we view government, then we can control business power the way we do government power. That is the premise behind Ralph Nader's drive to "constitutionalize" the corporation and related proposals for corporate democracy.

A democratic system cannot tolerate any permanent concentration of political power in private hands—or anything it perceives as such. Business freedom can be preserved only if corporations are seen as voluntary associations among individuals in pursuit of noncoercive ends. If corporations are classifed with government as agents of coercive power, then the framework of rights will necessarily be applied against them. Indeed, this pattern is occurring already in regard to worker and consumer rights.

Consumers are demanding that products be safe to use and reliable. Workers want variety and autonomy in the workplace. One way or the other, business will have to deal with these pressures, but it can make a difference only by framing the issues properly. If public demands are accepted as rights against the corporation, then workers and consumers will not hesitate to enlist the aid of government in securing them. That is what government is for, after all—to secure our rights. But these demands on companies cannot be rights. Someone must produce reliable goods. To claim a right to them is to claim a right to the efforts of those who produce the goods—no one has such rights against other people.

Companies can make this negative and deflating point in a positive way. In the first place, corporations compete for customers and employees and have every incentive to provide as much of what they want as is economically possible. Product competition with the Japanese, for example, has spawned various experiments in worker participation. Second, people differ in what they want. Some consumers want more safety features in products than others do. Consumer advocates trumpet these demands as the norm, but many people don't want to pay the higher price of added safety for all products, a point well dramatized by Monte Throdahl in a tongue-in-cheek issue ad about a $17 pencil. This excellent ad showed what would happen to the price of pencils if consumer advocates got worried about the dangers of these sharply pointed objects.[3] In the same way, some workers prefer the chance for rapid advancement in a growing company that cannot afford the job-security benefits of an already established corporation. Everyone is better off if all parties are free to work out cooperative arrangements on a voluntary, individualistic basis. A government-enforced "bill of rights," in contrast, would impose a uniform standard—satisfactory at best to a bare majority—and ensure that neither workers nor consumers would ever receive more than the legal minimum.

A second and equally pressing issue is the alleged political influence of business. Several years ago, an opinion research project organized by Louis Banks at the Massachusetts Institute of Technology's Sloan School found that "the only point of sharp conflict (between journalists and business executives) came in questions about the *power* of business in American life. The corporation executives believe that business has very little power, and the journalists believe strongly that business has too much."[4] We can understand the difference in opinion by looking at benchmarks against which the two groups measure results. Journalists often assume that government has an unlimited right to control economic activity and thus see business success in escaping controls as an exercise of power against the public will.

As Robert Hessen has shown,[5] that was the implicit argument of Charles V. Lindblom's influential book *Politics and Markets*:[6] if they are still free to operate as private entities, corporations must have manipulated the political process and even popular opinion so as to prevent the political control over them that would otherwise have occurred by now.

Business executives, on the other hand, naturally see any success as an act of self-defense, an attempt to ward off injury rather than gain positive benefits from the political process. In this light, business is not very powerful. Consider the areas of alleged influence. With some notable exceptions, such as the milk producers, most lobbying has only limited the damage of anti-business legislation. Regulatory agencies have in some cases been captured by the industries over which they were supposed to serve as watchdogs—older, industry-based agencies like the ICC and the FCC. But the government is currently deregulating these very industries.

Newer agencies like the EPA and OSHA have functional mandates ranging across the economy, and industry certainly hasn't captured them. Finally, as Peter Drucker has noted, many of the widely publicized cases of corporate bribery and illicit campaign contributions are really cases of extortion by government officials wielding discretionary power over business.[7]

I do not want to make the waters seem less muddy than they are, but to the extent that business's political activities have been defensive, it is important for business to stress the point. As many commentators have observed, a strong vein of populism makes Americans easy prey for theories about the political conspiracies of large corporations. But there is an equally strong feeling for the democratic right to have one's interests represented in Washington and for the constitutional right to petition government for a redress of grievances. These are possible bases of popular sympathy for business. Whether companies can earn that sympathy depends on how the public measures the true nature of their political influence, and that depends on which conceptual framework companies bring into play.

Mistaken Policies

It has commonly been said, especially in standard texts for "Business and Society" courses, that external corporate relations will be an important, perhaps the most important, function of management in coming years. But the observation usually implies that the political and ideological environment is a given to which business must adapt. In the short run, this is doubtless true. But as the basis for a long-range policy, it is mistaken on two counts.

First, we should not assume that business can adapt to any environment just by being nimble and pragmatic. The capitalist system and its private, voluntary organizations have existed only in the last 200 years and only in a few countries. They cannot survive indefinitely in a culture with a collectivist outlook, in a culture that regards the pursuit of self-interest as evil and the pursuit of wealth as dangerous or dishonorable. These are the attitudes that have impeded progress in the developing nations and that are struggling for ascendancy in the West.

If business leaves these attitudes unchallenged, the growth in political control over the economy will continue unabated and the corporation will not have to worry about its external relations: it will simply dissolve into its political environment. The offices and trademarks may remain, but the corporation as a locus of genuinely private decision making will gradually disappear.

Second, companies should not assume the inevitability of an anti-business ideology. The current environment is largely the product of anti-capitalist ideas that have flourished among intellectuals for a century and been absorbed by the "new class" of journalists, foundation executives, public-sector professionals, and the like. Assuming that intellectuals are necessarily antibusiness or anticapitalist is a sociological fallacy. Those attitudes are the product of historical trends, and they are subject to change. Indeed, small but promising signs of change are already showing up in a new generation of economic and political theorists. Change is slow at these altitudes, however, and the process by which new ideas trickle down, slower still. Business could speed things up by putting some new ideas to use now.

Thus, it is both possible and desirable for business to become active in approaching the ideological environment—at least to the extent of insisting on a framework of discussion that is hospitable to the case it tries to make in its own communications to the public.

Notes

1. From a Wharton symposium, quoted in *Business Week*, April 13, 1981, p. 13.

2. See "Corporations are Defending Themselves with the Wrong Image," *Fortune*, June 1977, p. 194.

3. See "The Pencil Problem—1990," Milliken & Company, New York.

4. See Louis Banks, "Taking on the Hostile Media," *HBR*, March–April 1978, p. 123.

5. See *Does Big Business Rule America?* (Washington, D.C., Ethics and Public Policy Center, 1981).

6. *Politics and Markets: The World's Political-Economic Systems* (New York, Basic Books, 1977).

7. See "What Is Business Ethics?" *The Public Interest*, Spring 1981, p. 18.

24

Business Calls Opinion Surveys to Testify for the Defense

SOLOMON DUTKA

The disciplines of survey research and statistical sampling, which historically have been used to support marketing decisions, are rapidly gaining currency in the courts and other legal tribunals. In lawsuits and regulatory hearings, U.S. corporations are turning increasingly to survey findings to buttress their positions. In effect, the companies use the weight of consumer opinion as a legal aid.

Business has applied survey research principally to cases centered on allegations of misleading advertising. But the technique also has found application in antitrust actions, rate cases, arbitration hearings, and IRS appeals.

At the same time government agencies, particularly the Federal Trade Commission, are using this type of research to substantiate allegations of misleading advertising and other unfair practices. Sometimes the regulators commission their own research, but more often they reach into corporate files for evidence to support a charge.

Although efforts to introduce surveys as evidence began in the 1870s, it was not until 1954 that a litigant succeeded in getting one admitted as evidence. In his ruling the presiding judge in the case reasoned:

> A party endeavoring to establish the public state of mind on a subject, which state of mind cannot be proved except by calling as witnesses so many of the public as to render the task impracticable, should be allowed

to offer evidence concerning a poll which the party maintains reveals that state of mind.

Legal Action

The Federal Trade Commission requires an advertiser to make "reasonable inquiry into the truth or falsity of a representation before it is published and uttered." The public's perception of the claim (explicit or implicit), rather than the message itself, is what matters.

The FTC has vigorously pursued its mandate to challenge false or misleading advertising. In some cases the advertisers have used surveys to defend themselves, to wit:

☐ The FTC charged that advertising for Hi-C fruit drink created the false impression that the product contained more vitamin C than citrus fruit juices do. But a series of consumer surveys, conducted by the maker of Hi-C (the Coca-Cola Co.) prior to the FTC action, had shown that individuals who had seen and recalled the Hi-C advertising *did* understand the message and were not misled. Hi-C prevailed.

☐ Firestone Tire & Rubber Co. employed a similar survey to refute an FTC charge that the slogan "the safe tire" would lead consumers to think that the tire is safe regardless of driving conditions or the manner in which a vehicle is operated. Consumers, the study found, thought the safety message was reasonable and did not raise unwarranted expectations. The FTC decided that no corrective advertising was necessary.

The use of surveys in legal matters is broadening beyond the scope of advertising. For example, before it sought a rate increase from a state regulatory body, a large utility surveyed residential and business customers in order to develop a price-demand elasticity model.

To cite another instance, when a major credit card company changed procedures on billing and interest charges, it notified cardholders by an enclosure mailed with statements. A class action suit held this to be insufficient notice. But a company study centering on a similar notice in another mailing established that most cardholders had read and were aware of its contents. The company won its case.

Trademark Cases

Surveys can also play a role in trademark clashes. In one case, the National Football League charged a manufacturer with unauthorized use of NFL team emblems on patches, equipment, and clothing. The court enjoined the defendant from manufacturing or selling emblems bearing identifying marks of NFL clubs or anything "confusingly similar thereto."

Survey findings used in the case were derived from interviews of 1,000 persons eight years of age or older who were shown the unauthorized patches. Some 80% identified the patches with NFL football teams, and of those people, 64% believed them to be official.

The makers of Lysol spray disinfectant used a survey to argue that users would confuse their brand with Listerol due to similarities in the trademarks and packaging. A national probability sample of 1,785 female heads of households who use spray disinfectants was randomly divided into two groups. Both groups were shown a booklet displaying different brands of peanut butter, dishwashing liquids, and household spray disinfectants.

For both groups, the three peanut butter and the three diswashing liquid brands were identical. But the spray disinfectants were different: Group A saw the Dow, Listerol, and Ajax containers, while Group B was shown Dow, Airwick, and Ajax. The Lysol container was not displayed to either group. Only 4.3% of Group B confused any of the brands with Lysol, but 17.5% in Group A recalled seeing Lysol in the picture. The makers of Listerol were obliged to change their packaging.

Trademark action also has extended to the area of secondary meaning. Here the issue is not the word portions of trademarks but graphic elements that are confusingly alike. In proceedings before the U.S. Trademark Trial and Appeals Board, the producers of Yago sangria used a survey to measure the extent to which consumers, when shown only the pictorial elements from six brands of the drink, identified the rendering of a matador and bull with the Yago brand.

The sample consisted of 3,522 individuals, 18 years of age and older, who had drunk sangria. Some 37.2% of the group associated the pictorial elements with Yago, while the next highest score among the six was 2.6%. The government agency, convinced that Yago had a case, rejected the applications of several sangria producers seeking to register trademarks that bore similar bullfight scenes.

Survey Design

Survey findings may be suspect on the ground that (a) the methodology was geared to produce a desired result or (b) the findings were unrepresentative of the pertinent universe. Of course, any indication that either is so renders the findings legally inadmissible.

To avoid such a disastrous error, the sponsor must design the survey with care. First there should be a meeting of the minds between legal counsel and the researcher. Based on the points of law that may apply, counsel will want answers on certain questions of fact. It is then up to the researcher to design a survey that is unassailable from a statistical standpoint and totally objective in its methods.

Management review of survey arrangements for legal use should address the following:

Adequacy of the sample. The crux of any survey is designing and selecting a sample that will statistically represent the pertinent universe.

Questionnaire construction. Scientifically drawn questionnaires address questions of fact and opinion in an unbiased manner. Multiple-choice or open-ended questions may be necessary to demonstrate that respondents have not been biased toward answering in ways that benefit the survey sponsor.

Pertinence of findings. After the questionnaire is complete, the parties should make a final review of it. A set of dummy tables will show the exact appearance of the findings. Although the dummy tables contain no data, they will still enable legal counsel to decide whether the findings will elicit the desired information.

Conduct of the survey. Professionals conducting the field interviews should adhere strictly to the sampling procedures. Because the interviewers usually have no knowledge of the survey's purpose or the client's identity, they can be objective in collecting the data. (If field procedures are questioned in the legal proceedings, the interviewers can be called to give testimony.)

Documentation of all material. Since work material will be subject to scrutiny by experts employed by the other side, it must be scrupulously prepared. Coding and the processing of data should be meticulously accurate and tightly controlled.

The investigator's qualifications. Opposing counsel invariably question the experience of the person chiefly responsible for the design and execution of the survey. Any witness unaccustomed to the rigors of cross-examination may founder. One way to handle this situation is to have an expert witness other than the principal investigator provide the analysis. Such an expert could justify the generalization of survey results.

Above all, the company using a survey to back up its claims against an adversary will want to avoid what Pepsi-Cola experienced last year. In a hearing by a panel of the National Advertising Review Board, Pepsi charged that a Cola-Cola advertising slogan, "Coke is lighter than the challenger," created a false impression.

Since the commercial indicated that Coke had 5% fewer calories, Pepsi maintained that consumers would interpret the message as a dietary claim. But based on further analysis of Pepsi's *own* survey data, the NARB decided that only 2.7% of those sampled mistook the claim in that manner. The panel ruled that this percentage was insufficient to warrant action.

PART FIVE
THE ROLE OF THE EXECUTIVE
AN OVERVIEW

For several years, executives have been counseled that they need to spend more time on public issues; in fact, many chief executive officers of companies now claim that they allocate as much as 50% of their time to dealing with the public. The problem is not with the amount of time, however, as it is with the way in which executives have gone about it. Few are able to drop their suspicions about the motivation of various elements of the public. And what they end up doing with all their time is confirming the prejudices of the world outside the corporation rather than winning it over.

What is needed is more candor and honesty, as well as a willingness to take the criticism that will necessarily be directed at the executive from the particular group that feels offended by his point of view. While in a perfect world the right side will always win out, in our very imperfect society, the self-interest of many blinds them to what is apparently right. Given that reality, executives cannot bury their heads, but must go on the record with the truth; it is always better than sending up an initial smokescreen.

This section of the book contains articles that first admonish executives to go public with their point of view, because, as Norman Adler points out in "The Sounds of Executive Silence," the nation is being deprived of a valuable resource. Recognizing that many executives demur from public comment because they think it might reflect poorly on their companies, Adler suggests that they be given the right to make wholly personal statements about vital issues, without jeopardizing either their careers or their organizations.

David Finn, in two articles, "The Price of Ignoring Posterity," and "The Public Invisibility of Corporate Leaders," hammers away at his long-standing position that executives are both missing out on a chance to fulfill themselves more deeply in a personal way by hiding their opinions and accomplishments from the public, and that they will only be accepted by that public when they learn to stop hiding their human qualities behind the mask of public relations.

In "Corporations Cannot Continue to Be Faceless," L. L. Golden embellishes this by suggesting that the public would be more receptive to business and its concerns if they related to the individuals at the helm of the business rather than to the corporation as manufacturing plants and products. The success of Lee Iaccoco and Irving Shapiro both in gathering public support behind their positions and enhancing the value of their corporations seems to buttress his point made almost ten years ago.

Dan Fenn's ideas are less philosophical in "Executives as Community Volunteers," but no less important. He admits that businessmen have offered their services as volunteers in charity organizations for years, but have often been dismayed that this "good work" goes unnoticed and unrewarded in a public relations sense. Fenn maintains that the reason is that executives do not participate in effective ways, but rather prefer to remain in the background. He recommends that companies develop policies to encourage their managers to actively join community groups and lend their very real expertise to helping with the management of these groups.

25

The Price of
Ignoring Posterity

DAVID FINN

People in business have long been taught that fame is not something that they should actively seek, though it may be thrust upon them. In this article, however, David Finn argues that such a pursuit is more than acceptable; it is laudable. Executives seeking renown, whether they achieve it or not, can enjoy a deep sense of pride in their accomplishments (and improve the reputation of their companies). And they become motivated to seek the greatness that can earn the respect of future generations. The author also discusses how fame differs from celebrity and true greatness, its value to society, how it can be achieved, and the historical importance of an interest in posterity in all fields.

Very few businesspeople alive today can look forward to a prominent place in the history of our era. This prospect is not likely to upset even the most ambitious corporate executives, since posterity is not one of their major concerns. Yet the remoteness of fame as a possible reward for an executive's achievements is troublesome both in terms of his own self-expectations and the values that could be passed along to future generations.

To contemplate the possibility that one's name and work might be remembered after one's death is uplifting. It is a way of transcending the distractions of the present and focusing on what might be important to the future. Only a handful of artists, writers, scientists, and statesmen in any era succeed in becoming famous, but almost all have dreamed of fame and would consider winning it their ultimate success.

Businesspeople do not usually think in these terms, although those who played a major role in American economic development in the late nineteenth and early twentieth centuries may well have had a larger vision. Rockefeller,

---

Author's Note. I use the masculine pronouns throughout to allow for easier reading.

333

Carnegie, Vanderbilt, and Morgan all knew that they were changing the face of the country and drew satisfaction from the contribution they thought they were making to the nation. Their achievements are commemorated in the names of universities, libraries, museums, and other institutions. There is no doubt that today's manager differs markedly from his predecessors in both his personal aspirations and the record he leaves behind. The subject cannot be examined without a few definitions.

What Fame Is—and Is Not

Fame is not the same as greatness, although they are closely related. Greatness implies an objective judgment of supreme worth. One might imagine, along with John Milton, that only God can judge greatness. Milton wrote:

> *This is true glory and renown*
> *When God*
> *Looking on the Earth, with approbation marks*
> *The just man, and divulges him through Heaven*
> *To all his Angels, who with true applause*
> *Recount his praises.*

Thus one can be great and not be famous. God would recognize his worth even if mankind might be blind to it.

Fame, on the other hand, is the badge mankind gives, rightly or wrongly, to those achievements it considers to be great. It is widely believed that over a period of time history will recognize true greatness; there is, however, no guarantee that this is so. Since we cannot know what God thinks, history, with all its faults, is the best judge we have of who is great and who is not. So when a person hopes to be famous, he is really saying he aspires to the quality of greatness that future generations will appreciate.

Being a celebrity is not the same as being famous. A celebrity is a person who is very much in the public eye at the moment. But a popular baseball player or television personality or political candidate may be forgotten tomorrow. *Time* magazine cover stories feature men and women who are in the news; they become even more celebrated by virtue of having their pictures seen by millions of readers, but they will be famous only if their names remain well known for a long time. Fame is associated with having done something memorable. Celebrity is the result of being in the news for sensational but not significant reasons.

Thus on a scale of public values, true greatness, as judged by God or some other absolute measure, is the rarest quality of which human beings are capable. Fame is next, since history is less rigorous (or less accurate) an evaluation of individual accomplishment. Celebrity lies below that, since it can be won by that comparatively large number of people whose names and faces come into public view for short periods. Anonymity is the state in which the bulk of humanity lives. (The scale is in some ways a circle since great people can be anonymous and anonymous people great, but history has no way of identifying and rewarding these exceptions.)

Fame or Celebrity?

Businesspeople may give little thought to fame, but they dislike anonymity. Lack of recognition can cut the price of a company's stock, impede the sale of its products, hurt its competitive position, undermine the confidence of employees, and jeopardize management's continuity. Facing up to these problems is the practical rationale behind public relations efforts to achieve visibility for a company's accomplishments. It also justifies community and cultural activities that win public plaudits. And it encourages business executives to do their part to help build the stature of their companies—serve on boards of directors of important institutions, make gifts to universities, serve on business school visiting committees, advise presidents or governors, make speeches to important audiences, grant interviews to the press, publish articles or books, agree to be honored by such organizations as the Boy Scouts and the United Way, have their portraits painted for boardrooms, and see their biographies recorded in corporate histories.

These are not likely to produce fame. They're not intended to. No businesspeople I know give much thought to the possibility that their publicity will outlast them. Seeking visibility is mainly a strategy for accomplishing specific business objectives.

A Place in History

Professional managers pride themselves on their realistic outlook, yet this commonly accepted point of view betrays a deeper shortcoming. Although it may be self-centered, egotistical, even selfish to want to perpetuate one's own name, shying away from the attempt leaves the forces of history to others who are less reserved about establishing their reputations and to those who prefer to effect changes anonymously. I don't mean to imply that any person—artist, poet, scientist, or businessperson—should be consumed by the desire for fame. I do suggest that the possibility of creating something of lasting value can be ennobling for both the creator and the public for which it is created. And there is no reason to believe that this sense of nobility is incompatible with a responsible business outlook.

The accepted corporate approach to seeking recognition is to depersonalize the credit as much as possible. If Alfred Nobel had felt that way when setting up the Nobel prizes in his name, the impact they have made during the past century might have been greatly diminished. More important, if he hadn't determined, on the basis of his convictions, to use his fortune for this purpose he would not have had a place in history.

The Pritzker award for architecture is a more recent example of a program in the Nobel tradition, yet, true to contemporary management thinking, there was considerable reluctance on the part of the person responsible for developing the award to use his family name (rather than "Hyatt," the name of one of his better-known enterprises). One can easily speculate about the debates that took place before Norton Simon, Inc. was named after its chief executive officer (and the Norton Simon Museum too), and before the Helmsley Palace was named after its builder.

It is not only one's name that is at issue, although without attaching one's name to inventions, paintings, symphonies, awards, corporations, books, real estate projects, and so on, one is far less likely to be a candidate for fame. What is most important is the drive to pursue one's personal goals in this world and to associate one's name with the things one is accomplishing. Why not take the credit for it and make an effort to have it remembered? If a person in business doesn't do so, the world will never know how much individual businesspeople have contributed to the betterment of society. It might also be a much less pleasant place in which to live.

Things to Consider

To decide what point of view corporate executives ought to have toward posterity, we must first answer three questions. First, how durable is fame likely to be? Second, why have men and women in other fields sought fame? Third, how is fame won?

How Durable?
Any realistic examination of fame must begin by acknowledging its unreliability. Poets have long bemoaned its changeable nature. They recognize that it is often whimsical, volatile, fickle. Keats called it a wayward girl, a gypsy, a jilt. In *Paradise Regained*, Milton wrote:

> *For what is glory but the blaze of fame,*
> *The people's praise, if always praise unmixt?*
> *And what the people but a herd confus'd,*
> *A miscellaneous rabble, who extol*
> *Things vulgar, and well-weigh'd, scarce worth the praise,*
> *They praise and they admire they know not what;*
> *And know not whom, but as one leads the other. . . .*

The "blaze of fame" may burn brightly in one age and fade in another. History has seen many shifts in attitude toward the great figures of the past. In ancient Greece, Pericles and Themistocles were equally revered—Pericles was the Athenian leader under whose aegis the Parthenon was built and who led the defense of his state against the Spartans; Themistocles made Greece a great naval power and successfully defended his country against the Persians. In the histories written over the next few centuries by Herodotus, Thucydides, Plutarch, and others, the biographical biases changed. As the centuries passed, the Age of Pericles came to be described as the pinnacle of Greek history and Themistocles' popularity faded.

This ebb and flow of reputation was not the result of a studied emphasis given to their roles in history by succeeding generations. Fame graphs can be made of every heroic figure of the past showing similar fluctuations. Even those who today supposedly have their places fixed in history—Alexander, Napoleon, Michelangelo, Rembrandt, Beethoven, Bach, Shakespeare, Goethe, Plato, Newton—have not escaped ups and downs in their reputations from age to age.

Often the fluctuations are drastic, ranging from the highest degree of recognition to total anonymity. In the time of Napoleon, Antonio Canova was considered not only the greatest artist of that era but also the greatest sculptor who had ever lived. Today some of his masterpieces are hidden away in cellars and crates. Renoir considered Bouguereau the greatest painter of his time, yet in subsequent generations Bouguereau became all but forgotten and Renoir achieved recognition by every schoolchild in the Western world. Verdi's *Rigoletto* is beloved by all opera fans, but Victor Hugo's play *Le Roi S'amuse*, written almost 20 years earlier and on which Verdi based his opera, is far less celebrated.

Why does a person's reputation rise or fall with the changing scenery of history? In studying the process we see that famous people of the past are symbols that have a special meaning in the lives of later generations. Since their lives are over, the people who stand out in history are not responsible for holding our attention. We remember them for our sake, not theirs. Fame follows an erratic pattern through the centuries because perspectives change and people need different symbols in different eras.

In our own era we can watch the rising fame of the poet Sylvia Plath, the photographer Diane Arbus, the painter Egon Schiele. Somewhere in our unconscious there may be an awareness that the tragic deaths of these gifted artists were in themselves important commentaries on our time, and this awareness heightens our appreciation of their works.

On the other hand, we may wonder about the future reputation of Albert Schweitzer, whose lifelong medical service to the African poor and his phrase "reverence for life" meant so much to the world in the 1950s and 1960s. Yet for no apparent reason, he appears to be barely known to the present college-age generation. Perhaps young people today are impressed by different kinds of devotion and are looking for symbols more meaningful to them.

The most powerful and widely heralded have sometimes suffered the most from the unpredictable tides of fame. "My name is Ozymandias, king of kings:/Look on my works, ye Mighty, and despair!" were, according to Shelley, words engraved on a pedestal found in the desert. Ozymandias's boast was in vain. All that was left of his immortality were "two vast and trunkless legs of stone." Nothing beside that "colossal wreck" remained.

Why Is Fame Coveted?

The second question, why have people sought fame, takes on a special poignancy in view of the unreliability of fame over an extended period of time. In Greek mythology the goddess Fame was the daughter of Hope, and it was thought that the most extravagant hope one could have in one's life was to become famous. Aristotle believed that achieving glory legitimately was "the greatest and most valuable of external goods." Cicero agreed. "For what, indeed, is there," he wrote, "in all this so slender and brief span of life, [that] may move us to such great labors, [but] that the memory of our name be not lost with life, but extended to all posterity."

Milton himself wanted to "leave something so written to after-times, as they should not willing let it die." He wanted to write, "as men buy leases, for three lives and downward." Shakespeare had faith that his "powerful rhymes" would outlive "the gilded monuments of princes." Ralph Waldo Emerson wrote that "it is to this itch of being spoken of, to this fury of distinguishing ourselves which seldom or never gives us a moment's respite, that we owe both the best and the worst things among us."

Psychologists have pointed out that the desire for praise has its origins in the child's need for parental approval. Children identify with the heroes of the past and believe that they will become heroes in their own lifetimes. They dream of immortal fame as a way of conquering awful death. While the dream fades as children grow into adulthood, it never completely disappears. Although logic tells us that true fame is reserved for only a tiny percentage of those alive in any period of history, the souls of many ambitious and creative people harbor some vestige of the archetypal vision of themselves in heroic form.

Whenever we receive a degree of public recognition for some achievement, no matter how trivial, the pride we feel is an echo of that grand image of ourselves. We may not think that we have been immortalized, but at least we have a sense of the projection of our personalities beyond the intersection point of here and now. That's why most people like publicity, awards, titles, tributes, and trophies. Beyond any tangible benefits they may bring, these plaudits feed our egos by giving us a taste of fame.

One of the most stirring speeches I ever heard was given by Dr. Louis Finkelstein, then chancellor of the Jewish Theological Seminary. He confessed before a large audience that people accused him of having a messianic complex. With arms outstretched and fire in his eyes, his voice reverberating with the thrill of genuine prophecy, he cried, "It's true! I want to make this world a better place!" I think hearts stopped in the audience at that moment and his listeners would have followed him as the mice followed the Pied Piper. What made this charismatic exclamation particularly moving was his utterance of the name of the Messiah, evoking images of immortality with which almost all of us can identify.

How Is Fame Achieved?

If this desire to be immortal is why poets, statesmen, and other ambitious people are attracted to the prospect of fame, how is fame achieved?

The biographies of famous people in various fields suggest that there are several characteristics that generate fame. Most important, of course, is the actual quality of greatness that is the essential ingredient of fame. But coupled with the quality of greatness are a passion for the work one is doing and a hunger for recognition of its value. One must also have a sense that the accomplishment is worth preserving for future generations. Unless one thinks of oneself as deserving a place in history and has a desire to win it, posterity probably will not oblige the fame seeker. The desire to be remembered is the thread most often found in the life stories of all famous people. Often couched in terms of some grand social or cultural goal, it is almost always implicit in their ambition.

Next there is the tenaciousness with which they pursue this ambition. It almost seems that those who try hardest to be remembered—or to make someone else famous—are the ones who succeed. Vincent Van Gogh's brother, more than the painter himself, demonstrated the necessary tenacity to achieve fame, in this case for another. And that is true of many others who have taken a prominent place in history. One of the greatest men I ever knew, a man who made an extraordinary discovery in the field of art and psychology, cared little about personal recognition and died almost unknown. Since his death, his wife has devoted her life to winning recognition for his ideas, and she may succeed. Virtually every person who has become famous has either had such a passion himself or has been the beneficiary of dedicated efforts by someone else who believed in the subject's greatness.

Another characteristic of people who have become famous is an uncanny ability to seek out those who are in the vortex of history. This is not unlike the successful businessperson's instinct to speak directly to the top executives of other companies if he wants to make a deal. Some people are reticent about approaching those who are the most influential in their field; they feel more comfortable dealing with persons in less imposing positions. But the ones who prefer dealing with the top people are likely to get the best results. When this tenacity is combined with the interest in posterity, a sort of radiating effect reaches from centers of influence to ever larger groups of people who are impressed by what they see and hear.

Even in so reserved a man as Einstein, this tendency was unmistakable. We can see it at work between the time his first article on relativity was published—with no fanfare—and the next six years, during which the leading scientists of his time began to recognize the importance of his ideas.

Still another factor leading to fame is the dramatic nature of one's life story aside from one's achievements (that is, poverty, illness, premature death). This could include changes in the course of history (Columbus "discovering" America); mythical acts that never took place (St. Patrick ridding Ireland of snakes); and figures who become famous—or infamous—as part of a legend (Count Dracula).

In sum, fame is an illusion, not at all the surrogate for immortality we wish it to be. It is not always conferred on those who deserve it. The poet Rainer Maria Rilke gave it the most cynical definition when he wrote, "Fame

is but the summary of misunderstandings which cluster around a new name."
And there is every likelihood that even the fame of those who are remembered for long periods of time will eventually be viewed differently by future
generations.

Yet the deep-rooted interest in posterity found among gifted people
has proven to be a potent prod toward greatness. Without it, mankind would
not enjoy the benefits of history, and civilization as we know it would probably not exist.

Guidelines for Executives

How then can a businessperson add a vision of posterity to his ambition in
order to connect the desire to succeed to the continuity of history? Here
are some guidelines taken from experiences in other fields of endeavor.

The intense drive to succeed found among so many executives should
be recognized as an essential requirement for winning a place in history. Let
the skeptics use the disparaging word *workaholics* if they are mistakenly
convinced that the compulsion to overwork is a disease. Those who take a
longer view recognize that history is made as a result of such compulsion.
Some call it an obsession and believe great things cannot be achieved without
it.

Of course, to be worthy of a place in history, something more than
making a sale must be the goal of one's hard work. It is not easy for businesspeople to do something memorable in the course of conducting their affairs,
but it's no easier for poets, scientists, or statesmen. Simply trying hard to
accomplish great works will not ensure fame. If some executives are to
succeed, however, the corporate environment should be hospitable to those
who are driven to make a positive impact on the world around them.

The appetite for public acclaim, so often considered immodest and
unbecoming, should be acknowledged as a healthy component of the individual's personality. Some executives do not like to see their names in print,
in which case they should be left to enjoy their privacy. But those who feel
otherwise should be no more embarrassed about it than an artist who hopes
for a favorable review of his or her work. And as with an artist, recognition
must come as a result of a person's actual accomplishments, not someone
else's imagination. Posterity does not look kindly on artificially promoted
personalities.

People in business should make a special effort to develop an appreciation for achievements in other fields that have endured through the ages
and for those of today with the greatest promise of lasting into the future.
The ability to appreciate such accomplishments is, of course, no less than
a hallmark of an educated and cultured person drawing inspiration from the
greatness of others. Such appreciation not only enriches one's own life but
also helps one to discover deeper capacities for achievement that may lie
within. As part of this process businesspeople should also be exposed to

those who have already won fame in their own time. The greatness that one recognizes in famous men and women can be infectious. One can be ennobled when in the presence of people who have a keen sense of their own posterity. It helps one to become aware of one's own potential and to focus on a purpose that might in some way measure up to what one sees as worthwhile in others.

A Sense of Posterity

The contemporary businessperson is not, for the most part, inclined to place a high priority on these aspects of life, and this lack of interest in fame suggests a limited vision. He may believe that it is more practical not to pursue the "illusory" values of posterity, but, in truth, this kind of thinking is shortsighted. It inhibits his ability to be a true shaper of society.

By ignoring the deeper meaning underlying the idea of fame, modern executives deprive themselves and society of the benefits to be gained from potentially memorable achievements that might survive beyond the present. They content themselves with superficial forms of recognition, going through the motions of being a historic figure but failing entirely to focus their energies on anything history would be likely to remember. Thus the businessperson's honors are rarely the type that are likely to endure. Boardroom portraits are almost always poor works of art and shallow representations of personal character. Corporate histories tend to be "puff" pieces, produced by undistinguished writers. Corporate titles are too numerous to be meaningful, and guests of honor at luncheon or dinner functions too obviously chosen for fund-raising purposes to be memorable. No one is particularly concerned about such shortcomings since projects of this sort are designed for short-range purposes. There is little if any interest in what future generations will think of the honored guests and the certificates they have received. They may enjoy the help that being celebrities for a short time gives their careers, but they do not care very much if their honors are forgotten after they have disappeared from the scene.

The unpredictability of fame does not mean that it is foolish to pursue it. The quest for fame is the only means at our disposal to establish the proposition that man is capable of some kind of greatness. The vagaries of fame force mankind to recognize that he cannot be the judge of either his own or his fellow man's true worth, but the emergence of famous people in every era reminds us that this is how history is made. A sense of posterity is the best method we have to look beyond the horizon of our own lifetime and estimate the ultimate value of our accomplishments.

Falsifying Fame

Executives are not alone in their superficial approach to posterity. An unprecedented variety of devices have been invented in recent years to simulate fame. The forest of plaques found in many contemporary hospitals promising distinction to generous contributors; the names on buildings of schools and universities around the world; the "halls of fame" in different fields; the awards and prizes given for outstanding achievements; the space in newspapers and magazines devoted to biographical sketches; the number of places in which all sorts of minor accomplishments are exhibited—movie houses, department stores, YMCAs, grade schools, churches, libraries; all these testify to modern man's inclination to dabble with fame rather than take it as a serious and lofty goal.

The incredible increase in the number of annual *Who's Who* volumes, from fewer than 10 in 1880 to more than 130 in 1970, tells its own story. Indeed, the development of public relations as a business has contributed an increasing number of ways in which the appetite for recognition can be fed. So prevalent has this characteristic been that the difference between being a minor celebrity and being a truly famous person has become blurred. The idea that reputations can be created out of thin air has also gained currency.

Respect for lasting fame and posterity has diminished while attention to publicity and momentary recognition has increased. Andy Warhol, the pop artist, wittily recognized this trend when he predicted the day when everybody would be famous for five minutes. What he didn't add was that none might be famous for much longer.

No Place in History

Because we show so little interest in historic achievements, we could be living in an age that will be considered a minor period of history. Lewis Mumford hailed "the death of the monument" as a positive development for society. And artists are producing works that are dismantled as part of the process of creation, like Christo's celebrated "Running Fence" or Robert Rauschenberg's "Erased Drawing by de Kooning," which involved the destruction of a work of art that might have been preserved for generations, and now the blank paper is admired as a record of the act. There is also a renewed interest in the collective work of art, similar to medieval workshops, where no individual wants to get the credit for the achievement.

Wise men have always given a high rating to the satisfaction that comes from the inner sense of a job well done. But surely the quality of that satisfaction is greater if one feels that the thing one has accomplished may have some enduring value. The prospect of fame inspires one to produce the stuff of which history is made. The question as to whether one will in fact achieve fame is not important, for one is not likely to be around to enjoy it. As Keats put it in a poem on fame, "Make your best bow to her and bid adieu,/Then, if she likes it, she will follow you." What can make a difference in one's life is the sense of history, both past and future, that one feels when striving to achieve something that is worthy of posterity. Such an effort can be inspiring even if one contemplates the possibility that the world will ultimately come to an end and that all human achievements will be consigned to oblivion.

This, unfortunately, is a vision that cannot be experienced by those who see their work and daily lives in terms of short-range values rather than as part of the continuity of history. To the extent that our society abandons the effort to produce things that may last for centuries, we will lose touch with the sense of posterity. This seems to be the fate of our contemporary business community with its heavy emphasis on such immediately tangible, but unenduring, values as the price-earnings ratio and the return on investment. The dream of fame will not affect the price of stock and will pay no dividends to stockholders.

The truth is that it does not *pay* to be famous. Thus portraits for the boardroom and company histories are produced only to give an appearance of heritage rather than a real inheritance. They do not represent a genuine respect for the past and a serious concern about the future. That is why they are so poorly done and so little attention is paid to them. Nobody really expects them to be around for very long, so why bother?

Beyond the Here and Now

This is not to say that it is impossible for men and women in business to take a longer view of themselves and their work. There are exceptional individuals in the business world who have demonstrated an interest in seeing beyond the ROI. It is not farfetched to imagine that when J. Irwin Miller of Cummins Engine worked out a plan to pay the fees of internationally known architects to design schools, libraries, churches, and other buildings in Columbus, Indiana, the small town in which his company is located, he entertained the hope that posterity would look kindly on his efforts. David Rockefeller may also have had such thoughts when he initiated Chase Manhattan's program of acquiring contemporary art. Irving Shapiro clearly demonstrated a sense of history when he used his position as head of DuPont to play an important role in national and international affairs.

One cannot predict whether these men will actually be remembered by posterity. But they have acted as people who care about the future, and in that sense have ennobled the present by their vision.

In a recent speech to the Society of Applied Economics, Toshinori Hayashi, president of C. Itoh and Company (America) Inc., cited two ancient oriental proverbs to explain his philosophy of "management beyond ROI." The first was, "The full evaluation of one's life is not complete until the lid covers one's coffin." The second was, "We must look for true friends after 100 years." He believes, therefore, that one's business decisions should be made with future generations in mind.

There can be little doubt that contemporary management dogma argues against this type of thinking when it insists that everything management does must be rationalized in terms of bottom-line results. The currents of our time, even in the arts, also seem to be running against the quest for fame. We seem to be determined to make our epoch an undistinguished stretch of history.

Perhaps the one signpost to posterity that remains for the business executive is the strength of one's inner conviction about the importance of what one is doing. Somewhere it has been said that one can feel one is doing God's work by performing so simple a task as throwing stones into the sea. To sense the potential of posterity in one's daily business life, one has to feel deeply about some aspect of one's work. One has to be committed to do or create something that will accomplish some good in the world.

It doesn't matter if this achievement is tangential to one's primary responsibility in business—it still may prove to be the most important thing one has ever done. Nor should one be concerned about the apparent perishability of one's acts. A speech written on the back of an envelope and taking a few minutes to deliver we all remember as the Gettysburg Address. The key ingredients are dedication to a profound idea and the determination to carry it out.

Perhaps the winds will shift and some of the spirit that moved the original entrepreneurs who built America will be revived in a new form. Maybe the time will come when we will see more poetry, philosophy, and statesmanship in business for their own sake, and not for the dollars they might produce. If so, it would make the world of business a more creative and qualitatively enriching place to work and would attract men and women of genius who could help give our era better prospects for posterity.

26

The Sounds of Executive Silence

NORMAN A. ADLER

Because most executives shun personal involvement with important and controversial issues not directly related to their businesses, "the nation is being deprived of the collective insight, experience, and judgment of one of its most responsible and potentially influential leadership groups." From this premise, the author discusses the reasons for such reticence and restraint and suggests a possible approach for resolving the dilemma of "the sounds of executive silence."

While folklore has it that ours is an egalitarian society, there is little doubt that in our social structure—even as in the socialist mecca of the Soviet Union—some people are more equal than others. At the very least, it cannot be seriously argued that our national interest is best served if the opinions of the local service station attendant and the corner druggist are actively solicited and gravely weighed while the views of the executives of our largest corporations are seldom expressed on the important and controversial social and political issues of the day.

The stridency of both the radical left and the radical right is increasing. The silent majority may or may not have the numerical preponderance that some have attributed to it, but it is certainly in the process of losing its reticence. At the same time, the academic community—students, faculty, and administrators—has become increasingly vocal, and we listen with varying degrees of attention to both our junior and our senior citizens. The underprivileged and the overprivileged get in their licks, and politicians on all levels of government are rarely at a loss for words.

But from most executives—chairmen of the boards, presidents and assorted vice presidents, directors, and managers of our largest, richest, and most powerful corporations—are usually heard only the sounds of silence. By and large, they are reluctant to join the national debate. With some notable exceptions, they shun expressing publicly their positions on the vital issues that now affect and will increasingly determine the well-being not only of the enterprises they serve but also of the country and the world in which they live and which, for better or worse, their children will inherit. This is the lamentable, but nonetheless true, state of affairs in our country today.

Some outstanding industry leaders have, from time to time, spoken out. For example, in 1969, Dr. Frank Stanton, President of the Columbia Broadcasting System, strongly rebutted Vice President Agnew's criticism of the television networks. He warned of the threat to all free journalism implicit in the Vice President's words and in the related actions of other highly placed government officials.

More recently, the heads of three other of our largest industrial enterprises—International Business Machines, DuPont, and Bank of America—criticized our continued presence in Southeast Asia and deplored its severe impact on our social and economic structures.

Unfortunately, these expressions are among the exceptions that underscore the much more prevalent practice of reticence and restraint.

In this article, I shall first discuss the reasons why most executives are silent on controversial social and political issues. Then, I shall offer the premise that the voice and conscience of the executive group is a valuable national asset that should not be wasted. Finally, I shall suggest how the problem of silence at the top might be approached.

Self-Imposed Celibacy

A *New York Times* report of the results of a survey made by the Businessmen's Educational Fund points up the timidity of most top corporate executives to stand up and be counted.[1] This organization attempted to elicit opinions on whether our foreign policy was outdated and whether it no longer continued to serve the national interest.

Specifically, 25,000 top executives were mailed copies of a statement by General David M. Shoup, retired Marine Corps Commandant, and were asked whether they agreed with his opinion that the United States has become militaristic and aggressive. Only 1,700 of those queried replied. Of this number, about 1,100 expressed agreement with the general, but asked not to be identified.

Latent Potential

The melancholy result of this self-imposed intellectual and social celibacy is that the nation is being deprived of the collective insight, experience, and judgment of one of its most responsible and potentially influential leadership groups.

If we take *Fortune* magazine's 500 largest industrial corporations and add the 50 top commercial banks, life insurance companies, retailing companies, transportation companies, and utilities, we arrive at a total of only 750 separate companies. Even if we limit ourselves to these very large corporations and arbitrarily but modestly assume that the top cadre of each such company amounts to no more than 50 executives, we arrive at the considerable aggregate of 37,500 people who are in this select and influential executive group. Compare this number with the 64,000 names of persons, from all occupations and walks of life, including officers of large corporations, listed in the current edition of *Who's Who in America.*

The head count, however, is not important. The numbers would obviously be much greater if we included all of our substantial business enterprises and all of their managers in responsible positions.

What does emerge with stark clarity and powerful impact, however, is the enormous power of this group to influence the national destiny. When its many voices are silent or expressed anonymously, the great national debate proceeds without the benefit of one of the most important segments of our society and one that could make a significant contribution.

With society becoming increasingly polarized—with the far left and the far right rapaciously devouring the moderate middle—we can, as a nation, no longer afford such calm detachment in the eye of the hurricane. Moreover, even on the basis of the self-interest of the managerial group and the well-being of their companies, this widespread abdication of social responsibility is unwise and insupportable.

Nonrisk Involvement

This is not to say that many of our more enlightened corporations do not involve themselves in community affairs and urge their executives to devote substantial amounts of their time and energy to public service. Indeed, one of our largest companies has recently announced a plan to encourage its top managers to accept positions with the federal government by guaranteeing against their loss of corporate status or seniority.

But, for the most part, such involvement is on the community or local level and in noncontroversial civic, charitable, and cultural areas. A substantial and needed public service is, of course, thereby rendered; and since everyone is for good and against evil, the corporation discharges its social responsibilities while at the same time enhancing its image. Even the most profit-motivated stockholder can have no legitimate cause for complaint when the corporation contributes reasonable sums in support of the public weal.

Without denigrating the quality or scope of this type of corporate and executive involvement, it is apparent that there is no comparable devotion of money, mind, or spirit to the resolution of far more fundamental and vital—and controversial—social problems. It is in this area that the commitment of the concerned citizen is most urgently needed, but it is precisely here that the top echelons of our most influential corporations shun both the commitment and its expression.

The rationale is clear, albeit shortsighted: since it is impossible to please everyone, avoid involving the corporation in controversy. The stockholders, consumers of the corporation's goods or services, and possibly also government officials may react with varying degrees of criticism or hostility. Thus it is the better part of executive valor to remain neutral and silent.

Thread of Controversy

Only those completely out of touch with reality can fail to perceive the enormity of the problems urgently awaiting analysis, definition, and solution. Consider:

☐ Are our national priorities positioned correctly, or have we got them backward?

☐ With concededly finite resources can we support an enormous defense budget and at the same time redress our domestic deficiencies?

☐ Should we explore the solar system now or first provide adequate interurban mass transportation?

☐ What can we do about the decay of the cities; our educational needs; the correction of our ecological posture; our crime, drug, and racial problems; and the alienation of our youth?

The list is very long indeed. And people of goodwill and of impeccable patriotism differ—and the disagreement is often deeply felt—not only in their estimates of the nature and dimensions of many of the problems but also in their ideas concerning the best means and methods required to effect solutions or ameliorations. Throughout the whole challenging array, however, runs the common thread of acute controversy.

Vast and profound philosophical issues are in the process of resolution. The judgments we make, the priorities we set, and the actions we take had better be the right ones. We may not have another chance to correct our mistakes.

In a democratic society based on the consent of the governed, our policy makers—the President and the Congress, and their counterparts on the state and local levels—if they are to be effective, must not only lead but also make their thrust and direction an expression of the national will. And the electorate—all of us whose fate is at stake—can express its views only to the extent that, and as soundly as, it is well informed.

Reasons for Status Quo

The officers and managers of our large corporations are well qualified—by education, training, expertise, and responsibility—to make contributions to the decision-making process. Certainly, they realize that nothing less than their lives and fortunes are at stake. Why then are most of them silent?

The answer, it would seem, can be found in two interrelated pressures. The first is the executives' understandable reluctance to do anything that may jeopardize their own success or security within the organization. The second is the very real concern that, by their own involvement or its expression, they will identify their corporations with their personal views. These are serious problems.

Let us examine the basis of each and then look at a possible solution. If we accept the premise that the voice and conscience of the executive group is a valuable national asset that should not be wasted, then the dilemma obviously should be resolved.

Executive Jeopardy

The climb up the organization is long and hard, and the path is full of pitfalls. A misstep can be serious and sometimes fatal. Even if we put aside for the moment the problem of identifying the corporation with the individual's speech or conduct, the concerned executive usually feels it necessary to tread carefully. Conformity and orthodoxy are solid and respectable.

The espouser or supporter of unpopular causes or dissenting views is generally regarded with suspicion. At the very least, he stands out. Controversy, especially in matters not immediately or directly related to the activities of the corporation, may be regarded by his boss as an unnecessary dissipation of the executive's energies. After all, he is paid to do his job.

And finally there is the real danger that his immediate superior or those all-powerful figures at the summit may have deeply felt contrary convictions and may be offended.

It is a truism that the unpopular cause of today often becomes the orthodox and accepted position of tomorrow—and history is replete with examples of such changes in attitudes. But executives who want to avoid bad marks on their corporate report cards may not be willing to gamble on the long term. Instead, they play it safe and do not make waves.

Of course, not all decisions to keep clear of involvement or controversy can be explained by such cliché-ridden terms or by all of the foregoing reasons, but the end result is the same. Unless, as is too infrequently the case, the highest corporate level is deeply committed to the right of free expression and unless top management actively encourages commitment by both words and deeds, lower echelons will inevitably practice the expediency. of abstention and silence.

Corporate Neutrality

The primary reason, however, that expressions of conscience do not usually flourish in the corporate environment is the difficulty of maintaining the neutrality of the corporation—as distinct from the people who serve it. It goes without saying that such neutrality should, if possible, be preserved. The corporation should not be identified with the views of an executive on matters which do not reasonably and substantially relate to its business— unless he clearly speaks for the company.

The rationale is obvious. A corporation is a separate legal entity. Its business is carried on and its objectives pursued within the framework and limitations of its charter and bylaws.

For example, when a responsible executive of a public utility defends the construction of a power plant against charges of potential ecological damage or when the president of a broadcasting company speaks out against the threat of government censorship, such utterances are in the areas of the direct and substantial interests of their enterprises. Both statements, to be sure, have profound social implications. Honest men may differ with the statements, but since, in each case, the business is directly affected, no one challenges the propriety of the executives speaking for their corporations.

The trouble arises, however, when an executive's views on controversial social or political matters not clearly within the company's province are imputed to the company. Then not only the position taken but also the propriety of the executive to take a position can become subjects of controversy.

The consequences of this straying off the corporate reservation can be serious, indeed, if the issue is one about which there is substantial public disagreement. The stockholders will undoubtedly be heard from, since in a large corporation their views will probably reflect the divisions of society as a whole.

Moreover, many who do not disagree in substance will feel that harm has been done by involving the company. The consumers or users of the corporation's products or services may weigh in with boycotts or shifts of allegiance. And if the subject is politically sensitive, there is always the risk of offending government and inviting retaliation.

How, then, can the corporation best preserve its neutrality?

A corporation's basic mission is to supply an honest product or service of good or superior quality at a fair price—and in the process to make a reasonable profit. If it accomplishes this objective, it has performed a needed service for its customers, discharged its obligation to its stockholders, and operated in the public interest within our economic framework.

Since the enterprise is not a bloodless automaton, it obviously can reach this result only through the efforts of its employees operating under the direction of its management.

Toward a Solution

How well the corporation accomplishes its mission is, for the most part, readily ascertainable. And its executives should be identified with the enterprise only in connection with corporate performance in the pursuit of its objective. In all other areas—thoughts, fears, aspirations, and judgments—their lives should be their own.

Thus, as concerned citizens, when they become involved with, and express themselves on, controversial issues not directly related to their businesses, the overwhelming presumption should be that they speak for themselves—unless they make the contrary clear.

If we agree with this principle, then it follows that corporate neutrality and integrity will best be supported if freedom of personal involvement and expression are encouraged. There is no reason to believe that the differences of opinion among executives on controversial matters will not roughly approximate the divisions in other segments of the population having comparable socioeconomic status.

Accordingly, the more widespread the participation and the more varied the expression, the more commonplace personal involvement will become; and the greater then will be the acceptance of the executive's personal freedom.

Kingman Brewster, former President of Yale University, has stressed the need for institutional neutrality in order to protect academic freedom. In reply to an expression of concern about his statements on controversial issues—especially when they did not relate to Yale—he stressed his conviction that institutional neutrality will be better protected if personal opinions may be outspoken.

If free expression for executives becomes the rule, rather than the exception, there should be little reason for one who selects a pair of shoes to look beyond quality, style, and price. An automobile manufacturer's views on Vietnam have as much bearing on the performance of his cars as does a surgeon's attitude toward sexual freedom on her skill in the operating room.

The Road May be Bumpy

The problem is not susceptible to ready or total solution. A good starting point, however, is for the corporation to adopt and enunciate a clear policy of free expression for its executives. In so doing, the corporation admittedly runs some risk that the personal views of its executives will be interpreted as the official corporate position. The mood of the country is such that almost any position taken on any important issue is bound to evoke hostility from some quarter.

But in a democratic society there is no satisfactory substitute for the airing of all points of view. If sensible judgments are to be made and a sound national consensus arrived at within the framework of our sociopolitical system, we need the contributions of all concerned citizens.

The corporation may not always succeed in preserving its neutrality by encouraging personal executive expression. But institutions have come under attack even when their people walk on eggs. Despite stringently enforced standards of institutional independence and reportorial professionalism, the most prominent news media—both print and electronic—have been assailed for allegedly slanting the news to express a bias unfavorable to the particular complainer's views.

One wonders, in passing, whether the news media's institutional neutrality would not be more effectively protected if the personal views of reporters and commentators on controversial issues were known to the public. At the very least, this would provide an additional benchmark which could be helpful in appraising the fairness and objectivity of the news and the cogency of the commentary.

Conclusion

In the last analysis, however, the problem of "the sounds of executive silence" will be resolved only on the basis of the corporation's enlightened self-interest. And in this regard an additional and compelling consideration comes to mind. A paramount obligation of top management is to provide for its succession—to recruit, train, and develop tomorrow's managers.

The colleges and universities are, of course, the most important source of embryonic executive talent. And it is there that many of the most creative, involved, and articulate young people are finding corporation careers less attractive than other occupations. The competition for the top graduates of colleges and graduate business schools is keen. The best will not join an organization where the atmosphere is one of intellectual sterility.

Indeed, there have been numerous cases of upper-level executives themselves leaving intellectually sterile corporations to work for social service institutions where freedom of expression flourishes. One can thus assume that, if their personal viewpoints on issues not directly affecting their companies had been encouraged, such felt personal needs might have been filled, and at least some of those executives might have stayed on.

The quest for improvement of the human condition started at the beginning of history and will be with us for a long time to come. Silence and conformity are hallmarks of a totalitarian state. They prop up the facade of tranquility. But, in a democracy, social progress flourishes only in a climate of free expression of diverse views.

Notes

1. May 30, 1970.

27
Public Invisibility of Corporate Leaders

DAVID FINN

Why do top corporate executives get such poor press—or, worse, no press at all? The reason, believes the author of this article, is not their lack of potential for interesting the public, nor their motives or personalities. It is their diffidence. Somehow the business world has taught them to hide their human qualities behind masks. They should not worry so much whether their decisions to do business in style will be seen as "ego trips." They should not be embarrassed that their enthusiasms spring from family contacts or friendships. They should let themselves be seen as they are—human beings with loyalties, passions, pet projects, fears, concerns, and aspirations that, though meritorious, have no origins in economic analysis or return-on-investment calculations. If they would be more candid and open about such motives, believes the author, the public could respond to their leadership more than it has been doing.

A major cause of U.S. business's persistently low score in public opinion surveys, I believe, is the failure of corporate executives to convincingly present themselves as persons who truly care about the state of the world in which they live. In fact, this absence of *visible* concern among top managers seems far more significant to me than does the widespread lack of public understanding of how the profit system works, although no doubt such a lack exists. Great salespeople that corporate managers are for their products and businesses, they have done a poor job of selling themselves. It is widely believed that they would sacrifice public interests for the benefit of the companies they head, and that their primary goal is to make as much money as they can—for themselves as well as those who put them in power.

Even sophisticated and socially minded executives have not been recognized as effective leaders of society. They don't seem to know how to
fire the public's imagination with enthusiasm and excitement about life's
potentialities. They rarely inspire public confidence in their judgments about
how to cope with great social problems. They don't propose goals for mankind to which all can aspire.

This is not to belittle the value of the many social and cultural contributions which corporations have made in recent years. It is rather a commentary on the lack of credit business executives have received for these
contributions and the responsibility of management itself for this failure.
Instead of winning public respect for their many public services, businesspeople have been condemned for the supposed venality of their motives,
their lack of honesty, integrity, and character. Good deeds done in the name
of corporate social responsibility do not persuade the public that those who
head large corporations are people of conscience. The good deeds are considered by many as little more than strategies to deflect attention from a
company's antipublic policies—"charity to hide a multitude of sins," to
quote Thoreau.

Thus, the audience boos a concert in the park when the announcement
is made that a large oil company is the sponsor. Critics accuse museums as
well as public television stations of selling out because corporate funds
underwrite spectacular exhibitions or programs; they charge that standards
of excellence are compromised in order to provide corporate publicity benefits. Some editors refuse to mention a corporate sponsor's name in reviewing
an art exhibition because they believe the company is only trying to use the
museum for its own purposes. Critics of business warn against the corruption
of our social, educational, and cultural institutions by ruthless, self-interested
wielders of corporate power whose irresponsible ambition will destroy our
most valuable assets if they are not watched at every turn. These critics
often have a flair for publicity and convincingly represent themselves as
individuals who care deeply about the welfare of society.

What are business executives' responses? Strong affirmations of innocence. Anger and frustration at the scant attention paid by the press to
their defense. Increasing pressure on communications advisers to find some
way to get the corporate story across. Expanding business advocacy programs to teach the virtues of the private enterprise system. But precious
little to win support for themselves as people who care at least as much
about the welfare of society as those who attack management. So they are
branded as villains, evil people, even murderers who deserve public retri-
bution for the deaths caused by their products and policies.

Business executives ridicule any suggestion that they are criminals.
But anyone exposed to daily news coverage on television, radio, and the
print media, or who reads contemporary novels about business, or who
watches movies on television or in theaters dealing with corporate life finds
plenty of support for such an accusation. The public learns about a congres-

sional report stating that "industry has shown laxity, not infrequently to the point of criminal negligence, in soiling the land and adulterating the waters with its toxins." It hears that pharmaceutical companies "dump" drugs in Africa which are so dangerous that they have been withdrawn from the American and British markets. It reads that tens of thousands of a particular automobile have been recalled because of shoddy workmanship that can cause fatal accidents.

The suspicions are heightened when the media quotes management's denial of wrongdoing with the seemingly endless refrain that the charges are based on "inadequate information," denials which seem transparently self-serving and irresponsible in the face of "incontrovertible facts." It is not surprising that the public considers these anonymous people who run our giant corporations to be people without consciences, capable of the worst crimes against humanity.

Occasionally a public relations adviser suggests a new solution to the problem, and for awhile the public is exposed to a barrage of advertisements, booklets, films, audiovisual guides, buttons, banners, and exhibitions proclaiming the virtues of the free enterprise system. Many of these programs are no doubt useful; they help clear up misconceptions (like the exaggerated notion of how much money American corporations make and what those profits are used for). But such advocacy programs are not likely to create a substantial following, at least not until business leaders prove to the public that they care more about what happens to society than what happens to their companies.

That a great many business leaders do care there can be little doubt. The problem is that they hide their human qualities behind a mask of corporate anonymity. A reversal of deeply entrenched ideas about corporate behavior is needed to change the public perception of who business leaders are. Only if this change is made can the executives who preside over our large corporations provide effective leadership for the nation.

My aim in this article is not to prove a case or present fresh findings. My aim is simply to offer a point of view based on many years of working with business leaders and observing public reaction to their behavior. Let me stress that my viewpoint is based on assumptions about executive behavior that, however heretical they may appear to much of the public, will seem quite familiar and obvious to most *HBR* readers. Since it is management I hope to influence in this article, not the public, I shall rely mostly on simple examples—examples that, I believe, could be duplicated over and over. I make no claim that these vignettes are newsworthy, only that they are real.

Criminals or Public Servants?

Imagine a newspaper columnist writing the following about the CEO of, let us say, General Motors:

> [Mr. Smith] has demonstrated something we have forgotten in America
> and even tried to deny; that a solitary individual with strong convictions
> and noble aspirations still touches the heart of a vast continental nation.
> . . . What [Mr. Smith] has done . . . is to make people in high office
> realize the force of moral conviction. To make them remember that they
> are not merely bureaucrats who propose laws, but they are also custo-
> dians of the nation's ideals, of the hopes and fruits that sustain it from
> one generation to another.

This is what James Reston wrote on October 5, 1979 about the visit of
Pope John Paul II to America. No one could doubt that whatever other
purpose the Pope had in mind, he presented himself to America as a human
being who wanted what was best for the world as a whole. Chief executive
officers of large corporations may feel a similar sense of devotion to humanity, but since most of their public statements have to do with how many
products they sell and how much profit they have made for their stockholders, it is difficult for them to "touch the heart of a vast continental nation."

Business leaders do in fact care about the higher values in life; this
can be seen in the many nonbusiness aspects of their lives. Businesspeople,
as board members, make possible the effective functioning of a substantial
majority of the country's hospitals, universities, museums, and churches
and temples. This is a dimension of human concern that is generally hidden
from public view because board members perform their functions as individuals or in the name of institutions rather than as officials of their own
companies. But the business executives themselves, I have observed, feel
a keen sense of responsible leadership in these public service functions.
They are truly selfless in their community activities. They give generously
of their time, take no personal compensation for their work, and respect the
knowledge and dedication of professionals who are modestly paid but highly
trained.

It is unfortunate that the leadership talents business executives display
in their extracurricular lives are considered peripheral to their jobs as executives. Rarely are the trustees from business visible to the public as corporate executives. Nor are they given credit by their companies or stockholders for their accomplishments as citizens who perform outstanding services
for the community. Although their communal activities may appear in their
official biographies (and perhaps eventually in their obituaries), they are not
mentioned in annual reports, articles about the company, or communications
to employees. There seems to be a tacit understanding that volunteer work
should have a low visibility in business communications lest executives be
criticized for taking time away from company responsibilities.

Lights under a Bushel

The result is a split personality for the business leader. The greatest victim
is the corporation, which loses the opportunity to have its top executive

recognized as a caring public servant. It also deprives the business community of those values, nurtured by our public institutions, which ought to be respected by all. In universities, museums, hospitals, and religious institutions, it is common to think in terms of truth, beauty, honor, and mercy, but these values seem out of place when the executive is at his or her office. The community-active business leader accepts them in one world and ignores them in the other.

In business, for instance, "truth" means explaining why the corporation's point of view about a controversial issue is correct and does not mean searching for that elusive quality in which no person or organization can have a monopoly. But in academic, cultural, and scientific circles, "truth" transcends self-interest and expresses humanity's unending search for meaning in life. "Man can embody truth but he cannot know it," wrote Yeats as the summation of his own lifelong quest for something to believe in. I believe that businesspeople generally understand such insights when they sit on university boards and wear their intellectual and cultural hats; if they could introduce the values into their business lives, public perception of their characters might be altered.

Business leaders do not actually leave their high principles behind when they enter the office; they just don't like them to be talked about. I have seen innumerable manifestations of high personal values, consideration of fellow human beings, respect for other people's opinions, concern about ethical behavior, and all the other admirable traits found among men and women of integrity in other fields. But while these virtues are heralded as significant marks of character in academic life, medicine, law, and government, they are usually considered irrelevant in the appraisal of an executive's way of doing business. Even when business leaders do make important decisions on the basis of human rather than "bottom line" motivations, they don't like to admit it.

One sharp businessman I know, for instance, recently acquired a company headed by a friend of his who had borrowed heavily to buy into the company and was having great difficulty in meeting his obligations. Because the acquiring businessman was considered one of the shrewdest financial managers in the country, it was widely assumed he had seen some extraordinary opportunity in this new acquisition. Although he was perfectly happy with this explanation and hoped it would turn out to be true, his personal motive was different: by acquiring the company, he had helped his friend solve his financial problems. The acquisition might or might not prove to be a good decision in financial terms, but both executives felt that the act of friendship was its own reward.

The point of this simple story is that the human element in business decisions—in this case, a personal friendship—is often masked by official corporate dogma. Again and again behind the scenes I have seen executives show profound concern for the welfare of the public when questions arise about the health or safety of their products. But when conscientious top executives of tobacco companies consider the smoking patterns of young people, or thoughtful top executives of utility companies consider the location of nuclear power plants, or sensitive top executives of chemical companies consider problems of environmental pollution, their public statements on these issues are always carefully composed by lawyers, scientists, public relations specialists, and other advisers whose job it is to keep the company out of trouble. In a sad way, we public relations advisers who try to help the companies we work for often do harm by preventing the true personalities of top management from being seen by the public.

What is missing is the human element, which can come only out of the minds and hearts of the leaders themselves, expressing what *they* feel about the issue at hand and its possible consequences to society. No wonder they appear to be heartless individuals who have no concern about what happens to the rest of the world as long as their companies prosper.

Off the Record

Some time ago, six chief executive officers of multibillion-dollar companies and six leading environmentalists held a one-day, off-the-record meeting. A condition of the project (laid down by one of the executives) was that no records be made and no summary of the meeting identifying the participants be published.

The question arose as to whether life on earth faced the prospect of total extinction. The environmentalists said yes, and the CEOs said no. Then one of the more conservative executives surprised everybody by saying, "Whatever any of us may think, it seems to me we ought to agree that there is a *possibility* that the world as we know it may end. It doesn't matter how remote that prospect is; the fact that it is a prospect at all must have top priority for each of us. We business leaders should therefore agree that anything our companies do which has the slightest chance of bringing that prospect closer should not be done, *no matter what the cost might be to our business.*" To the astonishment of the environmentalists, all the executives present agreed.

What a pity it is that such an affirmation was not made public. The popular impression is that executives would sooner see the world blow up than have their profits jeopardized. That attitude, in the view of much of the public, leads them to support nuclear power plants, heavy defense spending, and other threatening developments in our society which fill the coffers of their companies.

I am convinced that the attitude of the six business leaders at the confidential meeting is far closer to reality than the public impression of demonic industrialists. How are corporate executives to correct the popular misconception? The need, it seems to me, is for them to integrate their community and business lives—to speak up publicly as business executives when they serve on third-sector boards, and to speak out as culturally and intellectually sensitive individuals when performing their management functions.

Daring to Be Wrong

Sound management can be, and often is, a product of consensus decision making. Policies may be produced by boards, committees, and task forces rather than by dynamic individuals. Leaders have a hard time becoming visible in such an environment. They feel something is wrong with their way of doing things if they dare to assert individual responsibility in public for a major corporate decision. While press announcements may be made in their names, it should be clear to all that this is only a formality required by corporate etiquette. Actually, many executives have the ability to project their personalities but hesitate to do so because they feel corporate statements should always reflect collective judgment and not individual sentiments.

One Sunday, for instance, the president of a major television station read a critical review of his station's summer programming and was upset about some misstatements in the article. He tried to reach several members of his staff, including his public affairs director, to ask them to draft a reply, but no one was home. In desperation he sat down at his typewriter and dashed off a lengthy letter to the editor. It was published the following Sunday.

Afterward, the president complained because he had had to handle the responsibility by himself. If his advisers had only been available, he said, he was sure a much better job could have been done. They felt guilty about their failure. I was present at the postmortem discussion and, as an outsider, ventured the suggestion that a committee-written response could never have achieved the clarity, directness, and persuasiveness of the president's own statement. This suggestion met with general agreement. The executive was startled to think that he had done better than his professional staff could have done.

When top executives make decisions that they believe are right despite widespread opposition from below (or even from their boards), they may give shape and "character" to their companies. From time to time they may be wrong, just as political, academic, and religious leaders sometimes are wrong. But unless there are times when they are so convinced they are right that they dare to be wrong, and say so publicly, they can't expect anybody to follow their lead.

One company chief executive I have known for some time is a good example of a businessman who is not afraid to be himself even when it gets him into trouble. He is a superb salesman, and he does everything in business with great flair. He doesn't hesitate to spend large sums of money for excursions with customers to expensive resorts or major sports events in different parts of the world. His competition consists of companies much larger than his, but because of his natural showmanship he more than holds his own in the marketplace.

His dramatic bent and expensive tastes are sometimes accompanied by a short temper and disdain for critics, creating difficulties with governmental legislators who follow his industry and with reporters who cover stories about his activities. His advisers try to steer him away from controversial statements, and although he tries to listen to their counsel, he feels that if he can't be himself he might as well give up his job.

Because he is always so candid about how he feels, and because he always insists on the best no matter what he does, he has built up a tremendous loyalty among employees and the people with whom he does business. He has given a decisive and dynamic character to his company. It is not colorless and impersonal. Its leadership is not seen as remote and institutionalized.

"Ego Trips?"

Such people are often thought to possess an abnormal ego and are criticized (perhaps by jealous competitors) for trying to take the center of the stage. The opposite of showmanship is secrecy, and that is a far more common attribute among corporate executives.

An executive of a large real estate company prides himself on the anonymity of his company and feels no obligation to provide details of his company's operation to the public. As far as he is concerned, his company's financial performance speaks for itself. In a recent discussion with him, I mentioned another developer who has articulated a social philosophy about his real estate projects. "That man is just on an 'ego trip,'" said the executive scornfully, as if that were the worst label one businessperson could give to another. "All he wants to do is make speeches and get his name in the papers." I asked, "What's wrong with that? Isn't ego the basis of all drive and ambition, even for you and for me?" The executive was embarrassed. He agreed that everybody had a right to his own ego, but he couldn't help feeling that responsible business leaders should be more private.

Coincidentally, the developer accused of being on an "ego trip" suffers from the same malady affecting so many other CEOs. If his competitors think he is making speeches and seeking the limelight as a way of promoting his company, they are wrong. As a businessman he constantly talks about the need to justify everything he does in terms of bottom-line results. He makes speeches and gives lectures because he passionately believes in society's need for better urban planning, but he tends to make these statements as an individual rather than as the head of his company. Thus the business community is losing another opportunity to win credit for visionary leadership.

In another case, a large multidivisional company suffered from a lack of identity in the business community. Part of the problem was that its name was an acronym taken from its original stock exchange listing, consisting of letters that meant nothing. It is extremely difficult for such a name to make a lasting impression on anybody, and it is hard to have any concrete feeling for the company behind the name.

A leading firm specializing in corporate identity programs tried to find a solution, but none of the names it recommended was acceptable to management. However, in a follow-up study which asked, "What is the first thing that comes to mind after hearing the name of the following companies?'' a surprisingly high percentage of financial analysts mentioned the name of the founder and chief executive officer of the company. It was clear from this and other questions that the founder was the primary bond that tied this diverse enterprise into a single unit.

Another study tested the potential receptivity to giving the company the name of the founder-CEO. In reply to a query on this subject, the highly respected Swiss author Charles H. Tavel wrote a letter in which he stated, ''I am a firm believer in the decisive importance, especially in the years to come, of the personality of the leaders.'' He went on to point out that ''there is little doubt that what the public, and especially those who contest or challenge our type of society, dislikes the most is anonymity.'' He felt that the proliferation of acronyms in the business world has led to confusion; he believed that management must be seen as human beings, not ''anonymous committees or implacable reckoning machines.'' He concluded that naming a business after its founder gives it ''a name and a tradition which [can] survive through the years as a unifying factor.''

As a result of these studies, a recommendation was made that the company change its name to that of the founder-CEO. The recommendation was met with enormous resistance—first by the CEO himself, who stated that he and his family placed a high priority on privacy, secondly by members of the board, who were worried that such a change would be perceived by others as—again that wicked phrase—an ego trip. (As of this writing, the matter is still being considered, but my guess is that eventually the recommendation will be adopted.)

Esthetics of Leadership

In quite a few instances, chief executive officers of major corporations have spent more money on their headquarters facilities than some of their more spartan associates thought they should have. But, in other cases, the opposite was true. Spending lavishly on symbols of authority is not an essential ingredient of leadership, and, for every Buckingham Palace, White House, Versailles, or Vatican, there is a Henry Thoreau cabin or Thomas Paine cottage where a person with no desire to live in a grand manner affected the course of history.

But leadership does mean exercising the courage to create an environment that reflects a top executive's image of the way he or she wants to do business. It means resisting the temptation to be inconspicuous and anonymous in order to avoid reporters' questions and public gossip. Sometimes corporate leaders act as if they fear a raised eyebrow more than a deficit.

The academic world is more successful in creating this environment. A new college president is inducted with a convocation of eminent scholars. Graduation exercises are formal affairs at which distinguished speakers make memorable addresses. The church, too, is more successful. Religious leaders speak from pulpits in great churches to their congregations. In contrast, the business world has no such ritual benefits, and there are few opportunities for top executives to convey a sense of dignity about the positions they hold. They do enjoy fancy offices, chauffeured cars, company airplanes, and many other luxuries. But there are few symbols available to them which can impress their audiences with the seriousness and significance of their roles.

Building in Style

To make up for this lack, some executives have developed a sense of style in the way they conduct their business lives. When that style comes from a genuine quality in the character of a top executive, it can contribute to the effectiveness of leadership. The chief executive of a $700-million-a-year company, which has its headquarters on a large tract of land in the Midwest, has designed his corporate facilities in authentic colonial style. No one can visit the premises without feeling management's respect for the values embodied in American history. The chief executive's interest in America's traditions also has led to substantial contributions to Williamsburg and other historical restoration programs as well as to a museum of nineteenth and twentieth century American products.

The head of another large corporation decided he wanted the greatest contemporary architect to design his company buildings, the greatest landscape architect to design the environs, the finest industrial designer to design his products, and the work of the best artists and craftsworkers to adorn the halls and walls of his offices. When I visited the company headquarters, I asked an employee how he liked a new sculpture in front of the building. "Not much," he replied, "but if our chairman picked it, it must be the best."

I spent hours with the head of another multibillion-dollar company, trying to decide the best place to put a new Henry Moore sculpture that his company had acquired for the front of the new headquarters. We looked at the proposed site from every conceivable angle. He eventually decided to relandscape the entire front area of the building, which was a long stretch of lawn, trees, pathways, and a pond, in order to make sure the work was placed in ideal surroundings. In fact, he wasn't satisfied until the sculptor himself came to visit the site and give his approval.

Beyond ROI

Esthetic judgments of this sort can be expensive, and when they are it may be difficult to rationalize them in terms of return on investment. The company is not likely to see any direct financial benefit from relandscaping corporate headquarters to accommodate a new work of sculpture. Nevertheless, such an approach can produce an indefinable and immeasurable character for the company; it may enable the chief executive to introduce a sense of style into corporate operations. The result will not show up as some specific asset on the balance sheet, but it can have a major effect on the lives of those working in the company and in the surrounding community.

Certainly I am not suggesting that executives should develop a style in their businesses in order to create an artificial face for their companies. In 1962 I wrote an article for *Harper's* entitled, "Stop Worrying About Your Image," hoping to put to rest the misleading idea that by assuming a contrived public posture a company can solve basic problems in business. My effort was in vain because the unfortunate use of the word "image" has become more deeply embedded in our language than ever.

There is, however, another meaning of the word image. Yeats wrote, "Man is nothing till he is united to an image," referring to an image as an ideal or model that can help people plan their lives. An image to Yeats was not the result of an artificial pose but an inspiration, an expression of what a man seeks to become. So can it be for corporations. The esthetic judgments of business leaders can reflect what they are trying to accomplish for society.

What about Personal Motives?

Most top executives seem to be embarrassed to have their personal motives identified with important decisions and policies. I agree that there are limits of good taste and appropriateness in this regard. For instance, one executive of a large furniture company is anxious to further a friend's career as an actress, and he is not above assigning his company public relations personnel to publicize and promote her performances. Another executive tells his public relations advisers that their most important responsibility for the year is to see that his wife's picture appears in the newspaper the day after opening night at the opera. It is hard to justify activities like these. But they are not, in my experience, typical. The more typical personal motives are not irrelevant or inappropriate, and I think executives make a mistake in trying to conceal them.

For example, one chief executive has learned a great deal about photography from his son, a fine artist in that field. Stimulated by this experience, he has sponsored a series of major photographic exhibitions as part of his company's public relations program. It is an exciting, forward-looking program that has won great respect for his company and many admirers for his imaginative leadership. But since he is a highly competent professional who places a high value on ojective judgments in business, he is embarrassed about any implication that his personal interest in collecting art and his son's involvement with photography have influenced him. He shouldn't be. Why shouldn't parents and children learn from each other? It is an experience to be proud of.

Arguments have been made against management's use of stockholders' money to support activities in which an executive has a personal interest. I accept these arguments when the interest is as personal as publicity help for friends, but not when the interest leads to leadership in the community. The long-term outlook for stockholders depends on the emergence of effective leaders in the corporate world. If business fails to produce such people, the public will follow other leaders who command its attention and inspire its loyalty.

Conclusion

No one knows today, any more than Thomas Carlyle did in the nineteenth century, what makes a leader a leader. Carlyle provided the rhetoric that helps us recognize the importance of leadership in history; all I can add to his insight is that no one can be a leader if he or she doesn't permit his or her deepest instincts as a human being to manifest themselves at work and use those insticts to capture the public imagination. Business managers who, for the most part, have concentrated all their efforts on obtaining financial results for their constituents have done comparatively little to develop the gift of public leadership. This has undoubtedly contributed to the low esteem in which business leaders are held.

I believe that executives have a great potential for inspiring leadership in contemporary society. But they need to let people see what kinds of human beings they are, what they believe in, what they want to accomplish through their business activities, and what values they want to achieve for society through their efforts. To accomplish these objectives, business executives with a talent for leadership should:

1 Integrate their communal and business lives so they can gain credit for their public services and be credible when making statements about their businesses.
2 Develop an appetite for being in the public eye as individuals who represent the character of their companies.
3 Speak publicly and convincingly about human needs and values as well as economic benefits when discussing business policies.
4 Have the courage to initiate company programs that grow out of their personal interests, and become the public spokesperson for those programs.
5 Develop their own sense of style about the conduct of their businesses without worrying that they may be catering to idiosyncratic tastes.
6 Persuade their stockholders that it is important for managers to be human beings who have deep concerns about the health and well-being as well as the material comfort and financial security of their fellow citizens.

The public may approve or condemn a specific corporate action, but if it knows what kind of person is responsible for the company's policies and what values he or she believes in, it is possible to be responsive to that leadership. Instead of being anonymous instruments of impersonal corporate interests, top executives can be understood as conscientious individuals doing their best to fulfill responsibilities to society which they believe to be of great importance.

28

Corporations
Cannot Continue
to Be Faceless

L. L. L. GOLDEN

In a speech not long ago, the chief executive of one of the country's largest corporations called for a return to the philosophy of Adam Smith. He insisted that our prime concern must be a continuation of the free enterprise system, and he urged other heads of major corporations to stand up and be counted.

Although the speaker believed his theme was new and striking, the speech received little public notice. He seemed to forget that *The Wealth of Nations* was published two hundred years ago; that long before he was born we were in a mixed economy, with the private sector steadily shrinking to smaller dimensions; that Americans are a practical people uninterested in doctrinaire theories.

This executive is not the only one who insists on talking to himself. Yet he and too many of his peers wonder why they are "misunderstood"; why the press, the politicians, and the public hold them in low esteem. By their silence on subjects of prime social concern, business leaders buttress public suspicion that they consider themselves apart from national problems that do not impinge on the day-to-day operations of their company.

Who are the spokespeople for business the public heeds? It is difficult to name one, a fact very dangerous to the health of large businesses.

One reason that business executives refuse to speak out on issues of wide national concern is that as they climb higher in the hierarchy of the largest companies, they tend to lose touch with their origins and become isolated from all but a few—even in their own companies. Outside the company, they associate mostly with their peers who themselves are cut off from the currents of change.

The businessperson who becomes chief executive fails to perceive that his former companions of high ability now hesitate to press their opinions on him. He asks their views less and less often if they tend to disagree with him; soon he even begins to think he holds his post because he is a superior person.

As top business executives lose touch with the opinions of those who disagree with them, their ability to face the facts of social change becomes dulled. As they ride higher, they forget that the corporation must identify itself with society as a whole and not with a single group, that in the final analysis no business can survive without the consent of the public.

Another reason that many corporate officers do not speak out on subjects relevant to the public's interests may be that they do not believe that business's concerns lie outside the operation of their enterprises. Fundamentally, they believe that this talk about business and society is so much rubbish; that the business of business is business; that only one thing really matters, maximization of short-term profits. Many avoid their clear obligations as business leaders by hiding behind their misunderstanding of Milton Friedman.

How can they believe that business, which is so central to our society, stands outside it? How can they believe that national problems are the concern of the nation but somehow not the concern of our largest for-profit institutions?

He Spoke for Business

In 1948, Frank Abrams, chairman of the board of Standard Oil Company (New Jersey), told his stockholders in the company's annual report:

"No business exists in economic isolation. It is part of the social climate of its time. Its policies and actions affect the character of that climate. In turn, that climate—which is, after all, simply the ideas and goals of large numbers of people—influences any business importantly. It can even determine whether the business is to prosper and survive or decline and disappear.

"Corporate citizens have, therefore, come to accept many of the obligations traditionally imposed only upon the individual citizen. Today companies concern themselves with employee and community welfare and with many other activities going beyond a strictly economic concept of business functions. The management of this company is devoting an increasing share of its attention to the social problems affecting its business. We believe that in this way the continuity of the enterprise may best be assured and its economic health sustained."

Jersey Standard had established a public relations department early in World War II. One of its prime objectives was to demonstrate the company's patriotism and explain that its contracts with a German company, I.G. Farbenindustrie, dated more than two decades before the outbreak of World

War II. But Abrams believed that a public relations department was not enough. So when he became chairman in 1946, he took on the burden of speaking out for Jersey.

It was common sense, he thought, that the head of the corporation should represent the company, with the support of the board of directors and the advice and concurrence of the public relations department. The chairman of the board, he said, "is in an ideal position to represent the company and be its prime contact with the public. If he can't do it, who can?"

Abrams worked with stockholders, with governments, and with educators. He did not rely on hired lobbyists; he went to see congressmen himself. He did not wait for subpoenas, but volunteered to testify before congressional committees on subjects affecting Jersey. The more critical the jounalists, the more anxious he was to meet them. He would ask for appointments to learn the reasons for their criticism, give them his company's viewpoint, and explain why Jersey took a certain course of action. He did not hide behind a smoke screen; he believed that cosmetic jobs were very ineffective as well as dangerous.

Abrams campaigned to raise the salaries of school teachers at all levels and to provide financial help to private colleges and universities. His company began supporting the social sciences in colleges, as it had supported chemistry and physics. Abrams was the motivating force in the founding of the Council for Financial Aid to Education. Earlier, when the legality of unrestricted corporate gifts to education had been in question, he had instigated what became the Smith Manufacturing case. The result was a landmark decision that now permits a corporation to aid the arts as well as education in areas unrelated to its business.

At the period of Abrams's chairmanship of Jersey Standard—which extended to 1954—he spoke for business in social areas as well as for his company in business matters.

Who Speaks for Business?

Of the many qualities necessary to run the affairs of our huge multinational companies, big insurance companies, public utilities, and banking institutions in this period of great changes in our social structure, two qualities must be added: an ability to grasp public moods and an ability to argue the corporation's case.

Business executives are constantly complaining that if the people were only told how good the companies are, business's trouble with the public would disappear. Communication is bad, big business says. So what does it do? It hires more public relations consultants. It adds to the number in the Washington office. It retains law firms with politically influential partners. It puts more energy into trade association activities. It expands its use of advertising to tell the corporation's story. But senior officers shy away from going out front themselves, from carrying the burden as Frank Abrams did for Jersey.

The corporation cannot continue to be faceless. It must have senior officers, chairmen, or presidents who can do more than read carefully drafted texts. They must be able to meet the toughest kind of questioning by senators with presidential ambitions And they must deal with issues that lie beyond the immediate confines of business and in which the public has an interest. Repetition of the profit creed without relating it to what the public conceives as its interest is simply fanning the wind. It may provide jobs for surrogates but its value is minimal.

To avoid serious injury to the private sector, chief executives must shed their habit of hiding behind lesser mortals while they continue on their old ways. The crisis in business credibility is so serious that our major corporations cannot much longer avoid searching out candidates for president or chairman who can do the job. Today's climate of opinion demands more than one Frank Abrams.

29
Executives as Community Volunteers

DAN H. FENN, JR.

When he joins a community action group as a volunteer, the businessman does not provide leadership. Instead, he winds up doing things that do not challenge or attract him, to the detriment of his performance. The author recommends measures to correct this wasteful situation—measures for the community organization, for the company, and for the executive volunteer himself.

For generations, business executives have served on the boards of hospitals, schools, the United Fund, the Y, and a host of other community organizations. This service has become part of the corporate executive's way of life, and business leadership of voluntary groups is generally accepted as an important and desirable part of the American scene.

But a recent study of businesspeople in action in community groups discloses some characteristics which challenge several of our traditional assumptions about the nature, effectiveness, and purpose of that service. For example:

☐ The executive turns out to be a follower instead of a leader, an implementer rather than an innovator. He reacts to the initiatives of the paid staff of the voluntary organization, rather than managing it.

☐ Both the businessperson who gives her time and the company that permits—or encourages—her to do so take a notably pragmatic view of the process, and of the benefits that may come to them through this kind of involvement.

☐ There is a serious lack of understanding between business executives and organization staffs. The study shows that nearly one half of the corporate executives who are active in these organizations feel underutilized.

☐ Most businesspeople find some very thorny obstacles to working successfully with the newer, activist, heterogeneous community organizations, though these groups eagerly seek their help.

☐ A person's age, and the nature and especially the attitude of the company, have a notable impact on the nature of the voluntary service.

☐ There is a pronounced lack of systematic planning by both companies and managers for participation in voluntary organizations.

These are some of the findings which have emerged from an extensive study of the business executive as a leader in voluntary organizations which I completed in conjunction with Daniel Yankelovich, Inc.

The study, conducted for and sponsored by the Center for a Voluntary Society (a division of the NTL Institute for Applied Behavioral Science) in Washington and by *HBR*, was focused on the executive's role as a policy maker in nonprofit organizations. It involved over 400 personal interviews in 10 cities throughout the country. The respondents were active executive volunteers from business, top corporate executives of voluntary organizations, and managers who are not currently doing volunteer service.

One central fact about this service emerged immediately from the interviews: business executives' participation in community activities is increasing and becoming more meaningful, in the views of both executives themselves and the voluntary organizations they serve. Nearly 75% of the staff members of voluntary groups interviewed, for example, said they believe that business participation is on the upturn; only 10%, that it is merely holding steady.

Furthermore, this involvement is not of the "letterhead" variety. Some 80% of the business executives feel that token involvement is inadequate, and the interview reports are replete with strong quotations rejecting this kind of participation. Additionally, although the organization staffs do have some difficulties with their business members, as we shall see, they do not list chairwarmers as a serious problem.

"Within my own span," one business executive said, "it's changed. We can't pull down the shades and play within our companies anymore. We understand, even if we are reluctant about accepting it, that we are a part of the matrix. This has not always been true, but it sure is today."

The range of involvement and the staying power of business directors are now considerable. Some 83% of the businesspeople surveyed said they were active in two or more organizations, and, as Exhibit 1 shows, they tend to serve a long time. (I might note that this exhibit breaks voluntary organizations down to *traditional* and *contemporary;* the distinction, which

Exhibit 1.   The Staying Power of Executives as Volunteers

	Percentage of executives who have served:		
Type of organization	Less than 2 years	2–5 years	More than 5 years
Traditional	34%	36%	59%
Contemporary	62	56	44
Total*	96%	92%	103%

*Multiple responses.

I shall explain later, is not important here—just the size of the numbers.) I see no reason to think that this tendency toward longevity and multiple involvement will change. Virtually all the businesspeople now active say they would enlist again if they were given the opportunity to remake their original commitment to help.

How did they become involved? Almost all respondents were originally recruited—there are few true executive "volunteers." In explaining why they agreed to join up the first time, our respondents told us that it was because "I knew the work [they] were doing was badly needed" (47%); because "their concerns are the same as mine" (44%); because "the organization appeared to need the expertise or skills I could offer" (36%). Surprisingly few cited a reason such as "I wanted to oblige the friend who asked me." There is a message here for the organization looking for business help.

It is interesting, incidentally, to compare this record of involvement with the picture of the business leader in politics.[1] In the case of politics the businessperson is just as enthusiastic about the importance of his involvement with campaigns and candidates and just as articulate in stating his reasons. But there is a big difference. When you look for him in the smoke-filled rooms, he is not there. When you look for him in community organizations, he most assuredly *is*.

All this is fairly obvious to anyone surveying the business scene today. Not quite so obvious, perhaps, are the reasons for it. And here we get into some of the most interesting—and promising—aspects of the study.

Altruism and Self-Interest

Altruism, of course, plays its role. So does a sense of the seriousness of our current social situation; the responsibility of business for parts of it; and the obligation business and business leaders have to lend their talent to ease, if not cure, our social ills.

One top manager expressed his reason for his extremely extensive involvement in a very moving way: "Aside from the altruism, you know, you get involved for selfish reasons. Sometimes I wake up early in the morning and wonder what I'm really here for. If it isn't to make a contribution, I don't know what it is." Most of us would characterize this as altruism of the highest and most undiluted form.

But an impressive number of people with whom we talked view their participation as no longer a matter of choice. "More businessmen *must* become involved and help voluntary organizations," said over 85% of our respondents. They amplified this statement with comments like these:

"Given our social difficulties, businessmen have to unbend and lean more toward the idealistic and not to be too hardheaded. They say, 'We can't afford it,' but this might be one of those things you *have to* afford."

"Businessmen who do *not* serve on voluntary boards are doing society and the community a grave disservice."

"Business is an important citizen in the community, and, because it has developed considerable expertise, it is obligated to contribute this expertise to community needs. As industry contributes, so shall it reap."

"The businessman should return to the community that which he has gained in the form of services."

Equally, on their part, the staffs of voluntary organizations explained that the increased interest they see is due to the business executive's greater awareness of social problems and greater concern about them, as well as the multiplication of organizations needing help.

Attitude of the Corporation

There is, however, another very powerful (and relatively new) force operating here, and that is the corporation for which the executive works.

Businesspeople themselves overwhelmingly reported that "companies are sanctioning personnel participation more and more, and are even encouraging it." Organization staffs also feel that corporate approval is on the upswing. Exhibit 2 shows the percentage of companies that are seen by their

Exhibit 2.   The Effect of Company Policy on Executive Participation

Company policy	Percentage of executive participants from:			
	Large companies	Small companies	Manufacturing companies	Service companies
Favorable policy	71%	19%	62%	62%
Stated	59	15	50	50
Unstated	12	4	12	12
No policy	28	73	37	37
Respondents uncertain	1	8	1	1

managers as having positive attitudes, stated or unstated, toward executive involvement in community organizations.

Why this increased permissiveness about the use of executive time? Clearly part of the reason is the general rise in the level of corporate participation in community affairs, as documented by a number of reports—notably, Jules Cohn's *HBR* article.[2] In this context of corporate participation, top managers told us that:

"If we can improve the community we live in, we can expand our business here. Otherwise we'll have to decentralize to other parts of the country, which we don't want to do, or make ourselves into a fortress."

"This is our headquarters, and we are constantly bringing people in from the field to work here. They simply won't come if it isn't a decent place to live."

"If we don't do this kind of thing voluntarily, we'll get coercion from the damn government—and we know our problems better than any Washington bureaucrat, and can deal with them better."

"It has taken us a couple of years to see that we couldn't buy ourselves out of our community problems—that they are going to require our time and expertise."

"In the past, we could disregard public opinion. With the economic and ethnic revolution going on today, the businessman must devote time outside his business or there won't *be* any business."

When describing the specific effects which participation has upon the business executive, corporate spokespeople typically took such viewpoints as these:

"You know, a lot of the management jobs in this business aren't all that interesting. Unless people are expending their energy, leadership, and creativity outside the company, they are going to get pretty frustrated."

"This kind of participation sharpens your skills at working with people. I'm better at my job because of my experience in dealing with different kinds of people and situations outside the firm."

"This kind of activity broadens our young people."

How much does this kind of positive company attitude influence individual participation? The staffs of voluntary organizations feel it is important. By a score of 67% to 13%, they indicated that it makes a "favorable difference in the active involvement of a businessman volunteer." Staff members went on to point out that "by serving, he can achieve points in his own firm," and that "he feels more at ease and freer to take the necessary time."

The evidence on this point, however, is even more direct. As Exhibit 3 shows, when one compares the numbers of participating business executives who work for companies having *stated* positive policies with those working for companies where there is no such clear mandate, the difference is most impressive. It is clear that the existence of an explicit policy stimulates—or releases—someone to participate in more than one nonprofit group.

Exhibit 3.   A Favorable, Stated Corporate Policy of Participation Encourages Service in More than One Voluntary Organization

Company has stated policy favoring participation	Percentage of company volunteers serving in:	
	One organization	Two or more organizations
Yes	40%	64%
No	60%	36%

Effect on Executive's Career

This direct evidence, of course, relates to the general climate of the company, the model provided by the top managers, and the priorities a company sets for itself. But there is a more precise reason for the strong relationship between corporate attitudes and executive behavior, one that points to a powerful strain of pragmatism in the motivation of the individual business executive.

That reason, of course, is the relationship between an executive's opportunities for promotion and the level of community involvement. This may be the key link in the chain that has drawn executives into increased participation and bids fair to hold them permanently involved.

More than one third of the businesspeople reporting that their companies have specific written policies on voluntary service stated that pay and promotion benefits are built into that policy as incentives. And one can confidently speculate that the actual linkage (at least, as seen by those now in top management and those aspiring to it) is even closer, although it may not be spelled out as such. Here is what top managers say on this point:

"It is the intention of senior management at this corporation that participation have an impact on a man's career."

"We encourage our executives to be active. It makes them more visible in the company and thus contributes to their promotion."

"I'd be surprised if a good executive on the way up here weren't also a leader in his community."

"Yes, we put civic activities on the score sheet."

Thus, while it is true that very few companies *formally* state that there are pay and promotion implications in their executives' community involvement, it is also true that almost everyone we talked with was conscious of a startling coincidence between progress up the corporate ladder and significant community leadership. It is perfectly clear that the existence of this relationship is not lost on the would-be president of a company.

First of all, then, this study indicates that business executives are increasingly involved in the leadership of community organizations, that their staying power is great, and that it will continue to be so, since virtually all those who are involved would participate again if they had the chance.

Second, I learned that there is a strong undercurrent of pragmatism here both for the company and for the individual executive. This motivation has its roots in the corporation's conviction that it must itself participate in the community; the result is a real (if perhaps inexplicit) relationship between an executive's community activities and promotion potential.

These two findings should be good news for the hungry organization staff director on the prowl for business leadership—there is a larger and more responsive market than he or she may realize. It also means that active business voluntarism is a permanent part of the American scene.

Who Are the Active Volunteers?

The study found that the patterns are not uniform across the face of U.S. industry. Quite the contrary: there are some extremely interesting and significant differences by age of the executive, size of the company for which he works, and kind of industry with which he is associated.

By Age. In the first place, the active executive volunteer is likely to be at least 35 years old—only 7% of the active men interviewed were younger than that. In fact, he is probably 46 years of age or older (65%). Thus, in what follows, I use the term "younger" to refer to those 45 and under, and "older," obviously, applies to everyone else.

The older men usually started their volunteer service in the local branch of the major national charities—the Red Cross, the United Fund, and the Salvation Army, to name a few.

The younger men, on the other hand (46% to 29%), are more likely to have started with community welfare organizations, often of the newer type, such as the Community Action Agency or groups dealing with housing or minority problems. The newer agencies confirm this, incidentally, by indicating that they are more interested in the younger executives who, they believe, will roll up their sleeves, than in the older, established executives.

I might mention that some respondents felt this is a constructive development. They pointed out that the federal government is now involved in many of the activities—like hospitals, welfare groups, and schools—that used to be more or less exclusively the concern of the local community; in their opinion, this federal involvement has resulted in the increasing centralization of decisions once made by local boards. Thus, they argue, strong local representation is especially important now if community concerns and mores are to be preserved within the guidelines of national programs.

By Company Size. This seems to be a principal factor determining the level of a company's executive participation—well over half (57%) of the active volunteers came from large companies, compared with only 16% from companies at the lower end of the size range. (Size was based on number of employees and the national status of the company.)

Furthermore, people from large companies are far more likely (up to a spread of 15%) to believe that businesspeople should be involved, that companies are increasingly sanctioning participation, and that mere letter-head association is not enough.

Perhaps the most dramatic evidence that company size influences participation level showed up in the discussions of corporate policy. In these discussions, 71% of the men from large companies said their companies favored executive participation, while only 19% of those from small companies so indicated. (These figures are presented in Exhibit 2.) Given the clear evidence that company attitude is important, these figures signify that the chances are the volunteer will come from a large company.

Finally, the community organization staff is more likely to find the performance of a person from a major company satisfactory. When we asked, "Where does your most helpful volunteer come from?" 88% of the responding staff members named a large company. Conversely, when we asked about the size of the company for which the *least* helpful volunteer worked, 48% of the answers specified middle-sized or small.

Incidentally, in the same question, staff members were asked about the management level from which the best and the worst volunteer came, and the somewhat surprising finding was that 83% of the most useful volunteers come from top management, while about 30% of the *least* helpful board members come from middle management.

This was especially interesting because of a pair of myths which have wide currency: (a) that the top person in a company is too busy to be of any real use to a voluntary group; and (b) that the active and successful volunteer is the man who cannot cut the mustard in his own company and is seeking an outlet elsewhere. Judging by the responses to this question as well as other material in the study, neither of these commonly held views appears to possess much validity.

By Industry. One staff member to whom we talked had this to say: "Manufacturing guys are the hardest to involve; the men from service industries are more people-oriented."

The figures bear him out. Of our panel of active volunteers, 60% came from the service industries and only 23% from manufacturing, although there was no difference between the two industries as to whether there were policies, stated or unstated, favoring executive involvement.

What Does the Volunteer Do?

We have seen where the volunteer comes from and what motivates him. The next question is: What does he actually do for these community organizations?

In answering, there are some major distinctions to be made between the traditional, old-line agencies and the newer ones, which I call the "contemporaries.'' These differences carry some extremely serious implications, and I shall dwell on them shortly. But, first, an overall look.

Exhibit 4 describes the tasks that executive volunteers perform. As the figures show, their tasks tend to be associated with the internal administration of the organization, with the obvious exception of fund raising (nearly 70% have joined the search for dollars during their service).

When the active volunteers were asked what tasks they had been engaged in, they strongly emphasized items such as "establishing operating procedure," "budgeting and fiscal control," and "organizational staffing."

Executive volunteers, then, concentrate their attention on the *internal administration* of the community organization. The sense of the study is that they do not get very deeply involved in specific programs—not even in external relationships (between the organization and the public). And this is a somewhat surprising result, since supposedly one of the functions of a board of directors in an organization of this kind is to provide a tie between it and the community within which it operates.

This orientation toward internal administration is easy to understand if one considers that, by and large, businesspeople *like* to tackle this kind of problem. When asked where the most challenging problems were to be found, executive volunteers voted overwhelmingly for internal issues. As a matter of fact, the distinction between administrative and external projects

Exhibit 4. Tasks Undertaken by Executive Volunteers in Community Organizations

Task	Percentage of executives who have:	
	Engaged in task	Headed task
Fund raising	68%	36%
Establishing operating procedures to accomplish a particular goal	64	25
Enlisting support of other persons or groups to achieve a specific aim	64	25
Budgeting and fiscal control	62	29
Balancing organization so that different points of view are represented	57	18
Public relations and promotions	55	20
Recruiting more or new volunteers	54	23
Providing liaison with other community groups	53	23
Designating committees; recruiting	51	25
Organizational staffing	47	16
Providing liaison with local officials	45	17
Providing liaison with local business	45	13
Providing legal advice	12	8

was even more marked when these executives expressed their preferences about tasks than it was when they listed the tasks they actually perform. Exhibit 5 categorizes tasks perceived by executive volunteers as challenging into *internal* and *external* activities; and the executives' preferences are clearly for the first.

Thus, *Establishing operating procedures* was mentioned by 26% of the sample; *Organizational staffing,* by 16%; and *Budgeting and fiscal control,* by 9%. "I really like long-range planning," one man said, "and I gravitate to that in these organizations."

Executive Not a Leader

But beyond the specific functions he performs, what kind of a role does the executive volunteer play in the organization? One staff member has this to say:

> We have to do all the planning and the spadework on a project and present it to our business 'leadership' as a fait accompli. For example, we can't say to the man, 'Please head up a committee to see if we ought to have a stadium in this town.' He just wouldn't be any good at working through that kind of problem. Rather, we take that decision and then go

Exhibit 5.   Executive Perceptions of Challenging Tasks in Volunteer Work

Problem areas	Percentage of executive volunteers perceiving area as challenging*
Internal to organization	
Establishing operating procedures	26%
Deciding promotional approaches	19
Organizational staffing	16
Planning and executing fund-raising campaigns	11
Budgeting and fiscal control	9
Balancing organization to reflect differing points of view	8
External to organization	
Obtaining support of other groups	18
Liaison with local businesses	4
Liaison with other community groups	3
Liaison with local officials	1
Miscellaneous specific problems	32
None	15

*Unaided multiple responses.

to him and say, 'We are going to have a new stadium. Will you head a committee to decide where it should be and how it should be financed, and get it built? In other words, the businessman is an excellent implementer, but he is neither a leader nor a generator of ideas.

Distressing as this view of a business executive's role may be, the study supports it. Furthermore, this seems to be the case even in the areas in which the businesspeople are most active and which they find the most interesting and challenging (internal organizational problems). To see this, compare the figures under *Headed task* with those under *Engaged in task* in Exhibit 4; the contrast is indeed startling. In fact, the only project where even one third of our active volunteers took the leadership was in fund raising.

Another quotation-in-evidence is from an organization staff director whose board is dominated by businessmen. He said, somewhat mournfully:

Oh yes, they solve problems, all right, but they just don't deal with basic procedures and systems. I wish they would take some leadership in issues like that. They get too involved in day-to-day matters, to the point where they establish relationships directly with members of my staff, but they do not seem to be able to identify what policy is and take some initiative on the big issues.

Thinking of the executive who explained that "I really like long-range planning," one can speculate that unless organization staff initiated an effort of that type, he would never have got the chance to work out this particular enthusiasm.

In short, when the businessman walks into the board room at the Y, or the hospital, or the school, or the Community Action Agency, he apparently leaves his leadership hat outside the door—even in the areas he knows best and likes best.

Communication Breakdown

Some people with whom I have discussed this finding have asked, "But isn't that the way it should be? When I serve on organizations like these, I don't presume to tell the staff what they should do, or to start any new initiatives."

Perhaps it should be that way, but the staffs of these voluntary organizations do not think so. They respond to and appreciate leadership, and they are quite definite about it. When a staff described its most helpful volunteer and its least helpful volunteer, the members consistently indicated that (a) the capacity to provide leadership and (b) a strong motivation to become involved and serve usefully are the two criteria that make the difference.

For example, they said that the most helpful volunteer "provides leadership and creativity," "pilots projects," "is effective in fund raising and recruiting," and "supplies a special skill." With respect to personality, they characterized the most helpful business volunteer as "enthusiastic," "a leader," "sincere," "thorough." They criticized the least helpful business volunteer as "lacking interest," "lacking dependability," "too preoccupied," "not self-assured."

It would appear, then, that the staff members of these organizations have been unable to communicate to the executive volunteer what it is that they hope he will provide for them. By the same token, the business manager, in his *community* role, is less aggressive in stepping forward and assuming leadership than he could be. This represents a real breakdown in communications.

Misuse and Underuse

In this connection it is particularly interesting and important to note the answer received when the active volunteers were asked to identify the aspects of their service that troubled them the most. Nearly half said they felt underutilized: "My skills and abilities are not used to their fullest."

It may also be that these men feel misused. Of the activities that businessmen characterize as most interesting and challenging, *Planning and executing fund-raising campaigns* ranks fourth out of six internal task areas and fifth out of ten in the total list (see Exhibit 5). Still, according to the data in Exhibit 4, this is exactly the task he is most frequently called on to undertake and chair.

Exhibits 4 and 5 do not match in a number of other respects as well. According to Exhibit 5, for example, the executive volunteer feels a real attraction to deciding promotional approaches. But according to Exhibit 4, he is more likely to end up working on at least four other tasks—tasks to which he is less attracted.

On the whole, then, not only are the executive volunteers' leadership skills being underutilized, but they are asked to lead and work on projects for which they have only secondary enthusiasm.

In short, this failure of staffs to communicate with their business directors and vice versa means that managers are not contributing anything like what they could or want to. But this is not the only area where crimped communications lines are costly to both groups.

For example, especially in the traditional community organizations, considerable emphasis is placed on giving the executive personal recognition as a reward for participation. How many of us have received plaques, scrolls, or other wall hangings after serving as a community fund raiser! But the study throws doubt on the efficacy of this kind of reward—or incentive, depending on where you stand.

Newer groups say explicitly that they have found this sort of recognition to be an ineffective incentive in recruiting and retaining active business help. As for the executives themselves, the need for personal payoff is put at the bottom of their list of requirements.

To probe the frustrations and disappointments inherent in volunteering, the study asked the active executive volunteers to respond to this statement: "I feel that the personal rewards for real accomplishment are not as frequent in voluntary organizations as they are in business." This criticism came out ninth in a list of nine, with only 20% agreeing. (This was a multiple-response question.) Further, for those volunteers who were not currently active, this was a concern of but 11%—again, way down at the bottom of the list.

No Vestibule Training.

Still another area in which the business executive has some problems is recognizing organization needs and understanding organization programs. Staffs apparently do not appreciate the fact that these problems exist. When identifying their major complaints, a full 45% of the active businessmen said, "It takes too much time and trouble to learn what the organization wants and requires of you." Only 15% of these men reported that they had received any formal (or informal) training or briefing to prepare them for the tasks they were being asked to identify or perform. (Traditional organizations, incidentally, do a little better on this point than the newer ones.)

Now let me turn to what may be the most important series of findings in the entire study: those that stem from the differences between the traditional organizations and the contemporary ones.

Traditional and Contemporary

At this point I need to define these two kinds of organizations.

By "traditional" I do not necessarily mean old or established; one could start a settlement house today in the standard pattern, and it would qualify as "traditional" for my purposes. Equally, an old organization like a state welfare advisory board that is dominated by "Establishment types" could be reconstituted to include representatives of the poor and thus become "contemporary."

Thus the real difference is between the essentially homogeneous organization whose orientation is toward determining and then implementing programs to serve others, and the essentially heterogeneous organization that seeks to combine different elements in the community, especially those who are to be helped, in the planning and serving process. In contemporary organizations, representation of the beneficiaries may range all the way from slightly more than token representation to virtual domination.

From everything that I learned, one strong signal comes through: businesspeople are far more at home in the traditional organization than they are in the contemporary, and they seem to be more active there, although, in fact, the contemporaries want them more than the traditionals.

What do the business executives themselves say about these groups? Here are a few of their comments:

We businessmen are not so effective in minority-group problems. We are willing to support their ideas, if they have any, but it's like walking in a swamp. The social organization of these people is so different.

When business people talk to business people, someone will give up his autonomy. But these organizations are emotional, basically, and won't take a good, hard look at a problem. These social-political problems—we could solve them as we do issues like the expansion of an airport or the renewal of a downtown area, if we were given the reins. But they don't give us control.

I was a director of our local poverty program, but there was just a fantastic amount of frustration. I was on another board which legally had to be enlarged to include representatives of the poor—and it was awful. These people have an enormously long learning curve, they are ignorant of procedures and of how things really get done, and they used our board as a forum to grind their own axes. They can't see what you are trying to do, because they are so bugged by what is bothering them at the moment.

As a result of my experiences, I believe in self-perpetuating boards, in benevolent dictatorships, because they don't break down the way the democratic ones do.

I served on one of those boards that was suddenly changed to include neighborhood people. It was kind of an experience to meet with them, and now I feel I know them. But when they began to take over, to do things like setting meeting times when they knew the businessmen couldn't come, we all agreed that it was hopeless to try to work in that setup and decided we would just supply funds instead.

Under such circumstances, one may suspect, the contemporaries would have more difficulty than the traditionals in recruiting business executives (which they do) and demonstrate less desire to have business board members (which they do not).

Recruitment Goals

For recruitment, the contemporaries indicate that they rely primarily on personal solicitation and secondarily on recommendations from other groups.

But the traditionals put these two methods at the bottom, using instead suggestions of present members and public appeals. They simply remind the potential board member that "we do important work for the community," and stress how well run they are. The contemporaries, on the other hand, emphasize their role in "helping this community survive."

The traditionals place heavy stress on "starting at the bottom" and testing the leadership potential of volunteers over a period of time. The contemporaries tend to use a "task force" approach, which puts a premium not on the generalists sought by the traditionals but, rather, on people with specific interests and expertise who can be immediately put to work to head up a particular project. In their appeals, they stress the job that has to be done rather than the general usefulness of the organization. Clearly, the contemporaries are not on the grapevine, do not have established reputations on which to rely, and have a tougher time getting help.

But they want that help. To be sure, they are a little apprehensive about businesspeople as volunteers, expressing concern lest they will seek to make the group "less liberal, more traditional, more hidebound"—a fear the traditionals, needless to say, do not share—but they do want them nonetheless.

As a matter of fact, when the interviewers asked the two groups whether they wanted or could use more business volunteers, most traditionals said *no,* and the contemporaries emphatically said *yes.* I might note another interesting difference in this area: those traditionals that did want more executive volunteers indicated they had existing vacancies they wanted to fill, while the contemporaries said they wanted help so they could expand their activities and undertake more and new projects.

Executive Temperament

I stated earlier that business executives are less comfortable and less productive in contemporary groups. For one thing, in discussing the frustrations they experience in dealing with voluntary organizations, managers emphasize precisely the kinds of characteristics the contemporary organization is likely to display:

"It means dealing with incapable volunteers who slow down accomplishment and can't be fired" (70%).

"Everything moves slowly compared to business. Time is wasted" (61%).

"It is difficult to provide leadership for groups or committees of different kinds of people trying to work together" (54%).

Second, as we have seen, the traditional businessperson is primarily interested in the internal management of these groups rather than programs as such. The contemporaries, however, give administrative concerns a clearly secondary priority. In their eyes, procedures, systems, and controls are far less important than getting houses built or welfare standards changed or dropouts placed into productive work-and-learning situations.

This difference relates to the final, and possibly the key, point. Unfamiliar with the techniques and procedures for working together effectively and propelled by a great sense of urgency and immediacy, many of the contemporary groups are searching for effective, democratic, skillful, and empathetic leadership. In such situations, a dedicated and experienced executive would be highly useful to such an organization if he would take the initiative in helping the group pull itself together.

But, as we have also seen, this is precisely the role our business volunteers are loath to play. They are willing to implement but not to propel; they are not the ones to see a need and seize an opportunity to fill it. They just do not feel at home in situations where they have to step forward and take charge.

As participants in the contemporary groups, particularly, they look for staffs to guide them and procedures through which to channel their contributions—and neither one is there. No wonder they feel they are in alien territory. And the one thing they could do to extricate themselves and the organizations from the confusion they feel is the one thing they like to do least: *take the lead.*

To my mind, this is a serious problem. If, as I suspect, broadened representation and a diminishing role for the elite are the orders of the day for all society, and especially for our urban society, the businessperson who cannot function effectively in the heterogeneous, disorderly, activist, and contemporary community organization may find his influence increasingly restricted. As one thoughtful top manager put it:

> I am uncomfortable about the amount of leverage the business community has in this city. It has filled a void in the political leadership up to now, and has, in general, done it well and constructively. And the community as a whole has gone along. But is this really the right way to do things? And *how long will it work?*

Given the rising corporate sense of the importance of precisely this kind of involvement, this restriction of influence could pose a real dilemma— and one which is well worth further research.

The study, happily, supplies one more piece of information, already mentioned, that may diminish this difficulty; that is, the younger business executives are more involved in community groups (as opposed to national charities) than were their predecessors.

My hunch is that the bulk of the active volunteers so prized and sought after by the contemporary groups are just these younger people, who do seem to be able to relate readily to the concerns and needs of the contemporaries. They may be the ones to build new bridges between the business world and a dramatically changing community.

What Are the Implications?

In summary, what does the study mean operationally (a) for the voluntary organization, (b) for the company, and (c) for the individual businessperson? I trust each reader will draw useful conclusions for himself—here are some of mine.

. . . For All Organizations

1 Pay more attention to briefing and informing business volunteers.
2 Plan systematic ways to bridge the communication gap so that the executive volunteers know what you want of them and you know

what they want to contribute. You must assure them that you really do want to exercise some positive leadership and take some initiative. You may find this kind of role definition a much more useful incentive than the engraved brass plaque.

3 Target your recruiting at the company. This may be risky unless you structure your approach so as to maintain your freedom of ultimate choice. But the corporate attitude is so clearly significant in the performance of your volunteer that it is foolish to neglect it.

4 Recruit actively. Very few people will come to you.

5 Recruit selectively to mesh the particular interests of the business-people with the needs of the organization and the job you want done. Face-to-face conversations that identify the problem and define how any particular executive can and wants to contribute are likely to be the most effective method. To carry out a program of selective recruiting, you may have to make a more systematic analysis of where you are and where you want to go than you have up to now.

6 Get over any hesitation you may have about recruiting business-people. You have a more receptive and ready market than you think, and you probably will have this market for a long time to come.

7 Make sure you go to the large service companies that have stated policies on executive involvement—these companies are likely to be your happiest hunting grounds.

If your organization is contemporary in nature:

☐ Look for the younger executives. Apparently, they are most responsive to your appeals.

☐ Use your business talent in organizational and goal-setting functions, as well as in running specific projects.

☐ Because you are probably attached to the business establishment grapevine, you will need to pay special attention to recruiting. Setting up such a program, incidentally, is an appropriate responsibility to give a business executive volunteer.

☐ Orientation is especially important for your businesspeople, for they are moving into a universe which they may not readily understand.

If your organization is a traditional one, these possibilities should be considered:

☐ The danger of staff-run organizations is high. If you allow your permanent employees too much control, you will misuse or underutilize your business talent.

☐ The increasing trend toward national guidelines, reflecting the introduction of government funds in a wide range of health and welfare programs, calls for a stronger board focusing less on administration and more on policy. It also speaks for a new aggressiveness on the part of the board in ensuring that government officials permit latitude in the interpretation of guidelines in the interest of the local community.

☐ If, indeed, business volunteers—especially younger ones—are given more responsibility sooner by the contemporary organizations, that policy may be worth emulating. Otherwise, the pool of lively, ambitious, and helpful people may dry up.

. . . For Companies

1 If you want your executives to be active in the community, tell them so—explicitly, directly, and in writing. You need not tie it in with promotion implications; they are able to close that loop for themselves.
2 Develop in-house routines for putting people and organizations together. This is worth the investment of a few dollars, since the participation of your managers in community activities benefits their professional development and the company itself.
3 You might consider making a special effort to encourage a selection of your younger executives to work with these organizations. This will combat the danger that the company and the business community in general may become isolated from the contemporary organizations. Further, some investigation of what makes for constructive participation in these groups and what is ineffective hedges this investment of effort.
4 You might run a communitywide conference that brings traditional *and* contemporary organizations together with interested executives to discuss the needs of the groups and the interests of the managers.
5 Devise a regular method by which your volunteer executives can feed their information and insights into corporate decision making.

. . . For Executive Volunteers

1 If your company does not have a written policy on volunteering, encourage it to do so. An explicit, positive policy is likely to give you confidence in undertaking community activities.
2 As a volunteer, suggest areas of organizational activity which you think need attention, and *offer to tackle them.* Point out that you have both experience and an interest in projects other than fund raising.
3 Do not restrict your volunteering to the traditional groups. You may find quicker leadership opportunities in some of the contemporaries. And once you get used to taking the initiative in community work, you may well find you like it.

4 Do not expect a voluntary organization to operate like a business. You will be disappointed if you do.

5 Search out opportunities that have a professional usefulness for you. Such activities will be the most beneficial to you and to the organization you are trying to help.

Notes

1. See my article, "Business and Politics" (Problems in Review), *HBR*, May–June 1959, p. 6; see also Stephen A. Greyser, "Business and Politics, 1964" (Problems in Review), *HBR*, September–October 1964, p. 22, and "Business and Politics, 1968" (Special Report), *HBR*, November–December 1968, p. 4.

2. "Is Business Meeting the Challenge of Urban Affairs?" *HBR*, March–April 1970, p. 68.

PART SIX
FINANCIAL RELATIONS
AN OVERVIEW

Dealing with the financial public (most importantly, shareholders and investment analysts) is not only the newest activity in the realm of corporate public relations, but also the one that potentially has the greatest long-term impact. Taking your case before those who may or may not support you financially has a practical importance that executives can readily grasp. And so, initially at least, they were more ready to participate than they were in other kinds of public relations activities.

As in their relationships with any public, however, executives have gradually come to look on the management of these kinds of relations with the same mixture of boredom and disdain. In short, they don't relish this intrusion either. They usually fight it or leave it to the public relations professionals, with the result that the financial analysts and shareholders often know very little about the reality of corporate action. The value of the company may become downgraded in their eyes not only because they misunderstand the rationale of a particular move, but also because they suspect that they're not being told the whole truth.

A perfect example is the way that the stock market almost instantaneously downgrades the value of the stock of those companies pursuing aggressive acquisition strategies (outside of their area of industry expertise). If the investment community understood the underlying notion of the company's strategy in making the acquisitions, it might be more likely to "wait and see" rather than reacting in such a knee-jerk manner.

The articles in this section give out some sound advice on how much a company should disclose to its financial publics and how much it should leave back. Glenn Saxon's classic, "Annual Headache: The Stockholders' Meeting," recognizes the disruption that dissident shareholders can make on the meeting and counsels a thoughtful approach. He gives examples to show how substantive presentations and discussions by officers can diffuse some of the wilder kinds of outbursts. By setting aside periods for discussion and rigidly controlling the format of the meetings, the chairman can also control the kind of discussion that ensues.

In his generic article on the subject, "Crucial Role of Investor Relations," Robert Savage reports on the necessity for companies to make direct links with the financial community. He offers sound advice on ways to diffuse the impact of bad news on share price as well as to make certain that good news is understood for what it is and not necessarily for what it appears to be.

Fred Foy in "Annual Reports Don't Have to Be Dull," and Joseph Mancuso in "How to Name—and Not Name—A Business," tackle issues that most top managers would rather leave to the professionals. Yet each author shows how the executive must monitor the process in order to see that it achieves the correct ends. In a detailed analysis of several annual reports, Foy points out the necessity of discussing the figures in more detail and breaking down the data into more segments to facilitate analysis. Attempting to hide bad news with consolidated figures only gives the image of stonewalling and almost never achieves the desired results. Financial news that is big enough to hide will always be found out. Mancuso's short piece offers some good advice that should make most readers reassess the way that their company is named, especially those in small businesses.

The article, "Public Responsibility Committees of the Board," by Michael Lovdal, Raymond Bauer, and Nancy Treverton, does not talk about the relations between a company and its investors, but I'm including the article here because it deals with the board of directors. In fact, the authors call on companies to establish standing committees that act as a bridge between the concerns of the public and the shareholders, as represented by the board. In their survey of 35 organizations (at that time) with such committees, they discovered that the committees can give managers a more effective way to analyze a range of new social and political demands. Also, they offer cogent suggestions on how to run them properly and avoid unnecessary pitfalls.

30
Annual Headache: The Stockholders' Meeting

O. GLENN SAXON, JR.

Few things bring on an executive headache more quickly than the contemplation of the annual stockholders' meeting. Companies would like to be able to go about their business without having to explain actions to anyone, especially tiny groups of dissident shareholders. In this thoughtful piece, Saxon shows how some organizations (most importantly General Electric) have redesigned their concept of the annual meeting, reorienting the format and inviting stock analysts to participate. The company offers clear periods for discussion and makes certain that the presentations of the officers are meaty. The result can be informative and substantive, without too many disruptions.

With the Roman circus "season" about to burst forth in a shower of sparks on the American business scene, top executives of a number of leading companies are getting the aspirin ready for their own day in the "ring"— the annual stockholders' meeting. And well they might, for they realize all too painfully that, despite their most diligent preparation efforts and close procedural adherences, the meeting may turn out to be one colossal headache.

I am referring, of course, to the strange and growing phenomenon of a small minority of shareowners turning the annual meeting into a chaotic shambles by their disruptive actions. It does not matter whether they are misguided in their efforts or whether they are seeking to gain publicity, promote their own interests, or just hear themselves talk. The effect is the same—the meeting fails to achieve its legitimate purpose. Consider:

☐ It is not at all uncommon for a few individuals to consume 80% of the stockholder discussion at a meeting. They come prepared with lists of dozens of questions, many of them irrelevant. They "rise to the notice of the meeting" early in the proceedings. They comment on every matter to be voted on. They are not hesitant to interrupt or to be personally abusive to the chairman. At the 1965 IBM meeting in San Jose, California, one stockholder from New York City was quoted in the press as having asked Board Chairman Thomas J. Watson, Jr.: "Do you realize what an ignorant vulgarian you are?"

☐   At several other major annual stockholders' meetings in 1965, one or two vociferous individuals so dominated the proceedings that the audiences grew restive, and calls of "Throw him out!" and "Shut him up!" were heard. Many of the more impatient shareowners simply got up and walked out. By the time the chairmen finally gaveled adjournment, less than half of the beginning audiences remained; the other shareowners had long since gone, many with parting expressions of disgust to ushers or company officials.

The current crisis stage in the annual stockholders' meeting is at least partly caused by top management itself. Beginning in earnest about 1953, businesspeople started to view their annual meetings as forums for review which provided a unique opportunity to create loyalty toward, and support for, the company. In the ensuing decade-plus, largely because of aggressive promotion, the annual meeting has experienced an unprecedented growth in popularity. And with this growth have come problems.

Reappraisal Required

What is needed now is to take a fresh look at the annual meeting from the viewpoint of the crucial shareowner audience whose interests it should serve, and then to try to offer some solutions to the problems that are hampering its effective use in obtaining the regard not only of the current owners of record, but also of the security analysts, financial institutions, and potential investors—all of whom are important to current shareowners. This article is devoted to just such an endeavor.

At the outset, however, I wish to make it clear that while the annual stockholders' meeting is important in its own right and serves as the focus of the discussion which follows, it is but one segment of a company's total investor relations program. Today the modern investor relations program is a balanced array of activity which includes annual reports and other shareowner publications; communications such as dividend enclosures, proxy solicitations, and shareowner correspondence; professional investor relations, or relations with security analysts and institutional investors; and counsel and feedback to top management.

It is important to realize that disruptive antics at the annual stockholder meeting are no longer merely isolated occurrences in American business life. Generally speaking, the larger the company, the bigger the meeting, and the more extensive the publicity, the greater seems to be the likelihood that the annual meeting will become a showcase for show-offs.

To some extent, stockholder meetings today are in turmoil because many companies have been much better and more efficient at making arrangements for large and well-publicized sessions than at logically thinking through the real reasons for these annual meetings and what they should be trying to accomplish.

Executives' Dilemma

Talks with officials of many companies reveal great concern and wide disagreement about how the annual headache and its complex problems should be met. Some executives have even gone so far in their thinking as to question whether these meetings are actually necessary. While a few of these reactions may be attributable to pique or the inability of the chief executive to "take" a certain amount of abuse, most of the concern goes far deeper. Many serious questions are being asked in top management circles. For example:

☐   What does, or should, or can an annual shareholder meeting represent or accomplish? Is such a meeting really of value to the company and its shareowners?

☐   Is the general assumption justified that the major cause of the annual meeting headache is a direct result of the activities of a small handful of individuals? Or have the disruptions only served to bring to the surface some underlying weaknesses of the manner in which annual meetings are being conducted—weaknesses that would be present even if the disrupters were not?

☐   How can an annual meeting be created which will accomplish for the majority of shareowners in attendance what they have come for—one which will enable top management to communicate effectively what it considers to be important to the owners, permit widespread audience participation, and yet not be construed as an attempt to restrain unfairly any individual shareowner?

In groping for the answers to complex questions such as these, top executives are finding it necessary to learn how to lessen the adverse impact of the few disrupters on the majority of shareowners, while simultaneously enhancing the positive effects of the good things which do take place in the annual meeting. Admittedly, the task is difficult, but top management is not wholly in the dark in its search for workable solutions. Close analysis of the experiences of many companies indicates that while none has yet discovered techniques and policies which will absolutely guarantee a successful meeting, a logical initial step has been taken.

Constructive Beginning

This positive start, undertaken by the General Electric Company in 1963, holds promise for helping other executives solve some of their own annual meeting problems. In its advance planning for the annual stockholder meeting that year, GE decided to place new emphasis on the business and economic content of its officers' presentations, and to tailor the presentations specifically to the audience's interests as shareowners and participants in the private enterprise system.

Furthermore, in line with this thinking the GE officials decided to invite security analysts to attend its annual meeting. The purpose of this move was twofold: (1) to provide the analysts with more representative information about the company, its management, its character, and its prospects; and (2) to encourage the investment community to transmit this information to the many millions of Americans who invest or have the wherewithal to invest.

It is perhaps helpful to note that, prior to 1963, security analysts rarely attended GE's annual meetings. This lack of interest on their part was generally explained away by comments to the effect that they did not care to waste their time on "public relations type" meetings. It is obvious that the analysts would not have bothered to attend the 1963 meeting either if the company executives had not taken positive steps to encourage their attendance.

Analyst Participation

Each of the more than 100 analysts who regularly called on the company was contacted, either in person or by telephone, and invited to the meeting. A more creative approach to the annual stockholder meeting was discussed with each analyst in considerable depth. And from these individual discussions—most of which lasted about an hour—there developed widespread agreement and understanding about the importance of the annual meeting to the analysts and about the need for the company to get the presentations back on the right track.

The GE representatives in these discussions also pointed out that the meeting was the only occasion in any given year when the analysts would have the opportunity to see every member of the executive office, all vice presidents, and the directors assembled in the same place at the same time, and to ask questions and get answers from the very men responsible for each major area of the business. Furthermore, the annual meeting could be of significant help to the analysts in performing one of their more important but often most difficult evaluations—namely, that of rating the company's top management personnel. The annual meeting would provide an opportunity for them to form impressions about the ability, character, and versatility of the company's leadership.

The analysts with whom these matters were discussed agreed that the GE plan to put greater emphasis on the technical side of the business in the executive presentations might be a worthwhile step toward creating a better annual stockholder meeting. A total of 54 analysts later demonstrated their belief in the idea by attending GE's 1963 meeting. Several of the analysts actively participated in the session, asking questions on such matters as the index of company prices, technical considerations concerning participation in the Apollo contract, and the impact of changes in the economic climate of the European Common Market. These were thoughtful questions asked by professionals, and the answers to them were well fielded by the various GE officers.

Shareowner Feedback

Although there had been some company apprehension in the early planning stages that the technical and highly business-oriented questions asked by the analysts might be of little interest to the less knowledgeable shareowners, a follow-up mail survey showed that 95% of the audience had been interested in the financially oriented questions, and two thirds of the respondents indicated that they would like more of the same in future meetings. When asked about their overall reaction to the meeting, again 95% said they considered it worthwhile and their time well spent. One shareowner commented: "It was my first opportunity to confirm the opinion formed by reading reports. I feel 'closer' to the company. The participation of management other than directors and officers at the speakers' table was most informative, and I would suggest more of this."

The total results achieved at the 1963 GE meeting were encouraging. There had been honest criticism and disagreement expressed in floor discussions concerning certain management policies and practices. However, these question-and-answer discussions neither dominated nor disrupted the meeting, nor did they set an unpleasant tone.

In the two ensuing years, General Electric followed the same general pattern, but in 1965 no analyst asked any questions in the meeting. The reason for this, as several analysts indicated recently, was that they felt there had simply been no opportunity for them to participate because of the domination of the meeting by two shareowners.

This kind of a positive approach is, therefore, no panacea. However, when successful, it does offer economic and business pluses, and it helps to pull individual owners' and security analysts' interests together, which should be of mutual benefit.

Guidelines Essential

Assuming the potential exists for business executives to put more substantive content and business interest into their own company presentations, and thus make their annual meetings more meaningful, the question then arises: Can the annual meeting also be made more orderly within the existing framework without disenfranchising the very small vocal minority?

Technically, at least, the annual meeting is really the one time a year when individual owners can themselves probe into matters which they feel may affect their investments, and this is a valid function of the meeting. But it is apparent that one individual's honestly motivated question may be just a hollow, self-promoting gimmick if posed by another. The questioner who should be allowed to have his inning—the somewhat less aggressive individual or even the security analyst—too often is denied a turn at bat, not by the chairman but by a dominating shareowner who won't let others participate. In the interests of the passive majority of owners in attendance, as well as of more active owners who may wish to participate, some rules and guidelines are essential.

Structured Format

What is needed is a format for the future which will enable fuller, more democratic participation, prevent any one individual or small group from monopolizing the floor, and allow for orderly presentation of the business of the meeting. But how can the meeting be structured so as to serve the best interests of all present without denying anyone a reasonable opportunity to speak?

There has been a great deal of annual meeting discussion in recent years which centers around the "right" of the disrupters "to be heard." We should be very careful in the use of such words in this connection, however. Certainly, there are good reasons for defending an owner's right to ask certain kinds of questions—or to make certain kinds of comments, or to criticize and even berate some management decisions—if she so chooses. But the "right to be heard" implies some sort of obligation on the other owners to listen. And if this interferes with the purposes for which they have come to the meeting, it is clearly not sustainable.

Proposed Approach

With adequate preparation, many future annual stockholder meetings can be made far more orderly and fair to all than has been the case in recent years. Clearly, even with the best of preparations some meetings will not be successes. But there are a number of things which—in combination with greater emphasis on the business content of the officers' reports—most companies can undertake to strengthen their annual meeting. One proposed approach currently being considered in business circles includes the following four steps.

1. *Redesign the agenda format to eliminate weaknesses and assure a reasonable, businesslike tone for the meeting.* Top management should keep in mind that the real objectives of the annual meeting are to serve the legal purpose for which the meeting has been established; to provide a forum

for the dissemination of news and information; to make effective contact with, and gain the confidence of, the financial opinion leaders and share-owners, including those unable to attend in person; and to allow the share-owners to speak up, but in such a way as not to interfere with the rights of the majority.

2. *Recognize the authority inherent in the role of the chair, and re-solve to use it appropriately.* This can be accomplished by anticipating and rehearsing situations where such authority should be asserted; by giving the chairman the kind of preparatory assistance that will enable him to run the meeting in the best interests of all; by making full and complete preparations to enforce the chairman's decisions quickly and efficiently; and by avoiding actions which might enable any disrupter to be cast in the light of a martyr.

3. *Schedule the most constructive aspects of the agenda at the be-ginning.* Since the meeting may run long, the scheduling of those items which experience and surveys show are of the most interest and value to share-owners—the officers' reports, discussion of operations, balloting, and so on—in the early part of the agenda will enable those who may have to leave before the conclusion of the session to do so without missing what they have specifically come to hear.

4. *Provide for set discussion periods to encourage shareowner par-ticipation.* The initial question-and-answer period might well have a set time limit, with a limit also placed on the number of questions asked by any one person. Furthermore, by having this discussion period restricted to the general business of the company, it should help to establish a businesslike tone, lessen the likelihood that the meeting will be dominated by an individual or small minority group, and get a greater number of shareowners and an-alysts to participate. Strategic placement of a number of microphones throughout the audience will also make it easier for all who so desire to participate. The chairman should cut off all further discussion when the time is up, indicating that there will be an opportunity for additional discussion at the conclusion of the formal agenda. Shareowners attempting to speak out at other than the specified times should be ruled out of order. If they persist, they should be warned, then removed from the premises if necessary.

This proposed annual meeting format has several advantages over what many companies have used on previous occasions:

☐ By giving adequate notice and establishing reasonable ground rules, it provides every shareowner an opportunity to accomplish his purpose in attending the meeting, including the chance to question top man-agement or to discuss company operations.

☐ It enables the chairman to establish a firm position in case one or more individuals try to disregard the rights of others and take up too much time.

☐ Psychologically, at least, it will most certainly be a less frustrating experience from the viewpoint of the top company executives.

The Future?

Only about 120 companies have been targets of the disruptive minority of their shareowners. Of these, some top managements will certainly be willing to make an investment for a better future, recognizing that the lightning may strike their company again any time. Others seem willing to endure their one-day-a-year abuse rather than risk a head-on encounter. Companies which have no annual meeting problems as yet (and these are the majority of listed companies) are generally quite satisfied to let those who have such headaches solve them, and have shown little inclination to become involved.

Those companies which are on the firing line probably have a responsibility to all industry, as well as to their own investors, to be the leaders in promoting a reasonable approach. There is much to be gained. If the disrupters are successful in picking off companies on a one-by-one basis, they will have things more and more their own way in the future. If there is general adherence to a reasonable, businesslike policy, however, one or two years of sustained effort should result in more orderly and worthwhile meetings.

Conduct of Meetings

The first steps in promoting this approach are already well under way. The American Society of Corporate Secretaries has drawn up a list of guidelines for the conduct of meetings (see appendix). Informal groups of company experts in this area have agreed on the nature and importance of the problem. Several talks at recent professional management seminars have recommended a more aggressive and realistic company approach.

These constructive steps will not, of course, of themselves solve the annual meeting problem. Much more work needs to be done in many areas. For instance, what level of free company promotion should rightly be accorded those few individuals who make proxy proposals? Should companies be required to print the names of sponsors of proposals in proxy statements?

Usually the first step for a shareowner who intends to be disruptive at the meeting is submission of a stockholder proposal. This kind of proposal stems from an SEC regulation, modified in 1953, which remains almost an invitation to disruption. In the case of most proposals which are submitted to a number of different companies each year, there seems no necessary connection between a particular proposal and the company to which it is proposed; in other words, these proposals are treated by their proponents primarily as a way of achieving a certain special status at an annual meeting where they wish to take a major part. As proponents these individuals have semi-official status, limited but important to them. In addition, by the mere act of submitting a proposal the sponsors are allowed a 100-word supporting statement and may have their names and addresses printed in the statement mailed to all owners.

More thinking is needed on the nature of the proper role of the shareowner at an annual meeting and his rights and duties. How can every owner be allowed to participate actively, if he so desires, without destroying the meeting? How can owners assure themselves that the kinds of questions which will best protect their interests have the opportunity to get asked, and that irrelevant ones will be sidetracked? How can shareowners really use the meeting to enhance their appraisal of the worth and future of their investment in the company?

Management Challenge

These, then, are some key investor relations challenges which face executives today. Companies must create annual reports and other investor publications which will attract the readership of their shareowners and will make them more knowledgeable. Top management has to develop better procedures for satisfying the needs of a growing number of financial analysts, and to understand, and act more in keeping with, the needs and interests of owners.

Further, executives must increase their understanding of, and belief in, the fundamental mutuality of interests between owners and management. Top management must strive for creative new relationships with shareowners to gain their confidence and support. Only in this way will shareowners become more effective in the use of their rights and opportunities to help further the success of the businesses in which they have invested.

Appendix

Suggested Guidelines for the Conduct of Meetings of Stockholders, as Set Forth by the American Society of Corporate Secretaries

1 The corporation should furnish each stockholder attending a meeting an agenda, and the chairman should announce that the meeting will be conducted according to it.
2 The chairman need not follow any set of parliamentary rules. (They were never intended for meetings of stockholders.) Furthermore, the imposition of such rules would place a premium on specialized skills and knowledge which it is not reasonable to expect stockholders to possess.
3 The chairman of the meeting has a duty to conduct the meeting in a fair and impartial manner, and has corresponding authority to make such rulings as are necessary to achieve that end.
4 The chairman should ask stockholders to confine their questions or remarks to the subject under discussion. Remarks or questions not pertinent to the business of the meeting or personal in nature should be ruled out of order—whether directed to a member of management or to any stockholder.

5 The chairman should, within reason, give all those who wish to speak an opportunity to do so. However, no individual stockholder should be permitted to monopolize the time that can reasonably be devoted to any particular discussion to the exclusion of other stockholders. The chairman should require each stockholder to confine his remarks or questions to one subject and should give others an opportunity to speak before returning to the same stockholder. If it becomes apparent that a stockholder is continuing unreasonably, the chairman should fix a reasonable time limit for the stockholder to conclude his remarks or put to a voice vote of the stockholders a suggestion for a time limit to be generally applicable to remarks by stockholders.

31
Crucial Role
of Investor Relations

ROBERT H. SAVAGE

The purpose of investor relations, says the author, is to establish—and maintain—a fair market value for a company's securities. He presents the essential ingredients of a successful investor relations program, discusses the necessary expertise of the executive who fills this post, and assesses some of the benefits, which can be substantial, of an investor relations effort directed at long-term growth. It is of utmost importance, he maintains, that companies foster strong lines of communication with the financial community in good times as well as bad, for it is only through such continuous effort that credibility is established—and credibility is the investor relations executive's most important asset.

During the 1969–1970 stock market decline, Wall Street's thermometer, the Dow Jones Industrial Average, dropped a chilling 30% from a high of 968.85—by far the worst decline since the 1930s. Millions of investors lost billions of dollars. The fact that the losses were "paper" losses afforded small consolation to those who saw their visions of sugarplums turn into nightmares. Thus:

☐   In unnumbered corporate suites, executives gazed, dull-eyed, at stock options, granted at what seemed at the time to be bargain prices, but subsequently packed with all the investment appeal of Czar of Russia securities.

☐   The investors who used to complain about being locked in—that is, they'd made so much profit on their investments in less than six

Author's Note.   I wish to thank my associate, Victor A. Liston, Manager of Investor Relations, International Telephone and Telegraph Corporation, for his contributions to the preparation of this article.

months that they couldn't afford to sell because of the tax bite—later
sobbed uncontrollably because they had not sold out.

When they were not in a state of total shock, many disillusioned stockholders
sought to ease their wrath and pain by writing letters to corporation presidents, demanding an explanation for the horrendous decline in stock prices,
and asking what management proposed to do about it. Occasionally, a stockholder even asked the corporation to take back the stock and refund the
purchase price.

In times of crisis, when this tumult and weeping are heard both inside
and outside corporate offices, the lot of an investor relations executive is
not a very happy one. Let the stock market fall out of bed, or even show
an inclination to do so, and he is a very harassed man.

As many investor relations people will attest, when the stock market
is going up and up and up, few stockholders bother their department. The
volume of mail and phone calls from stockholders mercifully declines. At
such times, except for the continuing flow of inquiries from and meetings
with professional investors, the investor relations executive can go fishing,
for all anyone seems to care.

Of course, investor relations is an ongoing function, important in good
times as well as bad. The successful executives in these posts spend the
relatively quiet time organizing programs, continuing their missionary work
by maintaining close touch with their flocks in the financial community, and
keeping on the alert for the next stock market drop.

It is important that publicly held companies recognize the necessity of
employing a continuous investor relations program, as opposed to instituting
stopgap measures when faced with negative reactions like those mentioned
earlier. Credibility can only be established through consistent dialogue with
the financial community—and this credibility is essential when stock prices
turn downward.

Every publicly owned corporation needs and should have such a policy
and program. The scope of the program will depend, among other things,
on the size of the company. Billion-dollar corporations operate full-scale
investor relations departments. Considerably smaller companies either employ an investor relations executive or, if the budget will not permit, des-
ignate a company officer to handle the assignment. In brief, all publicly held
companies ought to subscribe to the *concept* of investor relations as an
obligation owed to those who have invested in them.

In meeting this obligation, the wise chief executive is also fully aware
that (a) the future expansion of the company will almost certainly require
additional infusions of equity capital, (b) the competition for the investor's
dollar is extremely tough, and (c) the only way to raise additional funds in
the market is to offer a good performance record.

Right now, it is estimated that U.S. manufacturing companies will try
to raise at least $100 billion of new capital expenditures during the next five

years. Those companies that have established reputations as practitioners of sound, reliable investor relations will have considerably less difficulty in obtaining the additional capital they need. From this standpoint alone, any management of a publicly held corporation that fails to meet its responsibilities in the area of investor relations does so at its peril. Consider some of the other benefits:

☐ A company whose stock enjoys widespread acceptance attracts key executive talent because its stock options hold promise of substantial appreciation.

☐ Employee morale is high, especially among those who are participating in the company's stock purchase plan.

☐ A company seeking to grow and diversify through acquisitions on an exchange-of-shares basis is in a strong bargaining position.

☐ Stockholders who are pleased with an investment can be counted on to support management in a proxy battle.

In this article, I shall examine the role of investor relations as a vital link between publicly held companies and the financial community. After a discussion of the functional elements of sound investor relations and the essential characteristics and duties of the executive who will direct the program, some guidelines will be offered to help companies avoid pitfalls and assure a viable investor relations policy.

Changing Needs

Achieving—and maintaining—a fair market value for the company's publicly held securities is the primary objective of investor relations. This concept dates back to Graham and Dodd, coauthors of the standard text on security analysis.[1] It was their position that corporate management has a responsibility to shareholders, not just to manage the company profitably and to pay out in dividends a fair return on investment, but to assume the additional responsibility of assuring that the stock commands the best market price. This responsibility, in the view of Graham and Dodd, is both a legal and an ethical one.

Although the foregoing commandment may strike some as a belaboring of the obvious, the time was—and not *that* long ago, either—when this dictum was regarded as black heresy. Until relatively recently, the securities market was the exclusive hunting ground of the very rich. The wealth of the nation, expressed in terms of capital expenditures for the factories and mines from which goods poured in awesome quantity, came from the treasuries of the rich, who, we can be quite sure, made these outlays only after assuring themselves that the investments would multiply during the round trip back to their coffers.

Gradually, and not always peacefully, the old order gave way. Slowly the opportunities to become part owners in company profits were made available to those with the price of admission. Stocks moved out of the hands of the few and became the possession of the many. It took time, but at last count by the New York Stock Exchange there were 30.8 million stockholders in the United States.

Reporting to Stockholders

The change in the elitism of stock ownership to broad public ownership necessitated a concomitant change in the entire process of reporting corporate financial results. The language and presentation of the annual report and of financial statements, for example, had to be reformed for a new audience. Since the report's original purpose was to enlighten those on the inside without informing those on the outside, its arcane phrases and terms needed to be augmented and clarified.

Federal agencies entered the scene, their sworn purpose to make certain that the newcomer to the stock market was given at least a minimal chance to understand what the game was all about. Prodded by such government agencies as the Securities and Exchange Commission and nudged along by the New York Stock Exchange (whose founders, on receiving the news of "people's capitalism," spun like crazed compasses in their graves), publicly held companies gingerly welcomed the growing influx of new owners.

Faced with an entirely new type of ownership, one composed of many bodies owning modest amounts of stock each, in contrast with a small but select group of major stockholders, corporations sought to shake themselves awake and appear attentive to this new breed. Formerly desertlike annual reports now bloomed with pictures of the company's plants and products, and becomingly benign portraits of the chairman and president added notes of grace to the annual letter to the stockholders.

Some unsung genius made the discovery that these stockholders were also potential customers for the company's jams and jellies, its innerspring mattresses, or its canned hams. Through the medium of the annual report and inserts in dividend envelopes, companies began to push sales with—since they're still at it—what could only have been gratifying results.

But the change from elite ownership to broadbased public ownership of business did not come about swiftly, nor did all corporations hearing the chants of the "people's capitalism" necessarily get the message. In fact, just a few years ago when a former general-turned-chairman of the board of one of our major corporations was asked at the annual meeting of stockholders to divulge how many shares of the corporation's stock he personally owned, he replied in effect: "None of your business." However, during the 12-month period between meetings he demonstrated an aptness for learning and, at the next gathering of the corporate clan, volunteered the information about his holdings.

As we have seen, with the dramatic turnabout in ownership of public corporations, there have been changes in the corporate posture as management has sought new ways to bring its story to the investor's attention. For example:

☐ The more readable annual report, with its highlights of the year conspicuously located up front for the too-busy-to-bother stockholder, and with its footnotes to financial statements tucked away in the back where those who dote on such mysteries can read themselves into madness.

☐ The diligence with which most companies court financial reporters of the daily newspapers and the national business magazines.

Either through written reports prepared and distributed by the company itself or through news releases appearing in the press, corporate management strives to keep past and potential owners informed.

Essential as the written word is, however, it does not create a reciprocal communication system between the corporation, its stockholders, and/or the general public. The word goes forth; it is read or not read. Or, being read, it is understood or not understood. True, the person sufficiently motivated can write a letter or even telephone the company and ask for further information or clarification. But quite apart from the time lapse involved in this instance, what about the audience that did not read the message or, reading it, did not grasp its significance? And if three or four people took the time to seek further enlightenment, how many others just did not bother?

The corporation's effort to inform its stockholders—commendable as it is—is not enough. Today, especially, prudence dictates that attention must simultaneously be given to informing that vast audience of nonstockholders from which future stockholders will be enticed.

Wooing "The Street"

Stockholders are not a captive audience, and woe to the company president who supposes otherwise. Stockholders are not indentured servants. Stockholders can and do sell out stock with maddening perversity.

It has been asserted that a stock is worth only what someone else, as well informed as the stock's owner, is willing to pay for it. Thus no great mental exercise is required to arrive at the conclusion that any corporate president who wishes to keep the company's stock readily marketable at a fair price will not neglect the investor who may buy when a stockholder decides to sell.

But company presidents, limited by time and other responsibilities, are not free to roam the financial ranges, buttonholing likely customers and extolling the attractive features of an investment in the company's securities. Besides, such behavior could well turn off investors in wholesale lots.

This is not to say, however, that the company's chief executive officer is cut off from possible future stockholders who might replace those defecting to apparently greener pastures. He can reach the audience of potential stock-holders far more effectively by approaching those through whom the buyers and sellers of securities transact their business—the financial community.

Those who serve the investing public, as well as those responsible for making momentous investment decisions for mutual funds and for invest-ment accounts of banks and insurance companies, welcome management representatives from reputable and growing organizations. This welcome is extended with equal enthusiasm to lesser-known companies that appear to have good growth potential but have not been in operation long enough to establish outstanding records of performance.

Role of Investor Relations

Investor relations links a publicly held company and the financial community of stockholders and would-be stockholders, security analysts, portfolio man-agers, investment departments of banks and insurance companies, and mu-tual funds. The objective of investor relations is refreshingly uncompli-cated—get the price of the stock up to where it realistically belongs and keep it there.

As stated earlier, in more sedate prose, the purpose of investor relations is to achieve a fair market value for the company's securities. This means that the stock should command a market value at least equaling the market value of those stocks from companies with comparable records and pros-pects. There is no rule against doing better, of course, and no investor relations executive worth her salt is content to have her company's stock dwell peacefully in the herd when, as she sees it, that stock is uniquely qualified to outperform the others and move to the top of its industry group.

Professional Standards

Investor relations, in common with all other areas in which one can scratch a living without either high capital investment or formalized qualification standards, has drawn its share of innocents-at-large and charlatans alike. There are no laws to prohibit abysmally unqualified persons from setting themselves up in either the public relations or the financial relations business. Maybe someday such legislation will be passed.

Meanwhile, professional organizations such as the Public Relations Society of America and the Investor Relations Institute are to be commended for their determined efforts to raise the competence of their membership. Concurrently, the security analysts have made great strides in raising their professional standards for admission to the guild through 41 local societies and their parent body, the 13,000-member Financial Analysts Federation.

Because the Investor Relations Institute came into existence only this year, it has not had time to assess just how many full-time investor relations officials are on the payrolls of U.S. companies or to conduct an in-depth study into such matters as average age, salary, years of experience, and professional background.

Without this data, I would guess that not more than 15% of the companies listed in *Fortune* magazine's "The 500 Largest Industrial Corporations" have an executive assigned full time to the investor relations function. This is not to say that the remaining 85% are indifferent to the need to communicate with the financial community. Many companies call on their chief financial officers or treasurers to double-in-brass as their spokespeople. In some instances, the president retains this function; in others, it is the vice chairman, the corporate secretary, or the chief of public relations.

Criteria for Choice

Obviously, the chief executives of corporations cannot spend all their time carrying the gospel of financial progress to captains of the investment industry; nor can they, in turn, give all their working hours to such meetings. Acknowledging this, both sides have independently delegated the day-to-day conference function to others within their separate organizations: (a) the security analyst for the investment community and (b) the investor relations executive for the corporate community.

Acting for their chief executives, the security analyst and the investor relations official establish and maintain a system of close communication that is essential to both of their organizations. Only on infrequent occasions do their respective chief officers get together for formal reviews and discussion; and, when they do, each relies heavily on the rapport initiated and nurtured so carefully during the interval by their deputies. Useful and continuing relationships between a company and the financial community can only be successful if this system is fully understood from the outset. It follows, then, that the selection of individuals who will act for the company and the financial community must be carefully considered.

In the Financial Community. Security analysts, working from their organizations' research departments, are the delegates-at-large for the financial community. Selection of the appropriate representative is relatively simple because the great majority of manufacturing or service companies can be catalogued easily according to industry, such as heavy manufacturing, retail, construction, and utilities. Security analysts, in turn, tend to become specialists in one or more major industries; there are steel analysts, insurance analysts, office equipment analysts, and so on, who are experts in their chosen fields. When a brokerage house decides to look into the investment attractiveness of a company, chances are that the industry specialist for the line of business in which that company is engaged will take on the assignment.

In the Corporation. Investor-relations executives are the security analysts' counterparts in the corporate structure. But, since many companies do not understand the nature or importance of this function, choice of the investor-relations official is not so cut-and-dried, and examples of haphazard or in-appropriate selection are quite numerous.

Aside from those companies that assign to the investor relations func-tion whoever happens to be available (one major corporation, for example, gave investor relations duties to a retired chemist), many organizations make one of two common errors:

1. Some companies will decide that investor relations are properly a part of public relations. They are unaware that many security analysts feel uncomfortable when talking with public relations people because, rightly or wrongly, analysts are generally suspicious of being "snowed."

2. Other companies assume that the best candidate for the investor relations function is found in the treasurer's or the comptroller's department. Security analysts, they reason, are figure-happy, and who is better qualified to throw around statistics than the person who has lived with them? Such reasoning is unsound, and if it accomplishes nothing else, it serves to dem-onstrate that the chief executive of the company has not got the message of what investor relations is all about. A moment's reflection will reveal that knowledge of the figure does not, per se, establish ability to communicate that knowledge effectively.

The solution to be found lies somewhere between these extremes. The best candidate for the investor relations post will have had experience in both public relations and the financial phases of a company's operations. Such a background might include:

☐ Special courses—often at night school—in finance and security analysis which, of course, include the fundamentals of accounting.

☐ Experience as a security analyst in a brokerage research depart-ment, or performance of the same function in the investment depart-ment of a bank or insurance company.

☐ Experience in financial news writing and/or in public or community relations.

No matter what their backgrounds, investor relations executives who earn the respect and confidence of the Street will have to be on familiar ground when they are talking with security analysts. They must be able to empathize with these people and to appreciate the nuances of sophisticated comments and inquiries.

Responsibilities of Management

Generally speaking, the person assigned to investor relations reports directly to the president or, if the company is a major one, to the chief financial officer. Whatever title he holds, the investor relations executive must have direct and ready access to top management. He must be fully informed on top-level policy and planning.

These requirements should be self-evident, but unfortunately there are occasions when the investor relations function is not clearly understood by top management. At the risk of sounding cynical, I have also known instances in which top management has appointed an investor relations executive, given him a high-sounding title, and then proceeded to methodically ignore him.

It should not require a great deal of time for the experienced investor relations professional to find out whether top management is genuinely dedicated to the investor relations function or is simply using him and his position as so much "window dressing." He will quickly determine this should he discover that although he surely has a need to know, he is usually the last to know!

When the investor relations executive has the good fortune to be associated with a top management that is sensitive to his function, the experience is an uncommonly rewarding one. Such management never makes the error of considering the investor relations role unimportant or delegates the position to a low man on the executive totem pole. On the contrary:

☐ The investor relations executive is privy to top management's thinking and planning.

☐ He is a trusted member of the inner circle.

☐ His advice is always sought on any proposal which directly affects the financial community.

It is no exaggeration to report that, quite frequently, an aware upper management will modify, or even abandon, a proposed policy or action because the investor relations executive has advised that the reaction of the financial community would be a negative one. He maintains consistent two-way communication with representatives of the financial community and is able to obtain valuable feedback concerning the receptivity of investors to a proposed plan. Consider the following case:

A major automobile manufacturer was experiencing difficult times and faced a deficit. As a result, top management decided to omit a dividend as a conservation measure. The investor relations executive knew, however, that many institutions required a consistent dividend record, or they would not buy or continue to hold stocks. Consequently, he urged a token dividend—and won. Thus, an unnecessary drop in the company's stock price was avoided because management maintained a sound investor relations program and was sensitive to it.

Similar examples, both positive and negative, are numerous. But suffice it to say that when the financial community doesn't like a proposed policy, acquisition, or what have you, the stock price of the company concerned is likely to drop. It is the investor relations officer's job to find this out ahead of time. It is in management's interest to listen to him.

Operational Machinery

On a day-to-day basis, the principal function of the investor relations executive is to serve as an information center for the financial community. It is her responsibility to help the investment analyst understand the company and to provide all the information—and interpretation of that information, when necessary—that she can ethically divulge or discuss.

She should not, however, do the analyst's homework for him. While most analysts are conscientious professionals, all too common is the analyst who says, "I'm new to your company. Tell me all about it!" Whatever procedure prevails elsewhere, at ITT we tend to take a hardnosed line when confronted with this situation. Our response is granite-firm. After loading the supplicant up with annual and interim reports, prospectuses, proxy statements, and any other informational literature, we lead him to the elevators and suggest that he get in touch with us again after he has digested the background material.

Among investor relations people there is a continuing debate on just how much an analyst is entitled to be told, and whether all analysts should be treated alike in the disclosure of information. For the record, let me hasten to report that the investor relations executive should not tell one analyst something unless she is prepared to give the same information to any and all analysts.

As with so many other policies, however, this one works beautifully—in theory. Neither analysts nor investor relations people are robots or computers. The superficial analyst is not likely to inspire enthusiastic responses to his routine questions. By the same token, the analyst who demonstrates a lively, informed interest will bring out the best in the investor relations executive. There is a difference between being ready and willing to give responsive answers to inquiries and compulsively volunteering reams of data to any and all comers.

Arrangement of Meetings

As the links between their companies and the financial community, the investor relations executives become involved in numerous meetings and information sessions. These generally take one of three forms: (a) speaking engagements of the chief executive or other corporate officers, (b) management-analyst meetings, and (c) individual analyst briefings.

Speaking Engagements.   The chief executive officer and, to a lesser extent, those close to the president's office, receive more invitations to address analysts' societies than they can fulfill. Not the least of investor relations responsibilities is to decide which invitations ought to be accepted by the chief executive and which can be delegated to other officers.

When the chief executive speaks to a group of analysts, investor relations is usually responsible for preparing the formal remarks. If the actual speechwriting is done elsewhere—in the public relations department, for example—investor relations will still have a firm say about the content as well as the form of presentation.

These sessions with analysts' societies tend to be as formal and as rigidly programmed as *Swan Lake*. After lunch or dinner, the president of the society introduces the guest speaker and other ranking officers of the corporation. The president of the company then makes a 20- to 35-minute address, followed by a question-and-answer period.

Experience has established that time given to making sure the chief executive's speech covers all major points of interest is time well spent. This is particularly true when a delicate or complicated subject will almost certainly be raised during the question-and-answer session. If the president has covered the point as carefully as circumstances permit, then he can always refer to his formal remarks, and thus avoid being drawn into saying more than he had intended. For example:

A few years ago, the president of a large corporation appeared before a financial analysts' group for a question-and-answer period that followed his prepared speech. In response to a question from the floor, he indicated that the current quarter would be disappointing. Members of the audience literally raced for the telephone to communicate the news, leaving the unfortunate president to ponder the impact of his inadvertent remark. The stock subsequently dropped sharply—a decline that could very likely have been avoided had the subject been covered more accurately in his formal speech.

Meetings with Management.   While most meetings with security analysts' societies are full-dress parades, less formal gatherings are frequently arranged by the investor relations executive. Often the chief executive sits down informally with a group of investment analysts who are quite sophisticated in their knowledge of the company and its industry. They will wish to go beyond generalities and to probe all sorts of esoterica. While such sessions are of great value to management and analysts alike, care must be exercised to avoid even the appearance of giving company information only to selected audiences lest the "full disclosure" rules be violated.

This brings up the diplomatically delicate subject of when to grant and when to deny requests for a session with the chief executive officer. Fortunately, most experienced security analysts are not title-happy. They are quite content to deal with an informed, responsive investor relations executive. Usually the investment analyst who asks for a brief meeting with the company president will outline what she would like to discuss at such a meeting. The investor relations executive soon develops antennae which instruct him whether the meeting would serve a useful purpose or not. If the signal is "go," he will arrange an appointment with his chief executive.

In this respect, analysts are beginning to realize that one does not always need an audience with the president to obtain reliable information about a particular company. In fact, analysts seeking in-depth knowledge of some particular aspect of company operations, would probably be better off talking with marketing, research, and/or technical heads.

Individual Briefings. The investor relations executive spends much of the working day in meetings with individual analysts. In major companies, these sessions are usually on an appointment basis. They may be held either in the analyst's office or at the company offices; the latter arrangement is usually preferable because the investor relations executive has ready access to the files and records should they need to be referred to during the meeting.

Sessions with individual analysts can last from 10 minutes to several hours. On the one hand, perhaps an analyst merely wants to "touch base" on a number of key points, having discussed the company in detail on previous visits. On the other hand, an analyst who is calling on the company for the first time, or is preparing a multipaged report for an institutional client, will request considerably more time. To avoid scrambled schedules, it is advisable when making the appointment to get some idea of what the analyst has in mind and to arrange the day's appointments accordingly.

Internal Functions

In addition to the responsibilities already outlined, the investor relations department performs a number of duties which are primarily internal. The functions of a sound investor relations department would include the following:

☐ Monitoring stock transfer sheets and reporting to top management on any significant changes in ownership.

☐ Preparing daily as well as monthly and quarterly studies on stock market performance and trends.

☐ Working closely with public relations in the preparation of annual and interim reports, financial news releases, company fact books and other publications.

☐ Advising and reviewing all financial advertising programs.

Periodic analysis of the stockholder list is another important responsibility. It is always a sound policy to know who your stockholders are, what percentage of total outstanding shares are held by institutions, for example, and how this percentage compares with past percentages. Such attention provides comparative data and helps uncover weak spots that the investor relations department should attempt to build up. Thus:

Five years ago, my company made an analysis of holdings and concluded that those of banks were far from impressive. We appointed a fulltime investor relations man to call on the nation's banks. The success of this move is evidenced by the fact that at the end of 1969, bank holdings of our securities accounted for 30% of total shares outstanding—three times the number of shares held by banks in 1965.

Critical Appendage.   When, in their wisdom, the officers of the Investor Relations Institute select an artist to design a coat of arms or great seal symbolic of the profession, a place of honor in that design will have to be accorded to the telephone. The telephone is as essential to the investor relations executive as the stethoscope is to the physician. For the marketplace is a volatile, frenetic, unpredictable force that produces constant communication:

☐   Questions demanding immediate answers pour from scores of brokerage houses during the hours of trading.

☐   An item on the Dow Jones broad tape generates a flood tide of inquiries.

☐   A would-be buyer of a large block of stock calls for help in locating a seller, or vice versa.

These and similar situations call for prompt, informed, responsive action on the part of the investor relations executive—and the situation is similar in large corporations everywhere, since the telephone ties all of these companies to the financial community.

Conclusion

I have emphasized the function of investor relations as the communications link between the company and the financial community. In this respect, executives who perform this function occupy the role of "devil's advocates." That is, they must always bear in mind that, while they are paid by one master, they must conscientiously serve two masters. The investor relations executives express top management's point of view in the financial community. But they also represent and speak for the financial community in the company, expressing the point of view of the investment world to their employers.

A Word of Caution

As I mentioned earlier, a sound investor relations program, continued through good times as well as bad, can produce substantial benefits. That this is so cannot be mathematically demonstrated—if, in fact, investor relations could be reduced to a formula whose application automatically resulted in higher stock prices, the formula would be universally used.

In a more realistic vein, however, the following admonitory points can help assure a successful program:

☐   An investor relations program should not be undertaken if management's objective is "window dressing." Nor should such a program be launched with an eye to the fast buck, or conversely, as a last-gasp defense. Wall Street has a long, long memory. (In the Wall Street version of the Lord's Prayer, the phrase "as we forgive those who trespass against us" has been omitted.) Credibility is one of the most important assets of the investor relations function; and it can only be established through consistent, honest dealings with the financial community.

☐ Investor relations programs which have not been planned for the long term are worse than none at all. In this connection a survey conducted by Hill & Knowlton, Inc. is noteworthy. The public relations company conducted a poll among the chief executives or top financial officers of 112 corporations, none of whom was a client of the firm. More than 70% of the poll participants reported they are devoting as much time and effort to investor relations during the current stock market recession as they did during the 1967–1968 bull market. Nearly 25% have actually increased their investor relations activities during the last two years.

☐ Investor relations should not be a shared function. In the same way that most companies' press relations are handled through the public relations department—thus discouraging newspaper reporters from buttonholing any and all of their executives—inquiries from the financial community should be directed to the investor relations department. Otherwise it is impossible to maintain any degree of consistency.

I think anyone who carefully examines the developments in investor relations over the past 20 years has to conclude that there has been a steady movement toward improved financial reporting, wider dissemination of financial information, and fuller disclosure of relevant data to help the investor become better informed. Contributing to this—with acknowledged assists from the Securities and Exchange Commission, as well as the accounting profession—has been an increasing awareness on the part of corporate management that investor relations is an essential service. The investor has always had a need to know. Through the investor relations function, management acknowledges the investor's right to know.

Notes

1. Benjamin G. Graham and David L. Dodd, *Security Analysis* (New York, McGraw-Hill Book Company, Inc., 1934).

32

Annual Reports Don't Have to Be Dull

FRED C. FOY

The annual report is one of the most important documents a publicly owned company produces—at a cost of tens of thousands of dollars. Yet the "return" on that investment is quite low; one survey reports that 40% of stockholders spend five minutes or less reading reports and another 15% don't even bother to look at them when they arrive in the mail. Too many corporate reports are aimed at the analysts and neglect the Aunt Janes, the author of this article contends. To attract the latter group, reports must present easily absorbed data and plainly written prose in a more sprightly and expressive fashion, and in a livelier and more readable format. He gives many examples of annual reports that rate high marks in their attention to the wants and needs of the "once-over-lightly, once-a-year stockholder reader."

A majority of corporate annual reports to shareholders really are not written for shareholders. Much, if not most, of what's in them is there because market analysts, investment advisers, and professional investors have asked for the information.

Yet the format, the pictures, and the whole package are aimed at the individual shareholders. They don't reach them, however. Too many stockholders simply don't read reports or give them enough attention and time to find out what's in them.

Recently, Georgeson & Company, an investor relations firm, made an extensive survey of report-reading habits of stockholders and of security analysts. The firm found that 40% of the stockholders surveyed give the reports five minutes or less and 15% don't read them at all.

When you consider that the average annual report contains numerous financial tables, from 4,000 to 8,000 words, and a dozen photographs, obviously the report has failed to communicate as far as two out of five potential readers are concerned. Five minutes is simply not time enough.

Another 26% give it six to fifteen minutes. This may be enough, even for readers who have anywhere from a few hundred to some thousands of dollars of their money bet on the, they hope, able management of the company, and who in most cases depend on a regular cash dividend.

The remaining 34% give the report from fifteen to more than thirty minutes. It would be foolish to try to involve them more than that. There's probably not that much of real interest to read about anyway.

The analysts are different. They have to know all they can, good and bad, about companies they are interested in. About 60% of them give reports they read more than an hour and only 8% less than thirty minutes. But three fourths of them read fewer than 200 reports a year.

It has been suggested that one report can't intrigue or satisfy both groups, that maybe we need two reports. It has even been suggested that we concentrate on the professional and forget the individual stockholder, who isn't that interested in the company anyway as long as dividends continue and the price of the stock doesn't fall out of bed.

I wonder. It's possible that the planners and writers of corporate annual reports have a much better image of their analyst reader group than of their stockholder reader group. They seem to edit pretty well for the in-depth people, but pretty badly for the once-over-lightly, once-a-year stockholder readers. How do we reach them?

Hit the High Spots

The typical stockholder is, I believe, a "highlight" reader. The annual report has to compete with magazines and newspapers for his time and attention. With the report, as with them, he starts by glancing at the cover, which in most cases gives him no reason at all to look inside. The contents page is about as intriguing as the dictionary but, if done well, could move him inside. He may even pause at the letter to stockholders, but only if the first couple of paragraphs grab him. If he ends up reading something inside, it will be only if it catches his interest as he skims through.

Even for the highlight reader, the five-minute explorer, maybe the foregoing sequence of events is assuming too much. This type of reader wants information quickly and easily. For my money, the masterpiece of instant business information transfer is that jewel, the second column under "What's News" on the front page of *The Wall Street Journal*. There, in a few concise paragraphs, the reader finds condensations of what's inside the *Journal* for the day. Each item is keyed to the appropriate inside page.

Why not issue an annual report that starts with a cover designed to pull readers inside to a discussion of general interest? It could be the story of a meaningful new product or research development (not like the frequent overselling of the mini-breakthrough); or perhaps a candid, in-depth discussion of corporate goals, management philosophy, or developments in the struggle involving business, government, and Congress.

Companies do treat such subjects in their reports, and some have done it well. In its 1971 annual report, Cummins Engine presented its highlights right at the start and in readable form. Inside, the report discussed conditions affecting Cummins—such as rigorous air pollution standards—and U.S. business in general, and how Cummins is coping with them. The report outlined the company's strategy for continuing this role in the future.

Koppers talked to large and small stockholders, in plain language, on its mission, on the public utterances and views of its leaders, and on its 10-year progress. This information is helpful to investors in deciding whether to put or keep their money in the company.

Koppers made ingenious use of its cover by starting its shareholder letter right there in large, easily read type. It is reproduced on the facing page. At this point, if they were interested, the readers could turn the page and, in two pages of the same large type, find out what the company "proved." The whole letter totals about 400 words, normal reading time one to four minutes. On page 3 they found, still in jumbo type, comparative figures for 1971 and 1970 in a simple, easy-to-read table.

At this point, the readers knew something of what was in the report and whether it interested them enough to read further. If they turned to the statment of mission or the quotes, they found them written simply, succinctly, and understandably.

For those analytically minded shareholders who sought more detailed information, the financial and operating reviews were explicit and complete, yet written in clear and uncomplicated language. There was also a table of proportionate sales and profits by divisions—a departure for Koppers that is being provided by more companies each year.

(Some readers may think that I am overselling a report in which I have a more than ordinary interest. Or they may even be suspicious that, partly at least, I was the author or architect of it. I was not; I didn't even see it until it was in final form. I just think it was a well-planned report that served both shareholders and analysts better than most.)

Tell More with Numbers

Let's talk figures. Both the SEC and the New York Stock Exchange require that the annual report contain, in comparative, columnar form, numerical statements for the past two fiscal years which, in the opinion of management, adequately reflect the financial position of the issuer at the end of each year and the results of operations for each year. In practice, this usually has meant the minimum: a balance sheet and an income and expense statement, as well as any necessary explanatory footnotes.

For years, analysts have argued that this is not nearly enough. One thing is clear. The more figures given and the more pertinent the figures are, the more usable information they disclose and the better the reader will understand the company.

Figures can usually tell what happened in less space than words can. Furthermore, when figures are tabulated comparatively over a period of years, they record the story of a company's progress, or lack of it, quickly and exactly.[1]

What they don't tell is what caused changes and why. Here only words can do the job. So how can figures and words be combined for the quickest, most useful stockholder impact?

The first inside cover could be a newsy, paragraphical, highlights page, such as I described earlier. I have written one, based on the 1971 General Electric report. It is shown in Exhibit 1.

The facing page could feature the required two-year comparative figures, printed in big, easily read type and organized to highlight the guts of the business. A sample is shown in Exhibit 2.

Some will argue for inclusion in this simplified table of extraordinary items and other income as a separate entry. Why, unless it is at least 5% of total income? Below that level, nonrecurring income neither distorts the figures nor influences dividend decisions. When we include such parsley, we lose the mildly interested stockholder. Let's face it: 40% of shareholders who give annual reports five minutes or less probably don't want to know more than what is in this table.

For the next group, those who are neither analysts nor once-over-lightly readers and want more information but not inundation, let's put the 10-year figures on the next two pages and tabulate them in the same fashion. But let's set the table up so that it explains itself, as Exhibit 3 does with Koppers Company's results for the 1962–1971 period. (But you won't find them actually presented in this manner in the company's annual report; the company developed much of the data expressly for this article.)

Businesspeople, sophisticated investors, bankers, and analysts may say that explanatory notes like those in Exhibit 3 insult the reader's intelligence. I don't think so. I have asked many ordinary, garden-variety investors how they evaluate year-to-year figures. Many say, "They ought to go up." That's not completely true. Some ought to go up, some ought to go down, at least relatively. Why not clue them in on this? Once they know how to read and understand short- and long-term comparisons, maybe they'll want to know more.

While a long-term historical record like Exhibit 3 tells a great deal about a company's performance, it is not always self-explanatory. An example is the 10-year rundown in General Tire's 1971 report, which showed that sales in the decade had risen from $959 million to $994 million. What kind of growth is that?

Exhibit 1. Sample Highlights Page Based on GE Annual Report

WHAT'S INSIDE

Sales of $9.425 billion, earnings of $471 million, and $249 million paid in dividends made 1971 GE's biggest year. Biggest year, too, for stockholders who benefited by a dividend increase from $1.30 to $1.40 a share beginning in April while most union employees got a 15¢ an hour pay increase in March, 8¢ for cost of living in October.

*   *   *

Threats of future power shortages, brown-outs, in various parts of the U.S. have been predicted. GE is a big factor in keeping it from happening, has shipped as much steam turbine generator capacity in the last 10 years as in the preceding 60, leads in nuclear plant operating experience. GE customers started up four new nuclear plants in 1971; company built the two largest operating reactors in the world.

(see page 14)

*   *   *

GE jet engines are performing exceptionally in new Douglas DC-10 Trijets, will also power European twinjet airbuses, the Navy's new anti-submarine fighters, Army's transport helicopters.

(see page 18)

*   *   *

We're up to our ears in cleaning up our own environment and in research and development on products and services to help others clean up theirs, to take the noise out of household appliances, industry's engines.

(see page 22)

*   *   *

Company provided jobs for 363,000 people at home and abroad, increased number of women, minority workers, and veterans on the payroll during the year, paid nearly $4.5 billion to suppliers, thus creating thousands more jobs.

*   *   *

A GE refrigerator today sells at the same price as a 1950 model, has double the storage space, such additional features as automatic defrosting, adjustable shelves, a coil free back, choice of colors; tangible evidence of GE success in the war on inflation.

(see page 10)

*   *   *

Adjustment to increasing costs will be helped by Government Price Board approval of 2% average price increase on domestic operations.

(see page 4)

Exhibit 2. Sample Two-Year Comparative Statement

1972 At a Glance	1972	1971
Sales	$172,045,539	$153,220,890
Operating profit	$ 11,612,434	$ 8,790,576
As percentage of sales	6.7%	5.7%
Net income	$ 6,009,155	$ 4,248,645
As percentage of sales	3.5%	2.8%
As percentage of investment	4.8%	3.5%
Earnings per share of common stock	$ 1.87	$ 1.32
Dividends paid per share of common stock	$ 1.03	$ 1.00
Taxes paid per share of common stock	$ 6.23	$ 5.24
Market price range of stock during year	$29⅞–17⅛	$23½–14¼

It's this kind! Net income went from $26 million to $48 million, earnings per share from $1.43 to $2.52, dividends from 36 cents a share to 98, and equity from $10.59 a share to $23.35. That's quite a performance on no sales growth, but for the casual reader the company offers no ready explanation.

A discussion in General Tire's 1972 report of how this was accomplished would interest shareholders and might even tell analysts something they hadn't realized over the years. Somebody at General Tire knew what he was doing and zeroed in on goals other than sales gains.

Segment Results

Only 7 of 32 reports I read before writing this article broke down sales and earnings by major product lines. They were Koppers, Time, Westinghouse, CBS, Eaton, General Electric, and International Multifoods. Of these, 3 gave such breakdowns as percentages of total sales or earnings, while the other 4—Westinghouse, Eaton, CBS, and GE—gave sales and profits in dollars by major areas of the business.

This is information that analysts have sought for years. Most companies have refused, usually for something they refer to as "competitive reasons."

Nonsense! Your overall figures make your competitors feel good or bad, but they won't spur them to do anything more to beat your brains out than they are doing already; nor will a breakdown by product lines. Sure, it will tell your stockholders, the analysts, or even your competitor where your returns are lowest. But so what? Most product lines or divisional breakdowns are so broad that they don't pinpoint any product where a competitor could hurt you anyway.

More likely, the result would be like that at Westinghouse. Donald Burnham, the chairman, told me, "We were concerned before we decided to give these breakdowns. So far we have seen no harm from it. Just the opposite: the groups within the company are competing against each other to make a better showing in the report."

The fact is, sometimes they're uncomfortable figures, so management would just rather not bare its breast and have to explain them. But even that could be good. Lloyd Workman, Senior Vice President, Marketing, of International Multifoods, said to me, "Publishing these figures has given us no trouble. Actually, they increased analyst interest. When we finished explaining them, both we and the analysts understood the company better." I'll say more about this subject later.

Words from Management

The annual report needs more than figures and tables, or even graphs, charts, or pictures. It needs candid, specific, readable statements of objectives, of difficulties and problems and how they are being attacked, of important new products or services, and of how management envisions the future of the business.

International Multifoods, whose 1972 report is by far the most interesting, most readable annual report I have seen, stated its case so that any stockholder could understand it. William Phillips, its president, stated its growth objectives as "10% per year in earnings per share and a 7% per year sales growth." What could be plainer?

In an interview with Richard King, the financial vice-president, these two questions were asked and answered:

Q. You have previously indicated a corporate earnings objective of 10% per year increase in earnings per share on a trend-line basis. This is the second year you haven't made it. Would you please explain?

A. At the start of fiscal year 1969 we set, and publicly announced an objective of, a 7% annual increase in sales and a 10% annual increase in earnings per share on a trend-line basis. What that means is that, over an extended period of time, this is what we are shooting for. We realized that, because of the character of our business, our ambitious growth plans, and the varying economic conditions, we could not hope to accomplish these objectives every year. Now let's look at the record. Since fiscal 1969, sales have increased at a compounded annual rate of 9%, net earnings have increased at a compounded annual rate of 18%, and earnings per share at 13%. Essentially, therefore, we're ahead of plan at this point and we're still committed to these same objectives.

Q. Didn't you have an objective of improving return on sales and return on average common stockholders' equity? What's happened?

A. You are right. These are specific objectives. Since 1969—when return on sales was 1.4%—we went to 1.7% in both 1970 and 1971, and this year we achieved a 1.9% return on sales. This has, in a large part, been accomplished through the replacement of lower margin business and with

Exhibit 3.   Ten-Year Selected Financial Data of Koppers Company (Dollar figures in thousands except for per-share and number of shareholders figures)

	1971	1970	1969	1968
This group of figures shows how the company has done over the years. The long-term trend of these percentages ought to be up.				
Sales and other income	$602,132	$ 535,698	$ 536,369	$ 451,789
Income before income taxes and interest charges				
Amount	$ 40,071	$ 28,784	$ 41,301	$ 29,472
As percentage of sales	6.7%	5.4%	7.7%	6.5%
Net income				
Amount	$ 18,693	$ 11,702	$ 18,357	$ 15,883
As percentage of sales	3.1%	2.2%	3.4%	3.5%
As percentage of investment	5.6%	3.6%	6.2%	5.9%
Earnings per common share	$ 3.29	$ 2.16	$ 3.70	$ 3.18
Dividends per common share	$ 1.60	$ 1.60	$ 1.60	$ 1.50
Taxes per common share	$ 4.54	$ 3.70	$ 5.38	$ 3.56
Annual market range per common share	$ 37-28¼	$ 46½-23½	$ 48¾-30¾	$ 46¾-31½
This group of figures shows the principal costs of running the business over the years. While dollar figures will rise as the business grows, the trend of these percentages should be down. You will note in the dollar figures that taxes are the only cost not under management control.				
Interest charges	$ 7,857	$ 8,741	$ 6,690	$ 4,552
Income taxes	$ 13,521	$ 8,341	$ 16,254	$ 9,037
Other taxes	$ 11,433	$ 10,695	$ 9,587	$ 8,102
Total taxes				
Amount	$ 24,954	$ 19,036	$ 25,841	$ 17,139
As percentage of sales	4.1%	3.6%	4.8%	3.8%
Selling, general and administrative, and research expenses				
Amount	$ 54,080	$ 53,710	$ 57,124	$ 48,210
As percentage of sales	9.0%	10.0%	10.7%	10.7%
Materials, supplies, and services				
Amount	$368,009	$ 324,890	$ 319,681	$ 275,469
As percentage of sales	61.1%	60.6%	59.6%	61.0%
Wages, salaries, and pension expenses				
Amount	$157,024	$ 150,502	$ 148,637	$ 121,720
As percentage of sales	26.1%	28.1%	27.7%	26.9%
This group of figures is for general information. Some stockholders and many investment analysts have asked for them.				
Cash flow to common stock				
Amount	$ 45,240	$ 33,401	$ 36,760	$ 33,487
Per share of common stock	$ 8.24	$ 6.48	$ 7.66	$ 6.96
Gross additions to fixed assets and investments	$ 27,364	$ 56,452	$ 39,913	$ 31,662
Net book value of assets	$194,486	$ 198,357	$ 165,766	$ 144,354
Earnings retained in the business	$ 9,211	$ 3,198	$ 9,963	$ 8,098
Long-term debt	$ 97,719	$ 115,790	$ 92,889	$ 76,396
Average common shares outstanding	5,492	5,151	4,802	4,811
Number of stockholders, year-end	16,937	16,943	16,437	16,831
Working capital	$135,994	$ 133,292	$ 119,915	$ 109,265
Book value per share of common stock outstanding, year-end	$ 40.13	$ 38.51	$ 39.16	$ 37.19

1967	1966	1965	1964	1963	1962
$ 450,495	$ 445,779	$ 386,436	$ 346,025	$ 302,500	$ 312,718
$ 24,044	$ 22,264	$ 22,200	$ 21,573	$ 16,164	$ 15,450
5.3%	5.0%	5.7%	6.2%	5.3%	4.9%
$ 14,608	$ 12,617	$ 13,226	$ 11,361	$ 7,825	$ 8,082
3.2%	2.8%	3.4%	3.3%	2.6%	2.6%
5.5%	5.0%	6.2%	5.7%	4.1%	4.1%
$ 2.83	$ 2.46	$ 2.63	$ 2.28	$ 1.53	$ 1.55
$ 1.40	$ 1.40	$ 1.20	$ 1.20	$ 1.00	$ 1.00
$ 2.56	$ 2.94	$ 3.13	$ 3.24	$ 2.79	$ 2.48
$ 45¼-26½	$ 33¾-22¼	$ 34½-27½	$ 29¼-19⅞	$ 21⅞-19⅝	$ 22⅜-16¾
$ 4,600	$ 3,347	$ 1,123	$ 1,356	$ 1,241	$ 1,252
$ 4,836	$ 6,300	$ 7,851	$ 8,856	$ 7,098	$ 6,116
$ 7,862	$ 8,081	$ 7,153	$ 6,431	$ 6,095	$ 5,802
$ 12,698	$ 14,381	$ 15,004	$ 15,287	$ 13,193	$ 11,918
2.8%	3.2%	3.9%	4.4%	4.4%	3.8%
$ 46,106	$ 43,268	$ 41,537	$ 38,732	$ 36,985	$ 37,008
10.2%	9.7%	10.7%	11.2%	12.2%	11.8%
$ 284,058	$ 282,036	$ 239,023	$ 213,271	$ 180,891	$ 193,261
63.1%	63.3%	61.9%	61.6%	59.8%	61.8%
$ 117,100	$ 118,990	$ 106,603	$ 92,098	$ 85,853	$ 85,207
26.0%	26.7%	27.6%	26.6%	28.4%	27.2%
$ 31,514	$ 26,296	$ 26,396	$ 25,560	$ 24,126	$ 22,672
$ 6.36	$ 5.38	$ 5.50	$ 5.42	$ 5.10	$ 4.71
$ 30,118	$ 48,742	$ 29,808	$ 15,720	$ 18,334	$ 13,744
$ 131,054	$ 121,837	$ 89,373	$ 92,565	$ 91,317	$ 92,097
$ 7,243	$ 5,342	$ 7,036	$ 5,216	$ 2,566	$ 2,742
$ 72,485	$ 67,966	$ 34,298	$ 28,062	$ 22,738	$ 29,711
4,957	4,891	4,795	4,715	4,733	4,812
16,959	16,890	15,646	16,183	15,818	16,307
$ 115,680	$ 111,064	$ 95,908	$ 84,136	$ 74,138	$ 80,157
$ 35.65	$ 34.32	$ 34.25	$ 33.42	$ 32.32	$ 31.63

the addition of higher margin sales in a variety of areas. We are still not at all satisfied with this level of performance.

Our return on average common stockholders' equity also has been going up—from 7.3% in 1969 . . . to 9% in 1970 . . . to 9.3% in 1971 . . . to this year's 9.6%. Here again we are working hard to improve our performance.

The Multifoods report resembled *Business Week* in its format. Its "advertising" consisted of ads which the company had run in newspapers and magazines. In addition to using the reporting and makeup techniques of newsmagazines, the report included columns by three guest contributors— a recognized securities analyst, an authority on food franchising, and a respected economist. The report invited comments from readers. More than 200 letters have been received, plus many phone calls and personal comments.[2]

The report was a grabber from the start. The contents page told, not just listed, what was inside and teased the prospective reader. It would be pretty hard to pass over an article on Multifoods' New York Stock Exchange listing subtitled, "The Big Cheese Comes to Wall Street"; or one on the company's industrial foods business subtitled, "Ugly Duckling Turned Swan."

Inside, the articles bore titles like "Ditching the Dodo Image" and "Rapidly Eating Up Yardage Lost in Court." In the articles themselves subheads like "In Touch With Youth," "Thinking Small," and "Weak Spots" helped hold the reader.

The company talked of its successes, but was also candid when it had stubbed its toe. In an interview, James Kallestad, a divisional vice president, spoke of "a disappointing failure." The article continued:

> It was Turkey Main Course—a frozen half turkey with dressing in a disposable pan enclosed in oven-roasting film. All the homemaker had to do was put it in the oven. It was an internally developed product which had a lot of things going for it. 'But we found that if you are not in the frozen food cabinet, and do not have frozen food marketing or distribution capability, you've got at least two strikes against you,' said Kallestad.

> As a result, the product failed. 'That taught us a valuable lesson—to move into other sections of the grocery store we had to have a marketing and distribution base rather than simply starting from scratch,' he said.

When the News is Bad

This brings me to a sore subject for most companies: what to say if there is bad news in the past fiscal year. The Georgeson & Company report said, "A great many stockholders complained that they were not getting accurate information from companies that were in trouble." Why not? If you have trouble, who can tell better than you what kind of trouble it is and why, and what you're doing about it. Read this from the Anaconda annual report.

It was the year that wasn't for King Foods

What a year it should have been for King Foods. But it wasn't.

Sales were up 17 percent for the premier producer of frozen portion-controlled meats. Capacity was doubled with the addition of a new plant at Norfolk, Va. New products, ranging from soups to sirloins, were being accepted. And the company was beginning to flex some merchandising muscles it hadn't developed before.

So why were King's earnings down sharply in fiscal year 1972? Howard Goldberger, the 32-year-old president of the fast-growing subsidiary of Multifoods, recently outlined the reasons in an interview.

"See that truck of meat out there?" Goldberger said from his office at the firm's plant in the St. Paul suburb of Newport. "A year ago the meat in that truck would have cost us $9,000. Today it costs $15,000."

In the past, King was able to buy meat when it was less expensive and then store it frozen. "But we've never had meat prices so high for so long before," Goldberger grimaced.

Caught With Its Prices Down! King would have been able to cope with the higher cost except for one thing. The price freeze caught Goldberger and his aggressive management team with its prices down.

"The high raw material cost began emerging in May of 1971," Goldberger said, but King held the line on prices as long as it could. Finally, on August 14, it raised its prices. But it was too late. The next day, President Nixon announced the freeze and King was stuck with higher costs it could not pass on.

"The freeze cost us over $250,000 in pretax earnings last year," he said.

That fact, plus startup costs at the new Norfolk plant, which went into operation in mid-summer, plus the continued upward trend of meat prices after the freeze, accounted for a major share of the dip in King's profits.

King Foods, acquired by Multifoods in December of 1969, was an early entry into the frozen portion-controlled meat business over a decade ago. From the time when King's first frozen portion-controlled hamburger patty was introduced up to its acquisition by Multifoods, sales grew from nothing to $25 million a year. Today King's sales are $29 million.

A Leader. King, today, is among the leaders in its segment of the food industry. With 500 employees in its two plants, it is well-known among its customers. They include many of the giants in the food

HOWARD GOLDBERGER
"See that truck of meat..."

service field — representing the fast food chains and variety stores and others.

"Our story is simple," says Goldberger, whose father founded King and taught him the business since he was a young boy. "We offer a uniform and very consistent quality product, and we have a first-class, nationwide distribution network," he explained.

King delivers frozen meats to any point in the country through 175 distributors working out of local warehouses. "This means that a King's chopped steak in Florida is the same quality as a King's chopped steak in California — and the price is exactly the same in both locations," Goldberger explained.

Among the things that make King unique is the fact that, "We don't develop a steak and then try to go out and jam it down the throats of our customers," he quipped.

Instead, King Foods finds out what the customer wants and then makes it specifically for him.

It is the old story of quality and service which has made the business prosper. "We want to be more to our customers than just a crown on our package," Goldberger concluded. ⑩

An ever-vending line

A variety of King Foods precooked portion-controlled meat products can be found in vending machines from coast to coast. The total away-from-home eating market, estimated at $43.9 billion in 1971, is expected to grow at more than 7 percent annually.

Although it has been in portion-control meats for only a decade, King already is one of the leading national suppliers of frozen meats to the food service market.

The portion-control meat business, a $680 million industry in 1971, is growing at an estimated 12 percent annually and is expected to be a billion dollar business in 1975.

King's Food Article

During 1971, Anaconda encountered the full force of political adversity in Chile. The expropriation of our Chilean investments had an impact of a magnitude that few corporations have ever had to absorb. It took away two thirds of the company's copper production and much of its earnings.

We have faced up to the hard realities of those circumstances. We have restructured our organization and resources, and thereby effected significant cost reductions, so as to revitalize and rebuild Anaconda. It is our belief that the company has a new sense of urgency, that it is stronger today—in terms of employees and their attitudes—than before Anaconda was deprived of its Chilean operations.

As a measure of the strength of Anaconda, the company was operating at a profit at the end of the year.

Further on, the report gave a more detailed discussion of problems in Chile and elsewhere during the year.

Even when it told the stockholders bad news, the International Multifoods report managed to end on the upbeat, showing them that the company was working at improving the situation. A page of the report that illustrates this positive tone (as well as the newsmagazine format of the 40-page document) is reproduced here.

Telling stockholders about problems and what is being done about them is not harmful but helpful. It can go a long way toward closing the corporate credibility gap.

Words about Management

A New York investment advisory service has this phrase printed at the bottom of every page of advice it issues: "Management Is Everything."

Who could disagree? But annual report writers seem to have forgotten it. Most list top management and directorial changes during the year, but with dull, uninteresting job title labels and no more. From such treatment there is no way that stockholders, most of whom never see these people on whom they're placing their bets, can learn about their strengths.

Why not use a little more space? Why not a profile, written so that stockholders can see them in their mind's eye and learn why these people have been successful? The business magazines do it; they must think readers want it.

Of the reports I studied, only three did more than name new officers and give their last preceding title and responsibility:

☐ General Motors listed its principal officer changes and traced their career posts with GM.

☐ Deere, which went outside for a vice president of corporate communications, told us he had been employed by the Bell System for 37 years, but nothing about why these years qualified him for his new post at Deere. Deere also told us the company elected its first woman officer, as corporate secretary. But it did not say how and why she got there.

☐ International Multifoods' interview of President William Phillips started by contrasting his button-down, conservative appearance when he was appointed 3½ years before with his long-haired appearance now. " 'I've been preaching change around here,' Phillips explained with a grin. 'A fellow really ought to practice what he preaches.' "

At most companies, one can only suppose, senior officers are too modest and retiring to okay colorfully written self-portraits in their annual reports. Or perhaps public relations people are skittish about doing full, honest portrayals of bosses they have to live with.

Maybe this difficulty could be overcome by hiring experienced business writers to do the profiles under by-lines. This sort of article gets high readership in business publications—the same ones many of your stockholders read.

Summary

Annual reports can reach stockholders. Reports can be laid out and written so that more stockholders read them and read more in them. They represent one expense whose productivity can be increased materially in most companies. To accomplish this requires four things of top management:

1 The decision to do it.
2 Insistence that the report be edited for individual shareholders, rather than for pros and analysts.
3 Support for readability and clarity at the expense of dignity—if necessary.
4 Determination to give the new look in the old book a chance, despite, perhaps, misgivings by the board of directors.

Notes

1. For an argument in favor of more data on companies' potential performance, see Henry B. Reiling and John C. Burton, "Financial Statements: Signposts as Well as Milestones," *HBR*, November-December 1972, p. 45.

2. Copies of the report can be had by writing to Quentin J. Hietpas, Vice President, Communications, International Multifoods Corporation, 1300 Investors Building, Minneapolis, Minnesota 55402.

33

How to Name— and Not Name— a Business

JOSEPH R. MANCUSO

Selecting the corporate name is a vital first step in launching a business enterprise—vital because the name is so visible. According to Internal Revenue Service estimates, there are more than 2 million corporations in the United States, and 350,000 incorporations are added annually. Most of the so-called good names have already been picked.

Many bad names have been picked too. Ego-tripping founders often christen fledgling companies in their own image. Also, many companies find themselves hampered in their expansion by restrictive names.

So, just because it's done one way doesn't make it right. Nor does it make my way right either. In a free enterprise system, everybody can do it his way and that's why it's so much fun. In a communist system we'd be numbering enterprises, not naming them. In a free enterprise system we even name hurricanes.

How Not to Name

I classify the ways entrepreneurs traditionally label their companies into four groups: big ego trips, little ego trips, nonsense names, and effective names. It's not hard to single out the three wrong approaches; how to pinpoint the effective name is more difficult.

☐ Big ego trips—These are the result of the irresistible urge of some people to grab every bit of the limelight. They want to become famous

428

and the business becomes the primary vehicle for their obsessions. This is a mistake, except in some service-type businesses. Even for most companies that succeed (acknowledging those with appellations like Ford and Du Pont), it is not a good practice.

Remember, most entrepreneurial ventures fail and when the business contains your surname, your name fails too. And when your name fails, to the public you as a person have failed.

You will recall the ill-fated Ford car, the Edsel. After wrestling with names like Phoenix and Altair for months, company management unwisely christened the new auto after Henry's deceased son. Think of the consequences for Henry's great-grandson, who carries the same given name as Henry's only son. If you meet him at a cocktail party (as I once did), you have only one possible salutation: "Are you *the* Edsel Ford?"

☐ Little ego trips—These enterprises are denominated by entrepreneurs who wouldn't be so crass as to put their own monikers on their fledgling businesses. However, their passion for glory moves them to almost name the organization after themselves.

Thus we have ARP Instruments, whose founder was Alan R. Pearlman. When he started Lestoil Products, Jacob Barowsky had three children, one of whom fortunately owned a given name starting with a vowel: Lenore, Edith, and Seymour.

People are so clever in constructing ways to get their immortality in lights without anybody knowing it. The funny thing is, though, that everybody eventually finds out why the organization is named whatever it's named and you don't really hide anything.

☐ Nonsense names are a third category of wrong choices. Naming a business is like naming a child; the tag lasts forever. You have only one chance to make a first impression, and choosing a meaningless name is hollow. It creates a facade that may cause uneasiness in your customer, supplier, investor, or new employee.

Choosing a business name without some tie to a business purpose or using a random selection of letters or numbers is like giving up without a fight. Better to have tried and failed than to call your company XYZ Corporation or NYETK Inc. These choices sound silly, but they exist. Can you guess what they make or sell?

One test in determining the effectiveness of a name for your business is the degree to which you think it will influence your customers to buy your product. The name can be one of your competitive edges, giving your company a marketing orientation right at the beginning. A nonsense name may have no meaning or apparent business connection, but if it is so distinguishable from those of competitors it is still worth considering. This is a rare exception to the rule. For example, the name Lux, for soap, is effective.

How to Name

Naming a new business is not easy, especially if you want the name to be catchy and memorable. Moreover, it has to be different from the titles of competitors and other organizations. Here are some principles to follow:

1 Name the business to be descriptive of what you make or sell. If possible, name it after what the business does better than other businesses (unique selling proposition, or USP).
2 Name it to be distinctive and easily identified and remembered.
3 Name it to be esthetically attractive and graphically appealing.
4 Name it with an eye toward future expansion—or at least do not name it in such a way as to forestall expansion.

Name the Business to Be Descriptive of What You Make or Sell.   The name is the first visible identification for the business. It sets the tone, so it must be appropriate. Bob Newhart's joke about "Helen Ferguson's Airline and Aluminum Storm Door Co." makes the point. Certain businesses have certain expectations. The name must match these expectations.

Which reminds me of a story told in the actual New Jersey towns of Red Bank and Long Branch: A financial institution in Red Bank bought out a rival in Long Branch, and people in Long Branch have been depositing their checks ever since at the Long Branch branch of the Red Bank bank.

A name with USP always takes the positive view of the product or business. The name Weight Watchers not only helps customers understand what is being sold but also gives a positive connotation to the product. "Fat Losers" or "Nonfat People" would be offensive as well as negative.

Some companies belong to the so-called high technology crowd and add suffixes like "onics" to a sophisticated root word. Industrialonics, Nucleonics, and the like are examples of this philosophy. Their long, hard-to-pronounce names are related to their products, which are usually also confusing.

Call your business after whatever it does best in order to help your customer know why to buy your products. It's one more reason to do business with your company. But don't get overly excited by this criterion, as you must also have a good business to succeed. In the rapidly expanding fast-food business, the leaders rank in market share as follows: (1) McDonald's, (2) Burger King, (3) Pizza Hut, and (4) Kentucky Fried Chicken. Notice that all but the leader have followed the rule. So a name with USP may make it easier to succeed, but it isn't always essential.

Here's a point to mollify anyone offended by my ego trip comments. In certain cases, most often in service companies or professional organizations, use of your own name may also be your USP. Because you're the hero—the thing that is different, the better ingredient—it's all right to name your funeral parlor, real estate agency, insurance firm, or law or medical practice after yourself.

Name Your Business to Be Easily Identified, Distinctive, and Easily Remembered. It should be all three, not just two out of three. Not long ago Missouri Beef Packers merged with Kansas Beef Industries. The combination was christened MBPXL, from Missouri Beef Packers and the Excel brand of Kansas Beef. The name looks more like a printer's error to me. It meets only two of the three tests.

George Eastman named his camera company in an appropriate way with an abrupt word that begins as it ends, Kodak. The same holds with Xerox. Both are excellent examples of words that are distinctive, identifiable, descriptive, and easily remembered. MBPXL is not.

Restaurants often have catchy, easy-to-remember names, in order to promote that vital element in a restaurant's success, word-of-mouth advertising. A favorite eating spot of mine is the No Name Restaurant, a popular place in Boston.

Insurance companies, on the other hand, have substantial-sounding names, and—because of the vast number of competitors in the field—the more distinctive the better. My favorite name of any company in the world is the John Hancock Mutual Life Insurance Co. I envision millions of insurance agents speaking to millions of customers and at that crucial moment of signing the contract, the agent proudly places it on the table and says, beaming, "Please put your John Hancock on this document."

It's an especially fitting name because of the intangible nature of the product. Customers for intangible products need continuing support and justification for buying the products, even after they have bought them. Notice that the other insurance companies also portray safety and shelter in their names and slogans.

Name Your Business to Be Esthetically Attractive and Graphically Appealing. While this may *sound* obvious, it's not. The process may require outside help. Having a complementary and compatible corporate name and logo right from the beginning can make a vital difference. Ralston Purina's checkerboard and Mercedes Benz's trisected circle are instantly recognizable.

Since each case is different, specific guidelines in this area are almost impossible. My advice is to solicit opinions from about 25 of your existing or potential customers. This exercise can be done in a few days and it is often immensely valuable in avoiding seemingly obvious foul-ups. It can be worth a great deal.

Name Your Business with an Eye toward Future Expansion. This issue may seem ridiculous when you are just starting out, but never mind. Consider the case of the magazine publisher in Knoxville, Tennessee, with the title of the 13–30 Corporation. Its original intent was to serve age groups between 13 and 30. But the magazine-reading market is growing older and the company is now focusing its business on persons from 40 to 70.

Or recall these prominent corporate giants: Pittsburgh Plate Glass Co., Radio Corporation of America, Columbia Broadcasting System, and National Cash Register Co. These companies grew into new businesses and their names became misrepresentations. So now they use only their initials, which are poor substitutes for descriptive titles.

On the other hand, First National City Corporation, which owns New York's largest bank, changed its name to Citicorp. In this way the company maintained an association with its previous name. But, more important, the new name also allows expansion into: Citicard, Citicash, Citicredit. It was a significant net gain without the loss of a historic tie.

So, should you name your new business to fit the criteria I have described?

34
Public Responsibility Committees of the Board

MICHAEL L. LOVDAL, RAYMOND A. BAUER, and NANCY H. TREVERTON

It is a rare company that has not been called upon to face important decisions involving community relations, charitable contributions, employee issues, or other similar matters. The number and type of social issues, as well as the degree of business involvement, both voluntary and otherwise, have tended to increase within recent years. And there have been corresponding changes in companies to meet these growing pressures. One recent trend is that of a standing committee of the board to ensure director attention to delicate and complicated social issues. Here, the authors discuss the establishment of a public responsibility committee, its composition, information sources, and activities that emerge from a research project involving 30 corporations which currently have such a committee.

As a result of government intervention, questionable corporate practices, and raised expectations from various sectors of society in recent years, most U.S. companies have had to face important decisions involving issues of social responsibility. To meet these pressures, many companies have, for example, added staff specialists or created new departments in such areas as urban affairs and affirmative action.

More recently, a corporate innovation has been instituted at the board level: a standing committee designed to deal specifically with complex and sensitive social issues. We call it "public responsibility," recognizing some companies have designated it "public policy," "public interest," "public issues," "social responsibility," or "corporate responsibility."

To judge the current impact and future potential of public responsibility committees at the board level, we examined—via mailed questionnaires and personal field interviews with directors, CEOs, and managers—the experiences of 30 corporations we had previously identified as having established such a committee. We also interviewed a limited number of directors in companies that had not established public responsibility committees.

This article, then, is a report on our findings of this Harvard Business School research project.

Nature of the Committee

What is a public responsibility committee? It is usually a standing committee of the board of directors initiated by a board resolution that details the committee's purpose, duties, and procedures. For example, the charter of one committee was as follows:

1 Identify the major constituencies—both internal and external—that normally judge the behavior and performance of the corporation; examine what they expect of the corporation's performance socially and environmentally.
2 Recommend specific issues for board and management consideration, and determine their relative priority.
3 Recommend corporate policy to respond to the priority issues.
4 Consider and recommend potential new areas of social responsibility and involvement.
5 Examine and report to the full board on corporate attitudes toward the needs and concerns of the major constituencies of the corporation.
6 Recommend where duties and responsibilities lie throughout the company with respect to the priority issues.

The typical public responsibility committee has five to seven members. While outside directors, primarily corporate executives, predominate, the committees in 24 of the 30 corporations we surveyed had inside directors and a few also included lower-level employees. Typically, the committee meets four times each year, considers a wide range of social issues, and receives its information through a designated executive on the corporate staff.

In our study the committees engaged in 10 basic areas of activity: general philosophy, affirmative action, communnity relations, pollution, product quality and safety, consumerism, occupational safety and health, employee issues, charitable contributions, and government relations. (A "working guide" that consists of appropriate questions for committee members in each area appears in the appendix for this article.)

Other than the foregoing generalizations, it is difficult to characterize a typical public responsibility committee. Most of those we studied are struggling with basic questions of purpose and direction, and they are in the process of defining various roles for themselves. This struggle reflects both the variety and the complexity of social issues that have developed during the past few years as well as the newness and the developmental state of many of the committees.

Despite this diversity, we have concluded that a public responsibility committee can be valuable for any corporation. In the balance of this article we shall explain why and offer suggestions for the successful establishment of such a committee.

Justification For

Why have a public responsibility committee? Because of the strident nature of widespread publicity and activity about business in relation to social issues—for example, consumer boycotts, proxy resolutions, and affirmative action lawsuits—some people might think that public responsibility committees are formed only in reaction to a crisis or severe pressure. This does not seem to be the case.

The primary reason for setting up a public responsibility committee is simply that a full board often cannot devote enough time and consideration to social issues. A director we interviewed expressed this feeling:

> It isn't easy to deal with sensitive matters in the boardroom where we might have 20 people involved. Our company has an increasing number of public policy issues and the full board is too large, with already too heavy a work load. We needed a separate committee to give special attention to sensitive matters.

By giving attention to social issues, a committee can indicate trends or situations which might not be perceived early enough by corporate management. We found one committee that identified consumerism as a growing issue for a large company and recommended the development of a consumer affairs department to handle complaints, screen advertising, and train managers to be responsive to consumer needs. Other committees we studied initiated the attention of management to issues such as industrial democracy, minority purchasing, and executive sabbaticals.

A public responsibility committee is also in a better position to monitor corporate performance in social areas than is the full board of directors. For example, we studied a committee that felt management's progress in achieving affirmative action goals was remiss. The committee insisted on changing the corporate incentive systems by factoring affirmative action achievements into managers' bonus calculations.

Through actions such as this, a public responsibility committee can indicate to all employees that top management is dedicated to social issues and can help spread corporate social philosophy from the top level down into the corporate structure.

Arguments Against

During the course of our research project, we encountered some opposition to the concept of a public responsibility committee. One director argued that the full board handles social issues in his company: "We report everything to all of our directors. To the extent that the board gets involved with these sticky issues, I want it to be the whole board, not just a committee." One author also has argued this same position:

> Fairly new on the horizon is a corporate responsibility committee. . . . While some companies may feel they need such a committee to show concern for the consumer, the community, and the environment, I feel that this function is so broad it should be the responsibility of the entire board.[1]

These arguments are of questionable validity. Social responsiveness is no less "broad" or elusive a concept when thought of managerially or strategically than is the concept of compensation, which has traditionally been a concern of specialized standing board committees.

Furthermore, the trend toward more board committees (the corporate strategy or objectives committee is one recent example) results from the necessity to handle the growing workload of the board. Thus a public responsibility committee is needed in an area that has significant policy implications.

Some people argue that a public responsibility committee would require specialization that most directors don't have. A few directors we interviewed expressed concern over their ability to assume responsibility on a committee for these kinds of activities. One director commented:

> None of the boards I sit on has a public responsibility committee. I think this is because the directors don't feel they have the expertise necessary to serve the board adequately in this area.

This argument is even more dubious than the others. Obviously, if the board feels it lacks the expertise to staff a committee, it is quite unlikely that the full board itself will be able to meaningfully tackle social issues. Furthermore, the expertise necessary for a public responsibility committee can be added easily to most boards; and, as we shall discuss later, members from traditional business backgrounds can indeed make a contribution.

Finally, a number of directors view public responsibility committees as but a passing fad established to counter a negative corporate image or adverse publicity. To the extent that this may be true, neither is it a valid argument against the establishment of such a committee nor does it mean that the committee cannot be an effective force in corporate social issues.

At the very least, the value of such an institution at the board level is to ensure that corporate directors and senior management direct their attention to delicate and complicated social issues.

Composition of Membership

Who should be on a public responsibility committee? Members may be drawn from inside and outside directors, as long as the balance is weighted in favor of outsiders, and both business and nonbusiness backgrounds are represented.

The Members

On a public responsibility committee, outside directors are necessary to provide broad perspective and to ensure independence of judgment and critical review of management's actions. Inside directors, on the other hand, have a high degree of knowledge about a company, and thus their representation on the committee encourages consideration of the problems of implementing social policies.

Moreover, since the recommendations of a public responsibility committee must, whenever possible, be compatible with the company's main business interests, these latter considerations should enter a discussion early rather than late—a contribution inside directors provided in several of the committees we studied.

As mentioned, members of public responsibility committees should represent diverse backgrounds, with some members having acquired their experience outside the world of business. The members of one committee we studied were described by a director as follows:

> Our members are individuals who have been exposed to, and have more sensitivity for, a wider range of activities than the typical businessman or lawyer who sits on a board of directors. For example, we have a university president on the committee who has had to face many conflicting interest groups in his job, and we have a black leader who is attuned to civil rights issues. They are a large part of why we have been successful.

However, members should not only be outsiders with a nonbusiness orientation. Experienced corporate executives, who are confronted continually with social issues in their own organizations, can add a necessary perspective. The value of having mixed backgrounds on the committee was explained by a senior officer of a large financial institution, who served as secretary for his company's public responsibility committee:

> I've discovered it's important to have a sense of realism and balance on this committee. We originally had three very activist, liberal members who kept pushing us further from reality. We finally added a manufacturing CEO from our board, and he asked the tough questions like 'Can we afford it?' or 'Does it fit with our strategy to take this position?' Having a balance between these two orientations is critical.

Specifying composition is always difficult for a board committee, given the constraints on talent available and each corporation's problems and board traditions. However, we believe that an "ideal" public responsibility committee would consist of five members—one senior inside director (preferably the chief operating officer), two directors drawn from the business world (preferably CEOs of large corporations), and two outside directors with nonbusiness backgrounds (academics or representatives of minority groups).

The thrust of this recommendation is not to suggest that a public responsibility committee must be a divided group with multiple constituencies. Rather, it is to suggest that special expertise, different ideological perspectives, and diverse backgrounds among the members simply lead to a more effective, vigorous committee.

The Chairman

While members with different backgrounds and philosophies are valuable on public responsibility committees, there is also the need for strong leadership. Besides the normal functions of setting the agenda and running the meeting, the committee chairman can make two other important contributions.

First, the chairman must often serve as the initiator of issues and ideas. In several of the committees we studied the chairman not only was the most knowledgeable and sensitive to social issues of all the committee members, but also was the most influential person in pushing the committee into new areas of activity.

Second, given the sensitivity of certain social issues and the expense associated with changes in social policies—for example, the costs of pollution control or the revenue lost through eliminating questionable foreign payments—a committee chairman must be the kind of individual who can at once act as a mediator between committee members and corporate management and, at the same time, be independent enough from management to recommend a course of action the public responsibility committee perceives as correct.

It goes without saying that the chairmanship of a public responsibility committee can be a most demanding job, requiring diligence, sensitivity, and persistence. Thus the choice of the best outside director for the position of chairman can be a critical decision.

Source of Support

What resources does a public responsibility committee need? Our study revealed that to be effective this standing committee requires basically two kinds of resources: internal staff support and funds for the hiring of outside expertise.

The Staff

Who should head the public responsibility committee staff and how much time would the job require? Most often, the key staff individual who serves the committee on a regular—although not necessarily full-time—basis is the general counsel/secretary or else the head of a corporate staff department, such as director of public affairs.

In some cases, we found several heads of corporate staffs serving the committee on an ad hoc basis. For example, if a committee needed information or work done in pollution control, it turned to a company's environmental affairs department. This arrangement seems feasible as long as there is one key staff liaison.

Certain basic duties must be performed by committee staff, such as helping to prepare the agenda, maintaining communication with committee members between meetings, following up on various committee requests and assignments, and communicating the committee's activities to the organization, the shareholders, and the public.

The staff should also be responsible for coordinating and reviewing written reports that go to the committee, and for giving guidance to operating managers who make presentations to the committee. In addition, three other factors are important for an effective committee staff.

1. *The staff leader must be able to devote an adequate amount of time to the committee.* This need may seem obvious; yet we studied public responsibility committees served by individuals who were either unable or unwilling to give the committee the attention and support it needed. An outside director described one case to us as follows:

For the first year our committee meetings were just disastrous. Our secretary was the company's chief legal counsel and he just never got things done. Reports were late, presentations were poorly prepared, meetings were a joke. I finally got on the CEO, and we got another chap who is doing a first-rate job. For this committee to work at all, you have to have some help from inside.

2. *The key staff person must have some sensitivity to social issues, especially in the early years of a public responsibility committee.* When committees are new and frequently searching for direction, the staff can be a source of expertise in determining committee activities. One staff person we interviewed mentioned the necessity to "prod the committee for suggestions of where it wants to go." Obviously, in order to do this there must be a feeling of rapport and mutual respect between members of the committee and its staff.

3. *Obtaining information and cooperation in fulfilling committee requirements is facilitated when the committee staff has a knowledge of the internal organization and occupies a position of significant corporate responsibility.* We found cases where committee staff members were viewed as "social oddballs" by line managers, operated largely in isolation from the rest of the company, and were consequently not able to serve the committee as effectively. Overall, the selection of the staff must be a careful

process of choosing personnel with time, expertise, and respect from company insiders.

Outside Expertise

Public responsibility committees should have the financial resources to hire outside specialists. We found outsiders useful to the committee because of their special talents, their ability to provide an independent viewpoint, or simply their providing committee members with the opportunity to test their own views. One committee we studied had hired 30 external experts in its three-year existence.

A range of outside experts can be used by public responsibility committees. These include opinion services to assess a company's public image or to survey employee attitudes, technical experts in EEO, pollution, or OSHA compliance, or auditors to certify activities in social areas such as an organization's charitable contribution patterns.

Of course, some directors felt that to use outside expertise would indicate a lack of faith in management, that inside staff should suffice for any committee-related work, and that bringing in an outsider could break down the communication flow within a corporation. Some directors even doubted the reliability of outside experts in social areas. As one argued: "I feel that there are no accepted measures of performance in this area. The consultants are biased, expensive, and their competence is often exaggerated."

We feel that these kinds of objections arise largely out of a basic uncertainty about the role of a public responsibility committee and not about the use of outside experts. The committee clearly needs the best possible information for the purpose of assessing and helping shape corporate social performance.

Thus the use of outside experts for this board committee ought to be no more unusual than an audit committee's contact with external auditors, or a finance committee's involvement with investment bankers.

Range of Activities

What issues should a committee tackle? Few of the public responsibility committees we studied were concerned with exactly the same social issues. This difference is understandable since all issues are not of equal importance to all companies. For example, a manufacturer in one industry might rank pollution control high as an area of concern, while another manufacturer in the same industry might rate product quality and safety as most important.

While certain topics may vary in importance from industry to industry, others such as affirmative action compliance or employee issues are common problems for most corporations. The activities of public responsibility committees are affected not only by the nature of the business but also by the interests of the particular committee and immediate pressures from special interest groups.

The dilemma, however, is simply one of where to start. Unlike other board committees such as audit or finance, a public responsibility committee faces an enormously wide range of possible activities. No board committee, given the restraints of time and capability, could possibly hope to tackle all the questions offered in the Appendix at once. To do so could result in superficial coverage at the expense of substantive input, and damage a committee's reputation with the board and the company.

Instead, we recommend that a new public responsibility committee, perhaps in its first organizational meeting, start by inventorying all the social issues facing the corporation. Then, priorities should be established. Obviously, the most pressing matters or those most likely to have the largest impact on earnings, employee morale, or company image should be dealt with first.

When a set of activities is chosen, then the committee should receive reports on each issue from appropriate corporate staff departments, coordinated by the committee secretary. The format for each report would be similar to that shown in the Appendix.

Once fully informed of the issues, a public responsibility committee can take on a variety of additional activities. The committee can serve as a screening group for the full board by judging the social component of regular board decisions—capital expenditures, acquisitions, divestments, reorganizations, and so forth. Also, it can be useful for the committee to meet directly with line managers one level below the CEO (e.g., functional and group vice presidents, and division general managers).

One company we studied, with four basic business units, had each of its division presidents meet once a year with its committee. The board chairman instructed them to report on social responsibility in their divisions. The chairman of the committee explained the practice:

> All I want is for these four guys to come in and give us their own perceptions of what corporate social responsibility means to them and what they are doing in their businesses. They don't get any guidelines for their presentations and there are no canned formulas for how to talk to this committee. The more open-ended and unstructured our dialogue, the more confident I am that we are getting the true picture.

The main value of this practice is that a public responsibility committee receives firsthand exposure to those managers most responsible for implementing corporate social policies. A chance to directly assess managerial performance and perceptions of social issues can be much more valuable to a committee than simply receiving all its information through corporate staff groups.

An extension of this philosophy exists in a few public responsibility committees that meet directly with lower-level employees. One board member explained:

> Directors always get their information after it has passed through many
> filters including the CEO. Once in a while every outside director ought
> to get face to face with a production floor worker or a secretary. This is
> the best way I know to get a true picture of life in a company.

Thus a public responsibility committee can serve as a device to open up
lines of communication between the board and various levels in an organization—to "unfilter" the board's information and to discover employee
concerns.

Pitfalls to Avoid

What problems can arise with a public responsibility committee? There are
several to which the committee is especially susceptible.

Because public responsibility committees represent a symbol of corporate commitment to social responsibility, they often receive high visibility
and create expectations for tangible results in social areas. If the results are
not immediately realized, committee members and staff can become frustrated; and lower-level employees, impatient to "see something happen,"
can become disillusioned. We found this problem in several cases.

While a certain amount of adjustment may be inevitable in any new
endeavor, certain steps can be taken to minimize this problem. First, everyone in the organization should be cognizant that it may take a while for the
new group to reach an understanding, take action, and produce results in
an area as ambiguous, controversial, and complex as corporate social
responsibility.

Second, as indicated earlier, the committee should place priorities on
its efforts and concentrate on one or two areas to achieve tangible results.

Third, it is important to publicize committee activity so others can
understand problems, conflicts, and delays—as well as successes. It is better
to be open about the uncertainties of developing such a new organizational
tool, rather than to be secretive and create the impression of deliberate
inaction.

A problem for any board committee, but especially for a public responsibility committee, given the range and complexity of social issues, is
the limited time of outside directors. As discussed previously, effective staff
support through maintaining follow-up and communication with directors
between meetings is one very helpful measure.

The committee might also have a problem with maintaining relevance.
In a few cases we studied, it was clear that the participants felt the committee
wasn't going anywhere. In order for a public responsibility committee to
remain relevant, there must be a periodic reassessment of goals and activities, especially in regard to changes between the business and the outside
environment.

The actual relevance, however, of this type of committee depends not only on how well it is manned and managed but on the commitment of other groups—the full board, top management, corporate staff, and line management—to social issues. Without a strong internal commitment from other constituencies within a corporation, a public responsibility committee can face a very difficult task.

Summary

We believe that public responsibility committees are a good idea. They offer an answer to the need of corporations to deal more effectively at the top management level with a range of new social and political demands for which existing organizational structures may not suffice.

Nonetheless, out of the thousands of American corporations, we have located just 35 that have established such a committee. Most companies are surviving without a public responsibility committee, and many of these are among the most socially responsive in the country.

Moreover, despite the existence of the well-publicized General Motors committee established in 1970, the concept of a public responsibility committee has not taken the boardroom by storm. To a certain extent this is attributable to the skepticism about such committees that we discussed earlier, but primarily, we think, to a lack of useful information about the committee's function and value.

Currently, public responsibility committees are in a developmental state. Companies with such committees have often gone through a painful learning experience in discovering problems and difficulties that they were not able to anticipate. Yet the committees with which we are best acquainted are becoming increasingly effective and are having an important impact on their corporations.

Perhaps public responsibility committees are in the same stage as audit committees several years ago, when they began. A number of companies were rejecting the concept as a passing fad, while a few creative pioneers were establishing and experimenting with audit committees.

Our judgment is that over the next few years the number of public responsibility committees will grow as corporations realize that a board-level response to more governmental regulation and increasing demands from various sectors of society is necessary.

Eventually, as with many board innovations, the idea will catch on and a rapid acceleration in the number of public responsibility committees will take place. Someday this committee will be as commonplace as the audit committee is today.

Certainly the decision to form a public responsibility committee cannot be taken lightly. It depends both on how well a company is currently handling social issues and on how willing it is to commit the necessary resources and endure the uncertainty of the learning experience.

We think it is worth a try, for a public responsibility committee can make a major contribution to a responsible corporation by directing high-level attention to public and social issues.

Notes

1. Ralph F. Lewis, "Choosing and Using Outside Directors," *HBR*, July–August 1974, p. 77.

Appendix

Here is a suggested "working guide" of appropriate questions for public responsibility committee members covering 10 basic areas of corporate activity.

1. *General posture and philosophy*

What is our company's philosophy regarding corporate social responsibility?

How has this been expressed—for example, in public statements, in annual reports, or in chief executive speeches?

Overall, is our posture one of meeting the letter of the law, of keeping pace with industry practice, or of trying to be a leader in this area?

Is social responsibility throughout the company regarded as a peripheral activity or as one with strategic significance?

How successful have we been in implementing social policies in the organization?

Are these issues largely handled by corporate staff, or are they considered a responsibility of our line units (divisions, branches, plants)?

What constituencies take an interest in our corporate social performance? What issues are they most concerned about?

Are social issues integrated into our strategic planning system and our control and incentive systems—for example, how much of a manager's bonus depends on performance in areas of corporate social responsibility?

2. *Equal employment and advancement*

Do we have an affirmative action program for the hiring, treatment, and advancement of minority workers and women?

What are our corporate goals for minorities and for women and how are they broken down—that is, by job classification, grade or salary level, division, or companywide? Who determines goals—personnel staff, line management, or a combination of the two?

How do corporate goals compare with current standing? Who monitors progress? Is performance in reaching goals rewarded? Are there penalities for nonconformity?

What plans exist for closing any gap between goals and current standing—for example, recruiting, hiring, and promotion policies?

Are there any current or prospective lawsuits against the company from employees or from the government?

What is the company stand on public disclosure of equal employment and affirmative action data?

Does the company require suppliers and dealers to have programs of affirmative action?

What special programs has the company initiated to improve performance in this area—supervisor training, special counseling, remedial education?

3. *Environmental quality*

What federal, state, and local environmental requirements—both current and projected—apply to our manufacturing operations?

What is the company's current standing in regard to those requirements?

What resources and costs will be involved in closing any gap and achieving state-of-the-art pollution control technology in all of our facilities?

How does our company compare with others in the industry?

Has the company developed plans for energy conservation?

Are there any current or prospective lawsuits against the company?

Who are the people responsible for environmental control programs in the company? How do they monitor progress? Do they have contingency plans for potential environmental disasters?

What procedures are used to assess the present and future environmental impact of company actions?

4. *Community relations*

How do we assess company impact upon the communities in which we operate in areas such as employment and location of facilities?

Do we know how these communities view the company? How do we gather this information?

If there are complaints from the community, what company action is taken?

How do we assess the propriety of our business practices abroad in comparison with domestic actions? Do we follow the same social standards and business practices?

Is someone responsible for community relations at each of our facilities?

5. *Consumerism*

What current and proposed consumer legislation will affect our company?

What are our policies in relation to our consumers—for example, product safety, advertising truthfulness, return procedures, warranties, product data?

Who is responsible for handling consumer issues in the company? What do they do with complaints and inquiries?

What is the nature of consumer complaints regarding our products and marketing practices?

6. *Product quality and safety*

What are our current standards of product quality and safety—for example, average product life, disposable and biodegradable products?

What is our current status in relation to existing and proposed federal and state regulations?

What are the plans for closing the gap between goals and current status?

Are there any current or prospective lawsuits against the company?

Are our new products and services evaluated for social relevance and utility as well as marketability?

What programs or systems such as product testing exist to verify quality and performance?

7. *Occupational safety and health*

What occupational safety and health hazards are of greatest concern in our industry and our facilities?

Who is responsible for OSHA guidelines in our company?

What is our record regarding occupational safety and health? How does this compare with local and national industry figures?

What plans exist to change company facilities and methods? What costs and benefits will be involved?

What programs or systems are used to ensure that the workplace is kept free from recognized hazards?

Are there any current or prospective complaints or citations?

Has the company been inspected by an OSHA compliance officer? If so, what were the findings? If not, what are our inspection preparations and expectations?

Should we follow or try to influence prospective trends by participation in various groups for setting national consensus standards?

8. *Employee issues*

What is our history in employee relations, including union and labor relations? Who is responsible for this area?

Are programs established to deal with particular employee problems—for example, family counseling, alcoholism, and drug abuse?

What is our policy in regard to employees when plants or facilities are closed?

Are the opinions and participation of employees sought when important decisions are made?

Should we have a corporate ombudsperson to facilitate our internal due process?

Is there a statement of employee rights to privacy, free speech, employment, and the like?

Do we have an internal code of ethics? If so, how is this enforced?
Are there guidelines on conflict of interest?

9. *Charitable contributions*
What community needs are not being effectively addressed by government and private action? Could we contribute to these needs?

What has been our history of contributions and how do the amounts compare with others in our specific industry?

About the Authors

Robert W. Ackerman *is currently president of Premoid Corporation and Whitman Products Ltd., manufacturers and coaters of specialty papers. He was formerly on the faculty of the Harvard Business School, where he taught business policy and from which he received M.B.A. and D.B.A. degrees. He has authored* The Social Challenge to Business *(Harvard University Press),* Corporate Social Responsiveness *(Reston Publishing Co.) with Raymond Bauer, and* Management and Organization: Text and Cases *(Richard D. Irwin) with Hugo Uyterhoevn and John Rosenblum, in addition to numerous articles in management publications.*

Raymond A. Bauer *is deceased. He was a professor at the Harvard Business School when he wrote "Public Responsibility Committees of the Board."*

Peter L. Berger *is University Professor at Boston University and a member of the Council on Foreign Relations. Mr. Berger is the author of numerous books including* The Heretical Imperative: Contemporary Possibilities of Religious Affirmation *and* Sociology Reinterpreted: An Essay on Method and Vocation.

Caroline Bird *was with Dudley-Anderson-Yutzy.*

Chester Burger *heads the New York management communications consulting firm of Chester Burger & Co., Inc. Earlier, he was national manager of CBS Television News, which he organized for the network, and was president of Communication Counselors, Inc. He has been a consultant to AT&T since 1955, and to many other organizations including the American Bankers Association. He received a Distinguished Service Citation from the United Negro College Fund and has been an adviser to the Black Executive Ex-*

The publisher was not able to contact all of the authors of the articles in this book and regrets the omission of their biographies.

change Program since its inception in 1969. He has written five books on management.

Alfred D. Chandler, Jr. *is Straus Professor of Business History at the Harvard Business School. Before coming to Harvard Business School he taught at MIT and Johns Hopkins. His major studies,* Strategy and Structure *(1962) received the Newcomen Award and* The Visible Hand *(1977), the Pulitzer and Bancroft Prizes and the Newcomen Award. Mr. Chandler is also the author of* Henry Varnum Poor, Giant Enterprise, The Railroads, Pierre S. duPont and the Making of the Modern Corporation, *and with Herman Daems,* Managerial Hierarchies. *He was assistant editor of the* Letters of Theodore Roosevelt *and editor of the* Papers of Dwight D. Eisenhower. *Mr. Chandler received his A.B. and Ph.D. from Harvard University.*

Dr. John T. Dunlop *is Lamont University Professor at Harvard University. He graduated with a Ph.D. from the University of California at Berkeley. Dr. Dunlop is the author of* Wage Determination Under Trade Unions, Industrial Relations Systems, Labor and the American Community *and, with Derek C. Bok,* Business and Public Policy. *He was also the editor of the* Wertheim Series in Industrial Relations.

Solomon Dutka, *Ph.D., is chief executive officer of Audits & Surveys Inc., a marketing research firm which he founded in 1953. He is also an adjunct professor of statistics at New York University's Graduate School of Business Administration. During World War II, Mr. Dutka was awarded a citation from the Secretary of War for his work in nuclear physics on the Manhattan Project. He served as an American Statistical Association delegate to the United Nations Sub-Commission on Statistical Sampling and was a member of the United States Census Advisory Committee. The author of many articles and a number of books on statistical techniques and their applications to marketing and marketing research, Mr. Dutka is a Fellow of the American Statistical Association and a Fellow of the American Association for the Advancement of Science.*

Dan H. Fenn, Jr. *is director of the John F. Kennedy Library in Boston and a lecturer at the John F. Kennedy School of Government at Harvard. Dr. Fenn served as staff assistant to President Kennedy in the White House, vice chairman of the U.S. Tariff Commission, lecturer at the Harvard Business School, and assistant editor of the* Harvard Business Review. *He graduated from Harvard College in 1944 and holds three honorary degrees and a masters from Harvard. Among other publications, he and the late Professor Raymond A. Bauer authored a book on corporate social responsibility published by the Russell Sage Foundation.*

David Finn *is chairman and chief executive officer of Ruder, Finn & Rotman, Inc., the largest public relations organization in the U.S. Mr. Finn has been responsible for many new techniques and concepts in public relations and* *publicity and has authored numerous articles and books on the subject in such publications as: the* Harvard Business Review, Leaders, Across the Board, Harper's, GEO, The Annals, Chief Executive, *and others. He is a member of the boards of The Institute for the Future, the MacDowell Colony, Global Perspectives in Education, New York Center for Visual History, American Energy Management, and on the Board of Overseers of Parsons School of Design. Mr. Finn is a graduate of the City College of New York.*

John Kenneth Galbraith *is the Paul M. Warburg Professor of Economics Emeritus at Harvard University. He has a Ph.D. in economics from the University of California, was a Social Science Research Council Fellow at the University of Cambridge, and has taught at California and Princeton as well as at Harvard.*

As deputy administrator of the Office of Price Administration in the early 1940s, Mr. Galbraith was principally responsible for organizing the wartime system of price control, which he headed until 1943. He was a director of the U.S. Strategic Bombing Survey, served in 1946 in the State Department, and was awarded the Medal of Freedom by President Harry S. Truman.

Mr. Galbraith served on the campaign staff of Adlai Stevenson in 1952 and 1956, was an early supporter of John F. Kennedy, and served on Kennedy's convention staff. He was the chairman of the Economic Advisory Committee of the Democratic Advisory Council from 1956 to 1960. During the Kennedy years, he was the U.S. Ambassador to India, and he has been variously associated with successive Democratic administrations as an adviser.

A former editor of Fortune, *Mr. Galbraith's most recent book is* The Anatomy of Power, *published in 1983. His other recent volumes include his memoirs,* A Life in Our Times, The Nature of Mass Poverty, *and* The Voice of the Poor. *His earlier well-known titles include* The Affluent Society, The New Industrial State, Money: Whence It Came, Where It Went, *and* The Age of Uncertainty. *All have been widely translated and are used in economics, business, and politics courses in colleges and universities throughout the world. He is a member of the American Academy of Arts and Sciences and in 1982 was elected, for literature, to the fifty-member American Academy of Arts and Letters, where he was given the chair previously held by the late Archibald MacLeish.*

David Kelley *is an author and lecturer. He has written extensively for* Barron's *and other publications, and spoken to business and academic groups on such topics as: media coverage of business, government regulation, affirmative action, the "fairness doctrine" in broadcasting, and the ethics of capitalism.*

He holds a Ph.D. in philosophy from Princeton University and has taught philosophy at Vassar College. His philosophical treatise, The Evidence of the Senses, *is to be published next year.*

His area of specialization is the media and the relation between economic and First Amendment freedoms. He is a member of the Media Institute's National Advisory Board and the author of Laissez Parler: Freedom in the Electronic Media.

Theodore Levitt *is Edward W. Carter Professor of Business Administration and head of the marketing area at Harvard Business School.*

Mr. Levitt is the author of numerous articles on economic, political, management, and marketing subjects, including the prize-winning article, "Marketing Myopia," in the Harvard Business Review. *He is a four-time winner of McKinsey Awards competitions for articles in the* Harvard Business Review; *winner of the Academy of Management Award for one of the outstanding business books of the year, 1962, for* Innovation in Marketing; *winner of the John Hancock Award for Excellence in Business Journalism in 1969; recipient of the George Parlin Award as "Marketing Man of the Year," 1970; recipient of the George Gallup Award for Marketing Excellence, 1976; and recipient of the 1978 Paul D. Converse Award of the American Marketing Association for major contributions to Marketing.*

Mr. Levitt is also the author of Innovation in Marketing, *(McGraw-Hill);* Industrial Purchasing Behavior: A Study in Communications Effects *(Division of Research, Harvard Business School);* The Marketing Mode: Pathways to Corporate Growth, *(McGraw-Hill);* The Third Sector: New Tactics for a Responsive Society, *(Amacom);* Marketing for Business Growth, *(McGraw-Hill); and co-author of* Marketing: A Contemporary Analysis, *(McGraw-Hill).*

Michael L. Lovdal, *vice president of Temple, Barker & Sloane (Lexington, Mass.) is a specialist in corporate planning and management development. Before joining Temple, Barker & Sloane, Mr. Lovdal was assistant professor at the Harvard Business School where he taught courses in business policy and engaged in research on boards of directors, government regulation of business, and corporate social responsibility. He has also served as a lecturer at MIT's Sloan School of Management teaching corporate strategy, policy, and planning. Mr. Lovdal is a Certified Public Accountant and he currently serves as a director of Beneficial Capital Management Corporation in New York.*

Walter P. Margulies *is a founding partner and chairman of Lippincott & Margulies Inc., which specializes in the areas of corporate communications, marketing, and design.*

Mr. Margulies originated the concept of corporate identity and corporate communications planning, and is credited with coining the phrase "corporate image." During its 40 year history, his New York City firm has worked with over 2200 major companies on corporate identity programs, and has developed close to 4000 corporate and product names. Industry Week *has referred to Lippincott & Margulies as "grandmaster of the name game."*

He is the author of Packaging Power, *writes a regular column for* Advertising Age, *and is founder of the Package Designers Council. Born in Paris, he was educated in Vienna, Rome, and Paris, where he graduated from the Ecole des Beaux Arts.*

Robert S. Mason *is deputy assistant secretary for public affairs at the U.S. Department of Housing and Urban Development. He was president of Mason Associates, Management Communications from 1973 to 1981; vice president of public relations and advertising at The Boston Company from 1970 to 1973; and director of public relations at McKinsey & Company, Inc. from 1964 to 1970. Mr. Mason has contributed articles to numerous publications, including* Harvard Business Review, Sloan Management Review, Bankers Magazine, Association Management, *and* Best's Insurance.

Mr. Mason's B.A. is from Harvard University and his M.A. is from Columbia University.

Joseph T. Nolan *is vice president, public affairs for Monsanto Company with overall responsibility for public and government relations, corporate philanthropy, and advertising.*

Before joining Monsanto in 1976, he had been an editor on The New York Times, *a Washington correspondent for UPI, a corporate communications executive, and a professor of journalism and public affairs at the University of South Carolina. He holds an A.B. from Holy Cross College, an M.A. from Boston University, and a Ph.D. in economics from New York University.*

In twenty-five years in the public relations field, Mr. Nolan has conceived and directed national and international programs, ranging from financial and labor relations to community service activities. Several of these programs have won recognition from the Public Relations Society of America and other professional groups.

William Safire, *who wrote "Financial Adventure of James Debenture: A Parody with a Moral" when he was a public relations man in the sixties, went on to become a speechwriter in the Nixon White House and is now a columnist for* The New York Times. *He won the Pulitzer Prize for distinguished commentary in 1978.*

George P. Shultz, *currently United States Secretary of State, has also served as Secretary of Labor and Secretary of the Treasury. He has also been dean of the Graduate School of Business at The University of Chicago and president and a director of Bechtel Group, Inc. Mr. Shultz's publications include:* Economic Policy Beyond the Headlines *(1978),* Workers and Wages in the Urban Labor Market *(1970),* Guidelines, Informal Controls, and the Market Place *(1966),* Strategies for the Displaced Worker *(1966),* Management Organization and the Computer *(1960)*, Labor Problems: Cases and Readings *(1953)*, The Dynamics of a Labor Market *(1951)*, Pressures on Wage Decisions *(1950)*.

His Ph.D. in industrial economics is from MIT.

George David Smith *is president of the Winthrop Group, Inc., a Massachusetts based consulting firm providing services in business and technological history. He is the author of a forthcoming book on the origins of the Bell Telephone System and is currently at work on a history of Alcoa and the aluminum industry since World War II. Mr. Smith holds a Ph.D. in history from Harvard University and, in addition to his consulting business, teaches courses in administrative and business history at New York University. His firm, the Winthrop Group, is currently engaged by several large corporations across a wide spectrum of American industry.*

Laurence E. Steadman *is president of Steadman/Coles, Inc., a Boston-based management consulting firm. Dr. Steadman earned his M.B.A. and D.B.A. degrees from the Harvard Business School, where he has held both research and teaching appointments in the field of corporate finance. He is active in three primary areas of Steadman/Cole's professional practice—market assessment, new venture planning, and management program development. Mr. Steadman's own management experience includes eight years as a marketing executive with a midwestern manufacturing company.*

Author Index

AUTHOR INDEX

Subject Index

83551